The Enigma of Diversity

The Enigma of Diversity

The Language of Race and the
Limits of Racial Justice

ELLEN BERREY

The University of Chicago Press
Chicago and London

Ellen Berrey is assistant professor of sociology at the University at Buffalo, SUNY, and an affiliated scholar of the American Bar Foundation.

The University of Chicago Press, Chicago 60637
The University of Chicago Press, Ltd., London
© 2015 by The University of Chicago
All rights reserved. Published 2015.
Printed in the United States of America

24 23 22 21 20 19 18 17 16 15   1 2 3 4 5

ISBN-13: 978-0-226-24606-2 (cloth)
ISBN-13: 978-0-226-24623-9 (paper)
ISBN-13: 978-0-226-24637-6 (e-book)
DOI: 10.7208/chicago/9780226246376.001.0001

Library of Congress Cataloging-in-Publication Data
Berrey, Ellen, author.
    The enigma of diversity : the language of race and the limits of racial justice / Ellen Berrey.
        pages cm
    Includes bibliographical references and index.
    ISBN 978-0-226-24606-2 (cloth : alk. paper)—ISBN 978-0-226-24623-9 (pbk. : alk. paper)—ISBN 978-0-226-24637-6 (e-book)   1. Cultural pluralism—United States. 2. Affirmative action programs—United States. 3. Race discrimination—United States. 4. United States—Race relations. I. Title.
    E184.A1.B4287 2015
    305.800973—dc23
                                                                2014038398

Diversity can be cringe-making, arbitrary, insincere and sappy. But take it away and you won't get more equality—you'll only get more privilege.

KATHA POLLITT, "Show Him the Money"

Creating a symbol or . . . identifying oneself with a popular symbol can be a potent means of gaining and keeping power, for the hallmark of power is the construction of reality.

DAVID KERTZER, *Ritual, Politics, and Power*

CONTENTS

"I have a dream" booms Dr. Martin Luther King Jr.'s voice. As the crowd shuffles into the University of Michigan's Rackham Auditorium, a video plays on a large screen. The film cuts to scenes of modern revitalization projects in Detroit, then to a young African American man singing, "The one thing I did right, was the day I started to fight. Keep your eyes on the prize, hold on."

The ornate auditorium is soon packed beyond capacity. More than thirteen hundred people, mostly students, fill the plush seats, sit in the aisles, and cram against the back wall. It is January 20, 2003, the day of the keynote speech for the university's annual MLK symposium. The university is in the midst of legal battles over its race-based admissions policies. In just a few months, the US Supreme Court will hear oral arguments in two cases against the university.

University president Mary Sue Coleman, a petite white woman dressed in a crisp beige suit, strides onto the stage to speak about the university's fight in the lawsuits and its staunch support for diversity. The legal cases, she explains, charge that the university unconstitutionally favors racial minorities. She tells of the university's adherence to law and its acceptance of only highly qualified minority students. The university's policies "seek out diversity," she says. They "consider a broad range of factors in admissions," with race as one of several criteria. The university has good reason to do so, Coleman continues. "Our research has demonstrated [that] essential values like respect, understanding, and goodwill are strengthened when students live and learn from people from many backgrounds."

Her closing brings the audience members to their feet, clapping and cheering. The university is working to keep the "doors of opportunity" open. "On this most important American civil rights holiday," she says,

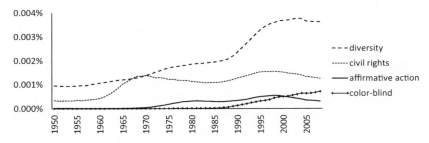

I.1. Ngram of references to diversity in more than eight million books, or 6% of books ever published, 1950–2008. *Source*: Google Books Ngram Viewer, http://books .google.com/ngrams, accessed March 31, 2014. *Note*: The terms *affirmative action*, *civil rights*, and *color-blind* are included as points of reference.

"I want to make our bottom line crystal clear: The University of Michigan has an absolute, unwavering commitment to diversity throughout our community."

Such talk of "diversity" abounds in the twenty-first-century United States, from the Oval Office to celebratory neighborhood festivals. Starting in the late 1980s, it became ever more common in public discourse, managerial trade journals, and published books (see fig. I.1).[1] In a 2003 national survey, nearly all the respondents said they valued diversity in their friendships and their cities or towns.[2] Organizational diversity efforts can be found in universities and schools, companies and communities, the military, and places of worship.[3] Civil and corporate leaders across the country, Mary Sue Coleman included, praise diversity in public speeches and mission statements, on websites, and in internal documents. Their diversity interventions range from affirmative admissions policies such as those at Michigan to mixed-income housing programs and corporate diversity training. These top-down diversity activities have been shaped and challenged by activists and thoroughly circumscribed by law. A consequential opinion in the 1978 US Supreme Court case *Regents of University of California v. Bakke*, authored by Justice Lewis Powell, established diversity's benefits as *the* acceptable legal explanation for those who wanted to proactively consider race in college admissions decisions, with ripple effects far beyond the admissions office.[4]

When political and organizational leaders speak of diversity, they could mean the many ways that people differ from each other. As evident in Coleman's remarks, delivered on a national holiday honoring an African American civil rights activist, however, they are often referring to racial minorities or specifically to black people.

These leaders are not repeating King's critique of racial discrimination, though. They are not echoing the demands made by civil rights activists in the 1950s and 1960s for political reforms to provide black people with full citizenship.[5] They are not calling for systemic intervention to remedy racial inequality, which was the stated goal of many early affirmative admissions policies in colleges and universities.[6] And diversity's advocates are not endorsing the color-blind ideal that race should be altogether disregarded.[7]

These decision makers are articulating a different vision of racial progress in America. Theirs is an optimism framed in terms of valuing and leveraging diversity, for everyone's benefit. And they have pursued this vision by developing an elaborate organizational infrastructure of diversity—diversity talking points, logos, programs, policies, spokespeople, and statistics—that beautifully symbolizes inclusion but only sometimes, and only partially, undoes racial hierarchies.

What This Book Is About

The enigma of diversity is the puzzle of what, exactly, political and organizational decision makers accomplish when they take on the goal of diversity. This book examines the ways political officials, organizational leaders, and activists have mobilized notions of diversity to manage racial integration and exclusion in the post–civil rights period. This notion of integration might seem outdated to some, but it encapsulates a critically important contemporary dynamic: the creation and ongoing negotiation of more egalitarian, racially heterogeneous environments. Integration is not simply the lifting of barriers. In the words of Dr. King, it is "a genuine intergroup, interpersonal doing."[8] The integration of people of color into predominantly white organizations and communities has been, and continues to be, a profoundly politicized phenomenon.

Integration also is not simply a demographic or political process. It is a cultural one—a meaning-making process produced through human agency and shaped by social relations, power dynamics, competitive markets, institutional interests, and other forces.[9] Diversity discourses and initiatives serve as organizing principles from which organizations and people improvise as they engage in and make sense of integration.[10]

This book takes these precepts as a starting point. It asks: How are diversity's enthusiasts constructing the meanings of race, racial progress, integration, and pluralism for the twenty-first century? The American racial landscape has changed tremendously since the landmark Civil Rights Act. People of color have made modest inroads into the economic and power elite, politics, and other domains where white people have dominated. The black middle class has grown, and new immigrants have arrived from Latin America and Asia. People of different racial groups have equal rights under law, and they coexist in closer physical and social proximity. Colleges and workplaces are more racially and ethnically heterogeneous, and communities have become somewhat less racially segregated.[11] Since the 1970s, the processes and people that directly propel racial integration have shifted, too. The action has moved from the streets to the corporate boardroom, from federal policy to the revitalization plans of the local chamber of commerce, from the "firsts" ever to be hired to those now hitting the glass ceiling. Some of the action is more intimate. Interracial marriages, no longer illegal, made up 8% of all marriages in 2008.[12]

The country has become more pluralistic in other ways as well. There are legal protections against workplace sexual harassment and discrimination based on disabilities, age, sexual orientation, and other statuses in addition to protections for race, sex, and national origin. Women participate in the labor force in much greater numbers and now make up 51% of managers, professionals, and related occupations.[13] Gays and lesbians have gained greater social acceptance and legal rights in some jurisdictions. Like women, they have become more visible in the American elite and more positively portrayed in the media.[14] Americans now practice a much wider range of faiths, with the percentage of those identifying as not religious at all increasing most precipitously, from 8% in 1990 to 20% in 2012.[15]

Amid these social changes, many of the fundamental dynamics of racial domination—of white privilege and racial minority disadvantage—have persisted, from where we live and work to whom we imprison.[16] The United States remains a racialized society. Racism, as a fundamental dynamic of systemic hierarchy and group subordination, continues to be foundational to the structure of the social system.[17] Many of the gains made following the midcentury civil rights reforms, such as improvements in black men's occupational status, have stalled.[18] This is all the more difficult to discern because color blindness—the ideological insistence that everyone be treated without regard to race, accompanied by a denial of the causes and consequences of racism—is pervasive in law, public policy, organizational routines, and individuals' accounts of their lives.[19] Conservative opposition to race-conscious policies has intensified, and court decisions have sharply limited organizations' ability to consider race in decision making.[20] Among many white people, a consensus has developed that being "racist" is unacceptable, yet they still perceive African Americans as culturally deficient and disregard the continuing white favoritism that greatly benefits them.[21] These inequalities are compounded by the widening wealth gap between rich and poor, with people of color represented disproportionately in the growing class of poor Americans but also, in very small numbers, among the wealthiest.

Why have organizations like universities and businesses interpreted such conditions and their own responses in terms of diversity? Whose interests are served, whose worldviews are represented, and what strategies of action are validated?

This phenomenon provides an opportunity to consider the role of culture in sustaining and legitimizing inequality—and, specifically, how organizational culture bears on racial hierarchies. Rarely do decision makers actively try to diminish the symbolic and tangible boundaries that divide people of color from white people and degrade their lives. How do diversity advocates engage in boundary minimization, and what are the consequences of how they do so? Which hierarchies, relations, and practices do they try to delegitimize, and which do they end up reifying in the process? These questions about legitimation and boundary minimization are questions about what diversity includes, what it excludes, and how power is exercised in its name.

The push for diversity also provides an occasion to assess contemporary racial politics and how they bear on social hierarchy. Does diversity exemplify the success of the civil rights movement or the movement's ultimate co-optation? What happens to the goal of remedying racial inequality when race gets folded into a celebratory American multiculturalism and taken up in neoliberal agendas? And how does the color-conscious push for diversity matter at a time of ideological color blindness, with its denial of both racial disadvantage and privilege? The stakes are high. As sociologist Sharon Collins writes, at issue here is "whether whites' monopoly over socioeconomic power and privilege, and the underlying ideology that supports this position, will be sustained. Or, conversely, whether positions of power and privilege will be reapportioned to let non-whites in."[22]

This book address these questions through a multicase study of the organizational push for diversity, based on a combination of six years of ethnographic research and historical sources dating to the 1950s. It provides a synthetic, sociologically grounded account of the diversity movement—an account that has not yet been written. At its core, it is an inquiry into the symbolic politics.[23] Symbolic politics is about the exercise of power: the ability to use and influence ideas so as to determine what should get done and to get those things done.[24] The symbolic politics of racial progress is how organizational and political actors exercise and contest power by advocating a particular interpretation of racial progress—be it legal equality, the expression of cultural identity, transcendence over race, or something else.

The book examines three cases: college admissions at the University of Michigan, housing redevelopment in Chicago's Rogers Park neighborhood, and human resource management in a Fortune 500 company that I pseudonymously refer to as Starr Corporation. Each case represents a fundamental arena of social life and a domain of activity targeted by civil rights activists and their opponents: the places people learn, live, and work. Each of these particular locales is known for its active promotion of diversity. The book investigates civic and corporate decision makers who advocate diversity—among them Mary Sue Coleman and other university administrators, developers, local political officials such as city councilors, company executives, and midlevel managers—many of whom are white men. It also documents the activists who question now-conventional notions of diversity.

The Drive for Diversity

The post–civil rights period, since the 1960s, has been characterized by new legal constraints on race-conscious policy, institutional pressures to show legal compliance, growing demographic heterogeneity, and the demands of neoliberal capitalism. These upheavals have created a new race problem for decision makers in many different settings: racial representation and the potential stigma of not representing race properly. The leaders of universities, companies, communities, government, and other domains confront a widespread expectation that some people of color, especially African Americans, will be present in a predominantly white context, measured either numerically or by their visibility or authority.

The issue of racial representation is most evident when people of color enter (or try to enter) social statuses and settings dominated by white people. This has been the case at both the University of Michigan and at Starr Corporation and in Rogers Park before the 1980s. Racial representation can also become salient when white people inhabit social statuses and settings as a numeric, cultural, or political minority, as has been the case in Rogers Park since the 1980s. Under either set of conditions, people of color and white people are relatively more likely to interact on more equal, less antagonistic terms and to coexist in closer proximity, both socially and physically.

Just as racial representation has become an issue—and, in part, *because* racial representation has become an issue—the representation of other marginalized groups has become important as well: women and people who are gay, lesbian, bisexual, or transgendered as well as immigrants, religious and linguistic minorities, and people with disabilities, among others. The new problem, then, is often also the broader issue of minority representation—how to promote group-based demographic heterogeneity and the incorporation of marginalized minority groups among majority ones. These problems are accompanied by the (unspoken) expectation that such minority representation should not threaten the status of white people and other dominant groups.

The decision makers in this study have responded by advocating diversity. As this book shows, they have constructed identities for their organization or community as distinctive for its diversity—as one of its distilled, essential characteristics.[25] Local community leaders, for instance, tout Rogers Park as "the most diverse neighborhood in Chicago." These identities are deliberately cultivated by decision makers who make concerted efforts to project a public image of the organization or community as unique yet recognizable, in hopes of shaping how others see it.[26] Sometimes they stem from and animate people's experiences of that locale. They may resonate with people's perceptions, or they may be perceived as disingenuous, especially if their production by decision makers is obvious. These identities are conveyed through pervasive discourses on diversity, as well as through programs, policies, offices, and other institutional-organizational structures that decision makers have deemed relevant to diversity. They are key elements of the diversity movement, which more broadly is made up of social relationships, material practices, and symbolic constructs that signify diversity.

As a component of an organization or community's identity, diversity serves purpose and constitutes meaning. Local leaders invoke diversity to describe heterogeneity, talk in code for black people, denounce minority exclusion, or build a concept of mutual gain. They "do" diversity in a variety of ways, from implementing effective policies to photoshopping. Their objectives vary as well, be they advocacy for race-targeted interventions, low-stakes affirmation, or legal inoculation. Regardless, *diversity* largely reflects the interests, worldviews, and experiences of powerful decision makers and their most important constituents—who may include people of color but by and large are white and well-off.

The corporate managers, community leaders, and other decision makers who champion diversity have redefined racial progress for the post–civil rights era, from a legal fight for equal rights to a celebration of cultural difference as a competitive advantage. Their aspirational ideal of diversity reframes racial integration as an accomplishment in which all parties benefit—not a zero-sum game or a moral imperative to help black people.

It claims the moral high ground, disavowing racism and discrimination. It diminishes the distinctiveness of race by couching it as one of the many cultural identities that make up America's valued pluralism. Decision makers' justifying rhetoric also emphasizes instrumentalist benefits. Diversity, they claim, is good for organizations, good for profits, good for learning, and even good for white people. Their programmatic interventions imply effective action and good intentions.

Not everyone is really included by the diversity movement. It is selectively inclusive. Cultural value is placed on the so-called diverse people who are most easily incorporated into a setting and who enhance institutional objectives such as prestige, distinction, or profit making. Desirable diversity is routinely characterized as the representation of high-status, upwardly mobile, or otherwise culturally appealing people of color and women. Having at least a token person of color on a corporate board, for example, has become in many settings critical for organizational and political credibility.[27]

Selective inclusion is compatible with prevailing institutional logics, such as capitalist accumulation and commodification, public service, elite-status gaming, bureaucratic management, or civic politics.[28] In this paradigm, racial progress is biased toward that which abets success in markets—markets for elite admissions, urban housing, skilled labor, and consumer consumption—or does not threaten such success. Diversity efforts are selectively inclusive when they favor such individuals. They frequently are oriented toward integration (or the semblance of such) at the upper rungs of the class ladder. Put differently, it is unusual to call for greater diversity in prisons or underfunded public schools.

As it turns out, selective inclusion—especially the *symbolism* of selective inclusion—is surprisingly low risk for the high-status white people who do the managing of diversity. It does not necessitate that leaders address racial inequalities throughout the organization or housing market. When diversity is confined to a small proportion of those who attend elite universities, own their homes or businesses, or work in the upper echelons of business, it helps lessen the risks of radical, race-class transformation that social justice may require.

There are both promises and pitfalls in treating race as diversity and the pursuit of selective inclusion. The drive for diversity seeks inclusiveness in some forms and satisfaction of the desire not to discriminate. It helps to legitimize the representation of people of color and other marginalized groups in difficult-to-attain positions and settings from which they have long been excluded. Some diversity policies effectively improve minority representation, and the concept of diversity can provide legal and political justification. The push for diversity also affirms a basis of commonality—a shared, self-reinforcing commitment to social cohesion—across group-based differences that normally divide Americans deeply.

But diversity advocates' efforts to minimize group divisions and expand the bounds of social membership have focused on symbolism more than on social causes. Much discourse on diversity leaves advocates without a language for talking about inequality.[29] Because selectivity is such a high priority, talk of diversity can normalize ideologies of color blindness and can favor of status-quo privileges. As Michigan president Coleman said in the speech that opens this book, only qualified people of color get admitted to the university. She was affirming the university's definition of merit—although activists and scholars have contended that this very definition is discriminatory.[30]

In practice, selective inclusion can lead to meaningful social change, such as greater racial minority representation at a college, but it is not widespread, substantive transformation, such as a remaking of the educated class. It resists fundamental change in the structures, practices, or cultures that guide day-to-day interactions and shape determinations of merit and value. It does not upend power dynamics or require those with privilege to relinquish their comfort in how things work. It is a mechanism of containing and co-opting racial justice, as it largely leaves untouched persistent racial inequalities and the gulf between rich and poor. This is the taming of the civil rights movement's provocative demands for integration, equality, and full citizenship.

The drive for diversity and the symbolic politics of racial progress unfold differently depending on the particular organizational and political context and the historical moment. The three case studies in this book illustrate those dynamics and sharpen our understanding of race, pluralism, and inequality in the twenty-first century.

The Cases and Unique Outcomes

In the sites studied—the University of Michigan, the Rogers Park neighborhood, and Starr Corporation—decision makers' push for diversity has focused on a core set of institutional practices critical to the successful integration of racial minorities into mainstream America. These practices are, respectively, college admissions, urban housing politics, and corporate human resource management. Across the three cases, institutional leaders advocated diversity as they tried to manage the challenges of attracting upwardly mobile people of color (especially in the university and the company) and appealing to and retaining white people. In two of the cases, local political activists weighed in as well.

University of Michigan

The University of Michigan, featured in chapters 2 and 3, is a predominantly white major elite public university located in the college town of Ann Arbor. Since the 1960s, the university's primary objective for racial integration has been to attract and retain some students of color. It first established race-attentive affirmative admissions policies in the 1960s, justified as providing opportunities to the disadvantaged. Following Justice Powell's opinion in the 1978 *Bakke* Supreme Court ruling, the university reframed those policies in terms of diversity and continued to do so through the 2000s.

In the late 1990s, plaintiffs filed legal cases challenging the university's race-conscious admissions policies at the undergraduate level and the law school. The litigation culminated in two major Supreme Court cases, *Gratz et al. v. Bollinger et al.* and *Grutter v. Bollinger et al.*, respectively, which were decided in 2003.[31] To defend its policies and counter the plaintiffs' call for color-blind admissions, the university elaborated a legal rationale based on Powell's opinion. It justified affirmative action in terms of diversity's benefits, arguing that diversity was a compelling state interest because it enhanced learning and that the university's admissions policies were appropriately tailored to achieve this goal. In *Grutter*, the Supreme Court affirmed this diversity rationale and found that the university could consider race in admissions decisions through an individualized review of each application, as the law school used. Subsequently, university leaders kept the law school admissions policy but retooled the undergraduate admissions process to follow suit.

The university's push for diversity has been a high-profile, politically controversial effort to integrate some people of color into an elite institution under jurisprudential constraints. In this effort, race is of utmost concern, but there is an inherent class bias because elite admissions favor affluent students.[32] Further, law plays a definitive role. Legal doctrine delineates the acceptable treatment of race in admissions decisions, subjecting race to the highest level of judicial review—in legal terminology, called strict scrutiny. Litigation structures the terms of debate over race, setting up an oppositional contest between those with the resources to mobilize arguments for color blindness and for diversity. And law is discourse defining. It establishes diversity's educational benefits as *the* acceptable justification for race-attentive admissions.

University administrators faced the challenge of pursuing a social-justice objective of racial minority representation within legal constraints while, at the same time, their priority has been to appeal to academically strong, majority-white students in an increasingly competitive admissions market. As shown in chapter 2, administrators in the 1980s eschewed their early rhetoric on affirmative action, which called for remedying minority disadvantage, and carefully cultivated a public image of the university as "excellent and diverse." Similar discursive shifts took place at universities and colleges nationwide.[33]

Michigan's identity became all the more important in the context of *Gratz* and *Grutter*, as it was a key mechanism by which the administration incorporated law into local institutional logics and routines, as chapter 3 documents. Administrators repeated over and again public relations sound bites on their legal argument for diversity. They gave compelling speeches, such as Coleman's at the MLK event, with rationalized justifications about the productive outcomes enabled by racial minority representation and storied descriptions of generative interpersonal interactions among people of different racial groups. Their messaging made the legal argument seem like a commonsensical description of campus life. That the student activists who opposed affirmative action actually adopted a version of the university's stance on diversity's educational benefits is strong evidence of just how dominant that message became.

The Michigan case is especially noteworthy because the administration's advocacy of diversity definitively shaped US law on race and admissions. In sum, the push for diversity at Michigan was a case of *preserving affirmative action* while *concealing the reality of racial inequality* through legal arguments and relentless messaging.

Rogers Park

Rogers Park is a racially and economically mixed residential neighborhood on Chicago's far North Side. In the 1960s, when Rogers Park was 99% white, civic leaders' basic motivation around racial incorporation was to retain white, middle-class homeowners in the face of new black in-movers. By the 2000s, the neighborhood had become mixed income and mostly racial minority, and the race-class dynamics of housing markets remained politicized. The neighborhood suffered from disinvestment and crime but was undergoing modest gentrification. Local political officials hoped to foster amicable relationships within the community and faced some political pressure to protect nonwhite, nonaffluent residents. However, the foremost priority of these officials was to win over middle-class and affluent home buyers, the majority of them white, while developers wanted to sell them units in new condominium projects.

The drive for diversity in Rogers Park has been disjointed and contentious, mobilized in the contexts of economic disinvestment and, especially, reinvestment. It has been shaped, foremost, through civic politics. As early as the 1960s, chapter 4 shows, activists advocated ideas of diversity and pluralism to construct a common community identity of diverse individuals and to argue both for and against low-income housing. By the late 1980s, developers and the neighborhood's alderman appropriated diversity rhetoric as they pushed for redevelopment of lakefront real estate and the conversion of low-income apartments into upscale condominiums.

As detailed in chapter 5, politicians, civic organizations, prodevelopment groups, residents, and many housing activists in the early 2000s all promoted an image of Rogers Park as a unique petri dish of diversity as they debated how to reverse the neighborhood's economic decline. For the alderman, mixed-income housing programs and residents' open-mindedness were protecting community diversity. For developers, the neighborhood needed *more* wealthy homeowners to truly be diverse. The ostensible push for diversity by the alderman and other pro-redevelopment groups was most conspicuous in their *talk* of diversity, not through the implementation of policy. It was low-stakes affirmation of difference. Likewise, while they praised the racial diversity of the neighborhood's population, their positions on housing were color-blind, with no recognition of the problems faced specifically by residents of color. For progressive housing activists, in contrast, diversity required low-cost, quality housing for poor, disproportionately black and Latino renters. Such debates and tensions over community identity are common in gentrifying city neighborhoods.[34]

In this cacophony of calls for diversity in Rogers Park, there was an almost universal theme: an appeal to a collective ethos of community and tolerance for social differences. However, for very poor renter-activists who relied on federal housing subsidies, most of whom were African American, the paradigm of diversity was entirely irrelevant to their group interests in civil rights protections, as chapter 5 also highlights.

Thus, in this case, the push for diversity amounts to a fragmented, political, and mostly rhetorical movement. It promotes a shared community philosophy while, in practice, largely favors white homeowners at the expense of the housing security of low-income, marginalized groups. The neighborhood is a case of *valuing tolerance* while *safeguarding property owners*.

Starr Corporation

Starr Corporation is a multinational Fortune 500 consumer products firm. Since the 1970s, the company leaders' primary organizational objective for racial incorporation has been to hire some managers and executives of color and retain them in this majority-white organization. These efforts began in the late 1960s and expanded in the early 1970s, when federally regulated affirmative action became mandatory for the company. Much like their corporate peers, Starr leaders initially framed the company's affirmative action programs as a corporate responsibility for minority opportunity, signaling their compliance with law and industry standards. By 1990, the company recast those programs as diversity management and justified them as beneficial for the bottom line.[35] As chapter 6 shows, Starr's new diversity management rhetoric sounded much like its decades-old rhetoric on diversifying the company's product lines and businesses, but applied to people.

By the 2000s, executives and managers depicted the company's identity as a profitable powerhouse with a proactive diversity strategy, proclaiming, "Diversity is a strength of Starr Corporation" on the company's website. Starr had a well-developed formal platform of diversity management, including a Global Diversity Management Department with five staff, employee affinity groups throughout the country, written policies and reports, and the like. Diversity management was most extensively institutionalized through support groups and professional development workshops for professional, managerial, and executive people of color—African Americans, Hispanics, and Asian Americans—and women (and, far less intensively, for gay, lesbian, bisexual, and transgender employees). In other words, diversity management constructed race and gender as the primary and parallel diversity concerns but, significantly, only of importance at the top of the occupational ladder.

The push for diversity at Starr was shaped primarily through the dynamics of managerial power, as chapter 7 explains. Its diversity platform was in many ways a symbolic artifice, disconnected from consequential employment decision making and overseen by personnel without much authority. Especially influential was the shift in the company's ownership structure that took place in the early 2000s, when a portion of Starr's stock was made available to the public. In the face of overwhelming pressures to improve the company's short-term stock value, diversity managers struggled to legitimate the enterprise of diversity management. They lacked the resources and authority to directly impact the predominantly white, male executives or the similarly situated supervisors who directly influenced the careers of people of color and women. In this context, diversity managers relied on the company's business case for diversity—a formalized boilerplate rhetoric—as a script to rehearse, perform, and (they hoped) validate the programs they oversaw.

Thus the drive for diversity in the company was a managerial move to encourage some upward mobility of high-status people of color and women, one that was hampered by limited managerial power and disregard of the majority of the lower levels of their workforce. This is a case of *pushing against glass ceilings* while *ignoring dirty floors.*

Political Activists Talk Back

Activists played a consequential role in the drive for diversity at Michigan and in Rogers Park. Chapter 3 discusses two campus activist organizations at Michigan that endorsed affirmative action; both of those organizations were politically progressive and had multiracial leadership. That chapter also examines two campus organizations that opposed racial preferences, both conservative-libertarian and led by white men. Chapter 5 on Rogers Park considers two tenant activist organizations, one a multiracial group of grassroots organizers and the other a small interest group representing very poor, predominantly black and female renters with government-subsidized housing vouchers. There were no comparable activist organizations involved in issues of race and human resource management at Starr Corporation—a point discussed in chapter 7.

Many campus and tenant activists disagreed vehemently with the political agendas that decision makers pursued in the name of diversity. They saw those agendas as narrowly conceived. Fundamentally, they took issue with whom decision makers favored for inclusion, decision makers' preferred strategies of action (or lack thereof), and the lack of substantive change. Most took the position that the prevailing optimistic discourses on diversity misrepresented the issues they cared about most. But by and large, these activists confronted an uneven playing field in which they were at a notable political disadvantage. They struggled with the constraints common to activist groups: limited material resources and time, restricted access to traditional channels of political power, a lack of legal resources or knowledge, and the difficulties of representing a worldview or constituency deemed unimportant by decision makers and the general public.[36] This raised a practical dilemma. How should they deal with a commonsensical, hard-to-argue-with concept that they found questionable?[37] As a leader of the Coalition to Defend Affirmative Action and Integration and Fight for Equality By Any Means Necessary (BAMN) complained, "You can't wage a war over diversity."

The ways activist organizations at Michigan and in Rogers Park did intervene was through protest, litigation, and always through symbolic struggles. They pushed for new words, alternatives frames, and contrary interpretations in order to align their constituents' understandings with their organization's objectives and to create controversies that would gain attention.[38] Across both settings, activists used one of three different rhetorical framing strategies to manage diversity. One approach was to endorse diversity while redefining it to fit an activist agenda. The Rogers Park Community Action Network championed diversity, social justice, and what the leaders labeled high-road development. A different activist strategy was to acknowledge diversity as important but avoid using the term. This approach was used by a short-term coalition of Michigan students who wished simply to publicly demonstrate campus support for affirmative action at the peak of the Supreme Court cases. A third strategy was to ignore the topic of diversity entirely, usually in favor of a focus on legal rights, as did the Rogers Park Section 8 Tenants Council.

In addition, almost every activist organization had a shrewd critique of popular diversity rhetoric. The activists participated in diversity politics through a tactic of *street-level semiotics*. Using classic techniques of counterframing and in the tradition of critical pedagogy—in which every individual can recognize the injustices of existing power arrangements—they dissected the words and ideas that decision makers preferred.[39] With an airquote gesture or an eyebrow raised, the activists would zero in on diversity, mixed-income housing, racial quotas, or another well-worn term in order to question decision makers' authority and credibility. In sum, the activist organizations illustrate the importance of *changing politics by challenging words*.

The Racial Order, Reimagined

The push for diversity at Michigan, in Rogers Park, at Starr Corporation, and beyond amounts to a political project to change the racial order. A racial order establishes boundaries around groups based on their phenotype and ancestry (real or assumed)—classifications such as white, black, Latino, Asian, Native American—positions those groups on a hierarchy, and structures their relations to each other.[40] The purpose of a racial order is the marginalization of minorities and the domination of white people and others with racial power. A racial order becomes consequential through various

mechanisms of inequality that enable dominant groups to monopolize resources, rewards, and respect—mechanisms such as opportunity hoarding
(by which people monopolize what is valuable for themselves and others
like them) and claims making (regarding what or who is worthy of recognition and rewards).[41] Racial orders are important elements of more general
inequality regimes—or interlocked practices and processes that result in and
reinforce class, gender, and racial hierarchies.[42]

Seminal scholarship on sociology of race, most notably Michael Omi
and Howard Winant's theory of racial formation, shows that such racial
categories and hierarchies do not simply exist; race must be *made* real and
impactful.[43] Scholarship on the cultural and organizational production of
inequality—by Charles Tilly, Pierre Bourdieu, and Michèle Lamont, among
others—builds on this point and provides nuance. As their work shows,
categorical inequalities are created, operate, and become impactful through
meaning-making practices that draw boundaries around groups and distinguish them based on their worth.[44] These distinctions become institutionalized and, therein, the basis and justification of inequality. Such distinctions
are, in part, social. Racial minorities are treated as less important, while
white people have far better life chances.[45] Group distinctions are always
also symbolic. Racial minorities are designated as *unlike* and *less than* white
people, while white people are racialized as superior.[46] The US racial order
rests primarily on racial distinctions that, socially and symbolically, advantage white people.

Through most of US history, the foundation of racial domination has
been a rigid and oppressive racial order established by state-sponsored
white supremacy and institutionalized through the economic system of
slavery, government-sanctioned extermination, property law, physical and
social segregation, and discriminatory political representation.[47] White
Anglo-Saxon Protestant men thoroughly monopolized material and social
goods and authority-bearing positions. The categorical distinctions between
racial groups strongly correlated with inequalities in people's positions and
opportunities. Such conditions create deeply institutionalized status hierarchies.[48] There was a pervasive ideology of white superiority, which categorizes the world into biologically or essentially different racial groups, denies
the humanity of those deemed nonwhite, and justifies exploitation and opportunity hoarding by white people.

Since the 1960s, with the diminishing of white men's monopoly on
power, the categorical distinctions that designate some groups as minorities and inferior increasingly do not correspond with their educational,

residential, and work positions. This is particularly so because enough members of these groups have moved into high-status positions. The world has become more "intersectionally complex."[49] Political scientists Jennifer Hochschild, Vesla Weaver, and Traci Burch argue that the US racial order also is diminishing in importance in some respects today.[50] People's life chances and social interactions are less likely to be determined by their racial-group membership than at earlier points in US history. Racial hierarchies have become more variable and more embedded in local social relations.

With these shifts, along with other historical shifts such as the rise of immigration, the racial order has been in flux.[51] Sociologists debate questions such as, Are some Asian Americans becoming "white"?[52] Is America's bifurcated black-white racial order morphing into a triracial system like that found in many Latin American and Caribbean countries?[53] While white Americans and their descendants by and large continue to enjoy many unearned advantages, the black-white divide so long at the crux of the American racial order has become far more complicated.[54] Scholars in this field largely agree that African Americans will remain disproportionately relegated to the bottom of the hierarchy, but even that marginalization is complicated by gender differences and the class heterogeneity within racial minority groups—which includes a few very visible outliers such as African American celebrity billionaire Oprah Winfrey and President Barak Obama, a biracial man who considers himself black. More generally, there is greater variation in inequality regimes, comparatively less policing of those regimes, and more contestation over them.[55]

While social scientists have stressed the demographic, social, and legal dynamics by which the US racial order is being *re-created* or *reentrenched*, analysts also need to attend to the cultural dynamics by which the racial order is *reimagined*. Changes in the social relations among racial group are accompanied by new ideas about what race is and why it matters and new conceptions of racial progress.

When decision makers project an identity for their organizations or communities as models of diversity, they give new meaning to the racial order. They reimagine the racial order as a peaceful, productive mosaic—not an exploitative hierarchy or a color-blind democracy. From this perspective, racial inclusion, especially the integration of black people into predominantly white settings, appears to be a fairly uncomplicated, universally positive process. These identities of diversity also give new meaning to American pluralism. Pluralism is not imagined as a regime of inequality (as some sociologists characterize it) or as divisive group making (as claimed by some critics of multiculturalism) but as an emergent social order in which cultural difference is as a social good and a competitive advantage, to be honored and appropriately managed.

For the cultural sociology of inequality, what is so striking about the push for diversity at this time of flux is that it has the pretense of minimizing categorical boundaries. Its proponents seek to make group boundaries less pernicious and thus expand social and symbolic membership—or at least they seem to do as much.[56] In the three cases studied, decision makers expressly reject prejudice and unfair barriers in the name of diversity. They denunciate some of the boundary-heightening tendencies common to organizations and communities.[57] The push for diversity does not reject racial distinctions altogether, though. Diversity efforts are almost always identity conscious. These efforts characterize (at least some) people and practices in reference to race, gender, sexual orientation, or the like, and they indicate that such differences should be recognized, valued, and actively promoted.[58] Further, diversity proponents revalue (some) minority group members as capable institutional participants, and they measure the worth of different racial and social groups as equal.

Diversity's expansion of social membership is inherently political and always incomplete.[59] The paradox of undoing boundaries in the contemporary era is that it is far easier for decision makers to make symbolic changes than to make social ones.

The changing racial order and the growing variation in inequality regimes across institutional settings greatly complicates the sociological analysis of how inequality is produced and the role of cultural processes therein. It calls for flexible analytic approaches and multimethod research strategies.

The Study: Relational Approach and Theory of Power

This book is theoretically motivated by an interest in organizations' symbolic politics.[60] Discourse is the most crucial medium by which ideas gain influence. As sociologist Ann Swidler explains, discourse is the "transpersonal ordering of symbols and meanings which sets the terms within which particular things may be said."[61] Discourse does not merely describe social life. It constitutes it.[62] It categorizes and assigns meaning to that which would not otherwise be meaningful.[63]

Through discourse, people with authority exercise power. Their conceptual categories, symbols, and linguistic devices enable them to control or limit others' actions.[64] Their discourse is ideological in that it is grounded in structural conditions, serves some groups' interests over others, and facilitates incorporation into a social setting.[65] Through discourse, decision makers legitimate and manipulate certain interpretations of social life. In fact, the ability to construct legitimate social realities is, in the words of political scientist David Kertzer, "the hallmark of power."[66] Perhaps these leaders are intentionally deceiving others, but their actions need not be premeditated or personalized and usually are not. This is their role. It is how they govern other people.

To understand the symbolic politics, discourse must be a central object of analysis, but it should not be abstracted from the social context of organizational, community, and political life. The meanings of any word, concept, action, or relationship derive from the social relationships and settings in which those ideas are formulated and expressed.[67] The relational turn in sociology provides useful analytic direction. The central precept of relational sociology is that social life takes place through interactive social relations.[68] To understand the push for diversity, then, this book attends to how people make meaning through the politics within and between organizations. Those meaning-making practices include people's ongoing construction of their interests and worldviews as well as their engagements with diversity structures such as initiatives, policies, programs, and offices.[69] The analysis centers on the interactive relationships between powerful decision makers, their constituents and audiences, and their detractors, as well as how those relationships re-create, mediate, or minimize social hierarchies and inequalities.[70] It also contextualizes symbolic politics in relation to history, political economies, laws, and systems of segregation. This requires attention to the cultures that define the field of action, the markets and institutional logics that influence people's priorities, and the power hierarchies and institutional conditions that shape people's opportunities and authority.

What This Book Is Not

The interpretive, relational approach of this book diverges from the standard scholarly treatment of diversity. Academics commonly refer to diversity as an inherently good thing, or they use the term to mean demographic heterogeneity. Those who treat diversity as a subject for analysis tend to do so from a distance through philosophical debate, polemics, or scrutiny of legal doctrine.[71] Many take sides in the political and legal debates over affirmative action.[72] Although this study is inspired by political critique and draws normative conclusions, it is not an attempt to develop an argument for or against affirmative action or any other policy intervention. It also is not a thorough attempt to understand those who ideologically oppose the objectives of diversity and diversity programs—those whose voices are exceptionally loud in the "comments" sections of online articles on the topic.

Nor is this book an attempt to assess the efficacy of diversity programs or heterogeneous workforces or to get inside people's minds to understand the social psychology of diversity.[73] It is not designed to do so. The results of such assessments are very relevant to the book's conclusions. I sometimes treat this line of social scientific research as qualitative empirical evidence: the research methodologies and scientific knowledge claims of the push for diversity.[74] Finally, this book is not an analysis of the institutionalization of corporate diversity rhetoric and programs, in the neo-institutionalist tradition.[75] While it complements such work, its central concerns are the symbolic politics of race and the role of culture in inequality, not the organizational and occupational reworking of law or processes of adoption and diffusion across organizations within an institutional field.[76]

Research Design and Methodology of Case Selection

The multicase research design is a hallmark of this book. The design rests on a relational conception of the object of inquiry: processes embedded in social context.[77] Specifically, the object of study is the organizational production of the notion of diversity, with sustained attention to its racial meanings.[78] That organizational process (or set of processes) serves as the analytic focal point and basis of commonality across the three very different cases. Such a focus is essential for managing the incredible heterogeneity in the data. The attention to process differs from a positivist focus on a static group, place, or program, which is typical of much sociological research. The research design also departs from a more traditional method of cross-case comparison, in which the researcher selects a number of cases, such as countries, that are similar on many variables but differ on others to explain variation across the cases.[79]

The research design builds on sociologist Diane Vaughan's approach of analogical theorizing, which in turn is inspired by Georg Simmel's argument for abstracting similar social forms from different social settings. Analogical theorizing develops explanations of social life through analysis and comparisons of a generic process across different sorts of organizations and at different levels of institutional activity.[80] It relies on a variety of forms of evidence, including thick ethnographic descriptions of single cases, and it benefits especially from historical data. The analyst generates theoretical explanations by looking for equivalent structures and processes while remaining mindful of the unique features of particular cases. Examining multiple cases forces the analyst to refine the argument in light of different sorts of data. It also helps to crystallize the broader social forces that influence local meanings and strategies of action.

The analysis of each case in this book centers on the activities that have the greatest bearing on the organizational production of diversity. With that focal point, it identifies common patterns and divergent themes in political participants' concepts of diversity and their strategies of institutionalizing those ideas (or lack thereof). The goal of the research design is to develop transferable sociological concepts, generalizable sociological explanations, and parallel demonstrations of theory.[81]

This is a multicase study of extreme cases, in which there is a lot of talk and action around diversity. With extreme cases, there is more evidence of the phenomena of interest, which enables the analyst to maximize the power of his or her observations.[82] The University of Michigan was one of the very first universities to pursue affirmative action in the 1960s, and the *Gratz* and *Grutter* cases were among the most important of that generation.[83] Rogers Park is one of the most racially and ethnically heterogeneous neighborhoods in one of the most segregated cities in the country.[84] Starr Corporation is among the most powerful companies in its industry in the world and has ranked in top slots in corporate diversity rankings. The cases here are not meant to be statistically representative of any other phenomena but, rather, are theoretically meaningful because they allow for logical inferences.[85]

The multiple cases require engagement with disparate areas of scholarship that scholars rarely bring into the same conversation—studies of higher education, urban sociology, and the sociology of work and organizations—to establish the relevant institutional practices, markets, patterns of stratification, and operative sources of power.[86] Because the push for diversity is structured in many ways through law, each case study has a strong legal backbone.

Each case study is qualitative and interpretive, based in fieldwork and historical evidence. I documented organizations' diversity activities through a variety of qualitative methods: ethnographic observations and interviews conducted between 2000 and 2006; analysis of contemporary organizational documents, legal cases, and media coverage; and historical research on those documentary sources dating back to the 1950s.[87] Following the tradition of theoretically engaged case-based ethnography, I developed the argument iteratively, through induction and interpretation while doing the field research and analysis and through the very act of writing. For instance, I

formulated the concept of the push for diversity by observing what organizations and participants in each case designated as relevant to diversity or
not. By investigating the topic from the bottom up, the analysis goes beyond
the glossy brochures that portray a unified agreement on diversity to show
how this push largely has been driven from the top down.

This book uses a few different conventions for protecting anonymity.
In the Michigan and Rogers Park cases, individuals are identified by their
real names if they consented to my doing so, were elected officials, had
public identities that could not be concealed, or made their remarks on the
public record. Each of those individuals is introduced by his or her first and
last name. First-name pseudonyms are used for all other individuals: a few
of the research participants at Michigan, most in Rogers Park, and everyone at Starr. The real names of organizations in the Michigan case and the
Rogers Park case are reported. A pseudonym is used for the company, per
my agreement with the company, and some specific details are concealed.
The appendix elaborates the research methods and methodological issues
in greater depth.

Forwarding the Cultural Sociology of Inequality

The Enigma of Diversity's analytic interventions help to explain a political
project that condemns (some) social hierarchies. In addition to its theoretical and empirical contributions to a variety of sociological subfields and
topics—higher education, affirmative action, urban community, workplace
organizations, and social movements—it engages theoretical themes that
cross cut various domains of social life. Building on insights from cultural
sociology and the study of stratification, the analysis elaborates the process
of boundary minimization. This process has received little scholarly attention compared to the voluminous research on the many ways that racial
group differences are invented, magnified, and used to exploit.

The book's attention to the symbolic politics in inter- and intraorganizational settings forwards social scientific research on racial ideology. That
field of scholarship by and large has neglected the meso level of organizational activity, and it has focused on identifying contradiction rather than
explaining causes and consequences. *The Enigma of Diversity* builds on constitutive theory of law, most notably the application of that theory by empirical critical race scholars.[88] The book shows how law manifests in social
life and, in turn, how law is produced, redefined, and reified or denigrated
through the meaning-making practices of organizations outside the formal
legal system. Likewise, it connects these legal practices to the reproduction

and dismantling of racial inequalities. And this book advances an emergent body of scholarship on the relational dynamics by which organizations influence inequality—scholarship developed by a network of scholars within which this book is situated.[89] By attending to the use of diversity rhetoric and the mobilization of diversity initiatives on the ground in organizations, it provides insight into the mechanisms by which organizational culture challenges some social hierarchies while legitimating others. These engagements with the sociology of race and organizations are revisited in chapter 1.

The unique research design of the study provides crucial analytic leverage. The multicase, multimethod analysis cuts across institutions and contexts and covers a span of fifty years. Thus it can show generality and variability of how integration is managed and how meaning making bears on inequality, and it can develop transferrable concepts. The triangulation of multiple methods, supplemented with secondary data on demographic patterns and quantitative outcomes, substantiates the book's claims.

There are six empirical chapters in this book, with two devoted to each of the case studies. The first chapter of each pair introduces the contemporary organizational or community of identity of that locale and elaborates the theme of boundary minimization. It traces the politicized development of that institutional identity over time, presented in a series of snapshots that provide a history of the present. It also explains the markets, segregation, and institutional practices relevant for the push for diversity. The second chapter of each pair centers on the key issue at hand—college admissions, housing policy, or human resource management—and the symbolic politics of racial progress. This chapter highlights the power dynamics among decision makers, those they oversee, and activists and the contentious fights and bureaucratic negotiations that ensue over discrete policy initiatives.

The ordering of case studies highlights a range of ways that racial justice is contained in relation to the mission of the mid-century civil rights movement. The Michigan case is closest to this original mission. In civil rights history, the Michigan case is a tragic Hobson's choice—a choice between what is available and nothing at all. Diversity efforts at Michigan cut off recognition of structural disadvantage to save a modest yet effective corrective policy. The Rogers Park case, where political leaders have less power over who lives in the neighborhood, is more complicated and more ambiguous in its consequences. Piecemeal gentrification takes place alongside a strong grassroots ethos of appreciating social difference. Starr Corporation marks the extreme neoliberal appropriation of diversity and the climax of the book's narrative arc. It is indicative of what is happening to workers in a market context that marginalizes people of color and treats lower-income people as of lesser value, irrelevant, and disposable.

When Mary Sue Coleman spoke at the MLK celebration, she was championing racial tolerance. She was endorsing the importance of racial minority inclusion and the university's obligations to support it. She was doing so without promoting King's core mission of dismantling racial and economic inequities or his radical denunciation of white supremacy. Such advocacy of diversity's value and payoffs provides an inspiring vision of racial integration. However, it presents integration as an accomplishment achieved or within close reach, one that is universally applauded and universally advantageous. In the name of diversity, American decision makers such as Coleman have upheld the civil rights movement's dream of a more just world while quieting its critique.

ONE

The Symbolic Politics of Racial Progress

The most clear-cut sign of social change is the development of a new vocabulary. As political scientist Thomas Rochon explains, a new vocabulary is more than just a simple change in terminology, and it does more than provide a unique description.[1] It enables the articulation and discussion of new concepts. It establishes a perspective from which the world should be viewed and a standard by which it should be assessed. Rochon writes, "Cultural change occurs when we alter the conceptual categories with which we give meaning to reality. It is a matter of *how* we think, not simply *what* we think."[2]

The post–civil rights period has been characterized by different political agendas and visions of racial progress—among them equality, color blindness, multiculturalism, diversity, and postracialism. Those politics are evident in the new vocabularies and concepts of race and difference that organizational leaders deem acceptable, the social relations they deem desirable, and the conditions of action that they deem normal. To explain how and why diversity advocates engage in the symbolic politics of racial progress, it is helpful to understand just what diversity is and its origins.

What *Is* Diversity?

In the American lexicon, the meaning of *diversity* is ambiguous. The Oxford English Dictionary defines *diversity* as "a range of different things." We speak of a diversity of people, objects, places, and ideas. In the national vocabulary, the word conjures the (usually positive) idea of social differences. It implies that a group, organization, or place can be composed of different elements that coexist amicably, without extreme conflict.[3] It is, if nothing else, a convenient shorthand that indicates a given fact of heterogeneity.

Diversity is also an abstract ideal. As legal scholar Peter Schuck writes, it is a normative principle that people associate with higher ends such as pleasure and competitiveness. Terms such as *community, democracy,* and *fairness* all share this same quality.[4] Who in the United States is willing to say that they do not value diversity?[5] The cultural ideal of diversity is "distinctively, if not uniquely, American," observes Schuck. "In the pantheon of unquestioned goods, diversity is right up there with progress, motherhood, and apple pie."[6] The popular rainbow bumper stickers urging "Celebrate Diversity" are a ubiquitous example. The word wears a halo.

When used without qualifiers, it commonly refers a heterogeneous mix of racial, ethnic, and language groups.[7] Often, it simply implies the presence of racial minorities, often just African Americans.[8] The same is true in popular media. In 2011, Marvel Comics announced a new Ultimate Spider-Man series featuring Miles Morales, a young man with an African American father and a Latina mother. The company's editor in chief explained, "What you have is a Spider-Man for the 21st century who's reflective of our culture and diversity."[9] It also may indicate a long list of somehow analogous differences, among them race, ethnicity, nationality, gender, sexual orientation, age, and other attributes as well as personal predilections such as viewpoint, lifestyle, and taste. Diversity might conflate race and class. It might mean race only sometimes.[10] It might not mean race at all. In addition, "diversity" is frequently a placeholder for a legal argument favoring affirmative action, particularly in high education.[11]

Diversity, we often hear, should be valued and empowered.[12] In the 2003 *Grutter* decision, the court established legal guidelines for how diversity should be conceived and treated in college admissions decisions. Beyond the admissions office, however, US legal doctrine, public policy, or even cultural norms provide little guidance on how diversity actually *should* be pursued in a vast range of settings.[13] Likewise, an organization's stated commitment to valuing diversity—like a commitment to building community or ensuring fairness—contains no clear prescription for action. The word wears a halo and also a haze.

With these features, *diversity* is what cultural sociologists call a keyword: an influential, binding term that is open to local interpretation but has some widely recognized associations.[14] For any person at any given moment, a keyword can have multiple meaningful associations that stem from different sources. The meanings of such a term depend on the social location of the speaker and his or her objectives, audiences, and context.[15]

Keywords become more important and more contentious in periods of cultural upheaval.[16] When people are less certain of the social conditions under which they live and the norms they should follow, broadly meaningful terms—whether *revolution, equality, the American Way, the nation,* or indeed *diversity*—provide touchstones.[17] They draw clarifying symbolic boundaries among groups of people that help to explain their relationships to each other and orient their actions. Not surprisingly, the organizational push for diversity emerged during a period of momentous cultural transformation—a time of uncertainty in the social status of marginalized groups and lack of clarity about the appropriate methods of governing those groups.

The Turn to Diversity

A cacophony of political, social, and economic forces propelled the organizational turn to diversity in different domains of American life in the late twentieth century. Many of these shifts directly or indirectly involved law. While the empirical chapters that follow specify the more proximate links between these shifts and decision makers' actions in the particular cases, there are some cross-cutting dynamics that created the historically new problem of minority representation and made *diversity* a useful keyword for managing it.

Midcentury Civil Rights Reforms

The antecedents of the turn to diversity lie, in part, in the political struggle for civil rights in the mid-twentieth century. Civil rights activists organized a massive challenge to the oppressive racial order of the United States.[18] Their political struggle gained momentum in the mid-1950s and reached an apex in the 1960s, calling for equality, justice, and full citizenship. Although the movement comprised multiple struggles, a basic premise was racial equality through integration: economic, political, legal, and social transformation that would open up to black people a proportional share of the country's resources.[19]

The activists achieved a major civil rights victory with the 1954 US Supreme Court case *Brown v. Board of Education.*[20] The Supreme Court decided unanimously that existing state laws that created separate public schools for black students and white students were unconstitutional under the equal protection clause of the Fourteenth Amendment to the US Constitution. Supporters interpreted the decision as both an embrace of the ideal of a color-blind Constitution and a call for the dismantling of the country's racial caste system.[21] While political debates in later decades framed these objectives as being in conflict, *Brown* supporters viewed opposition to racial classifications (the anticlassification principle of the equal protection clause) and opposition to systemic racial inequality as part and parcel of the same struggle.

The legislative victories of the 1960s made color-blind liberalism the primary legal foundation of racial progress.[22] The Civil Rights Act of 1964 and subsequent reforms prohibited discrimination and segregation based on race, ethnicity, sex, national origin, and other statuses in employment, education, public accommodation, housing, and other realms. De jure racial segregation—segregation required or allowed by law—was made unconstitutional. While lawmakers were motivated by mass mobilizations for black civil rights and long-rooted problems of black disadvantage, the new civil rights protections were premised on a paradigm of abstract color-blind liberalism, which frames racial distinctions as extraneous to the pursuit of equality.[23] Put differently, this paradigm insists that law treat racial-group categories as unimportant, both socially and symbolically. Lawmakers rejected the widespread use of race to denigrate people of color, especially in the Jim Crow South. The new laws granted formal equality and set fairness as the standard, based on the assumption that justice is best achieved through nondiscrimination and equal opportunity for individuals regardless of their membership in a minority group. Abstract liberalism still prevails in American law and politics.

This was not just an upheaval in black-white relations. Chicano activists, feminists, and gay and lesbian organizers mobilized in the 1960s and 1970s to more assertively demand societal acceptance and fair treatment.[24] Although African Americans remained the paradigmatic minority group, Hispanics and women, in particular, benefited from the extension of federal protections first conceived for African Americans.[25]

In the late 1960s and early 1970s, alongside this prevailing strategy of color-blind antidiscrimination protections, the federal government established some actions to proactively remove barriers to black progress. As sociologist John Skrentny shows, federal agencies adopted interventionist affirmative action programs in order to pragmatically demonstrate results of their efforts.[26] Unlike civil rights reforms, these programs—many of which are still in operation—openly recognized race on the grounds that such recognition is necessary to rectify unfair disadvantages experienced by racial minorities.[27] They distinguished different racial groups to undo racial inequities. The largest of these programs was workplace affirmative action requirements, detailed further in chapters 6 and 7.

In the realm of housing, attempts by the US Department of Housing and Urban Development (HUD) to implement prointegrative policies in the 1960s and 1970s were less successful. Deliberate government efforts to integrate African Americans into white neighborhoods have included racial-maintenance housing programs and scattered-site public housing (for poor people but primarily serving African Americans). However, there were few of these programs, and meaningful federal interventions were dismantled by the administration of President Richard Nixon.[28] Largely unrelated to those federal interventions, some universities and colleges in the 1960s and 1970s adopted affirmative admissions policies, which considered the race of applicants in order to increase the enrollment of African Americans.[29]

The government's proactive integration measures conceptualized race as countable minorities. In the late 1960s, the Equal Employment Opportunity Commission, which oversees implementation of Title VII of the US Civil Rights Act, began requiring employers to track and report the race of all employees.[30] It then used those numeric measures of racial representation to identify patterns of discrimination by a company or within a geographic region or industry. In 1977, this conceptualization of race was formalized by the US Office of Management and Budget, which issued guidelines for standardizing the federal government's collection of racial data for the purposes of gathering data and monitoring civil rights.[31] These guidelines codified a set of official racial categories that historian David Hollinger describes as the ethno-racial pentagon: African American, white, Hispanic, Asian / Pacific Islander, and American Indian.[32]

These government interventions rested on an ideology of remedial racial justice. They framed racial discrimination (and sometimes gender- and class-based discrimination) as a problem institutionalized systematically in organizations' practices and in need of proactive correction.[33] Similar assumptions about systemic discrimination and remedial justice undergirded a few key court cases. In *Griggs v. Duke Power Co.* (1971), the Supreme Court affirmed the legal theory of disparate impact under Title VII of the Civil Rights Act, finding that formally neutral tests could have a disproportionately negative impact on minorities, so employers that used such tests had to convincingly justify them as a business necessity.[34] The multiple decisions in *Gautreaux v. Chicago Housing Authority*, first decided in 1969, and the 1981 *United States v. Yonkers Board of Education* case sought to remedy discrimination and segregation by promoting residential mixing along racial and economic lines.[35] *Gautreaux* resulted in a large housing mobility program designed to help African American public housing residents to move to more affluent, majority-white communities, and that program became a model for at least fifty other desegregation programs across the country.

Although the keyword *diversity* emerged in the late 1960s, it was neither a cornerstone of civil rights reforms nor a principle of decisions such as *Griggs* and *Gautreaux*. Its earliest supporters were white college administrators and community activists trying to encourage black integration into exclusively white universities and neighborhoods. These leaders derived the notion of diversity to make sense of those experiences, deflect legal opposition mounted by conservatives, and—for the universities—to prevent federal interference in their admissions processes.[36] University administrators were retooling their admissions policies to be more inclusive.[37] Notably, the Big Three elite colleges—Harvard, Yale, and Princeton—took on a new goal of rapidly growing the number of black students.[38] They primarily explained their goals as an effort to develop Negro leadership, although they also stressed the notion of diversity and sometimes mentioned the need to compensate for historical injustices against African Americans.[39] Concurrently, some neighborhood activists who supported racial integration adopted diversity rhetoric in their efforts to appease resistant white residents and the antagonistic real estate industry.[40] This was evident in some transitioning Chicago neighborhoods such as Rogers Park, Hyde Park on the city's South Side, and suburban Oak Park—all white neighborhoods experiencing in-movement of black residents.[41] For the time being, diversity was associated positively with African American representation in white-dominated settings but did not yet have strong ideological associations.

Powell's Opinion in Bakke

In the 1970s, Allan Bakke, a white man and undistinguished student, had applied twice to the medical school at the University of California–Davis and was twice rejected. With some support from the nascent neoconservative movement, Bakke legally challenged the university's program that set aside sixteen seats for racial minority students out of the one hundred seats available.[42] Because the legality of affirmative admissions was uncertain, the *Regents of California v. Bakke* case garnered public attention.[43] In the Supreme Court's 1978 decision, a solo-authored opinion by Justice Lewis Powell established *diversity* as a keyword for race under law. The importance of his opinion for the push for diversity in higher education and beyond cannot be overstated.

There was no clear-cut majority opinion in *Bakke*. The nine justices were very divided. Five of the justices found the UC-Davis policy an unconstitutional racial quota—a numeric requirement based on race. Four of those took the stance that admissions policies should be altogether color-blind. For them, there was no meaningful difference between racial subordination and race-conscious remedies intended to counteract subordination. Justice Stevens argued for "a colorblind standard. . . . Race cannot be the basis of excluding anyone from participation in a federally funded program."

Four other justices in *Bakke*—called the Brennan Four, after Justice William Brennan—would have found the policy constitutional. For these justices, race could be considered in admissions for the purposes of remedying racial minority disadvantage. They opined that the government "may adopt race-conscious programs designed to overcome substantial, chronic minority under-representation where there is reason to believe that the evil addressed is a product of past racial discrimination." They argued against the color-blind position as well. Justice Harry Blackmun wrote, "In order to get beyond racism, we must first take account of race. There is no other way. And in order to treat some persons equally, we must as well treat them differently."

Powell was one of the five justices who objected to the UC-Davis policy, but he did not call for color-blind admissions; he agreed with the Brennan Four that affirmative action was sometimes acceptable. His solo-authored opinion was a nonremedial defense of affirmative action. He framed this defense in terms of diversity. Drawing on a brief submitted by Harvard, Columbia, and a few other prestigious universities, he reasoned that individual students bring different valuable qualities to the mix on college campuses and that race is one of many "pertinent elements of diversity." Universities could consider race in college admissions decisions, he wrote, if they treated a student's race or ethnicity as a "plus" factor and did so with the objective of diversity, which he described as socially beneficial. His opinion identified diversity as a constitutional rationale for accounting for race in admissions decisions. It provided an instrumentalist argument for race-conscious decision making: institutional benefits—"the robust exchange of ideas" central to the educational mission—ensue from an environment that is diverse along many dimensions. This was an argument for productive diversity.

Powell's opinion in *Bakke* was the US government's first major endorsement of diversity as a legal concept and the first legal justification for considering race based on diversity's functional and practical benefits.[44] For universities and colleges that wanted to practice affirmative admissions, his argument was safest to follow because it allowed race-conscious policies while setting the most restrictive parameters on them. Historian Nancy

MacLean writes of the response to *Bakke*, "Supporters grasped at the new language as at a life raft on a perilous sea."[45]

As the highest court in the country, the Supreme Court is the ultimate authority on federal law and the Constitution. One of the court's most important roles is to determine whether the Constitution protects a right and whether a constitutional right has been violated. Its judgments clarify law and establish precedent. They formalize parameters on what is lawful and what is not.

Yet it was not a foregone conclusion that universities or any other institution would follow Powell's lead. As social scientists Anna Kirkland and Ben Hansen note, Powell's argument about diversity "evolved as an alternative, not as an independently robust jurisprudential concept."[46] It provided what seemed like a legally viable alternative to an ideology of color blindness and a moderate alternative to an ideology of remedial racial justice. Over time, his opinion created a governing standard. It simultaneously put pressures on colleges and universities to frame their admissions objectives in the narrow terms of diversity, to signal that they were complying with law and not unlike peer institutions. Law enabled the turn to diversity but did not require it.

Powell's conception of diversity tapped into a long-standing ideology of cultural pluralism, which explicitly recognizes ethnic differences and venerates those differences as meaningful cultural attributes. Cultural pluralism has roots in the early twentieth century, when there were strong nativist pressures on immigrants to assimilate. Intellectuals and activists who wanted to counter these norms called for the preservation of peasant European immigrants' cultures.[47] The Jewish philosopher Horace Kallen articulated a vision of democracy in which immigrants to the United States retained unique aspects of their ancestry rather than lose those traits in a melting pot.[48]

Cultural pluralism experienced a revival in the 1970s, with support in many circles dominated by white people: Nixon's administration, local festivities honoring the American 1976 bicentennial, and the descendants of Polish, Irish, and other immigrants who began to identify as ethnic.[49] Its central ethos was a reverence for the distinctiveness of different ethnic group identities and histories. This was a play borrowed from black cultural nationalists.[50] Unlike black nationalists' calls for separatism, though, which criticized the very premise of a cohesive social order, the normatively white cultural pluralist revival posed cultural differences as a basis of national unity and universalism. Adherents also ignored activists' concerns about structural racism, sexism, and economic inequality.[51] Sociologists Nathan Glazer and Patrick Moynihan provided intellectual authority to this reactionary position by developing a theory of race as ethnic difference and by portraying the cultures of African Americans and Latinos as the root of those groups' social hardships.[52] Glazer's work depicted minorities as favored and white people as subordinated.

Powell's opinion in *Bakke* reiterates key themes of cultural pluralism with its characterization of black people as one of many valued cultural groups—among them, violin players and "a farm boy from Idaho." Powell posed an innocuous equivalence among those groups, suggesting that all could potentially add "an essential ingredient to the educational process." As did Glazer, Powell referred skeptically to "the white 'majority.'" He characterized white people as "composed of various minority groups most of which can lay claim to a history of discrimination."[53] And, for Powell, racial inequality was not a pressing concern, nor was its remedy a legitimate explanation for affirmative action.

Color-Blind Opposition to Race-Conscious Programs

The turn to diversity was also a defense against the rise of the conservative movement. By the early 1970s, following the movement of federal administrators toward a pragmatic model of workplace affirmative action, color blindness became a banner for white and Jewish right-wing activists who opposed affirmative action.[54] They stopped arguing in favor of white supremacy (which had been their initial stance) and began to decry so-called racial preferences, quotas, and reverse discrimination. Their color-blind position was that no racial group should be deliberately favored in order to protect individuals' constitutional rights and that racial progress is best achieved by ignoring race.

Over time, color blindness became a prevailing legal theory regarding race-conscious programs. In the 1970s, the Supreme Court tacked away from a systemic analysis of discrimination and became more hostile toward race- and sex-based affirmative action.[55] In *Bakke*, four of the five justices who found the UC-Davis policy unconstitutional—all the justices but Powell—endorsed color blindness by reasoning that *all* race-attentive admissions policies violated the color-blind standard established by the Civil Rights Act, even if the intent was to undo discrimination. With *Washington v. Davis* (1976), the court emphasized equal protection from racism that was intentional but not from practices with discriminatory effects. *City of Richmond v. J. A. Croson Co.* (1989) solidified this treatment by holding that a minority set-aside program was reverse discrimination because the remedy was not tailored to serve identifiable victims of past discrimination. Legal scholar Ian Haney-López argues that the color-blind standard established by these decisions is a form of institutional racism.[56]

As the neoconservative movement gained steam in the mid-1980s, civil rights organizations simultaneously lost members and power. Their rallying cry of fighting societal injustice was discredited and drowned out by their critics and had eroding legal support. To counter conservative opposition to race-conscious policies, some of the remaining civil rights activists turned to that keyword, *diversity*, and the meanings codified by Powell's opinion in order to counter conservative opposition. While this played out primarily in the legal contests over race-conscious admissions, elaborated in chapters 2 and 3, diversity served this purpose in realms beyond higher education; it could be easily adapted to the political contingencies of different contexts. For instance, in 1985, Alexander Polikoff, who served for decades as the lead counsel for the *Gautreaux* plaintiffs, was concerned about the countermovement against racial integration maintenance plans. With support from President Reagan, the federal courts, HUD, and other government agencies, conservative activists were openly questioning the constitutionality of those programs on the grounds that they promoted racial quotas and racial steering.[57] At a hearing of the US Commission on Civil Rights, Polikoff proposed that civil rights activists inoculate their prointegration efforts by calling them racial diversity efforts and by emphasizing "the positive value of diversity."[58] In its 1990 decision in *Metro Broadcasting, Inc. v. Federal Communications Commission*, the Supreme Court applied Powell's diversity rationale to the context of mass media.[59] It agreed that a diversity of views and information on the airwaves would uphold important First Amendment values and that the FCC's policies, which favored minorities applying for broadcast licenses, helped to achieve such diversity in addition to serving some remedial purposes.

Legal Compliance, Legitimacy Pressures, and Professional Endorsements

During the 1970s and 1980s, the shifting legal climate also created pressures within workplaces and professions that led to the institutionalization of diversity management. US corporations were anxious to show their compliance with new vague and broad government antidiscrimination mandates, but they were uninterested in institutionalizing the large-scale efforts to hire people of color and women that activists wanted. In the 1960s and 1970s, personnel experts within companies—in the words of sociologist Frank Dobbin—"invented equal opportunity."[60] The new equal employment opportunity (EEO) and affirmative action (AA) policies and offices were threatened when Reagan became president in 1980.[61] His administration oversaw major cuts to staffing and funding for monitoring employment discrimination, thus all but ending enforcement of affirmative action. Meanwhile, public support for the policy waned. Companies curbed their most aggressive affirmative action programs but maintained those specialists and their safeguards against discrimination.

Faced with the prospects of losing their jobs, human resources (HR) experts reframed EEO/AA and refashioned their skills under the banner of corporate diversity management. The diversity managers adopted a new instrumentalist, pragmatic rhetoric on the benefits of diversity: it would enable companies to recruit and optimize the skills of people of color and women as well as improve companies' abilities to reach an increasingly diverse markets by creating a workforce with more varied views and experiences.[62]

Companies' primary motivation for adopting these responses was not the upward mobility of people of color and women. They have shown little interest in figuring out which interventions are actually effective. And when put to rigorous scholarly tests, most of these initiatives—including the most popular one, diversity training—do not result in the movement of white women and people of color into management.[63]

Rather, employers adopted diversity responses because they facilitated companies' legitimacy. Such responses met the expectations of different audiences, including regulators, and conformed to industry norms.[64] The new diversity management programs, like the EEO/AA structures, were in large measure symbolic, as they were disconnected from core employment decisions.[65] Professional associations such as the Society for Human Resource Management and diversity consultants provided resources and pressure promoting diversity management as more effective than workplace affirmative action. These responses became institutionalized quite widely over time as they diffused across organizations.[66]

The turn to diversity found support among professionals outside human resource departments as well. In the 1980s, college admissions officers and New Urbanist planners began to depict their work in terms of what political scientist Daniel Lipson labels a diversity consensus.[67] Like the HR specialists Dobbin studied, these professionals came to see appreciation for diversity as part of their professional norms and expertise. On many college campuses, administrators embraced affirmative action as diversity policies, and those policies satisfied the various legitimacy pressures they faced from constituents such as African American and Latino communities.[68] There was not a comparable noteworthy effort by US mayors at this time to champion urban diversity, although large private foundations, most notably the Ford

Foundation, encouraged their grantees in urban communities to take up the objective of diversity.[69]

The Rise of Multiculturalism

Corporate diversity managers' predictions in the 1980s of an impending explosion of people of color and women in the workforce population proved overblown, but the country's demographics were changing momentously. Starting in the 1970s, more people of color joined the college-bound population, the professional workforce, and the middle class, in large measure because of university affirmative admissions and federal workplace affirmative action requirements.[70] The passage of the Immigration and Nationality Act of 1965 enabled massive waves of immigration from Africa, South and Central America, and Asia.[71] Movements for identity politics—advocacy of and by people of color, women, people of marginalized religions and geographic regions, and sexual minorities such as gays and lesbians—burgeoned in the 1980s. The country's growing heterogeneity was not a story of unadulterated success, though, as social inequalities persisted, ranging from an ongoing white monopoly on the best jobs and schools to lower wages for women and antigay violence. Economic inequality began to escalate while the concentration of poverty worsened in black and Latino city neighborhoods.[72]

An ideology of multiculturalism gained popularity in the 1980s and early 1990s as a framework for making sense of these changes. As Louis Menand argues, multiculturalism was a reaction to the demise of the Cold War and a universalist, majoritarian notion of American culture.[73] Multiculturalism calls for the equal esteem of the world's cultures and societies on grounds that those cultures are morally equivalent.[74] It carried on cultural pluralism's themes of revering minority cultures and treating the members of an ethno-racial group as culturally predisposed to hold certain worldviews.[75] Yet, unlike cultural pluralists, many multiculturalists were attuned to race, gender, sexual orientation, and, to a far lesser extent, class. They questioned the American ideal of a common culture as patriarchal, heterosexual, and Eurocentric. In literary theory, radical multiculturalism posed such a common culture as incommensurable with the culture of "others."[76] Multiculturalist sentiments became institutionalized primarily through curricula in elementary schools and college classrooms in the 1980s and early 1990s, where advocates challenged the selection of the literary canon and other treatments of elite white men's experiences as the pinnacle of legitimate knowledge.[77] Identity politics, an important component of multiculturalism, prioritized the recognition of distinct cultural groups over class concerns and the equitable redistribution of material resources.[78]

Talk of diversity was a part of multiculturalism. According to sociologist Antonia Randolph, in multicultural school curricula a theme of assimilating diversity took hold, one that was "color conscious but race blind."[79] Teachers' discourse celebrated diversity while it ethnicized racial minority status, relying on cultural explanations of black underachievement, favoring some immigrant children while sanctioning African American students and schools, and ever perpetuating whiteness as the normative standard. Over time, the term *diversity* became favored over *multiculturalism*—university and corporate multiculturalism were reconceived in the 1990s as diversity offices and initiatives—likely because diversity more evidently eschewed a social-justice view in favor of a view of productive, generative group relations.[80]

Neoliberal Capitalism and Commodification

The turn to diversity was driven by the emergence of economic neoliberalism as well. The core ideological tenet of neoliberalism is that individual liberties should be advanced through a neoclassical model of economics. Neoliberalism heralds unfettered capitalist markets and the retooling of government regulation to facilitate those markets.[81] An economic regime of shareholder capitalism justified on these terms developed in the latter half of the twentieth century. The US economy and the national economies of other countries became increasingly oriented to global economies and service provision, and global competition became more intense.[82]

Following the economic downturn of the early 1970s, corporations began to more vigorously undermine once-strong labor unions, and they advocated government deregulation.[83] These efforts gained momentum in the 1980s, especially with the election of Reagan. Maximizing shareholder value became of upmost importance to many firms as corporations began to rely more on institutional investors, the financial sector grew with minimal regulatory restrictions, and CEO pay became tied to stock options.[84] This economic regime prioritizes returns for wealth holders and eviscerates much of the power of lower-income employees. Endemic to it has been the deterioration of stable, livable wages for US workers, less job security, dramatic worsening of income inequality, and economic crises.[85]

While neoliberal capitalist growth processes seem, at first blush, not to be racial, they leverage racial meanings and racial exploitation in the service of generating profit.[86] Specifically, the racial logic of neoliberalism refashions race for niche consumer markets, often under the guise of diversity.[87] Ethno-racial differences get commodified to sell neighborhoods like Harlem, with Starbucks corporation promoting its new store there to symbolize its racial cosmopolitanism for white suburbanites, and products like the United Colors of Benneton clothing line, which began in the 1980s with provocative images challenging moral and political taboos.[88] Racial differences have also been mobilized in employment markets. Employers rely on them as indicators of employees' abilities to perform certain jobs at both the top and the bottom of the occupation ladder, whether in niche marketing or lawn maintenance.[89]

Thus the strongest forces propelling the turn to diversity can be summarized. Powell's opinion in *Bakke* established diversity's benefits as the legitimate explanation for those who wanted to proactively consider race in admissions decisions. A celebratory discourse on diversity and its instrumental benefits supplemented an ideology of remedial racial justice and became the primary counter to conservative calls for color blindness in social policy. The consequences rippled far beyond the admissions office. With the declining power of the civil rights movement, the growth of the neoconservative movement, and the erosion of federal support, those who supported race-conscious policies found Powell's diversity rationale very appealing. Likewise, in the face of legitimacy pressures, vague federal mandates, and new constituents, professionals such as corporate managers and teachers adopted a new organizational culture endorsing diversity. As the US population became increasingly heterogeneous, multiculturalist ideologies explained racial divisions as cultural differences. Likewise, a neoliberal capitalist regime encouraged a market-friendly notion of diversity as commodifiable differences and skill sets.

At the confluence of these shifts, institutional leaders have confronted new pressures to manage increasingly heterogeneous but persistently unequal student bodies, communities, workplaces, congregations, military units, and the like.[90] These pressures include the historically novel problem of racial minority representation. There is a widespread expectation (often shared by decision makers themselves) that at least some people of color will be present in the company of white people and treated with respect. At the same time, there is the expectation that racial minority representation can be achieved without major substantive social change and without unduly threatening the advantages enjoyed by white people. Sometimes, such representation includes a parallel expectation that women, gays and lesbians, and other marginalized populations will be respectfully included among or alongside majority groups.

The issue of racial representation has raised new challenges in political and organizational governance. Institutional leaders face the task of managing racially mixed environments unlike any before in history. Yet they have had little legal guidance on how to influence the representation of certain racial groups or govern intergroup racial dynamics. They must contend with legal and social restrictions. Quotas, for example, are forbidden. They need new language, strategies of action, and explanations of why representation matters. Further, organizational leaders and political officials have strong incentives to look like they are concerned with racial representation but not to change anything too drastically. In this context, some have found *diversity* a useful keyword.

Scholars across disparate fields and subfields have begun to identify positive outcomes associated with diversity—conceived alternately as programmatic interventions, demographic representation, skills and viewpoints, or social psychological beliefs. In a pathbreaking analysis, sociologists Alexandra Kalev, Frank Dobbin, and Erin Kelly demonstrate that workplace affirmative action and diversity management initiatives designed to hold managers accountable effectively increase the share of African Americans and white women—far more so than initiatives intended to reduce managerial bias.[91] Seminal research by William Bowen and Derrick Bok shows that affirmative admissions demonstrably improve the educational opportunities and career prospects of African Americans as well as the leadership capacity in black communities.[92] They find that affirmative action beneficiaries who graduated from elite universities have formed the "backbone" of the black middle class. A study by Cedric Herring finds that businesses with more racially heterogeneous workforces have larger consumer bases and higher relative profits; thus, in some form, the business case for diversity proves true.[93] In "soft" decisions that employers make about how to organize work, such as selecting members for a hiring committee, considering race and sex in decisions can create an integrated workplace environment where biases are lessened.[94]

Management scholars have shown that some workgroup performance outcomes are improved (and others not) by a greater diversity in the racial and gender composition, skills, and styles of various groups.[95] In his 2007 book, *The Difference: How the Power of Diversity Creates Better Groups, Firms, Schools, and Societies*, Scott Page reviews a large body of research and surmises that a diversity of perspectives leads to superior outcomes in product development, management, laboratory research, democratic governance, and beyond.[96] Social psychologists who study perceptions of diversity find that in workplace settings where white people express support for the positive recognition of racial and ethnic group differences, people of color are more likely to be psychologically engaged and to perceive less bias.[97] The opposite is true in workplaces, as well: where white people believe that race differences should be ignored, people of color are more likely to be psychologically disengaged and to perceive bias.

Meanwhile, some scholars interested in post–civil rights racial ideology, myself included, have turned a critical eye to popular discourses on diversity.

Bringing in Organizations to the Study of Post–Civil Rights Racial Ideology

Social scientists have examined new contemporary vocabularies of race, foremost by studying racial discourse. Racial discourses express the ideological foundation of a racialized social system.[98] They are systems of meaning that contribute to the maintenance of social hierarchies. Analysis of racial discourse speaks to what sociologist Howard Winant identifies as the core ideological paradox of the current period: pervasive symbolism of equality, diversity, and multiculturalism persists alongside the real-life realities of entrenched racial inequality.[99]

The most influential analyses of post–civil rights discourse have focused on the racialized rhetoric of color blindness and, increasingly, diversity. Methodologically, most of this research has been based on interviews, surveys, and analyses of organizational documents. Using interviews and surveys, Eduardo Bonilla-Silva and his collaborators show that people articulate a color-blind, abstract universalism that explains unequal social relations as natural, inconsequential, and a product of individual minorities' bad choices.[100] The neighborhood residents of different cities interviewed by sociologists Joyce Bell and Doug Hartmann speak of race as diversity, in a positive, abstract, and universalizing light.[101] Through a content analysis, sociologists Lauren Edelman, Sally Riggs Fuller, and Iona Mara-Drita find that professional management periodicals present a managerial rhetoric of diversity. This rhetoric equates social statuses that are bases of disenfranchisement with identities and skills that purportedly make for a more effective workforce.[102]

These analyses of narratives, wordplay, and rationalizations show deep disjunctures between the egalitarian world that individuals and organizations imagine and the world as it is actually lived and patterned by hierarchies. In one way or another, this research shows how discourses of color blindness and diversity are ideological expressions derived from unequal, expropriative relationships between subordinate and dominant groups.[103] Such discourses bolster power inequities by obscuring them, diminishing possible opposition, and providing beneficiaries with interpretations that they find plausible and satisfying. Color-blind racism denies the importance of white people's preferences for other white people. It alleviates white people of responsibility for racism. Happy talk of diversity betrays individuals' accounts of their actual relationships and interactions with other people. It interferes with their ability to talk about inequality. Corporate diversity rhetoric undermines the antidiscrimination intent of civil rights law.

By design, these empirical analyses end at the level of spoken words and written texts. This hampers our understanding of race. The power of discourse does not come alone from the world it imagines or its repetition by people with high status and bully pulpits. As sociologist Loïc Wacquant writes in his statement on the analytics of racial domination, "Discourses do not contain within themselves the social mechanisms that endow them with potency."[104]

While it is important for scholars to document what people *say* about race it also is necessary to understand what people *do* with such ideas and why. Without observation or contextual information about people's lives, scholars tend to attribute people's interpretations directly to their social status, organizational office, or legal doctrine, thus imputing motives from social structure.[105] Further, the scholarly critique of spoken and written racial discourse tends to end with the identification of contradiction, not an empirical explanation of causes, processes, or consequences.

Also missing from most major studies of post–civil rights racial discourse and from much of the larger, fruitful body of research on racial formation is in-depth attention to racial meanings at the meso level of intraorganizational politics.[106] Studies of the creation of racial groups and racial inequalities usually telescope out to show how race becomes codified at the macro level through state policy and labor markets.[107] They have zoomed in, too, to explore up close how individuals creatively negotiate their own racial identities at the micro level.[108] But they less often look to organizational routines, cultures, and forms. While organizational processes are foregrounded in research on diversity management by Edelman, Dobbin, and their collaborators, it is not for the purposes of explaining the exercise of power over race.[109]

Formal organizations—companies, universities, units of government, nonprofit groups, churches—are a key social domain in which race becomes meaningful, ideological, and consequential. In these contexts, racial boundaries are drawn and racial ideas gain authority through power relations, rules, routines, law, and formal structures.

Symbolic Politics and the Organizational Production of Diversity

At Michigan, in Rogers Park, and at Starr, decision makers have adopted new vocabularies of diversity. They have established diversity as an organizational-political perspective and a standard for managing minority representation. While these three cases differ in many respects, there are some commonalities in *diversity*'s organizational meanings, uses, and influences and the power dynamics therein. In so many words, there are crosscutting themes in the organizational production of diversity across all the cases. Many of these ways of producing and "doing" diversity facilitate selective inclusion. Some are squarely about race. Others are not. But in one way or another, all have relevance for the symbolic politics of racial progress.

A Buzzword, Symbolically Amplified

In the cases studied in this book, decision makers deploy *diversity* as a presumptively positive buzzword. They rely on it to symbolically amplify aspects of social life as of a higher and more venerable order.[110] These decision makers reference diversity to draw contrasts, too—to vilify aspects of social life as threatening, denigrated, or inferior.[111] *Diversity*, as they use it, is not our grandfathers' racism. It is not a lily-white suburban enclave, an impenetrable ivory tower, an old white boys' club, or a simple or bland homogeneity. Although diversity's substance remains unclear, they most consistently define *diversity* as a numeric measure of the proportional representation of minorities, with success defined as reaching some unspecified compositional threshold. On websites and in public speeches, local leaders repeat these statistics again and again. This is the halo and the haze, put to use.

That *diversity* is a memorable word is significant. This makes it easy to repeat, recognize, and market. Taken up in law, social policy, bureaucracy, and public relations, that word becomes powerful. It seems real, objective, and difficult to discredit. It also constitutes people's self-understanding, which is a mechanism of power albeit more indefinable, subtle, and self-imposed.

The Double Move: First to Race and Then to Culture

Diversity proponents do many things with *diversity*, and one of these is advocate for race-targeted policies. They have pursued such policies in hopes of involving modest numbers of people of color—foremost, African

Americans—and encouraging white people's positive reception. Couching their objectives in terms of *diversity* can help to insulate them—against legal challenges, against regulatory scrutiny, and against charges of racism or apathy. Diversity can thus be a cover for intervention targeted to people of color—which is one interpretation of racial progress and its achievement.

Organizations do the second move of diversity when they advocate diversity as a politics of inclusion that does not necessarily or solely involve racial representation. The very word suggests the representation of many different groups—people of color, women, immigrants, gays and lesbians, non-Christians, and people with disabilities, among others—and the creation of an inclusive environment. These groups are not the privileged majority, but purportedly have an important place among the majority. When someone complains, "There was no diversity" in an organization or at an organized event, that person often is referring to an absence of women, people of color, and perhaps other minority groups. That person is suggesting a failure, on the part of someone in charge, to include those groups. According to sociologist Mitchell Stevens, this prevailing interpretation of *diversity* relies on an unmarked category of whiteness and treats that category as the (purportedly) neutral referent for defining other people and things as diverse.[112]

The second move of diversity, away from a justification for race-based intervention, frequently is accompanied by a change in *diversity*'s meaning: *diversity* tends to refer to cultural, racial, and other types of difference.[113] More specifically, it tends to refer to cultural identity. Further, decision makers construe success as the expression of cultural identities in interpersonal interaction and toward shared institutional objectives.[114] This sentiment is evident, for example, in the popular photograph of hands of different colors grasping each other in unity (see fig. 1.1). When diversity is a matter of culture, particularly in organizational rhetoric and quasi-pedagogical activities, it can extend to vague and superficial differences. In diversity training at Starr Corporation, cognitive approaches and idiosyncratic personal preferences, such as being a "daytime" or "nighttime" person, are presented as forms of diversity valued by the company.[115]

Racial progress, understood as such, is a mutually beneficial outcome. And it is just one element of a larger accomplishment enjoyed by many groups. In some versions of that popular photograph of the interlocked hands, the hands visibly belong to women and men or the young and old. This conception of diversity is especially evident in the identities that decision makers at Michigan, in Rogers Park, and at Starr construct for their organization or community, as an epicenter of diversity. From this perspective,

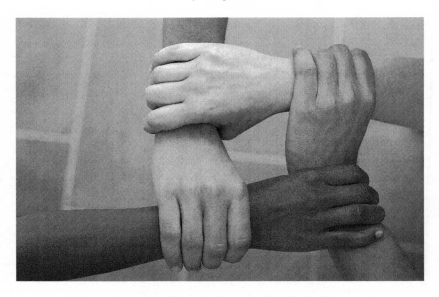

1.1. A popular symbol of diversity. *Source*: Joachim Wendler/Shutterstock

a cohesive yet always-evolving social order is generated through the interaction among minority and majority groups.[116] Different cultural groups seem to coexist peacefully and cooperatively for their mutual benefit and the good of the institution writ large.

This cultural conception of racial progress is reiterated in organizations' justifying rhetoric on diversity's instrumentalist advantages.[117] Starr Corporation's business case for diversity is typical in stating, "A culturally sensitive, diverse workforce is better able to . . . generate the wealth of ideas that are key to innovation." Such rhetoric suggests that pluralism is productive, in service of the bottom line. The legal rationale for diversity similarly emphasizes diversity's pragmatic payoffs for learning, for the benefit of people of color *and* white people.

This second move, toward a politics of inclusiveness and a cultural conception of race, can animate advocacy for redistributive race-targeted programs. It can affirm social heterogeneity contra a majoritarian preference for what is white Anglo-Saxon and traditional; sociolegal theorist Mariana Valverde calls this affirmation the "rainbow nation" version of diversity.[118] Diversity's emphasis on shared benefits is an ideological counter to the now widespread view among white people that racism is "a zero-sum game that they are now losing"—the view that antiwhite bias has risen over the last six decades as antiblack bias has declined, such that racism against white people is a more serious societal problem than racism against African Americans.[119] Further, this organizational paradigm of diversity prompts social psychological responses from white people that may translate into their greater support for diversity initiatives.[120] Overall, white people perceive ethno-racial multiculturalism as exclusive of white people. But an ideological message that white people, too, have a place in diversity can give them a sense that they personally belong.

The second move can make room for some dissent as well. With diversity, there is a presumption that minority groups should be seen and heard. Some political activists, like those with the Rogers Park Community Action Network, have invoked *diversity* as a banner for the interests, rights, and political power of people of color, immigrants, poor people, and renters.

But by and large, the top-down diversity movement does not pursue racial progress by undoing structural obstacles. Sometimes, diversity advocates are designating collective group interests—to foster cohesion, minimize strife, to inoculate, or for political appeal. Routinely, though, their talk is low-stakes affirmation of cultural difference, for the purposes of very selective inclusion. These leaders may simply imply diversity by photoshopping. One example is college brochures in which students of color are overrepresented compared to their actual numbers on campus.[121] In a recent scandal, the University of Wisconsin–Madison doctored a photo of an otherwise all-white crowd at a football game to include an African American student, Diallo Shabazz, and then published the photograph on the front of its admissions brochure.[122]

There are critics of decision makers' production of diversity. For many observers, race-based intervention is *the* objective of the diversity movement. Conservative and libertarian critics see a numbers game: illegal hiring quotas and rigged admissions systems unfairly biased toward people of color and to the disadvantage of white people.[123] On a University of California–Berkeley blog post on affirmative action, a graphic image depicted a row of tall, colorful crayons alongside a short white one with the heading: "Diversity: Guess who was promoted to CEO?"

Meanwhile, many progressives consider diversity's cultural view of race a fundamental flaw.[124] They denounce its superficiality. They argue that this view undermines the midcentury civil rights framework, in which race is a basis of legal disenfranchisement, institutional discrimination, and economic disadvantage. Critical race scholars see the diversity rationale cutting off any conversation about this country's history of racism.[125] Shabazz challenged Wisconsin's diversity photoshopping with a lawsuit asking for a "budgetary apology." He succeeded in winning $10 million that the university had to earmark for diversity initiatives, including the recruitment of students of color. Literary theorist Walter Benn Michaels raises a different critique. The preoccupation with racial identity and cultural diversity, he claims, is a distraction from the more dire economic inequalities of capitalism.[126] From these perspectives, the symbolic politics of racial progress rest on elision between numbers and culture, between intervention and celebration, and between what is and what is desired.

Racial Ambiguity, without Acknowledging Structural Inequalities

Another common theme characterizes the symbolic politics of diversity at the University of Michigan, in Rogers Park, and at Starr: tremendous ambiguity about what decision makers are doing, if anything, about race or problems of racial injustice. These leaders' endorsements of diversity make the realities of race difficult to discern. While diversity is strongly associated with African American representation, the issues at hand are almost never just racial and are sometimes not about race at all. This enables advocates to constantly jockey between the messages that "race matters" and "race does not matter"—as historian Bryant Simon puts it—depending on what racial proclivities and positions they deem desirable.[127] Official accounts of diversity suggest that marginalized groups' needs are being met, although those groups repeatedly report otherwise.

This ambiguity leaves lingering questions about how much decision makers actually prioritize racial representation and inclusion and whether they are really addressing problems of discrimination or unfair privilege. Moreover, diversity's boosters frequently downplay or outright deny structural problems of racial inequality. This was how Michigan defended affirmative admissions legally and how developers in Rogers Park solicited new home buyers. Diversity's symbolic politics of racial progress are thereby grounded in ambiguity and, many say, deception.

Archetypal, Market-Friendly Diversity

As shown throughout this book, the diversity movement favors certain types of people: those whom decision makers uphold as acceptable archetypes of diversity. In the Rogers Park neighborhood, desirable diversity is the enterprising Peruvian restaurant owner who serves a varied clientele, not the young black gang members who sell drugs or the protesters who disrupt realtors' open houses for condominium buyers. Other acceptable diversity archetypes include female professionals, gay and lesbian two-parent families, and multiracial children. These groups exemplify diversity through their unique business acumen, their family values, or their symbolic embodiment of triumph over racial prejudice. At the same time, a white person with a sensitive, open-minded disposition can be important for diversity. This is the "we" projected by an organizational or community identity of diversity.

The acceptable diversity archetypes can be interactions, experiences, and scenarios as well. The classic example is captured in that photograph in so many college brochures: young men and women of different racial backgrounds relaxed on a lawn or gathered around a professor, consumed in deep conversation. Those storied interactions are ones in which participants visibly represent different racial groups and perhaps other statuses, express their own identity and culture, and show appreciation for those of others. There are unacceptable archetypes, too, of prejudice and exclusion. The consummate example is a panel of business leaders composed only of white men.[128]

The acceptable archetypes are the symbolic material of selective inclusion. Desirable diversity is that which is commensurate with deeply institutionalized explanations of interests, relations, roles, and action. It is the least disruptive sort of inclusion. These archetypes also reflect the preference in the diversity movement for cultural differences that are market friendly. Diversity becomes associated with participating in seemingly exotic, out of the ordinary, or exciting minority "culture," such as eating tacos from an owner-operated Mexican taqueria. This sort of diversity is "stuff white people like"—according to the satirical blog of the same title.[129] Racial progress, imagined as such, is less threatening to the status of white people. White people may appear and feel tolerant, cosmopolitan, and cleared of potential charges of racism by virtue of their openness to minority groups and their cultures.

A Focus on Discrete Initiatives and the Circumscription of Contestation

In these three cases, decision makers stress that awareness and goodwill are crucial for creating and maintaining diversity. Moreover, they point to identity-conscious policy interventions as essential; these are organizational and political structures, such as affirmative action, that take into account demographic group identity, in contrast to structures that are identity-blind.[130] Such diversity interventions are especially important for the symbolic politics of racial progress, but not necessarily because they improve minority representation (their effectiveness is very mixed). The policies at hand tend to be small in scale and disconnected from consequential decision making, so they do not dramatically alter the underlying markets or institutional priorities that sustain inequality.[131] They, too, are shrouded in ambiguity. Their scope is often unclear and their efficacy unknown (but always asserted). Yet they are the focus of much organizational activity and political deliberation regarding diversity.

With the diversity movement, the symbolic politics of racial progress also includes the circumscription of political contestation. There are deep, fundamental conflicts between political and organizational actors stemming from their differing interests in the distribution of material resources and differing understandings of racial integration. These struggles are channeled into debates over discrete policies or political interventions and are carried out through formal institutional procedures. They play out as claims-making contests in which decision makers' normative support for diversity is reified as a moderate, sensible middle way—somewhere between, on the one hand, racist opposition or color-blind denial and, on the other hand, regulatory overreach or remedial racial justice.

Activists who want to contest diversity politics may find some leverage in law and in their claims to be the very diversity that is of such concern. Yet most activists are at a notable disadvantage, with high barriers to their participation and low probability of achieving the societal transformations for which they fight. To politically engage, they get involved in for-or-against battles over existing initiatives—battles that are difficult to wage, much less win, and that divert activists from pursuing more ambitious agendas for social change.

These dynamics—catchy lingo, the double move of diversity, racial ambiguity, denial of structural inequality, market-friendly archetypes, and circumscription of dissent—are defining features of the organizational drive for diversity. They amount to a very complex, contradictory politics of racial progress. They ideologically combine a diagnosis of how the world works and how it *should* work with principles for action.[132] Foregrounding the organizational context in which these ideological notions of diversity are mobilized provides theoretical purchase on the processes by which organizations legitimize and delegitimize inequality in the post–civil rights period.

The Organizational Legitimation of Inequality

By and large, organizational activity is not racially neutral. Much organizational activity generates and maintains hierarchies of race as well as those of class, sex, age, disability, and sexual orientation.[133] This happens in many ways, from administrators' quiet processes of cognitive bias to managers' blatantly discriminatory firing choices to the more expensive, exploitative home loans that banks disproportionately provide to people of color.[134] Many organizational practices seem, at face value, unbiased and meritocratic but are in fact preferential toward white people, men, and the affluent. Examples include college admissions policies based on standardized tests, political decision making through community input panels, and workplace hiring through employees' personal networks.[135]

An emerging body of scholarship is highlighting the relational dimensions of organizational inequality.[136] This work begins from the theoretical premise that inequalities are produced through the dynamic relations between people and positions in organizational environments—relations that are patterned by power differentials, organizational structures, interaction, and culture. It attends to different kinds of organizationally mediated relationships, such as an authority figure's exploitation of others or their claims that white people have superior skills. While the focus of this relational scholarship has been employing organizations, many precepts are transportable to educational and political-civic organizations.

One line of this research—and a line that is underdeveloped— foregrounds the dynamics by which organizational culture undergirds inequality.[137] Organizational cultures enable and validate the unequal distribution of recognition, resources, and rewards. That is an exercise of power, although it is different from decision makers' control over resources such as investment dollars or votes.[138] It is the power of legitimation: of mobilizing biases, establishing the decisions to be made, and preventing certain issues from arising. It is the power of manipulation as well: of giving definition to people's consciousness, wants, and values in ways that shape their acquiescence. Much can be learned about mechanisms of inequality by examining organizational culture and legitimated power. Such mechanisms range from the additional burdensome emotional labor that employees of color must do to the gendered assumptions as the basis of bureaucratic structures such as job positions to the concerns with efficiency that motivate some affirmative action policies.[139]

Some scholarship to date has demonstrated how the rhetoric and symbolism of organizational diversity programs are discursive mechanisms that reinscribe inequalities. Managers, community advocates, and developers speak of the diversity of people and places in ways that insulate their own power and white privilege.[140] Courts interpret the mere existence of diversity initiatives as evidence of nondiscrimination, despite the fact that most diversity programs fail to move people of color and white women into management.[141] When employers are faced with accusations of discrimination, they draw on a discourse of meritocracy that construes inequality as inevitable and justify their innocence in reference to purportedly neutral bureaucratic procedures, such as employee evaluations, while leaving most discrimination unabated.[142] Such insights nicely complement the study of postracial discourse. They show that racial ideologies reinforce organizational activities and decision-making processes that leave intact exploitation, opportunity hoarding, resource pooling, and other mechanisms of inequality.

This line of research, and the broader project of studying the organizational legitimation of inequality, can be advanced by a stronger theoretical grounding in cultural sociology. In organizational settings, culture constitutes social life in a variety of forms, ranging from formalized structures such as curriculum requirements to rituals such as awards ceremonies to physical arrangements such as architecture to organizational identities and rhetoric.[143] Put differently, culture is not simply a material artifact like a painting or a discernible custom, nor is it just rhetorics that are instrumentally mobilized. Rather, as cultural sociologists have well established, social life has cultural dimensions.[144] People are always making meaning as they do things, in order to do things. Meaning making provides people with interpretations, motivations, and recipes for how to act.

Those who hold positions of power impose a dominant organizational culture. That culture constructs meanings in ways that reflect their worldviews and interests and that lead others to accept the status quo.[145] Coupled with resources and power, those meanings commonly become entrenched; they become thoroughly institutionalized and structure widespread patterns of social behavior.[146] But decision makers' control over meaning is not absolute. Meanings are always fluid. Organizational culture are assessed and experienced in different ways by organizational and political participants, their audiences, and observers. In general, culture is open improvisation and contestation, depending on who is producing meaning, their methods of production, who is interpreting them, and their sociohistorical context.[147]

Under certain conditions, cultural meanings effectively influence people's thoughts, their behaviors, and social systems. This happens, for example, when those meanings exhibit particular qualities, such as when they are accessible and congruent with existing ideas.[148] As sociologist Amin Ghaziani observes, culture shapes social action when it is "resinous"—when it becomes associated with and sticks to certain organizational tasks.[149]

The chapters that follow bring together the study of organizations and inequality with a constitutive theory of culture. They expand the study of organizational culture beyond a focus on organizations' formal rhetoric and the symbolism of organizational structures. A broader, more contextualized view of culture reveals subtle on-the-ground cultural processes by which organizations constitute hegemonic social realities (and the role of formal rhetoric and program symbolism therein).[150]

Through historical-ethnographic evidence on how organizations take on, formulate, and pursue an objective of diversity, this book reveals new aspects of legitimation. Decision makers and their detractors draw on different cultural concepts of diversity as they engage in different sorts of organizational practices—such as reporting statistics, teaching talking points, or portraying the process of classroom learning. Diversity's meanings gain significance and become consequential by animating such practice. These are symbolic politics of racial progress at the meso level of organizational activity. By looking at these politics up close, in everyday organizational and political life, we can see more general processes by which decision makers simultaneously legitimate and delegitimate hierarchies and the negotiation and contestation involved.

PART ONE

Undergraduate Admissions at the University of Michigan

TWO

"Academically Excellent and Diverse"

"Michigan: Distinguished. Diverse. Dynamic." This is the headline applicants to the University of Michigan would see, in blue and gold lettering,
when they opened the Office of Undergraduate Admissions' website in
2004.[1] Alongside those words were images of a football game, a science lab,
and an orchestra. The text introduced the university: "A vibrant community
of intellectually adventurous students and renowned faculty who live and
learn in an environment of limitless possibilities." Videos and photos featured students of different racial backgrounds hanging out or engrossed in
deep conversation. Pullout quotes testified to the exciting challenges, welcoming environment, and diversity of the university and its student body.
"Be prepared, pay attention, speak up, and really think for yourself," advises
a young white woman with short red hair. "Diversity is one of the issues I'm
most passionate about," says Ewurabena Menyah, a nursing major from
Ohio.

On the admissions office website and in the university's other public relations and educational materials, campus leaders projected an identity for
Michigan as a trailblazer in academic excellence and diversity. Michigan was
"the leaders and best"—as the fight song proclaimed—not just in scholastic
achievement and football but also in its support of diversity.

This identity gained tremendous political importance at the turn of the
twenty-first century, with the *Gratz* and *Grutter* litigation detailed in the next
chapter. Before then, for decades prior, university leaders had cultivated and
mobilized it to mediate integration on campus. In the mid-1960s, a few university leaders took on a historically unprecedented objective: to encourage
the numeric representation and institutional assimilation of black students.
Over the subsequent half century, Michigan transformed from a nearly all-
white university to one in which white students, in 2013, made up 67% of

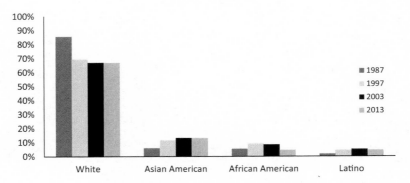

2.1. Representation of undergraduate students enrolled at University of Michigan–Ann Arbor, by race, fall 1987–fall 2013. *Source*: Based on data from University of Michigan, Office of the Registrar, Report 837, multiple years.

the undergraduate student body (see fig. 2.1).[2] Many administrators were deeply invested in spurring those changes. Administrators advanced them principally through organizational practices of affirmative action in admissions and explained them initially in reference to remedying disadvantage and then, by the 1980s, in terms of diversity's educational benefits.

The push for diversity at Michigan both enabled these changes and was defined by them. It was prompted by discernible forces in the university's external environment, namely Powell's opinion in the 1978 *Regents of University of California v. Bakke* case and responses to it in the field of higher education. In the context of the increasingly restrictive legal doctrine on race, diversity became a cover for a policy intervention to support people of color. But the university's adoption of diversity was not simply copied and pasted from Powell's opinion. Campus leaders made diversity the centerpiece of the university's identity. This identity linked both racial minority representation and campus pluralism with academic rigor, campus vitality, and the social good. In fact, in their organizational activities, administrators made far more of diversity as an image, ideal, and low-stakes affirmation than as a technical explanation for race-conscious admissions.

This chapter introduces Michigan's Ann Arbor campus and the university's identity of diversity. To establish patterns of stratification and institutional structures relevant to the administration's drive for diversity, it explains the politicized markets of selective college admissions and the policy of affirmative admissions. Then the analysis traces the historical development of the university's diversity efforts and identity over four points of time, starting in 1964. The administration's advocacy of diversity symbolically signaled that the boundaries of the student body were far reaching—not just inclusive of white people and not biased toward students of color—and in modest but impactful ways, their diversity efforts pragmatically opened up access to a white-dominated, highly coveted domain of privilege.

Welcome to Campus

The University of Michigan is a large, elite public university known for its football team and its prestigious faculty and resources. The main campus, in the college town of Ann Arbor, sprawls over about three thousand acres. In 2005, the university consisted of nineteen schools and colleges, enrolled forty thousand undergraduate and graduate students, and employed more than five thousand faculty members. Around the same time, its total research expenditures reached over $750 million.[3] It is among the most prestigious public universities in the United States. In 2004, *U.S. News and World Report* rated the Michigan undergraduate program as the third-best public university and among the top twenty-five colleges in the country.[4] The university has become selective since the 1970s.[5] In the mid-2000s, Michigan's first-year student admissions rate was around 50%, making the university more competitive than most large public schools but far more accessible than elite private schools such as Harvard or Yale.[6] Gaining admission required excellent credentials. In 2005, only 25% of admitted students received an SAT score lower than 1240. University boosters call it the "Harvard of the Midwest."

The student body at Michigan is predominantly white and affluent or middle class but still quite heterogeneous. In 2005, the undergraduate student body was 68% white, 13% Asian, 8% black, 5% Latino, 1% Native American, and 5% unknown.[7] In the fall of 2005, just over half of Michigan's undergraduates were female, and almost 5% were international students.[8] In 2002, 54% of first-year students reported a family income over $100,000, while only 14% reported a family income below $50,000.[9] About 13% of undergraduate Michigan students received Pell Grants from the US government for low-income students, which earned Michigan the third slot for economic diversity among the top American universities in a *U.S. News and World Report* index.[10] At the time of this study, in 2005, the cost of attending Michigan as an undergraduate was over $19,500 for students from within the state (compared to average cost of public universities nationwide of $12,115).[11] Students who were not state residents—about 32% of the undergraduate student body—were an important source of revenue for the university; they paid over $38,000 in tuition, room and board, and other costs.[12]

The university has a strong intellectual, social, and political culture. The university calendar includes hundreds of speakers, conferences, workshops, performances, and readings. Many university activities, guided by Michigan's mission as a public university, are oriented toward public service such as service learning for students. Student political and social activism has been vibrant on campus for decades and leans liberal. Students and graduates express a strong sense of identification with the university, especially its athletic teams, the Wolverines, which include the school's wildly popular football team and twenty-six other varsity sports teams.

"Academically Excellent and Diverse"

Diversity is portrayed as a core value in administrators' statements on the university's mission and guiding principles, paired with references to Michigan's commitment to public service and academic rigor. The University of Michigan Vision Statement set out seven aspirations for the university in the twenty-first century, among them "To be a source of pride for all people of Michigan," "To occupy a position of unique leadership among the nation's universities in research and scholarly achievement," and "To be recognized as a University that honors human diversity." The Senate Assembly, representing the faculty, passed a statement on the "value of diversity" in 1998 that posed diversity as conducive to knowledge:

> The goals of an institution of higher learning should be to generate new knowledge, to convey knowledge to others, and to involve its faculty, students, and staff in using this knowledge to address contemporary social problems. For the University to excel in reaching these goals, the rich diversity of contemporary society is a resource that needs to be tapped. . . . Our commitment to diversity means at the most basic level a willingness both to recognize the value of disparate experiences and visions and to weave them into the fabric of our institution. Because of this, we are committed to a policy of recruiting and maintaining a culturally and racially diverse student body and faculty that are representative of contemporary society, and to assuring that these diverse influences are respected and incorporated into the structure of the University.

Statements such as these are formulated for the purposes of articulating shared principles and, through their circulation in handbooks and online, become part of the university's public image.

The administration also carefully cultivated an image of the university as an incubator of diversity and excellence in its public relations materials. Speeches and statements by the university president made reference to the value of diversity as central to the university's mission. The university's promotional websites and brochures crafted an image of the student body as archetypically diverse. The Office of Undergraduate Admissions' 2004 Student Profile described the student body:

> University of Michigan students have a lot in common. They're intelligent, motivated, inquisitive, hard-working, open-minded, ambitious, and ready to be challenged. . . . Beyond that, however, you couldn't find a more diverse group. Michigan undergraduates come from all 50 states as well as 129 foreign countries. Think of the student body as a mosaic of races, cultures, languages, religions, and points of view.

One commonly circulated image showed President Coleman with James Duderstadt, a white professor who had previously been the president of the university, and Lester Monts, an African American professor in a high-ranking administrative role, ceremoniously on stage. All wear academic regalia, their colorful robes signaling their achievement of a PhD.

As in the Senate Assembly statement, university leaders routinely identified Michigan's admissions policies as crucial for creating diversity. A December 2002 e-mail announcement from the administration, explaining the current stage of the *Gratz* and *Grutter* litigation, stated that the undergraduate admissions policy "works very well in choosing a student body that is academically excellent and diverse in many ways."

The university's materials—whether formulating core values, marketing Michigan's people and environment, or characterizing its policies—also underscored the good that came of such diversity. The faculty senate diversity statement explained that, by fostering diversity, "we can provide students with the unique educational experience and intellectual stimulation that can only come from interacting with and learning to respect a broad range of people with differing backgrounds, life experiences, beliefs, and ideas." Such statements on productive diversity stressed the learning and growth that students experienced through their interactions with different types of people.

The university also made diversity an explicit organizing principle throughout much administrative activity, programming, and intellectual work. There were many ways to promote diversity and to achieve it. These included affirmative action in admissions and hiring, training and pedagogical programs for students, programming under the Office of Academic and Multicultural Initiatives, a presidential Diversity Council, and the National Science Foundation–funded ADVANCE program for female faculty members in science and engineering. Support services were provided for students of color, female students, gay/lesbian/bisexual/transgender students, students with disabilities, and international students. Faculty and administrators, some of whom were leading researchers on diversity, conducted major research studies on the effects of racial heterogeneity on student performance and best practices of campus diversity initiatives. The university published histories and time lines of diversity, suggesting a long-standing, deeply engrained institutional dedication to diversity.

Most Michigan students expressed similar views of the university. The Michigan Student Study, a longitudinal study of student and alumni perceptions, found that students expressed overwhelming support for diversity on campus. In 2004, the vast majority of seniors—from 68% of white seniors to 79% of African American ones—reported that diversity had "quite a bit" or "a great deal" of an impact on their college experience, and for most of those individuals, the impact was positive.[13] The 2004 seniors and alumni of the university, reflecting on their years on campus, felt their exposure to new and different people and perspectives had enhanced their intellectual development and awareness of other types of people. (However, as discussed in the next chapter, white students had more reservations about diversity and affirmative action, and many students of color experienced racist hostility.)

Meanwhile, popular media, college guidebooks, and institutional authorities on higher education spotlighted the university's academic rigor and diversity. Unigo, a popular online college guide created in 2008, ranked the university as one of the top ten "New Ivies" and committed to fostering diversity. The student reviews, which are referenced on the website of *U.S. News and World Report*, included comments such as "diversity here is amazing."

These value statements, images, testimonies, activities, rankings, and endorsements all seemed to be tangible evidence that Michigan was indeed diverse and a stalwart in the twin pursuits of excellence and diversity. It appeared to be a place where people of different backgrounds learn, work, and socialize peacefully and productively—where their racial, ethnic, economic, and other social differences enhanced students' learning experiences and the vitality of campus life. As depicted, students expressed their unique personal identities through enriching cross-cultural interactions with other students. The university seemed ever more prestigious for its groundbreaking support of diversity.

That Michigan administrators projected such a polished identity is not surprising. The university's ideas of diversity were derived from law on race in college admissions. In the context of major legal attacks on those policies in the late 1990s and early 2000s, an argument about educational benefits of diversity served as a legitimated, legalized explanation for its race-attentive admissions policies.

These notions of diversity and excellence had purchase beyond the political arena as well. At Michigan they were relevant, in particular, for admissions officers' work of recruiting students and selling the university to those students and their families. Administrators mobilized such ideas in branding practices as they vied for smart students and external funding, in competition with other selective universities.[14] This is part of the corporatization of higher education.[15] Over the last forty years, universities and colleges have increasingly commercialized research, instruction, and athletics.[16] In admissions, selective universities promise a coveted product (a degree) and sought-after services (elite education), and they have come to treat students as consumers with desires to satisfy. Like administrators at many other elite universities, those at Michigan made diversity, excellence, and leadership their sales pitches in the face of a market of elite college admissions—a market in which affluent students are essential and the demand for academically accomplished students of color is greater than the supply.[17]

Admissions Matters

Having a college degree matters. It affects a person's future income, occupation, and social relationships.[18] People of all racial backgrounds and poor people have better prospects with a college degree.[19] Racial representation and inclusion in higher education (and beyond) crucially depend on college admissions.

Racial and class inequality is endemic to college access. They are evident in who goes to college, where they go, whether they graduate, and their college experience. The college enrollment of black, Hispanic, and low-income students has increased notably since the 1970s, but these students are far less likely to go to college or complete it.[20] When they do, they are more likely to go to the low-status, broad-access institutions at the bottom of the higher education hierarchy, which have fewer resources and provide lower economic payoffs, such as future earnings.[21]

In a society where educational credentials are highly valued, college admissions is a gateway to full social membership. It establishes the social boundaries of the well educated—those discursively deemed skilled and competent. A number of institutional developments initiated between the 1940s and the 1960s fundamentally expanded access to higher education. The 1944 law establishing benefits for veterans returning from World War II, known as the GI Bill, provided free tuition and other educational benefits that almost eight million veterans used to go to college.[22] During this same period, elite universities began to shift from a system of admissions based on family lineage to one based on standardized tests.[23] The shear numbers of students applying and the qualifications for admittance ramped up.

Admissions matters most at selective colleges and universities because, by definition, those institutions reject a relatively high percentage of applicants. Selective college admissions is a competitive market. There are many good reasons families want their children admitted to a selective college or university. Those graduates fare better in terms of earning a professional or graduate degree, career advancement, and future income, and a degree from a superelite university can be decisive in employers' hiring decisions.[24] Selective institutions are resource rich and can invest in those things that keep them competitive, including students who have strong academic qualifications and can pay steep tuition.

Since the 1990s, administrators' admissions selections have been motivated in large measure by their university's standing in college rankings.[25] The *U.S. News and World Report* ranking is the most important of these. It gives tremendous weight to selectivity (percentage of applicants rejected), standardized test scores, and grade point average (GPA).

Two noteworthy trends in admissions have influenced the racial and class composition of prestigious institutions over the past thirty years.[26] By far the most influential of these trends is the ability of affluent families, the vast majority of whom are white, to advantage their children in college admissions. Selective admissions relies heavily on class-biased criteria—what some scholars call wealth preferences—particularly standardized test scores and high tuition rates.[27] Affluent families can more easily achieve these criteria through all sorts of strategies, such as paying for test prep tutoring and private schooling. As the United States has become more economically unequal, students at selective institutions have come from higher and higher income brackets.[28]

These wealth preferences also profoundly advantage white students, who are more likely to have material resources such as access to strong schools.

Their social networks connect them to other people who attend college, and they benefit from ideological support, including societal messages that they are normal and competent. Wealth preferences simultaneously disadvantage students of color, who are more likely to attend underresourced schools and to be tracked into remedial courses. Students of color are more likely to have parents who have not attended college. They score lower on standardized tests because of their lack of experience and their anxieties about fulfilling the stereotype that they are incapable.[29]

Universities' and colleges' objective of staying atop the rankings then puts enormous pressures on admissions officers that work in favor of the admission of affluent, white, Asian, and male students and against low-income students, women, and other students of color.[30] With declines in financial resources from state governments, public universities (particularly selective ones) have increased their tuition commensurately. For instance, in the 1960s, 80% of the University of Michigan's general fund, which is the budget for core academic programs, came from the State of Michigan. By 2012, less than 17% of that fund was paid for by appropriations.[31] Selective public universities have admitted a growing number of students from out of state, who pay as much as double the rate of in-state tuition. They have also shifted away from providing need-based financial aid while increasing funds for merit aid, which is not based on a student's family income. Elite education recycles privilege.

The other key admissions trend affecting the demographics of college campuses has been race-based affirmative action. Affirmative action is a form of decision making that intentionally considers an individual's race, ethnicity, or sex for the purposes of expanding opportunities for racial minorities and women.[32] When directed at students, it seeks to improve racial minorities' chances of being admitted to, attending, and graduating from universities and colleges. Affirmative admissions ranges from outreach and recruitment activities ("soft" affirmative action) to financial aid to admissions policies that explicitly give some favoritism to African Americans, Latinos, and Native Americans.[33]

Affirmative admissions is only operative at selective universities and colleges, and there it is practiced widely.[34] It has the support of top schools and national educational organizations such as the American Council on Education. Accreditation organizations evaluate colleges and universities based in part on affirmative action policies. In 2004, the racial composition of high school graduates headed to selective institutions was 72.5% white, 12% Asian, 7% Hispanic, 3.5% black, less than 0.5% Native American, and 5% multiracial or other.[35] Research shows that such admissions rates are only possible with race-conscious admissions policies that give demonstrable bonuses to black and Latino student applicants.[36] Affirmative admissions in higher education is an engine of opportunity for black and Latino students.

Still, affirmative admissions is a remedial add-on to the standard process of elite admissions. It is selectively inclusive. It is not an elimination of the fundamental class and racial biases of the standard process. Thus it does not challenge the presumption that the most resources should go to the most academically accomplished students, and it treats the merit of those students without regard to race. White students at every income level are still considerably more likely to be enrolled in a highly selective institution than their peers of color. In fact, contrary to popular depictions of affirmative action as a major obstacle to white students' admissions, white students' odds of enrolling in a highly selective college or university have improved over the past twenty years (as the United States has become more economically unequal), and standardized test scores have become more important.[37]

Unlike the admissions of wealthy students, affirmative admissions is further complicated by American jurisprudence. The law applies an extremely high standard for race-conscious decision making. Under the Fifth Amendment and the equal protection clause of the Fourteenth Amendment, race is a suspect classification, meaning that it is a distinction that routinely has been used to unconstitutionally discriminate. When a federal or state entity classifies people on the basis of their race, either explicitly or implicitly, the court subjects its practices to strict scrutiny. Strict scrutiny means that the policy will only survive judicial review if the government proves that the organization's practices are constitutional.[38] These practices must pass a two-pronged test: they must serve a compelling interest, and the institutional means to accomplish this compelling interest must be narrowly tailored to that end. In other words, if an educational institution that receives federal support relies on racial classifications, it must demonstrate that it does not have malicious objectives.

Whereas it seems quite obvious why a selective college would court affluent students—those students can pay expensive tuition, above all else—the reasons for doing affirmative admissions are more complex. The standard of strict scrutiny and other legal obstacles to affirmative admissions can be daunting. Nonetheless, university officials have come to see the presence of students of color as important to their organization's public legitimacy.[39] Activists and interest groups have put pressure on universities for enrollment of students of color, especially African American students. Many administrators understand race-conscious admissions as part of their professional norms and expertise.[40] A racially mixed student body has become one factor in a school's national reputation and is something that some students seek out when applying. *U.S. News and World Report*'s diversity index, separate from its academic rankings of selectivity, measures schools based on the proportion of racial minority students (although that can be at odds with selectivity measures).[41]

From the perspective of admissions officers at Michigan, affirmative action activities are essential for getting underrepresented minority students to even apply. Tyrone Winfrey, the associate director of admissions who ran the university's Detroit admissions office, contrasted for me the university's recruitment methods at different schools. In fall 2004, at a peak moment in the recruitment cycle, his team of counselors did three presentations in Troy, a predominantly white, affluent suburb with a sizable Asian American population. About two hundred students attended each of those presentations. "There was a line of fifty students who just wanted to *talk* to someone because they were applying," said Tyrone.

That fall, the same admissions recruitment team had already gone six times to Renaissance High School, a majority-black and poor public high school in Detroit that was one of the main "feeders" for black Michigan undergraduates. There, the recruiters had done informational sessions, reviewed students' in-progress applications, picked up applications, met with ninth graders to provide advice on preparing to apply, and personally told each applicant the university's admissions decision. And the recruiters would go back again for more sessions later that year. "At Renaissance, you could never just do a presentation alone," Tyrone told me. "You would never get any applications."

As we drove around Detroit, over potholes and past barricaded public high schools, Tyrone explained that he was proud to work for an institution that made such an effort to recruit students of color and, as the next chapter details, was defending affirmative action. Michigan, he remarked, stood for "excellence, diversity, and confidence."

The history of the push for campus diversity helps to explain the complicated terrain that Tyrone and other university officials confronted, their reasons for identifying the university as a champion of excellence and diversity, and the consequences of doing so.

How the University of Michigan Became Diverse

Issues of racial representation and intergroup relations on campus have been politically charged at Michigan since the 1960s. The administration adopted and held fast to a policy of affirmative admissions that was inter-mittently contentious and came under legal constraints. In the 1980s, the university leadership managed these and other challenges by developing an identity for Michigan as academically rigorous and committed to diversity. With this identity, university leaders construed racial integration as a highly desirable, complex endeavor, one that required deliberate interventions to bring in a small percentage of high-achieving students of color and that could generate a socially cohesive campus community where identity-based differences were a positive generative force.

Snapshot 1: Before Diversity—Minority Admissions to End Disadvantage, 1964

In the early 1960s, Michigan provost Roger W. Heyns announced a new objective for the university: "to improve the status of the American Negro in our society."[42] Institutions of higher education were undergoing radical changes, including rising student enrollments and greater selectivity by ad-missions offices, but they remained almost exclusively the province of white students.[43] African Americans, women, and foreign students had been ad-mitted to Michigan since the late 1800s, but there were less than two hun-dred black students on campus, and some discriminatory practices, such as fraternities' secret "bias clauses," were commonplace.[44] Title VI of the Civil Rights Act of 1964 forbade programs receiving federal financial assistance from discriminating on the basis of race, color, national origin, religion, or sex. Public universities could no longer exclude students based on their race, and most private universities followed suit.

Top administrators at Michigan and a couple of other universities, in-spired by civil rights activism in the US South, were beginning to see the racial exclusion on their campuses as a problem.[45] Michigan was one of the very first universities to respond by creating a race-conscious admis-sions policy. Provost Heyns and President Harlan Hatcher, with early sup-port from the Detroit Urban League, spearheaded this effort. They hoped to increase the numerical representation of black students and worked to garner institutional support from the university's other white, male leaders.

The Opportunity Awards Program, created in 1964, targeted Detroit students. The program consisted of recruitment, admissions, financial aid, special orientation, and counseling services. In its inaugural year, 1964–65, seventy black students were admitted, most of them without outstanding high school records.[46] It was soon formally expanded to other students of color and low-income applicants but stayed oriented to African Americans.[47]

With this program, the university's restrictive admissions process became two-track, with separate requirements for students of color.[48] To be admitted, mainstream (white) students needed to have a 3.3 high school grade point average and SAT scores in the top 25%, while students of color who had lower GPAs and test scores could be admitted if admissions staff saw them as having sufficient potential to succeed.[49] The enrollment of students of color rose to 3.4% by 1969.[50]

Early on, the most vocal critics of affirmative admissions policies were radical college students who wished to see more sweeping, faster-moving change.[51] At Michigan in the late 1960s and early 1970s, the Black Action Movement and other campus activists protested and organized an eighteen-day "smash racism strike." They demanded that 10% of the student body be black by 1973 and that the administration take other supportive measures such as addressing entrenched discrimination on campus and increasing the almost nonexistent Latino population.[52]

University officials acknowledged (but did not adopt) this objective and pledged financial aid to support it. They began to produce reports on the numeric enrollment of students of color and dedicated more funding and support to those applicants.[53] They faced ongoing criticism from activists, who wanted the 10% goal met, and from other constituents who believed the university was giving an unfair advantage to African Americans.

Much like their peers at other universities, supporters of the Opportunity Awards Program explained affirmative action as compensation for past and present racial discrimination. They cited such rationales as "improving the position of black students as well as that of other minority and disadvantaged groups" and "correcting social wrongs."[54] The program exemplified and operationalized remedial racial justice; by design and in its rationales, it located discrimination in the normal workings of admissions and required corrective organizational intervention in the form of new supplemental decision-making routines.[55] Rectifying racial subordination was the ethos of some national leaders who were calling for attention to problems of black poverty, racism, and social unrest. As President Lyndon B. Johnson said in his famous 1965 commencement address at Howard University, "Freedom is not enough. . . . We seek . . . not just equality as a right and a theory but equality as a fact and equality as a result." Thus the university's color-conscious approach to race at this time was defined by rhetoric on minority opportunity, an interest in numerical representation, and a programmatic focus on black students.

Even with these policy issues, Michigan's identity in this period was that of an institution "long recognized as one of the world's great universities," as one brochure stated. The university was distinguished by its leaders and faculties—nearly all them white men. Its identity was implicitly racialized as white and for the well-off.[56] In the public spotlight, university officials did not usually stress the connection between the university's identity and its new affirmative admissions policy, nor was public relations image making even important to admissions. The institution remained, according to a government audit, primarily for "rich white students."[57]

Snapshot 2: A Legal Rationale of Diversity's Educational Benefits, 1978

The US Supreme Court's 1978 ruling in the *Regents of University of California v. Bakke* case proved very consequential for the politics, the design, and especially the rhetoric of affirmative admissions at Michigan as well as other selective universities. The case was brought by a white man, Allan Bakke, who argued that he was rejected from the University of California—Davis medical school based on his race. The university's affirmative action program reserved sixteen of one hundred seats for students of color, and, according to his case, this violated the equal protection clause, a provision of the California state constitution, and Title VI of the US Civil Rights Act of 1964.

The court issued six different opinions, with no single straightforward majority opinion. A majority of the nine justices—five—found the UC-Davis policy to be an unconstitutional racial quota. Four of those justices would have altogether struck down the UC-Davis policy as a violation of Title VI. A different constellation of justices—again, five—believed that race-conscious admissions were acceptable. Four of those justices, called the Brennan Four, would have used intermediate scrutiny under the equal protection clause and upheld the policy. For those four, the objective of remedying past discrimination was a sufficient explanation for considering race in admissions decisions.

Justice Lewis Powell was the fifth justice on each of those majority opinions. He agreed that the UC-Davis program was an unconstitutional quota but opined that race-conscious admissions were sometimes acceptable. He reasoned in his solo-authored opinion that the program should be considered under the basis of the equal protection clause and that the two-pronged test of strict scrutiny should be applied. At this time, strict scrutiny was not yet the standard for affirmative admissions programs. It was being applied to adjudicate invidious uses of racial classifications (such as Jim Crow laws, which were malicious, hostile discrimination). But the majority of justices then were unprepared to say that strict scrutiny should be applied to benign uses of racial classification (such as the UC-Davis policy, which intended to remedy discrimination). Nonetheless, Powell argued for that standard and, under it, would have struck down the UC-Davis program because it was not narrowly tailored to meet a compelling governmental interest. He argued that three of the university's four stated goals failed this test: reducing the deficit in racial minority doctors created through the discrimination in the medical field, remedying societal discrimination, and improving health care services for underserved communities.

However, Powell saw a compelling interest in the program's fourth stated goal, which he characterized as "obtaining the educational benefits that flow from an ethnically diverse student body." Powell reasoned that diversity was a compelling goal in admissions decisions. He defined diversity as encompassing "a far broader array of qualifications and characteristics of which racial or ethnic origin is but a single though important element." Race could be considered in admissions decisions, but not race alone. According to Powell, a diverse environment improves the functioning of a university and serves the collegiate mission. A diverse student body, he wrote, promotes "the atmosphere of speculation, experiment and creation so essential to the quality of higher education."

Justice Powell's opinion allowed race-conscious admissions but with the most stringent restrictions. Unlike any prior court decision, law, or regulation, his opinion elucidated the educational benefits of diversity and identified the benefits of affirmative action for white people.[58] No other justice joined his opinion, so it was not binding under law. However, it was influential because it was a reasoned argument by a Supreme Court justice and articulated a comprehensible basis for sustaining affirmative action programs.

University officials at Michigan and elsewhere took notice of *Bakke*. The case had allowed the continued use of race-conscious admissions but left vague what sort of policy was not a quota, with Powell citing only a holistic policy used by Harvard. The university leadership remained committed to affirmative admissions. In 1977, during the case, President Robbin Fleming wrote that race-neutral policies would be insufficient for addressing "the continued cancer of racial discrimination embedded in our institutions."[59] In the wake of the case, Michigan held a conference during which the university's administrators, like their counterparts across the country, concluded that their admissions policy could consider an applicant's race but could not make race the most important factor.[60] After that, the undergraduate admissions office continued to run the Opportunity Awards Program and remained focused on numeric targets, which Fleming characterized as goals, not quotas. Administrators tweaked the admissions policy by adopting a new grid system for admissions, with lower SAT and GPA thresholds for admitting what the university called "qualified underrepresented minority (black, Spanish surname, Native American)" students.[61] A version of that admissions grids policy became the initial target of the *Gratz* and *Grutter* litigation in the mid-1990s.

Just as Supreme Court decisions establish formalized parameters on legally acceptable and unacceptable practices, they can also become a part of social life far removed from formal legal arenas, where they take on significance and new meanings. They can make people more likely to accept concepts they previously had not considered or had found objectionable.[62] They can be put to use in ways not originally intended by the justices or anticipated by analysts. In the years after *Bakke*, the Michigan administration adopted a new discourse on diversity to construct the institution's essential collective characteristics.

Snapshot 3: Diversity—What White, Black, and Brown Students Like, 1982

In the early 1980s, the administration continued to have a goal of increasing the numerical representation of racial minorities and devoted resources to that goal. For example, in 1983, 32% of the $24.2 million in university financial aid was targeted to students of color. However, affirmative admissions continued to be a separate program, with still only a few people in the undergraduate admissions office working specifically on it. Further, students of color were dropping out at high rates. In the early 1980s, the percentage of black students dipped to 5%, from a peak of 7.7% in 1976, and Latinos made up 1% of the student body.[63] Prodded by the research of an African American professor of sociology, Walter Allen, university decision makers became more cognizant of problems of retention, discrimination on campus, and the insufficient social support for students of color.

At this time, admission to Michigan was beginning to become more competitive, and the undergraduate admissions office became more focused on attracting academically accomplished students. Meanwhile, the student body was becoming more heterogeneous, with growing numbers of women, students from other countries, and out-of-state students.[64] The administration also began to attend more carefully to the university's public image. This was visible, for example, in the Undergraduate Admissions Office viewbook—that glossy 8.5" × 11" booklet distributed with applications, to introduce the university and entice applicants. The university revamped the viewbook in the early 1980s to make it more polished and resolutely positive (prior versions of the viewbook had featured students' "likes" about the university as well as their "dislikes," such as "large, impersonal classes and bureaucratic administrations").

The turn to diversity happened in this context. The administration began to represent race in terms of diversity and as a crux of the university's identity. From the outset, pushing for diversity meant asserting that Michigan valued diversity and was itself diverse. While this identity served to signal the university's compliance with *Bakke* and legitimate affirmative action, administrators tended not to talk publicly about affirmative admissions as diversity and not to publicize affirmative admissions much at all in the early 1980s.[65] The purpose of the Opportunity Awards Program was explained briefly in the 1982 viewbooks, toward the back on page 22: "to serve the educational needs of selected, academically promising students who need special academic support and whose numbers are greatly under-represented at this institution." According to the viewbook, the program was to aid primarily students who were "black, Hispanic, Native American, etc." and increase their representation.

Meanwhile, in the public spotlight and at meetings of the university regents, administrators eschewed their earlier racialized rhetoric on remedying disadvantage as a justification for affirmative action. Administrators borrowed directly from Powell's opinion as they made diversity a centerpiece of the university's public image. They projected diversity as an attribute of the student body, a shared value, and a purposeful organizational objective. The opening page of the 1986 undergraduate viewbook describes the Michigan student body as diverse and asks students to imagine themselves as part of that diversity: "When you become an undergraduate student at Michigan, you join a group of 22,000 young people with diverse social, ethnic, and economic backgrounds who come from all 50 states and more than 90 foreign countries." For the first time, the viewbook cited statistics on minority student enrollment, at 10%, and foreign student enrollment, at 5%. As sociologists Mitchell Stevens and Josipa Roksa observe, statistics on the racial profile of the student body function as "a proxy for the officially important but amorphous organizational trait of 'diversity.'"[66] The viewbook summarized: "This diversity is one of the assets of the University."

The subsequent year, the viewbook features a letter from university president Harold Shapiro that associates diversity with academic excellence and makes it both a central objective and a defining feature of the university's identity. The letter began:

> The University of Michigan is committed to being a racially, ethnically, and religiously heterogeneous community. This commitment stems from many

sources, including the conviction that such diversity is essential to creating an intellectual and social climate which promotes the freedom of thought, innovation, and creativity so fundamental to an academic community. Further, I believe the University has a special responsibility to seek this diversity and to nurture the sensitivity, tolerance, and mutual respect that are such necessary characteristics of a community in which all may thrive.

The text of these materials echoes important elements of Powell's opinion. Diversity meant students of color, but not only them. Diversity was a valued cultural identity of students and would provide cross-cultural exposure. Everyone would be better off with it—"as all may thrive." They intimated that diversity had instrumental payoffs, such as creativity, that could be achieved through the organization's proactive intervention.

In addition to these changes in the text of the viewbooks, the photographs in the 1980s illustrated principles of Powell's opinion. In earlier decades, most of the photos portrayed black students alone or with another black student. The 1986 cover photo, in contrast, shows three white students and a black woman sitting on benches in conversation, one with a school notebook open on his lap. This juxtaposition indicates a shift in the organization's thinking on race, from enrolling people of color as a distinct group and for the benefit of their personal development to projecting a productive diversity, with race evidently a part of it but still ambiguously so, where cross-cultural learning and the interpersonal exchange of ideas flourish, for the benefit of white and minority students alike.

In their admissions materials, administrators also constructed idealized images of Michigan student diversity—those acceptable archetypes of diversity. The typical Michigan student was, supposedly, academically motivated, appreciative of diversity, and somehow demographically distinctive. One viewbook in the early 1980s presented profiles of fourteen students, five of whom refer to Michigan's diversity positively. Linda Pulley, identified as a black sophomore from Southfield, Michigan, and a chemical engineering major, peers over her desk from behind oversized glasses. The quote next to her reads, "I chose to come to Michigan because of its excellent Engineering College, and because of the diversity." Benna Kushlefsky, a white female with wavy black hair and a warm smile, a sophomore from Edison, New Jersey, majoring in political science, is quoted as saying: "The best thing about U-M is its diversity. Where else could one take a course in Serbo-Croatian and another devoted solely to the study of *War and Peace*." Linda, Benna, and the others profiled exemplified diversity in their very personhood. Such representations insinuated that students, whether they were white, black, Latino, or Asian, could embody prized institutional role characteristics—studious, curious, engaged—and contribute to the campus community.

This construction of the student body was not altogether new. In the 1970s, the viewbooks described Michigan students as a mix, from different racial backgrounds and walks of life but united by their shared intellectual drive.[67] But post-*Bakke*, Michigan students became diverse. Through such imagery, words, and statistics and affirmed by the authority of university leaders, diversity was much more than just legal jargon. It apparently comprised the very fabric of campus life. "Diversity" made racial minority representation and amicable race relations seem endemic to the college experience while it helped to market the university for a new era.

These viewbooks are public relations depictions of the university and not necessarily empirically accurate. As such, they illustrate how administrators created an image of the university through the double move of diversity: they framed racial integration as commensurate with academic principles and indicated a higher-order objective of including different cultural identities, with race one among them. The administration's concept of diversity expanded the bounds of campus membership to include academically ambitious students of color. It also validated affirmative action as an explicitly racialized method of creating such membership.

Snapshot 4: Diversity Complements Excellence, 1988

In 1986 and then 1987, a series of racist incidents occurred on Michigan's campus that garnered national outrage. Twenty black women were gathered in a dorm lounge, perhaps as a meeting related to a massive civil rights march in the South two days earlier, when someone slipped a piece of paper under the door declaring "open season on porch monkeys."[68] The event was reported in the campus paper, and a few days later disc jockeys with the student-run radio station made offensive racial jokes that were broadcast to as many as ten thousand students. Student activists organized the United Coalition against Racism to protest. They issued a series of demands on the administration, including "a specific plan to guarantee a substantial increase in Black student enrollment," the establishment of "an Office of Minority Affairs with an autonomous supervisory commission elected by the minority campus community," and "a mandatory workshop on racism and diversity for *all* incoming students."[69]

Faced with student demonstrations, media attention, the involvement of state legislators and area ministers, and a campus visit by civil rights activist Reverend Jesse Jackson, then university president Shapiro gave a speech in which he decried "discrimination, harassment, exclusion, abusive or insensitive language, or any other manifestation of bigotry or racism."[70] He announced that the university would supplement its efforts toward these goals with $1 million for "programs designed to enhance and sustain the diversity of the university community."

Duderstadt, who became university president in 1988, built on this intention by creating "The Michigan Mandate: A Strategic Linking of Academic Excellence and Social Diversity." The mandate, announced in 1988, was a major plan to increase the representation of students, faculty, and staff of color and improve their campus experiences. It dedicated new resources such as university funding and created new staff and faculty positions and hires, administrative bodies, student recruitment, multicultural awareness training, and other campus programming. The text of the mandate justified this programming as an expression of Michigan's pioneering leadership in higher education:

> The fundamental premise of the Michigan Mandate is that for the University to achieve excellence in teaching and research in the years ahead, for it to serve our state, our nation, and the world, we simply must achieve and sustain a campus community recognized for its racial and ethnic diversity. But beyond this, we believe that the university has a mandate . . . to build a model of a pluralistic, multicultural community for our nation. . . . Embracing and, even more importantly, capitalizing on our racial, cultural, and ethnic diversity will be a critical element in the University's ability to achieve excellence in teaching and research while serving our state, nation, and world in the years ahead.[71]

The mandate borrowed Powell's ideas of diversity and applied them to the specifics of campus life. The document listed many forms of diversity—race, ethnicity, culture, religion, and nationality—although university leaders' early discussions of it focused on people of color, particularly African Americans, as did many of the more than one hundred programs that the mandate deployed.[72] The document cited various instrumental advantages of mobilizing "the human talent represented by its under-represented populations": academic excellence, successful democratic governance in the United States, the country's economic prosperity, and its standing among other nations. It envisioned Michigan at the forefront of creating a pluralistic, high-status educated class, inclusive of people of color.

The mandate was political, created in response to charges of racism on campus and developed by a president who wanted to create a defining legacy. It is significant for this story because it was a major statement connecting diversity with academic excellence, increases in racial minority representation, and university leaders' vision of a pluralist society. While the methods of affirmative admissions changed little, the mandate explicitly downplayed the need to remedy racial subordination, stating that in the country's future, "the full participation of under-represented groups in all realms of national life will not be just a matter of equity and social justice. It will be the key to the future strength and prosperity of America."[73]

The implementation of the Michigan Mandate corresponded with higher enrollment and graduation rates of students of color and the hiring of more faculty of color.[74] Between 1988 and 1998, the percentage of undergraduate and graduate students who were African American, Latino, Native American, and Asian grew from 15% to 25%, with increases in the representation of all racial minority groups.[75] By 1998, 9% of the undergraduate student body was African American.[76] Administrators later cited these numbers as indicative of the university's successful achievement of diversity. Internal changes in the undergraduate admissions office likely contributed to many of these changes. In 1985, the office created the position of director of minority admissions, who would integrate minority recruitment into the daily recruitment of all the professional and counseling staff and develop an extensive platform of recruitment programming.

Through the mid-1990s, the grid system of undergraduate admissions was still in place. The Opportunity Awards Program was folded into a larger Comprehensive Studies Program, which administrators then framed as inclusive of all students although it served almost exclusively students of color.

Meanwhile, the law school policy was overhauled under the leadership of the dean of the Michigan Law School, Lee Bollinger, a white man who later became university president. The revised policy reflected the language of Powell's opinion and stressed diversity, with specific reference to race. It called for "a commitment to racial and ethnic diversity with special reference to the inclusion of students from groups which have been historically discriminated against, like African Americans, Hispanics and Native Americans. . . . [Those students] are particularly likely to have experiences and perspectives of special importance to our mission."[77] The affirmative admissions process was incorporated into a holistic review of each individual student's application.

Like administrators in similar institutions, many at Michigan came to see race-based affirmative action as a professional norm and responsibility.[78] Meanwhile, they remained mindful of white students' perceptions of racial diversity. During a 1993 regents' meeting, a dean noted that white students came to the campus eager to experience diversity.[79] A subsequent survey of the class of 1994 found that 30% of white students cited Michigan's "racially and ethnically diverse student body" as an important reason in their decision to attend the university.[80]

The Michigan Mandate and the university's discourse on racial diversity served as templates for administrators' understanding of other marginalized groups and the development of other inclusionary policies. President Duderstadt's 1995 Michigan Agenda for Women, modeled on the mandate, sought "to create a University climate that fosters the success of women faculty, students, and staff by drawing upon the strengths of our diversity." In 1993, the regents added sexual orientation to its official bylaws on nondiscrimination and affirmative action—an action that regent Laurence Deitch, a white man, explained as making "a reality out of our commitment to diversity."[81] Hence, responsibility for diversity became ever more central to the university's identity, and the notion of diversity expressed a vision of pluralism in which group differences are socially desirable and pragmatically valuable.

Reimagining the Boundaries of the Student Body

In the twentieth century, the political fight for racial justice, integration, and equal access in higher education was met with a bureaucratic response by some of the nation's competitive white universities and colleges in the form of accommodationist policies. The signature intervention was a supplemental program of affirmative admissions, which Michigan was at the forefront in adopting. Administrators there presented affirmative admissions first as a means of creating minority opportunity and remedying disadvantage and then, in the 1980s, in terms of fostering the benefits of the diversity. They did so principally to defend, explain, increase, and market racial minority representation on a majority-white campus.

In this period, university leaders cultivated an identity for the university as a bastion of diversity. Their adoption of diversity rhetoric was a strategic response by the administration to a politicized legal environment. Given Justice Powell's opinion in *Bakke* and the contentious political environment, it was prudent for administrators to take on the goal of diversity in order to create the semblance of compliance with law. Yet, Michigan administrators did not simply label affirmative admissions in new language. They did the double move of invoking diversity. They made it a core element of the institution's raison d'être, alongside academic excellence. They incorporated diversity as a principle, an objective, a description, and a programmatic feature of campus life.

Michigan's identity as a champion of diversity posed racial minority representation and inclusion as crucial to its status as an elite public research university. That identity came to comprise many campus leaders' understanding of inclusion while also facilitating many politicized objectives. It projected a polished image of the school, served as a sales pitch to both students of color and white students. It both comprised and signaled visionary presidential leadership.

Michigan's identity as an innovator in diversity and excellence symbolically redefined the symbolic boundaries of the student body. It constructed inclusion as a common group interest for the community, one that could be advantageous for everyone involved and for the institution itself. It depicted racial minorities as culturally distinct from but culturally equivalent to white people. This identity provided a language for campus pluralism in terms other than a black-white binary or the remediation of minority disadvantage. It asserted baseline commonalities across students: academic skills and normative appreciation of cultural difference. It valorized those who fulfilled the idealized archetype of a bright, motivated, studious Michigan student.

Michigan's identity minimized symbolic racial boundaries by downplaying problematic differences between white people and people of color—whether that was the racial privilege enjoyed by so many white students or the academic and social obstacles experienced by so many students of color. Although administrators sometimes acknowledged racial inequality, their mobilization of diversity obscured it. They were ambiguous, if not deceitful, regarding what the university was actually doing to facilitate the incorporation of students of color. Further, Michigan students and faculty of color were still frequently treated as second-class citizens by their counterparts on campus, their full membership never realized.

Just as Michigan administrators were constructing racial representation as essential to an elite education and investing more resources in their affirmative action efforts, legal jurisprudence and politics were making universities' race-conscious policies far more controversial.

THREE

Gratz, Grutter, and the Public Relations of Defending Affirmative Action

"Good evening! I'm delighted that you are all here tonight!" boomed Ted Spencer, the executive director of undergraduate admissions for the University of Michigan. "Why are you here and why were you selected?" He was addressing 175 high school seniors and their family members sitting in a decorated ballroom in the Crowne Plaza, a fancy hotel in suburban Detroit. It was the winter 2003 Annual Pursuit of Excellence Student Symposium, an event the university had been hosting for more than twenty-five years. About thirty people in the room were white; the rest were African American. Many of the students wore ties or dresses, as did their parents, aunts, and grandparents. The racks outside the ballroom were loaded with wool overcoats and a few furs, with fedoras stacked on top. Admissions office staff hovered around the perimeter, wearing suit jackets and cheerful smiles.

The symposium was a major university event for recruiting students of color. The university invited "underrepresented minority students"— African Americans, Latinos, and Native Americans—who met a threshold for test scores and grade point average (GPA). This year, the university expanded its criteria to include some "majority" students with lower family incomes—$50,000 a year or less.

The admissions director, an African American man who was wearing a blazer and a favorite tie striped with the school colors, blue and maize, answered his own rhetorical question. "We've had an opportunity to look over information about you—your GPA and test scores. And what we've learned is that you have the characteristics that a typical University of Michigan student would have. . . . You are among the best and brightest."

He continued, explaining that the university had just adopted a new admissions process that fall, so applicants needed to provide more in-depth information than they had in years past. "This is the result of what I see as a very positive Supreme Court decision, which allows all universities to continue to consider diversity in decisions. Building a class means taking into account geographic diversity, different forms of diversity, bringing together many ways of thinking and ideas for a robust exchange."

The next speaker, Lester Monts, had an even more powerful position within the administration as senior vice provost for academic affairs, professor of music, and senior counsel to the university president for the arts, diversity, and undergraduate affairs. A solidly built black man with a thick beard and large square glasses, he said, "We interpret diversity very broadly. To touch on one part that you may not think about is intellectual diversity." He mentioned courses in different departments, including his own on world music. "Everyone in this room represents some branch of diversity. Sharing backgrounds and values is a very important part of what we do on campus." He closed boldly, "No one matches the University of Michigan in terms of its action and devotion to diversity."

Following the introductions were panels of faculty members, students, and financial aid administrators and an information fair. At the end of the evening, with everyone gathered in a large ballroom, an associate director of admissions charismatically led two rounds of the chorus of the Michigan fight song, "The Victors." People clapped along and pumped their fists in the air as they sang, "Hail! Hail! to Michigan, the leaders and best! Go Blue!"

The Twenty-First-Century Push for Diversity at the University of Michigan

Just six months before the Pursuit of Excellence Student Symposium, the US Supreme Court had announced its decisions in the two 2003 legal cases Ted Spencer referenced, *Gratz et al. v. Bollinger et al.* and *Grutter v. Bollinger et al.* These cases challenged the University of Michigan's admissions policies at the undergraduate and graduate levels, respectively. They were the most significant Supreme Court cases on affirmative admissions since the 1978 *Regents of the University of California v. Bakke.* In them, the Supreme Court decided that the university could use a race-conscious admissions policy so long as the objective was diversity and race was consulted as one of many factors, but not the decisive factor, in admissions decisions.

Law is powerful. It is an obdurate, highly consequential institution. It establishes formal rules, norms, and meanings for people to live by, both procedurally and symbolically. The Supreme Court is widely considered a credible, persuasive authority, and its findings establish enforceable governing standards. The peculiar nature of litigation creates an adversarial conflict between opposing sides, each of which undertakes to introduce and construe evidence and make arguments in a manner that favors its claims. This conflict gets reinforced by activists, public policy analysts, academics, and media commentators. Law also establishes the language of debate, as it defines the discourse that can be used.

All this held true for the symbolic and social politics of affirmative admissions at the turn of the twenty-first century. In the years after *Bakke,* the issue had crystallized into a polarized debate between clashing philosophies.[1] In that debate, conservative and libertarian opponents argue that affirmative action does more harm than good. These opponents' core argument is that admissions should be color-blind. They contend that *any* deliberate recognition of race in decision making—as they put it, any racial preference—is unfair and discriminatory and violates individual liberties protected by the Constitution. According to this color-blind position, actions that distribute resources to people of color in order to improve social conditions are legally and morally equivalent to actions intended to oppress a racial group.[2]

In the years following *Bakke,* the liberal defense of affirmative action argued that race-conscious decision making is necessary to achieve important societal goals. While some defenders of the policy insisted that affirmative action was necessary to counteract entrenched inequality and foster integration, the prevailing position was the value of diversity. With *Gratz* and *Grutter,* the issue of affirmative action was firmly entrenched as a polarized legal contest, and diversity was firmly entrenched as *the* defense against calls for color blindness.

Between the time *Gratz* and *Grutter* were filed in 1997 and the court's decisions in June 2003, the university administration developed an extensive legal defense of its admissions policies and engaged in a massive public education and relations campaign. With the objective of winning both the legal cases and public approval, the administration drew on Powell's opinion in *Bakke* to formulate the legal concept of diversity—what became known as the diversity rationale. They drew on that concept to moderate the heated political dynamics. This included the crucial work of explaining the cases, the university's involvement, and the outcomes to applicants like those at the Pursuit of Excellence symposium. Student activist organizations, four of which are examined here, engaged in the litigation politics as well. The activists tried to weigh in on one or the other side of the debate. One organization, the Coalition to Defend Affirmative Action and Integration and Fight for Equality By Any Means Necessary (BAMN), tried to shift the terms of the debate altogether. It spearheaded legal intervention in *Grutter* in the lower courts, arguing that affirmative action was necessary to promote integration and equality, although its claims were marginalized throughout the litigation.

This chapter discusses the legal and symbolic politics of *Gratz*, *Grutter*, and affirmative admissions in the mid-2000s. It begins with an explanation of the cases and the court decisions. It examines in depth the university's construction of its identity during the campaign leading up to those decisions and the engagement of the activist organizations. Then the discussion moves to the changes that the university made to its rhetoric and its race-conscious practices after the June 2003 decisions. Its defense continued long after the court's decisions were announced. To state what is perhaps obvious, the push for diversity at Michigan at this time was, above all else, the administration's defense of race-conscious admissions as an indispensable strategy for achieving racial progress.

Gratz, Grutter, and the Legal Rationale for Diversity

In 1997, the Center for Individual Rights (CIR), a libertarian public-interest law firm, filed two legal cases, *Gratz* against the undergraduate College of Literature, Science, and Arts (LSA) and *Grutter* against the law school. Over the previous fifteen years, opponents of affirmative action and their color-blind politics had gained political traction. Troubled by civil rights gains and the growing power of women and people of color, they had found support from the administrations of Presidents Ronald Reagan and George H. W. Bush and the increasingly conservative US judiciary. *Bakke, Wards Cove, Croson,* and other major legal cases were decided to their liking, finding affirmative action in admissions and employment to be based on racial quotas and limiting the policy or banning it altogether.

By the mid-1990s, there was some political momentum in their favor. The 1996 decision by the Fifth Circuit Court in the *Hopwood v. State of Texas* case found that the University of Texas's consideration of race, even as one factor among many, was unconstitutional, thus prohibiting affirmative admissions in Texas, Mississippi, and Louisiana.[3] The high-profile activist Ward Connerly and others pushed ballot measures to end race- and gender-based preferences in state hiring, contracting, and state university admissions. These campaigns succeeded in California in 1996 (Proposition 209) and Washington in 1997 (Initiative 200) and supported legislative restrictions on affirmative action in Florida. Soon CIR, which had gained recognition for its representation in *Hopwood*, turned its sights on the University of Michigan.

The *Gratz* and *Grutter* plaintiffs were white individuals who had applied to Michigan but were not initially admitted. Taking the color-blind position, they charged that the university gave explicit racial preferences to African American, Latino, and Native American applicants without sufficient justification, in violation of the equal protection clause of the Fourteenth Amendment, Title VI of the Civil Rights Act of 1964, and 42 USC § 1981.[4] They claimed that diversity was not a compelling state interest and that the university's policies were not narrowly tailored: "Diversity as a basis for employing racial preferences is simply too open-ended, ill-defined, and indefinite."[5] They argued, "The interest in diversity that the University asserts in justification of its racial preferences is based on stereotypes . . . [and] race-neutral alternatives to the preferences have not been meaningfully considered."[6]

Gratz contested two different race-conscious admissions policies that the LSA had used. One of these was the grid system, which consisted of thresholds for white and nonwhite applicants. That policy, in place until 1997, was a variation on a policy the university had adopted in 1980.[7] The other policy was the points system, which the university had adopted in 1998. Under the points system, applicants needed to earn 100 out of 150 points to be qualified for admissions. Crucially, the policy assigned 20 points to a student who was an underrepresented racial minority—African American, Latino, or American Indian—or from a socioeconomically disadvantaged background or a scholarship athlete. The *Grutter* case challenged the law school's policy of considering race as one of many factors in a case-by-case review of individual applications. (Although both the LSA and law school policies favored affluent students through criteria such as standardized test scores, only the race-based policies were brought into question.)

Gratz and *Grutter* hinged on the question of whether the university's affirmative admissions policies passed strict scrutiny. The test of strict scrutiny requires that the governmental policies that classify people based on their race must pass a two-pronged test. The practices must serve a compelling interest, and the institutional methods of achieving that interest must be narrowly tailored to that objective. Strict scrutiny had not applied when *Bakke* was decided. In 1978, the court had not considered the question of whether remedying societal discrimination or achieving diversity was a compelling governmental interest. In subsequent years, there was a move by federal judges, led by Republican appointees, to apply strict scrutiny to the government's use of both racial classifications.[8] Of particular importance for *Gratz* and *Grutter* was the 1989 Supreme Court decision in *City of Richmond v. Croson*. In that case, a contractor with the City of Richmond, Virginia, challenged the city's regulations requiring that its construction contractor subcontract 30% of its work to a business owned and controlled by people of color.[9] The majority of the justices decided that strict scrutiny should be applied not only to invidious uses of race (to discriminate) but also to benign uses of race (to counter discrimination). As Justice Antonin Scalia wrote for the majority, "Racial preferences appear to 'even the score' . . . only if one embraces the proposition that our society is appropriately viewed as divided into races, making it right that an injustice rendered in the past to a black man should be compensated for by discriminating against a white."[10] Justice Thurgood Marshall had presciently argued against such a move in a concurring opinion in *Fullilove v. Kirkland* (1980), when he cautioned that heightened scrutiny of benign racial classifications would be "strict in theory, but fatal in fact."[11]

The other major consequence of *Croson* relevant to the 2003 cases was that the majority found that "remedying past societal discrimination" was not a compelling governmental interest that could sustain a race-conscious program. Thus a governmental entity could not argue that its affirmative action program was intended to redress the effects of racism in American society and expect that program to survive judicial review.

When *Gratz* and *Grutter* were filed, the legality of the university's policies was an open question.[12] In the wake of *Croson*, it was not clear what would allow an affirmative admissions program to pass the test of strict scrutiny. It was not obvious what a governmental entity could argue about the purpose of its affirmative action program that would demonstrate a compelling state interest. Powell's opinion was not squarely a precedent, and lower courts had produced conflicting rulings based on *Bakke*. The court could have lived up to Justice Marshall's fears that strict scrutiny would be fatal in practice: it could have decided that nothing would pass the test.

The University's Defense of Diversity

The university administration mounted a massive defense of affirmative admissions at the undergraduate level and the law school by arguing what commonly is called the diversity rationale: that student learning improves and other benefits accrue when students interact with peers of other backgrounds, including but not limited to race and ethnicity, because such interaction exposes students to unfamiliar experiences and perspectives. It cited *Bakke* as precedent, claiming that the case allowed the consideration of race and ethnicity in university admissions. Further, the university mobilized an intensive effort to develop Powell's conclusion that diversity is a compelling state interest in higher education. It presented extensive research-based evidence on what administrators repeatedly referred to as the educational benefits of diversity. Maureen Mahoney, a white woman and lead attorney for Michigan in *Grutter,* told the Supreme Court justices:

> There is a compelling interest in having an institution that is both academi-cally excellent and racially diverse, because our leaders need to be trained in institutions that are excellent, that are superior academically, but they also need to be trained with exposure to the viewpoints, to the perspectives, to the experiences of individuals from diverse backgrounds.

The university argued that race-conscious admissions policies were essen-tial to achieving such diversity. It also claimed that its admissions policies were narrowly tailored because race and ethnicity were considered as one of many factors in admissions selections toward that interest, without the quotas or numeric goals that *Bakke* forbade.

In *Grutter,* the university also maintained that it had an interest in en-rolling a critical mass of African American, Hispanic, and Native American students who, without special consideration, would likely remain extremely underrepresented in the student body and thus unable to fully contribute to the law school learning experience or the legal profession. These arguments rested on a depiction of Michigan's identity as an institution in which aca-demic excellence and diversity were intimately connected. As the university argued, "The University considers a broadly diverse student body 'an inte-gral component of its mission' because such diversity 'increase[s] the intel-lectual vitality of [its] education, scholarship, service, and communal life.'"[13]

The adversarial dynamic in *Gratz* and *Grutter* put university leaders on the defensive. They hoped to win both the court's approval and public support. They were anxious to avoid liability and a tarnished reputation. Importantly, key university leaders also understood their involvement as an opportunity to defend a policy that they strongly believed was necessary and just.[14]

Once the *Gratz* and *Grutter* cases were filed in 1997, the litigation ab-sorbed the attention of many university leaders and soon permeated other aspects of university life.[15] The undergraduate and law school admissions offices continued to admit applicants under the guidelines in question—to the frustration of some undergraduate counselors, who preferred to tweak the policy from year to year. The university tried its best to shield the offices from the public spotlight. Political activists organized on and off campus, most of them in favor of affirmative action. A group of faculty members weighed in with their support as well. Student groups arranged panel discussions with participants in the cases. The media coverage was intense, with news crews combing the campus at critical stages in the cases. Meanwhile, a number of educators and administrators who ran campus diversity programs incorporated the lawsuits and issues of affirmative action and diversity into their pedagogical activities. The politics became ever more heated when the Supreme Court decided to hear the cases.

Over this period, leaders in the administration undertook a massive effort to accrue both evidentiary and political support for the university's position. Early on in the lawsuits, university executives convened a legal team to respond to the plaintiffs' charges.[16] The organization invested time, human capital, and financial resources—upward of $10 million (although some portion was covered by liability insurance). University leaders substantiated Powell's opinion with social scientific research, much of it conducted by their own faculty.[17] The university's lawyers and expert witnesses integrated these empirical findings into their legal statements and reports. This systemic evidence differentiated the university's defense from the earlier legal defenses by the Universities of California and Texas. Professor of psychology and women's studies Patricia Gurin, a white woman whose research was crucial to their case, served as an expert witness and public spokesperson.[18] In her expert report, quoted in the opinion, she described her argument's basis in an analysis of multi-institutional national data, a survey of Michigan students, and an evaluation of a classroom program at Michigan:

> It is clear . . . that interaction with peers from diverse racial backgrounds, both in the classroom and informally, is positively associated with a host of what I call "learning outcomes." Students who experienced the most racial and ethnic diversity in classroom settings and in informal interactions with peers showed the greatest engagement in active thinking processes, growth in intellectual engagement and motivation, and growth in intellectual and academic skills.[19]

Her study also identified students' positive "democracy outcomes," including greater motivation and better capacity to partake in a heterogeneous democracy.

In their campaign around the litigation, university officials strategically solicited business and political endorsements.[20] Before the cases were even filed, university president Bollinger embarked on a coalition-building effort to rally support for the university. In the late 1990s, he successfully elicited the backing of former US president Gerald Ford, who wrote a *New*

York Times op-ed that endorsed affirmative action, Michigan's policies, and the importance of diversity in college education.[21] Over time, he and other university leaders successfully used their professional networks to solicit amicus briefs, including a high-profile brief from sixty-five Fortune 500 companies and another from retired military officials, both of which were widely touted and proved consequential for the court's final determination. These and the other briefs filed in support of Michigan's policies reiterated versions of the diversity rationale. The brief from the Fortune 500 companies in *Grutter* stated that "the skills and training needed to succeed in business today demand exposure to widely diverse people, cultures, ideas, and viewpoints. . . . [We] need the talent and creativity of a workforce that is as diverse as the world around it."[22]

The public response to *Gratz* and *Grutter* overwhelmingly favored the university. More amicus briefs were filed for a single side than in any court case in prior US history. On the day of the oral arguments, tens of thousands of people participated in an April 1, 2003, march on Washington that was mobilized by BAMN.

These legal arguments and political activities worked to Michigan's favor. In June 2003, the Supreme Court upheld *Grutter*. By a 5–4 majority vote in *Grutter*, the justices determined that diversity was indeed a compelling interest and that the law school's admissions policy of individualized review was constitutional under the equal protection clause of the Fourteenth Amendment. The law school's interest in enrolling a critical mass of minority students and its consideration of individual applications toward that end were narrowly tailored. The law school had passed the strict scrutiny test. The court's majority opinion, written by Justice Sandra Day O'Connor, cited institutional benefits of diversity such as an enhanced educational environment, better national leadership, stronger national security, and greater competitiveness in the global economy. She wrote:

> Diversity promotes learning outcomes and better prepares students for an increasingly diverse workforce, for society, and for the legal profession. . . . The path to leadership must be visibly open to talented and qualified individuals of every race and ethnicity.[23]

In *Gratz*, the court found by a 6–3 vote the undergraduate admissions policy of assigning twenty points based on an applicant's race was unconstitutional under the equal protection clause. It concluded that the university's admissions process was not narrowly tailored because it made "race a decisive factor for virtually every minimally qualified underrepresented minority applicant."[24] But because of *Grutter*, Michigan and universities and colleges across the country could continue to consider race in admissions in the interest of diversity.

The university declared a victory. The presidents of major universities, congressional Democrats, civil rights organizations such as the NAACP, corporate leaders, and other allies of the university applauded the *Grutter* decision. Court decisions have legitimating effects, and the *Gratz* and *Grutter* decisions legitimated the legal concept of diversity and, in some circles, affirmative action. Newspaper editorials published after June 2003, compared to those published before, were far more likely to support affirmative action and to do so on the grounds of diversity—arguing that a mix of people from different racial and ethnic backgrounds enhances student learning and improves the nation's leadership ranks.[25]

Opponents of affirmative action were disheartened. Although the court had found the undergraduate admissions policy unconstitutional, it had not banned affirmative action. After the Supreme Court decisions in June 2003, some conservative analysts chastised CIR for not attacking the diversity rationale in court.[26] I mentioned this criticism to Roger Clegg, the animated white man who served as the general counsel of the Center for Equal Opportunity. His organization, which filed a brief supporting the plaintiffs, cast itself as "the only think tank dedicated exclusively to the promotion of color-blind equal opportunity and racial harmony." He explained that, foremost, his allies' constitutional argument had stronger legal grounds and it best reflected their ideological stance. Mounting an attack against the diversity rationale would require time-intensive research, he said. I asked him if conservatives had not developed a compelling critique of diversity. "Well, obviously," he replied, "we did not do a very good job, or we did an inadequate job, although I think it was sort of understandable. Because I think the conservatives probably thought that, 'Oh geez, nobody's actually going to buy this, are they?'"

During the Litigation: Turning Diversity's Educational Benefits into Sound Bites

In her press statement on the day of the *Gratz* and *Grutter* decisions, Mary Sue Coleman made a statement that illustrated a key element of the university's campaign around the litigation, one that deserves further analysis: "I am proud of the voice that the University of Michigan provided in this important debate," she said. "We fought for the very principle that defines our country's greatness. Year after year, our student body proves it and now the

Court has affirmed it: our diversity is our strength." To fight for affirmative action, the administration cultivated and publicized an identity for the university as the incarnation of key tenets of the diversity rationale—an identity evident in this statement. My fieldwork in the year leading up to the court decisions reveals just how they did so.

When CIR initiated the litigation, the Office of the Vice President for Communications put together a communications strategy targeted to alumni, donors, students, reporters, business leaders, and public relations personnel at other elite universities. The office disseminated the university's position through e-mail, personal meetings, press releases, newspaper clippings, and a public LISTSERV. It created an extensive website, still publically available, that contained the legal filings along with a vast array of information, most of it oriented to presenting the university's position in the most favorable light: statements from university leaders, overviews of the cases by Michigan's assistant general counsel, frequently asked questions, news media reports, supporting research, rebuttals to affirmative action opponents' critiques of that research, statistics on the student body, and press kits.[27] The university president, the provost, the director of undergraduate admissions, and others spoke at events such as panels sponsored by the communications office, a debate organized by the LSA student government, and off campus at venues ranging from undergraduate recruitment fairs to national meetings of various professional organizations. They published articles and books about the legal defense and campus diversity, such as *Defending Diversity: Affirmative Action at the University of Michigan.*[28]

As law and society scholars have persuasively shown, people in their everyday activities do not directly translate law from the written word.[29] They must interpret it. This interpretation happens through all sorts of decisions, actions, and cognitive processes, from businesses' informal resolution of contract disputes to media representations of out-of-control tort litigation to the schemas that form individuals' consciousness of the law.[30]

Michigan's sophisticated public education and relations campaign was a deliberate effort to translate a very complex legal argument into language that was comprehensible to its many audiences, especially those outside the court. The administration wanted to persuade these audiences to agree with its defense. To do so, administrators needed to ensure people understood basic elements of the cases and to shape popular perceptions of the university, the litigation, affirmative action, and diversity.

While litigation, in any setting, often fuels an organization's negative reputation, Michigan leaders tried to use the litigation to make a positive statement about the university. The coordinators and participants in the campaign, like the legal team that developed the university's argument, masterminded that two-step move of diversity. The campaign reframed the debate over race-conscious admissions—a controversial intervention to increase racial minority representation—as a fight for the more politically palatable objective of cultural diversity. University spokespeople presented the diversity rationale as legally sound, empirically verifiable, and politically righteous. Their campaign played up the university's identity as one of academic excellence and diversity, spotlighting those aspects of university life that best exemplified principles of the diversity rationale. Connected to the university's identity, the diversity rationale seemed like a commonsensical, valid description of the student experience at Michigan.

This construction of the university's identity was a fundamental component of the administration's work of garnering political, organizational, and corporate support for the defense. It was at the heart of a campaign that fueled relentless messaging of the university's legal stance.

On Message

My interview with Ted Spencer did not go as I had planned. When I arrived at the admissions office, Ted invited me into his large corner office, framed by large windows and walls decorated with awards. Sounding positive, he said he had heard about me from his staff members. After we made small talk, and before I asked my first interview question, he pulled out photocopies of two PowerPoint slide shows and launched into a presentation called "The Need for Diversity in Higher Education." One slide, titled "What has happened at the University of Michigan since its commitment to diversity," listed various positive consequences, such as "Academic quality has increased," "Diversity provides an educational benefit to all students," and "Corporate recruitment has not diminished."

I later learned that he presented this material to alumni and journalists. During the interview, I eventually worked in my questions, but this was not the interview that I had hoped for. His presentation exemplified just how carefully scripted and well rehearsed were university spokespeople's speeches, presentations, and public comments.

This careful scripting followed from the university's communications strategy, which included an internal Admissions Lawsuit Media Plan. The plan identified goals and tactics for communicating about the legal cases as well as talking points—in local parlance, messaging. Office staff had translated the legalese of the university's defense into accessible sound bites, concepts, and images. For example, one key talking point was: "There is empirical evidence that learning in a diverse environment benefits EVERY student, regardless of race." Communications and legal staff briefed the various university presidents, interim presidents, deans, provosts, attorneys, and other figures in the public spotlight on the media plan. James Justin Wilson, a white student and campus spokesperson for student activists who opposed racial preferences, complained in our interview, "If you listen to the comments of *every* university administrator . . . they all say the exact same thing."

According to Julie Peterson, the associate vice president for media relations and public affairs, the lawsuits communications team wanted to depict the university as taking a reasoned position rather than a polemical stance. A white woman with a calm demeanor and long red hair, Julie explained that the university wanted to "guide a national conversation about the importance of diversity. . . . Not so much to convince [people] that 'We're right and they're wrong,' but to say, 'We're thoughtful. This is an important social policy question. We need to have a really thoughtful and rational debate.'"

University spokespeople would characterize diversity's benefits as a shared point of agreement for all sides of that national conversation. In winter 2003, the day before CIR filed the *Grutter* brief with the Supreme Court, President George W. Bush issued a statement on his opposition to affirmative action: "I strongly support diversity of all kinds, including racial diversity in higher education. But the method used by the University of Michigan to achieve this important goal is fundamentally flawed."[31] Soon thereafter, at the MLK Symposium that opens this book, university president Coleman said:

> I was pleased to hear the President supports the importance of diversity in America's colleges and universities. . . . It also was gratifying to hear him acknowledge what our research has demonstrated—that essential values like respect, understanding, and goodwill are strengthened when students live and learn from people from many backgrounds.

Her reinterpretation of Bush's announcement suggested that the debate between opponents and proponents of affirmative action was not so polarized after all. By publicly asserting that diversity's educational benefits were premised on sound, authoritative knowledge, administrators tried to defuse their adversaries' criticisms.

On Stage

In addition to using carefully scripted talking points, those involved in the educational and PR campaign elaborated the university's diversity rationale by staging formal events at which university spokespeople spelled out the university's legal argument and legitimated it by invoking the university's identity. They drew on characterizations of Michigan's public reputation, displays of authority by its faculty, and performances of engagement by its students. Through such actions, university leaders presented the diversity rationale as a factual characterization of reality. They selectively portrayed campus life—the essence of being at Michigan—as comprising meaningful, enriching experiences that were enhanced explicitly by the expression of differing viewpoints and, implicitly, by the presence of students of color, particularly black people.

One such event was the fall 2002 Admissions Lawsuits Update forum, sponsored by the communications office, the Office of the Vice President and General Counsel, and the Ford Foundation.[32] That afternoon, people filled most of the plush red seats in Mendelssohn Hall. The audience quietly listened to an all-star cast of administrators, lawyers, and other spokespeople. The event was webcast, telecast on a local television station, and excerpted on radio stations across the state.

Marvin Krislov, a white man who was the university's general counsel and the moderator that day, opened by explaining that the event was intended to be an explanation of the university's legal defense and policies, not a debate. The simple structure of the panels—one called "legal experts" and the other called "educators/leadership"—presented the educational benefits of diversity, respectively, as legal argument and as established academic wisdom.

President Coleman began her speech by noting the high stakes of the cases and the university's prominence:

> As you know, university presidents across the country look to the University
> of Michigan as a model of what a great public university can be . . . where a
> deep, unwavering commitment to diversity goes hand in hand with a deep,
> unwavering commitment to excellence.

She noted the university's deliberate academic and pedagogical objectives for admissions: "We know that the kind of educational environment we enjoy here does not 'just happen.' It is carefully cultivated." At no point did she refer to "affirmative action" or the design of the admissions policies.

Instead, she noted their constitutionality. Her comments stayed focused on the diversity rationale, spelling it out as an expert insight into human behavior and commonsensical truth:

> More than fifty years of changes in higher education have taught us that the more diverse an academic community becomes—through every form of "diversity" you can name—the more vigorous its debates and discussions.

Differing viewpoints, she explained, were central to the learning enterprise. Coleman noted that race was one of many forms of diversity, relevant as a part of person's cultural identity and an influence on people's viewpoints:

> Recognizing the educational benefits of diversity does not mean that we equate a person's race with a particular point of view. It reflects the fact that race still matters in American society, as it influences our perceptions about the world and the people around us. To understand the impact on perception, there is no substitute for face-to-face interaction among students. It is the most powerful educational tool we know to break down stereotypes and overcome assumptions. It helps students see commonalities across racial lines and acknowledge differences within racial groups.

She also stated that benefits of diversity were instrumentally useful and widely shared, not an advantage enjoyed by any one group: "The experience of studying in a diverse community prepares students—all students—to participate in an increasingly diverse democracy and to compete in a global economy. . . . A diverse learning environment is a better learning environment for every student." Throughout the speech, Coleman reiterated scholarly underpinnings of the diversity rationale, mentioning Justice Powell's use of a quote from a former president of Princeton University, the empirical evidence of diversity's benefits produced through "rigorous, multidisciplinary social science research" by Michigan scholars, and the new research questions explored in the biological sciences after more women and people of color earned PhDs in those fields.

When interim provost Paul Courant spoke, he too invoked social-scientific discourse and his professorial expertise, citing examples from his own teaching and research. A middle-aged white man dressed in a gray suit jacket and wire-rimmed glasses, he told the audience definitively:

> There are enormous benefits in general associated with human diversity in a wide variety of contexts. I happen to be an economist, and a very important

idea in neoclassical economics is the division of labor. Diversity is very much about the division of labor and the division of labor is very much about diversity. If you want to solve any problem, you want to have a team of people who have a variety of skills rather than a clump of people who are essentially all identical.

The provost spoke simply of a diversity of perspectives, not of race at all. He recounted the payoffs of such diversity for classroom discussion, noting, "Everyone who's been a student or a teacher [knows] an enormous amount of teaching is done by students."

One objective of the university's media plan was to "humanize the university's position—attach human faces and first-person stories to our messages," and the two other educators/leadership panelists, Michigan alumna Judge Geraldine Bedsoe Ford and Michigan student Monique Luce, did just that. Both were African American, and both recounted how meeting different sorts of students on Michigan's campus had personally enriched their experiences at the university. Judge Ford, a distinguished woman with a gravelly voice, said in measured, punctuated phrases,

> I was here in the mid-'40s. And the new students coming back [from World War II on the GI Bill]—men they were, really—made a deep and abiding impression on all of us who were ordinary undergrads. I think the vitality, the sense of commitment of those older students did a lot to change the university. . . . And I think that in terms of meeting people who'd had *that* variety of experience, who were married—we didn't know anything about married people!—but here at the university, we met that variety of people.

Judge Ford, like the other panelists, was referring to many salient forms of diversity, experienced through the expression of different viewpoints. She made passing reference to race as something of the past, noting that there were only two hundred African American students when she was at the university. "The difference I see today is a much greater cross section of humanity." The judge was an acceptable archetype of diversity. She personified the university's argument that it trains people of color to be leaders in society.

Monique, an African American senior who served as student government president and a leader of a pro–affirmative action campus organization, embodied another diversity archetype: a smart, well-spoken black student. With a confident demeanor, she remarked, "Yes, I've been able to interact with people on a level that I never have before. White, black, gay, lesbian, all

those different types of things have been amazing for me in my development." Her presence and self-presentation reinforced the university's arguments that it admits only highly qualified students of color, while her
comments reiterated the university's argument that it cultivates a learning
environment where students are exposed to cultural differences.

Monique recalled how, after growing up in a predominantly white and
upper-middle-class community, she was eager to attend college with other
black students, noting, "Also having a chance to be around more people of
color, in particular more black people, has also been extremely valuable to
me." This comment, while not directly from the university's talking points,
hinted at an argument the university made in *Grutter*—that a critical mass
of underrepresented racial minority students was necessary to achieve diversity's benefits so that minority students would not be isolated or easily
stereotyped. "So, I guess I love the student body mix here."

Monique then veered off the official script and criticized the administration. She chastised the university for neglecting recent hate speech incidents
in the dorms and not addressing issues of minority retention: "Yes, the university has done its best in defending this affirmative action case and talking
about the importance of diversity, but. . . . this is still a very sort of racially
biased institution, just as much of America is a very racially biased country.
There are many more things that the university could do." The mood in the
room had grown tense.

The moderator asked the provost for his reaction to Monique's criticism.
Provost Courant spoke slowly: "Well, there's definitely more to be done. . . .
In order to be able to make the further progress that Monique just referred
to . . . we need to have the basic numbers." He also interrupted himself as
he spoke, noting: "I have to say that my earlier comment—that students
teach—was perfectly exemplified by Monique." He diffused the tension by
changing the topic and by not disagreeing with Monique (he later noted
that "our duty [is] to try to make this environment one in which people are
comfortable disagreeing with one another"). His parenthetical aside was
subtle, but it too deflected Monique's criticisms by reframing them as evidence of the educational benefits of diversity. That aside was a rhetorical
move I witnessed many times: administrators would tell storied lessons of
diversity in which they retrospectively characterized a tense interaction or
negotiation between people of different backgrounds as an instance that
produced new learning.

Organizational scholars have observed that managerial attempts to
define a singular, definitive organizational identity often provoke resistance

and conflict.[33] This is particularly true in academia in the United States. Universities are scientific institutions with varying priorities across disciplines, and faculty and students regard freedom of research and intellectual thought very highly. Many university leaders, admissions officers, and faculty members personally found the focus of the legal cases constraining. The litigation limited how they could talk about and manage affirmative action. The emphasis on race and ethnicity in admissions had been externally imposed on the university, they said, and they were eager to move beyond it. At another public panel about the cases, an audience member questioned the university's attention to racial diversity. Marvin Krislov replied, sounding exasperated, "We're talking about racial and ethnic diversity because we're being sued about it!" A few professors and administrators complained openly (or quietly) about the constraints inherent to the concept of diversity, as they believed that it wrongly cut off social justice arguments.[34] But the framework of the diversity rationale had tremendous flexibility. As the provost implied at the admissions update panel, even a critic of the university could contribute to campus diversity; an institutional identity of diversity and excellence allowed for circumscribed dissent.

(Constructing) the Student Experience of Diversity

As evident at the admissions lawsuit panel, representations of diversity in the student body were central to the university's official communications about the cases. Many other units within the university also were involved in producing public representations of Michigan students—such as theatrical performances and student panels—and some of these, too, reiterated tenets of the diversity rationale. For example, *Campus Diversity, Student Voices*, a documentary film produced in 2003 by the university's Dialogues on Diversity program, centered on Michigan students' experiences of identity formation through their interpersonal relationships and academic experiences. The brochure for the film explained: "In their own voices, students impart a close-up view of the scope and meaning of their experiences, and the significance of opportunities available in campus life to learn from difference." The documentary premiered in downtown Ann Arbor, with introductions by the provost and the dean of the graduate school before an audience of about 175 people. It featured eleven students who differed by their school, year in college, race, ethnic heritage, class, national origin, geographic origin, gender, and political orientation. The students talked about living with people of other racial groups and learning about those groups' cultures and social practices, describing those experiences as informative for their own self-understanding and identity. A white male of Polish ancestry remarked that he disliked the course he took to fulfill the undergraduate race and ethnicity course requirement, but he also admitted to learning much from it.

Did Michigan students really see diversity this way? The university made extensive efforts to gather information on undergraduates' views of diversity—some research-based, some anecdotal—for purposes that were political, public relational, scholarly, teaching-related, or some combination thereof. The longitudinal Michigan Student Study was among the most important of these efforts. That research, which was a basis for Gurin's expert report, generated systematic evidence about the student experience of diversity, although of a particular sort. The very design of the research, the methods used, and the topics explored rested on some similar assumptions as the diversity rationale: that diversity is expressed through viewpoints, is a source of learning, and is centrally about race, which is experienced as a cultural identity in interaction with others.

The Michigan Student Study showed that, by and large, students had experienced diversity as the students in the film had. In 1994, over half of all fourth-year students had had extensive exposure to diversity (meaning "information and activities devoted to understanding other racial/ethnic groups and interracial ethnic relationships") through their class and personal relationships.[35] A large portion—from 72% of African American seniors to 92% of white seniors—had had positive relationships with students of different backgrounds. However, notable portions of all the students, white students in particular (40%), believed that the university's emphasis on diversity inhibited the ability to "talk honestly about ethnic, racial, and gender issues."

The study found that Michigan seniors expressed very strong support for the principle of educational equity on issues of race and ethnicity; 80% of white seniors and 96% of African American seniors agreed that "universities aggressively remove institutional barriers that promote inequality." White students, though, showed less enthusiasm for specific affirmative admissions policies, with just 37% of white seniors agreeing that different admissions criteria for ACT and SAT scores may be justified for some students of color (compared to 74% of African American seniors, 58% of Latino seniors, and 47% of Asian American seniors).

The authors of the study also identified important divides between black students and white students. African American students reported a general satisfaction with their time at Michigan but a strong sense of alienation on campus. They saw institutional racism. They felt that students and faculty did not respect them intellectually and that the university did not sincerely support students of color. The white students hewed closer to a color-blind view of race. As the authors noted, those students expressed positive but ambivalent orientations toward diversity, agreeing with equity in principle while opposing affirmative action in practice. They voiced suspicions about groups' separate expressions of their cultural difference. The authors characterized these divergent positions as differences in students' experiences with and perceptions of diversity.

That Michigan had problems retaining students of color, that the campus was a hostile environment for those students, that white students held misinformed stereotypes, that black students felt isolated and disrespected—none of this was new.[36] These complaints dated back decades. Various programs had been implemented in the university in response to them, in addition to the undergraduate admissions office activities and Michigan Mandate plan. The university had a number of academic units, programs, and pedagogical requirements intended to teach students about race and diversity. These ranged from academic programs such as the Center for Afro-American and African Studies to offices such as the Students of Color of Rackham, from first-year seminars to special programming such as theme semesters and diversity trainings in dorms. Many of these initiatives dated to the high-profile racist events that took place in the late 1980s.

Two of these initiatives merit some elaboration here, as they each illustrate (and foreshadow) the politics of the two-step move around diversity. The LSA had a requirement that students take a course with a substantial focus on race and ethnicity. As stated in the 2004 LSA handbook, "A Race and Ethnicity course will ask you to consider the role that racism and ethnocentrism have played and continue to play in American society and throughout the world." In the late 1980s, a group of faculty members organized, most of them white, because they thought students needed to learn about racial inequality. According to one professor who had been involved, they originally wanted the course to be a "racism" requirement. For these faculty members, it was deliberately *not* about multiculturalism or diversity. Elizabeth Anderson, a white woman who was a professor of philosophy, explained that the requirement "needed to make connections to race. It was not about appreciating cultural differences." For this group of faculty, the course requirement should be premised on an ideology of racial justice in which race, intolerance, and discrimination are understood as bases of inequality. However, the university did not present it that way. Administrators instead labeled it a "race and ethnicity requirement," although in the guidelines for students, it was described as a course on "racial or ethnic intolerance." In the early 1990s, the admissions office called it a "diversity requirement" in its newsletter.

The Program on Intergroup Relations and Conflict (IGR), also founded in 1988, was a social justice program intended to improve the campus climate. It became nationally recognized for its semester-long, peer-facilitated dialogue groups with students of different "social identity groups." The objective was to teach students skills of respecting and understanding diversity, managing intergroup relations, and mediating conflict among people of different backgrounds. Social justice remained a central theme, and at least one of its founding faculty members was also a part of the group that pushed for the race and ethnicity requirement. Yet this program, explicitly designed to expose students to different perspectives to generate new learning, hewed closely to an ideology of diversity's benefits.

It was this ideological and politicized terrain that campus activists needed to negotiate as they tried to engage with the limited terms of litigation and influence the outcomes of the cases.

The Power of Diversity: Through the Eyes of Skeptics

From the inception of race-conscious admissions, political activists have played central roles in disputes over university policies. That engagement has ranged from the inspiration that the civil rights movement provided the college administrators who first established these policies in the mid-1960s and the picketing by student organizers who demanded for more aggressive policies in the late 1960s and early 1970s to the work of undermining such policies soon pursed by conservative-libertarian activists. The *Gratz* and *Grutter* cases, represented by the partisan CIR with support from other conservative and libertarian movement organizations, prompted engagement on Michigan's campus as well as by other activists across the country on different sides of the debate, especially those in favor of affirmative action.

Scholarly explanations of what activists do with diversity and why are important. They reveal how the push for diversity involves the circumscription of political contention by channeling conflict into disputes over discrete policies, pursued through formal institutional processes. Such explanations also point to what the campus push for diversity excludes—the issues only partially represented and the voices silenced. Activists commonly assign different symbolic worth to race and racial groups than do the decision makers who advocate diversity. They often have divergent understandings of how the social divides between racial groups should be managed.

Activists of any sort seek to establish their legitimacy as participants in a political debate. To engage meaningfully in affirmative action politics on campus, the activist organizations at Michigan could not avoid the adversarial dynamic that *Gratz* and *Grutter* established. They were compelled to take a side in the legal cases and to articulate a reasoned argument for their position. What's more, the litigation made diversity central, so all these groups needed to couch their argument on affirmative admissions in relation to the diversity rationale. And like administrators, the campus activists would speak of diversity as an ideal, an identity of the university, a policy objective, and a legal argument for race-conscious admissions policies.

Yet none of these campus organizations endorsed the diversity rationale wholeheartedly. Each took the strategy of either recognizing and avoiding diversity or adopting and critiquing it. Each of these organizations also engaged in the framing practice of street-level semiotics, scrutinizing the terminology used by university administrators, opponents of racial preferences, or both. That sort of critique is an important element of legal argument, in fact. Each activist organization's orientations to affirmative action and diversity and its political strategies show the range of acceptable debate within the parameters of *Gratz* and *Grutter*.[37]

BAMN's Fight for Racial Equality: "Race Has a Singular Importance"

"It is time to hear the voice of truth again with a new civil rights movement!" yelled Shanta Driver, a national spokesperson for BAMN, a militant and oppositional social movement organization. It was the 2003 Martin Luther King Jr. holiday. BAMN had organized a three-day conference and a rally headlined by Reverend Jesse Jackson. Shanta, an energetic woman in her forties with a raspy voice and ambiguous racial identity, was the first speaker at the rally.[38] Hundreds of people had packed into a university lecture hall. Many were white or Latino and college-aged or older, but most, like BAMN's membership, were African American and high school age. The activists had just finished marching through Ann Arbor to demonstrate their support for affirmative action and their opposition to what they called "the coordinated attack on affirmative action by the far-right" (see fig. 3.1).

BAMN is a national organization that was founded in the mid-1990s under Shanta's leadership in opposition to a decision by the Regents of the University of California to end affirmative admissions. It subsequently expanded its focus from California to include Michigan. BAMN activists organized conferences, training sessions for student organizers, legal action, and marches, including the large April 1 march on Washington. Many

3.1. BAMN poster

of BAMN's high-profile spokespeople were white. In 2002, the organization claimed to have over a thousand student members from forty-five high schools across the United States and approximately thirty-five colleges and universities, including a chapter on Michigan's campus.[39]

BAMN's agenda was radical. Its leaders framed the organization as a youth-led mass movement for revolutionary social change—as the rightful torchbearer of the civil rights legacy. Its name evoked the Black Action Movement campus organization, which organized strikes in the late 1960s and early 1970s (BAM I), black student activism in the mid-1970s (BAM II), and again in the 1980s (BAM III). Although race was their central concern, they called for the liberation of disadvantaged groups—people of color, women, poor people, immigrants, Muslims, and gays and lesbians—through political mobilization and a stated willingness to use violent action.

The case of BAMN reveals a central way that the push for diversity sanitizes modern-day racial progress: by making it very difficult for political participants to credibly assert a civil rights argument for justice. BAMN shared with the university administration a fundamental position: that race-conscious interventions helped to incorporate people of color into majority-white settings. But the activists had a very different understanding of the purpose of affirmative action. They believed that the policy advances equality and integration through race-based (re)distribution. Their ability to assert their claims was delimited by the adversarial dynamics of litigation and the strictures of legal doctrine. These politics made little room for radical activism. The organization and its claims were further sidelined by the moderate wing of the pro–affirmative action movement on campus.

The university administration, in its legal arguments and expert witness reports, did not (and could not reasonably) claim that their affirmative admissions policies countered racial inequality. The university's success at the Supreme Court in 2003 rested in part on convincing the justices that it was *not* practicing race-based affirmative action in order to remedy discriminatory practices or promote racial justice. When formulating their legal case, university leaders made a deliberate, not surprising decision to reject social justice arguments and treat Powell's opinion in *Bakke* as precedent.

The university's legal arguments depicted inequality in a way that BAMN activists found deeply problematic: as an issue in society at large and not a product of the university's institutional practices. The university argued that most young people grew up in segregated environments, which led them to develop different perspectives based on their experiences but limited their opportunities to interact across racial lines. Thus students often brought with them misconceptions, stereotypes, and mistrust that they needed to learn to overcome. The provost paraphrased this legal argument at the Admissions Lawsuits Update forum:

> We live in a *very* segregated society still. The vast majority of our students, the vast majority of high school students in the United States and certainly of high school students in Michigan, are raised in highly segregated environments. So environments in which there is racial and cultural diversity are almost automatically culturally and psychologically hot in this sense and lead to an improved learning environment in general.

The provost and other university leaders emphasized that affirmative admissions made it possible for *all* students, regardless of racial background, to benefit from interpersonal exchange with different sorts of people.

BAMN, in contrast, asserted that affirmative action remediates inequality and also proactively furthers the causes of integration and equality, foremost for the benefit of students of color and poor students. At protests, activists carried the organization's signature red and white posters at protests and marches: "DEFEND Affirmative Action and Integration. FIGHT for Equality."

BAMN's radical politics were far outside the mainstream. Many affirmative action supporters, including some within the university administration, were glad that BAMN made an argument about integration. However, the administration distanced itself from the organization and its militant stance. Another student organization that aligned with the administration, discussed below, openly disparaged it. BAMN had support from black Baptist churches, Jesse Jackson's Rainbow/PUSH coalition, the NAACP, the United Auto Workers, and some other national organizations. But mainstream civil rights groups kept a distance. They endorsed BAMN's April 1, 2003, march on Washington only in the final hour. BAMN struggled to get financial resources from those very organizations. The MLK Day rally and conference, for example, cost the organization $70,000, but donations covered only $50,000. BAMN leaders ran up debt on their personal credit cards.

One crucial way BAMN organizers engaged the politics of affirmative action was by entering the litigation and using that involvement and their legal expertise as a basis of political legitimacy. Early on, BAMN coordinated the student intervention in *Grutter* under the umbrella organization United for Equality and Affirmative Action Legal Defense Fund, along with Law Students for Affirmative Action and forty-one current and aspiring law students. The interveners were a third party in the *Grutter* case in the lower courts but not at the Supreme Court. Their legal filings codified BAMN's arguments, provided a nationally visible platform, and invoked the symbolic authority of law.

The *Grutter* interveners argued that affirmative action in admissions is necessary to offset historical and ongoing racial discrimination, segregation, and bias and to achieve an integrative, egalitarian ideal. They described affirmative action as a counter to "the cumulative effect of discriminatory tests, segregated education, social inequality, and the depressing effect of racial prejudice on the undergraduate grades and overall academic performance of minority students." Unlike the university and nearly all the organizations filing amicus briefs, BAMN charged that the Law School Admission Test (LSAT), the standardized test that is the primary criterion for law school admission, was not neutral and color-blind but racially biased against African American, Latino, and Native American students.[40]

The interveners argued for national unification through integration. Their position was that the proper legal precedent for affirmative action was not *Bakke* but rather the 1954 legal case *Brown v. Board of Education.* They translated this position and their legal arguments into punchy political rhetoric. As Shanta said in her opening speech at the 2003 MLK Day rally, the goal of *Brown* was "to force integration in this society" following centuries of "the dark days of segregation and inequality." Affirmative action carried on the *Brown* legacy, she said, but that legacy was now at risk with *Gratz,* *Grutter,* and other political threats. "Affirmative action programs were integration programs for higher education. They desegregated schools like this! But now *Brown* and affirmative action are under attack. . . . A small group of segregationists have been able to turn back the clock."

In their legal brief, the interveners extensively cited Justice Thurgood Marshall's dissenting opinion in *Bakke.* In that opinion, Marshall argued that affirmative action is a constitutionally acceptable remedy, even in cases lacking evidence that those who benefit from affirmative action have been targets of discrimination. For Marshall, affirmative action was justified because of pervasive societal racism and the necessity of working toward "genuine equality." The interveners recognized Powell's opinion in *Bakke* as precedent but claimed that the diversity rationale was actually a hindrance to social progress. Powell's opinion had "helped slow down progress towards genuine equality," they argued in their filing with the Supreme Court.[41] It "left affirmative action policies more vulnerable to legal and political attack" because it "obscured affirmative action's fundamental nature as a means of achieving integration and equality; and left university administrations with only a single partial . . . defense—intellectual diversity." According to BAMN, the diversity rationale might be necessary, but it was utterly insufficient for addressing systemic racism.

BAMN activists also critiqued the diversity rationale as derogatory to people of color. At a BAMN recruitment event in the cafeteria of a Chicago-area university, an audience member asked, "When is it acceptable for a school to say we need diversity to get a better education?" Jodi Masley—a white Michigan alumna, lawyer for the *Grutter* interveners, and BAMN organizer—replied that BAMN was grudgingly willing to use the term. "Diversity has been kind of a code word for a few but not everyone. . . . At first I found the diversity concept kind of insulting. It says: 'If you're white, young, male you might as well have some women around, some black people around.'"

Jodi, like other BAMN organizers, used street-level semiotics as a framing technique, a method of political argument, and a tactic of political training. With critical comments such as hers, BAMN leaders indicated that they had incisive analysis and the gumption to expose others' biases, including the administration's coded but nefarious diversity rationale. They also pointed to their constituents, particularly students of color, as evidence that BAMN represented an important but wrongly excluded constituency.[42]

Throughout the legal cases, the university administration treated the interveners with a calculated neutral stance.[43] For instance, the admissions update panel included Miranda Massie, the interveners' attorney. Endorsing the intervention would imply the university's defense was incomplete, but objecting to it would set the university in conflict with the students it was supposed to be representing. To the interveners' frustration, the university did not share with them any of its time for oral arguments at the Supreme Court, as the plaintiffs had shared with Theodore Olson, the solicitor general of the United States.

University officials visibly kept their distance from BAMN in particular. Before the Supreme Court decisions, the news media coverage of the cases often featured the BAMN and interveners, represented as a militant voice in the "debate." The university administrators did not promote BAMN activists as spokespeople. Nor did they include BAMN in educational and public relations materials intended as official documentation of the cases. They did, however, appropriate civil rights imagery from BAMN's activism. After the court decisions, the Office of Marketing Communications oversaw the creation of a traveling multimedia gallery exhibit about the cases, "Views and Voices: U-M's Case for Diversity," which chronicled the cases with historical documents, quotes, and video clips. The exhibit, including its signature logo, featured photographs of older, middle- and working-class African American women at the April 1 march on Washington. The women held BAMN's signature sign, with the tag line "DEFEND Affirmative Action" in clear view. The rest of the slogan—"and Integration. Fight for Equality"— was partially obscured by a gate. BAMN's name was not shown anywhere.

This analysis of BAMN highlights the conservatizing force of both the push for diversity and the color-blind opposition. BAMN's strategy of engaging in these politics, hamstrung by the legal cases, led the organization to focus on incremental policies rather than their agendas for structural transformation.[44] BAMN's involvement illustrates how the mainstream framing of race in terms of diversity denigrates issues of institutional discrimination. Activists who argue for redistributive justice face an especially high bar. To participate in post–civil rights racial politics, activists need material and cultural resources, especially a sophisticated understanding of law and a sophisticated engagement with political discourse.

SSAA and "The Student Voice": Simply in Favor of Affirmative Action

Students Supporting Affirmative Action (SSAA) began organizing in earnest in winter 2003, just a few months before the Supreme Court oral arguments. These activists had a very narrow goal: to demonstrate Michigan students' support for the university's admissions policies at the most crucial moments of the *Gratz* and *Grutter* Supreme Court cases.[45] SSAA's multiracial leadership, who represented over twenty different student organizations, characterized the organization as a short-term collective. As their name spelled out so clearly, SSAA leaders simply took two positions: they were the student voice, and they supported affirmative action. They presented a united front for the media and general public.[46] At the SSAA press conference in Washington, DC, on April 1, 2003, the day of the oral arguments in both cases, SSAA activists sang the Michigan fight song and chanted, "Go black. Go brown. Go yellow. Go blue. We need affirmative action, and so do you!"

With financial and public relations support from the university, office space and other resources of the Michigan Student Assembly (the campus student government), and assistance from national organizations, SSAA activists were quite successful in their objectives. They were featured in the peak moment of major media coverage of the court's decisions.[47] On June 24, 2003, the day after the Supreme Court's rulings were announced, the front page of the *Philadelphia Inquirer, Atlanta Journal-Constitution*, and other newspapers across the country ran an Associated Press (AP) photograph of two SSAA activist-leaders—a white woman and an Asian American woman—hugging joyfully.

SSAA activists projected student solidarity and the legitimacy of their organization by visually appealing to Michigan school spirit. Their most important messaging device was a dark blue T-shirt (see fig. 3.2). From the front, the shirts resembled university-sponsored Michigan paraphernalia: a large yellow "M" logo superimposed with the word "JUSTICE." That image could be seen in the popular press, including the AP photograph of SSAA activists hugging. The smaller slogan on the back of the T-shirts vaguely emphasized injustice: "Race must be a factor because racism is a factor."

3.2. Students Supporting Affirmative Action T-shirt. *Source*: Photo by author

SSAA organizers worked to display racial diversity and positive cross-racial interaction in the student body. At the planning meeting for SSAA's bus caravan to the April 1, 2003, march on Washington, held the day of the Supreme Court arguments, SSAA leaders reaffirmed an earlier goal they had set: to fill no more than 70% of each bus with students from the same organization.[48] Monique, an African American leader of SSAA who had sat on the Admissions Lawsuits Update panel, was blunt: "We don't want all the black student organizations on one bus. It isn't gonna look like diversity is working at all."

SSAA's stance on the litigation resembled that of the administration. However, when crafting their political platform, SSAA organizers deliberately decided *not* to endorse the diversity rationale or any other singular ideological justification of race-conscious admissions policies. They did this to keep their coalition cohesive and functional. From their perspective, convincing their member organizations to agree on a justification for affirmative action would be time consuming and unnecessary. Further, SSAA leaders worried that any efforts to develop a consensus would interfere with what they saw as a fragile but successful effort at multiracial organizing. Such efforts, the leaders told me, frequently fall apart because they are dominated by white students and mistrusted by students of color.

SSAA's press kit included pro–affirmative action quotes from seventeen Michigan students. Many made an argument of redistributive racial justice. Monique Perry, an African American woman who was vice president of the

Michigan Student Assembly, supported race-conscious policies because "institutionalized racism and inequalities still exist." A number of the students stressed the importance of access to higher education. Five mentioned diversity, four expressing a version of the university's diversity rationale. Angela Galardi, a white undergraduate and president of the Michigan Student Assembly, declared, "Learning from people who are different from yourself is such a large part of our college education. You can only learn so much from books and coursepacks." As organizers pointed out to me, their ambiguous public messaging was politically savvy. It enabled student participants to voice whatever justification for affirmative action they personally believed—their own expression of their viewpoints—and it provided the media with a variety of quotes from which to choose.

That SSAA did not have an official opinion on diversity did not prevent SSAA activists from critiquing it. Jackie Bray, a white leader, was one of many who viewed the diversity rationale as an inaccurate representation of students' experiences. She described her personal relationships with women of color: "Race comes up. My privilege comes up, and barriers come up. That's never warm and fuzzy. I've grown as a person tremendously from these relationships, but they don't invoke shiny sunny days where we're all sitting taking pictures together." Michelle Lin, an Asian American leader, had a more pointed criticism. For her, the diversity rationale was patronizing and discriminatory: "Students of color are on campus to educate white students? Like a tree, to add color?"

Many SSAA organizers disliked BAMN intensely. They viewed it as an unnecessarily confrontational, dogmatic group led by outsiders.[49] SSAA activists went to great lengths to point out differences between their organization and BAMN. At one meeting, a white male SSAA leader contrasted SSAA and BAMN: "We are the students. . . . They are not. We represent the University of Michigan students. They do not." Some SSAA activists referred to the organization as "BAM-N" to suggest that BAMN did not have a valid connection to BAM I, II, and III.

University officials were pleased when SSAA formed. SSAA was a sympathetic, unobjectionable ally. As Peterson explained, "It was really helpful when the SSAA took some leadership because that really was a student group and everyone in it were active students. So we could really engage them and represent them to media as these are . . . a group of U of M students who are, you know, expressing their views." The university promoted SSAA activists as spokespeople. Its press release immediately after the announcement of the court's decisions included five statements from Michigan students representing the student government and organizations for African American,

Latino, and Native American students, all connected to SSAA. Each of the student quotes reflected tenets of the university's diversity argument, referring explicitly to the value of diversity or else to the importance of learning from minority groups' unique perspectives.

SSAA illustrates the type of activist organization that is likely to be successful in the context of the organizational push for diversity. With financial and institutional resources, its members had a privileged status (as students at an elite university) and included many students of color. The interests of the administration and the dominant logics and practices of campus life, including coursework that encouraged critical analysis, were in SSAA's favor. The activists presented themselves as smart, engaged, high-achieving multicultural agents—quite like the archetypal idea conjured by the diversity rationale. Their very political participation could illustrate how student life was enhanced through the different viewpoints they expressed (although within a limited range, as all favored affirmative action). The administration did not need to photoshop student diversity; these activists were exemplary of it.

The Michigan Review *and YAF: "Diversity of Ideas Is What I Like"*

On the 2003 MLK holiday—the same frigid, gray day of the BAMN rally at which Shanta spoke—activists with Young Americans for Freedom (YAF) organized a counterprotest to demonstrate their opposition to racial preferences. Bundled in puffy jackets and thick mittens, about twenty-five activists with the *Michigan Review* and YAF, nearly all of them white men, protested the three-hundred-odd BAMN activists who marched through campus before the rally. Some of the counterprotesters walked backward in front of the BAMN activists to create the appearance of a face-off.

The anti–affirmative action activists carried handmade posters with slogans such as "Diversity is more than skin deep" and "Racial preferences = Not King's dream." As we walked, a young white male YAF activist told me that he believed that Michigan's race-conscious admissions policies were "state-sponsored racism. . . . You can't actually achieve true diversity because people are still looking at race." For these activists, race-neutral fairness and merit, not the benefits of racial diversity, should be the guiding principle for admissions.

The *Michigan Review* was a bimonthly student-run campus newspaper with a circulation of four thousand. Run by a politically engaged editorial board, the paper served as a mouthpiece for politically conservative, libertarian, and independent students. YAF at Michigan was one of many campus chapters of the national organization, which was founded in the early 1960s by a grandfather of the modern conservative movement, William F. Buckley. In 2003, its website listed chapters in eighteen states, many on college campuses. At Michigan, YAF was known for its incendiary, racially antagonistic direct actions lampooning affirmative action and illegal immigration. Many students belonging to both groups viewed themselves as marginalized outsiders up against a campus culture of political correctness dominated by zealous liberals.[50]

Despite their small numbers, activists with the *Michigan Review*—especially editor in chief James Justin Wilson—and YAF were often featured in the news in juxtaposition to affirmative action supporters. Working with the Michigan College Republicans, they succeeded in getting the Department of Student Affairs to fund two viewpoint-neutral buses in SSAA's caravan to the march on Washington.

These conservative and libertarian campus groups basically echoed the arguments for color blindness made by their national counterparts. The leaders of the *Michigan Review* and YAF characterized themselves as defenders of liberty and the US Constitution. For them, race was largely irrelevant for social life in contemporary America, and racial inequality was a non-problem (except for reverse racism, which they saw as inherent to affirmative action). Invoking an ideology of color-blind abstract liberalism, the *Michigan Review* and YAF activists characterized college students not as models of diversity but as constitutional subjects. The university's policies were racially discriminatory, these activists claimed, because they favored applicants of certain racial groups and thus violated individuals' constitutional rights.

In spring 2003, the *Michigan Review* held an anti–affirmative action bake sale in the middle of a popular campus walkway. It used the prices of bagels to mock the university's point system for undergraduate admissions. Because the point system gave up to twenty additional points to African American, Latino, and Native American applicants, the activists set the prices for bagels differently depending on the buyer's race. Black students were charged eighty cents for a bagel. White students were charged one dollar. Wilson told me, "You shouldn't be given base discounts on food because of your race. You shouldn't be given special admissions based on race. They're both discrimination. That's where we were coming from." The bake sale received national media attention, as did a similar one held at University of California–Los Angeles a few weeks earlier. Soon groups at Southern Methodist University, Northwestern University, and other universities hosted their own.

The campus opponents of racial preferences had financial support through their affiliations with extensive, well-funded national networks of conservative organizations, think tanks, and funders.[51] For example, the *Michigan Review* received funding from the Intercollegiate Studies Institute's Collegiate Network, which has helped to create "the great talent pools of the Right."[52] Neither the *Michigan Review* nor YAF had a direct relationship with the plaintiffs or CIR, but they drew on similar talking points and sometimes, it seemed, a carefully choreographed script—participating in what the progressive watchdog organization SourceWatch calls a neoconservative echo chamber.[53] For nearly every anti–affirmative action slogan and tactic used by the campus activists—from their appeals to color blindness to their bake sale—numerous comparable examples could be found in the conservative media, the literature of conservative think tanks, and the activities of like-minded activists.

The same was true of their talk of diversity. The *Michigan Review* and YAF characterized the university's commitment to diversity as a euphemism and a lie, arguing that diversity just meant race.[54] This antidiversity stance was potentially risky. The educational value of diversity was the university's official stance and generally popular. Taking an antidiversity stance could alienate faculty members and university officials, who might see the activists as hostile to foundational principles of tolerance and equality (these activists were, after all, still students). That would put them far outside the parameters of what it meant to be a good student at Michigan.

YAF and *Michigan Review* spokespeople managed these tensions by playing off the university's identity as champion of diversity and excellence: they denounced the goal of *racial* diversity but praised *intellectual* diversity. During their counterprotest on the King holiday, I asked a few for their opinion of the university's diversity rationale. One young white man responded, his breath foggy in the cold air,

> Diversity of ideas is what I like. If you have a diverse student body with diverse ideas, and it's a diverse place, it's a better place to go to school, in which to live, in which to pursue your education. . . . That's what the goal of diversity should be. Diversity is not based on race. It's based on ideas and experiences.

By "diversity of ideas," these activists usually meant conservative and libertarian viewpoints, which they saw as ostracized on campus. A 2002 *Michigan Review* editorial opined about the composition of the student body, "Slackjawed, conservative Southern Baptists are certainly under represented. Where are their diversity points?" With such statements, the *Michigan Review* and YAF activists interpreted diversity in terms much like the administration did: as a commonsensical value, a mix of people with differing viewpoints expressed in such venues as the classroom and campus speaker series, and a benefit for the educational experience.

The plaintiffs in *Gratz* and *Grutter* took the same position, arguing to the Supreme Court that the university "looks to use race as a proxy for genuine intellectual diversity that can be found directly in the different outlooks, backgrounds, experiences, and talents of each unique individual."[55] Other conservative activist organizations, media outlets, and think tanks were also calling for "intellectual diversity."[56] In spring 2002, YAF and the *Michigan Review* sponsored a campus talk by David Horowitz, a conservative move-ment spokesperson. Horowitz's organization promoted an "Academic Bill of Rights" calling for "an environment of intellectual diversity that protects and fosters independence of thought and speech."[57] Shortly after Horowitz's visit to Michigan, a representative from the Collegiate Network posted a comment in response to an article on the *Michigan Daily* website, "Congratulations to YAF and the *Michigan Review* for bringing true diversity to the University of Michigan."[58]

The experience of the *Michigan Review* and YAF activists illustrates the po-litical opposition to affirmative action, with its arguments for color blind-ness and the small but vocal and well-funded coalition of opponents working in lockstep. These activists' involvement draws attention to the bounds of a win-win legal argument for diversity. The diversity rationale was so central to affirmative action politics, the administration's public relations so effective, and the talk of diversity on campus so ubiquitous that even campus oppo-nents tried to say something positive about diversity. And, as it turned out, the cause of intellectual diversity was one that affirmative action opponents and supporters could actually share in the wake of the court's decisions.

However, these activists' appeal to intellectual diversity was not their core political platform or that of their national counterparts. Color blind-ness was the principle that guided ongoing legal and political challenges to affirmative action and the opinions of conservative justices, which have con-tinued to narrow the definition of discrimination and restrict race-conscious interventions.

After *Gratz* and *Grutter*: Replacing Race with Diversity, 2003–2006

Following the court's decisions in *Gratz* and *Grutter*, campus leaders made the legal notion of diversity central to the university's new undergraduate admissions policies, the design of other affirmative action initiatives, and their public discourse on the student body. Diversity became a guiding principle for the internal admissions process, and race remained an important factor in how admissions officers did recruitment. But in all these arenas, the administration publically downplayed the topic of race or stopped mentioning it altogether, instead emphasizing perspectives and geography in its statements about diversity. This was yet another two-step move around diversity, with the significance of race becoming ever more ambiguous and diluted, while the concept of diversity did even more administrative and public relations work for the university.

For the undergraduate admissions cycle starting in fall 2003, the Office of Undergraduate Admissions—in consultation with university attorneys, regents, and others—replaced the point system with new admissions procedures that emulated the law school's policy. The legal rationale of diversity was codified in the technical design of the new policy. The language of the admissions policy closely mirrored that of the *Grutter* decision, describing the new "holistic, individualized review of the many facets of every application." Under the revised review system, two or three people read each application and made an assessment, which included assigning a grade to the application. Many of the applications were discussed in smaller committees as well, and all were ultimately approved by a working group. Under this revised policy, the criteria that admissions officers would use to evaluate applicants were unclear, although internal guidelines stated a priority of applicants with the highest standardized test scores and "flawless academic record combined with demanding curriculum."[59] To accommodate this new, labor-intensive admissions review, the Office of Undergraduate Admissions expanded from approximately 80 employees to 133. It conducted extensive training for admissions counselors, staff, and outside readers that included in-depth briefing on the court's decisions.

Many elements of the new process reflected themes of legal diversity and reiterated the university's identity of diversity and excellence. The new 2003 LSA undergraduate application included more essays than in previous years, including an essay on diversity that asked students to answer one of the following questions: "At the University of Michigan, we are committed to building an academically superb and widely diverse educational community. What would you as an individual bring to our campus community?" Or "Describe an experience you have had where cultural diversity—or lack thereof—has made a difference to you."

Applicants to the undergraduate college picked up on themes from the legal cases. A study of applicants' responses to the diversity essay questions found that white students' essays tended to be more individualistic. Those students discussed how everyone is diverse, and they focused on themes of international cultures, religious differences, or the instrumental uses of diversity.[60] Students of color were more likely to write about race. Low-income students pointed to the tense and segregating aspects of diversity. The authors concluded that, across racial background and socioeconomic status, students commonly presented themselves in terms of a cosmopolitan post-racialism marked by an awareness of people's varied identities and elective cross-cultural affiliations. Students of color, they noted, were more likely to be left out of the popular diversity culture.

On campus, at internal meetings of application review committees that I observed, admissions counselors and faculty members (of different racial and ethnic backgrounds themselves) deliberated over which "borderline" applicants to admit. They discussed considerations such as admitting a majority of students from the state of Michigan, the strengths of applicants' schools, their test scores, and the content of their essays and their extracurricular activities. They also discussed applicants' contributions to diversity, —which encompassed demographic attributes such as race, nationality, language skills, socioeconomic status, family background, geographic origin, and parents' marital status. The committee members cited these various indicators of diversity to justify some admissions decisions. For example, the committee recommended that the university admit a student from South America whose parents were Taiwanese immigrants; one member noted, "He has very good diversity." Committee members criticized the lackluster diversity essay from another student who was unimpressive in many regards: "On cultural diversity, he said nothing." During another discussion, a member referred to a white male student who had written an essay about the lack of diversity in his white town, "Let's see if he can adapt to a non-white environment!" An admissions counselor half-heartedly described an Asian American student who had some eccentric hobbies as having a "diversity of interests." In this context, diversity provided a flexible, ambiguous standard of evaluation for assessing a students' qualifications.

Although the court decisions permitted the university to pursue the goal of racial diversity, administrators had far less leeway in how they could consider race when allocating organizational resources to students. Administrators amended the university's race targeting in campus support services, recruitment activities, and financial aid directed at black, Latino, and Native American students. They quietly changed the eligibility criteria to include white and, where relevant, Asian American students. The Comprehensive Studies Program (CSP)—into which the Opportunity

Awards Program had been folded in the 1980s—was one such support services program. In 1993, underrepresented racial minorities made up 99% of the first-year students enrolled in CSP, with African Americans in the majority (71%).[61] In 2004, CSP had 337 first-year underrepresented minorities— about the same number as in 1993—while the number of white students increased from three to one hundred, becoming over 22% of CSP first-year students, with the largest leap occurring between 2003 and 2004.[62] Likewise, recruitment events such as the 2003 Pursuit of Excellence symposium that had previously targeted applicants of color began to include lower-income students, students from different geographic regions, and first-generation college students.

The university's educational and PR campaign continued as well, although it was much scaled down. University officials gave speeches and presentations, such as Ted Spencer's during our interview, to explain the outcome of the cases and the revised admissions policy to the public. Administrators believed that there was public confusion about exactly what the court had decided, and they were concerned that people in Detroit and other black communities misunderstood the university's position (some privately intimated that BAMN had contributed to this misunderstanding by virtue of its criticisms of the university). In these public forums, administrators made the university's legal defense part of its public identity. They asserted that the university's fifteen-plus years of dedication to "strategically linking social diversity to academic excellence" in instruction, research, and service were pivotal to the court's favorable decision in *Grutter*.[63] They would reference the university's legal defense as evidence par excellence of the institution's genuine commitment to diversity.

University officials explained the amendments to the admissions policy and related programs in terms of their objective of diversity. The Pursuit of Excellence symposium is illustrative. Administrators engaged in a complicated organizational dance of pursuing diversity through affirmative admissions (evidenced in the invitation criteria stipulating students of color and low-income white students) while they explained the objective of affirmative admissions as the sharing of diverse viewpoints (evidenced in the remarks of both Ted Spencer and Lester Monts). In spring 2004, the university held its annual Spring Welcome Weekend, a recruitment event for students that had been admitted to the university. It previously had targeted underrepresented racial minorities, particularly African Americans, but was expanded that year to include lower-income white and Asian American students. Spencer told the visiting students, "We've broadened this day to be a special one for all kinds of students, all kinds of diversity." The Michigan

Scholar Award, a merit award worth up to $25,000 at the time, previously had been available to underrepresented minority undergraduates who lived out of state.[64] In fall 2003, any out-of-state undergraduate was eligible for this award as long as he or she "contribute[d] to the overall excellence and diversity of the university community."[65]

Admissions staff appropriated legal and public relations discourse about the utility of diversity to pitch the university to applicants and their families. At a spring 2004 information session for applicants to Michigan's engineering program, the recruiter—a personable African American woman—read an ad from a technology company: "Diversity powers our business. . . . As a global leader in communications, Lucent recognizes diversity as a business imperative." Michigan students had attended a university job fair earlier in the year, she said, and afterward, these students reported that the most common question that companies asked them was "How experienced are you with diversity?" The recruiter remarked proudly that the students could say that they had a great deal of such experience: "Because diversity is the cutting edge in business, we provide that cutting edge here."

University officials seemed especially sensitive to white students' reception of the policy changes. At the Pursuit of Excellence symposium, Ted described two good essays for the audience, both written by white students. One reported, "My diversity barometer is pretty low." The only nonwhite person in her rural community was an exchange student from Costa Rica whom she had never met. His second example was an applicant who worried, "I'm probably the last person you want." Ted went on, "But he wrote about how he could contribute to tolerance on campus . . . to help me and the readers to see what he could contribute to diversity. . . . So use [the essay] to tell us about yourself."

The shift away from a discourse and programmatic focus on race and toward the educational and economic payoffs of diversity was evident in the university's viewbooks and public relations materials as well. The Office of the Vice Provost produced a full-color, graphics-intensive brochure about the cases, called "The Educational Value of Diversity: A Landmark Decision," which was distributed at such events as recruitment fairs and posted on a companion website. The brochure squarely foregrounded the general idea of diversity, not race. While the brochure made some mention of race, such as in the summaries of the cases, the description of the university's admissions policies and fifteen of the twenty-four quotes in the brochure, which had been reprinted from the amicus briefs and other statements by world leaders, mentioned only diversity. The brochure highlighted campus initiatives for gender, religious, and political diversity. No initiatives were identified as specifically about race or even racial diversity. There was no reference to the race and ethnicity course requirement, while IGR was highlighted as the first of many "interpersonal experiences" on page 5. Near the end of the brochure, two of the main programs serving students of color, Multi-Ethnic Student Affairs and the Office of Academic and Multicultural Initiatives, were described as "open to all students."

In new initiatives, the administration championed intellectual diversity—a newly popular phrase for characterizing work that included issues of racial inclusion. Under Lester Monts, the university created a new Center for Institutional Diversity, which he described to me as reflective of the mission of his office, stating that it highlights "intellectual diversity and how that fuels into, feeds into the educational enterprise." He was eager to finish our conversation on the lawsuits and instead wanted to talk about the plans for the center, which, according to the website, would support the role of higher education in promoting "knowledge, justice, and opportunity in a diverse democracy and global economy."

Under Tyrone Winfrey, the staff in the Detroit satellite admissions office responded to the new admissions policy by spending considerable time explaining the new admissions process to applicants and high school administrators and providing additional support such as giving students access to computers in their office where they could complete their applications. They were very concerned about the impact on applications from students of color, as were people who worked with those students. In spring 2004, Michigan hosted an appreciation breakfast for guidance counselors from Detroit schools, and the counselors gave the admissions staff feedback about the new application. The counselors, nearly all of whom were African American women, said their students were "overwhelmed" by the application and had "issues about writing essays." At our table, a university representative asked, "Are they not relating to the questions?" One counselor replied, "They don't exactly sit down and think about their lives this way." For these counselors, the new essay questions created a greater obstacle to low-income and black applicants, demanding writing skills that their high school curriculum did not teach and that their counterparts in wealthier, predominantly white school districts were more likely to possess. The Detroit admissions staff worked to help those students manage the new demands of the applications.

The new admissions policy and discursive and programmatic shift to diversity did not pose serious obstacles to the enrollment of students of color. Between 2002 and 2006, the racial demographics of Michigan's undergraduate student body did not change dramatically.[66] The representation of black and Latino first-year students dropped by just under 1 percentage point each, while that of white and Asian American students slightly increased. However, more dramatic change happened a few years later, when affirmative action was banned across the state.

Continuing Challenges to Affirmative Admissions

As *Gratz* and *Grutter* wound through the court system, opponents of racial preferences continued their nationwide mobilization for color-blind admissions. After succeeding in California in the mid-1990s, Ward Connerly and his allies mobilized campaigns to end to race- and gender-based preferences in state hiring, contracting, and state university admissions in numerous states, almost always successfully (by 2013, seven states had bans or restrictions on affirmative action). Their activism helped to inflame opposition to such policies in general and to popularize the cause of color blindness. Soon after the *Gratz* and *Grutter* decisions, Connerly and Jennifer Gratz announced a campaign for a misleadingly named ballot initiative, the Michigan Civil Rights Initiative, or Proposal 2. The text of the initiative was lifted from California's Proposition 209.

In contrast to the affirmation action litigation, Proposal 2 was more squarely a civil rights issue, regarding the protection of minority rights. To fight the ban, the university assembled the One United Michigan coalition with major businesses and universities in the state. They framed affirmative action as a diversity issue with elite support—again, rather than a program of remedial racial justice or a matter of civil rights—and played up women's issues while minimizing racial ones.[67] In November 2006, 58% of the Michigan residents who voted approved an amendment to the state constitution that prohibited the state's fifteen public universities and other public institutions from granting preferential treatment based on race, sex, color, ethnicity, or national origin in public education, employment, and contracting. Political scientist Daniel Lipson concluded that the coalition leaders "may have erred by ceding rights-talk on racial issues to a colorblind cause."[68]

With the passage of Proposal 2, the university had to altogether stop considering race in admissions decisions. Administrators revised the admissions policies and program criteria to target clusters of high schools and geographic areas that were underrepresented at the university. They continued to couch the university's values and their admissions policies in terms of diversity, and the administration released a new strategic plan for recruitment and retention, called Diversity Blueprints.

Although the consequences at Michigan were not as extreme as at other public universities following the passage of similar state laws, the enrollment of students of color at Michigan dropped quite dramatically. In fall 2013, black, Latino, and Native American student made up 10% of the first-year class, which was the first class admitted solely under the post–Proposal 2 admissions policies.[69] This was a decrease from 15% in fall 2003, the last class admitted under the point system.[70] The percentage of African American students declined even more precipitously. In fall 2013, African American students made up 4.6% of the undergraduate student body—down from a peak of 9% in 1997 and below their 5% representation in the early 1980s.[71]

The decline in the representation of underrepresented minority undergraduates was surely compounded by the steep and rising cost of a Michigan degree and the university's deliberate recruitment of out-of-state students, who are predominantly affluent and white. In 2012–13, attending Michigan cost approximately $27,000 for in-state undergraduates and around $55,000 for those from out of state, who made up 40% of the undergraduate student body.[72]

As their numbers dwindled, students of color at Michigan found themselves ever more isolated and the campus acutely inhospitable. In fall 2013, sparked by a Michigan fraternity party that threw a "Hood Ratchet Thursday" party and invited on Facebook "bad bitches" and "ratchet pussy," black students with the Black Student Union launched a Twitter campaign.[73] The goal of Being Black at University of Michigan (#BBUM) was to voice "unique experiences of being black at Michigan." Students tweeted comments such as "Having to defend your oppression to someone who is willing to argue but refuses to listen" and "When every room you stand in on campus 9x out of 10 your the only one that is black." The group organized protests and issued seven demands, including 10% representation of black students on campus—harkening back to the demands of BAM I and II (although BBUM activists conspicuously did not use the same acronym). The hashtag quickly trended on Twitter and was covered in the national media. Similar campaigns at University of California–Los Angeles, Harvard University, and other predominantly white campuses creatively used video and photography to raise similar issues.

Meanwhile, the Supreme Court agreed to hear two more affirmative action cases. In the interim years since *Grutter,* the court had become even more conservative, more hostile to race-conscious decision making, and more willing to overturn prior court decisions. National politics were characterized by a broader climate of racist backlash against President Barack Obama, elected in 2008, and the rise of the libertarian-conservative Tea

Party. *Fisher v. University of Texas* asked the court to either find UT's admissions policy inconsistent with *Grutter* or to overrule *Grutter* altogether.[74] In 2013, in a 7–1 decision (with Justice Elena Kagan abstaining), the court upheld the holding in *Grutter*; it did not find all affirmative action in higher education unconstitutional, as many supporters feared. However, it returned the case to the lower court on grounds that that court had not adequately applied the standard of strict scrutiny. In doing so, the justices seemed to avoid the issue of affirmative action's constitutionality while setting the legal standard for affirmative action even higher. Citing *Bakke*, the majority opinion, authored by Justice Anthony Kennedy, stated that universities would need to prove and the court would need to verify "that it is 'necessary' for the university to use race to achieve the educational benefits of diversity." The court would need to be convinced that there was no viable alternative for creating a diverse student body.

The constitutionality of Proposal 2 in Michigan was also challenged in court. The challenge began as two cases, one of which was brought by BAMN and the other by the ACLU, NAACP, and other organizations in 2006. They were subsequently combined into *Schuette v. Coalition to Defend Affirmative Action* and heard by the Supreme Court.[75] The case, led by BAMN, did not directly concern university admissions, and strict scrutiny was not the primary standard. Rather, the challengers claimed that Proposal 2 violates the equal protection clause of the Fourteenth Amendment because it denies the right to political equality based on race. As they argued, the ballot initiative created a racially unfair political process: people of color, but not any other group, now must engage in an expensive, long-term campaign to amend the Michigan constitution if they want to contest a university's admissions policies to ensure that those policies reflect their interests.

In their brief to the Supreme Court, the BAMN-led plaintiffs incorporated an argument about structural racial inequality and corrective, redistributive justice that echoes themes from the interveners' brief in *Grutter*. They claimed that Proposal 2 relies on grade point average and standardized test scores as a seemingly neutral baseline but that "racial bias [is] captured, reflected, and often exaggerated" by these criteria. Their brief also provided an extensive ideological and legal critique of the notion of racial preferences. It problematized "preferences" and "preferential treatment" forty times, usually with scare quotes.

In spring 2014, in a 6–2 decision (with Justice Kagan abstaining), the Supreme Court upheld Proposal 2. The majority opinion rejected the plaintiffs' argument about political process doctrine—a thirty-year-old theory allowing people of color to advocate for public policies that support equality.

In doing so, it affirmed state-based voter initiatives to end affirmative action. The lead opinion, written by Justice Kennedy, argued that minorities should not all be assumed to have the same policy preferences. Justices Antonin Scalia and Clarence Thomas went further, making the color-blind claim that public policies can only consider race if they are tailored remedies for specific acts of intentional racism.

The *Schuette* decision exemplifies the court's steady dismantlement of the legal scaffolding that supports race-conscious, equality-seeking policies under Chief Justice John Roberts. It is yet another opinion that undermines precedent and introduces new arguments that can be cited in later decisions. It also illustrates the ongoing narrowing of the debate over race-conscious decision making, absent the option of legal claims for diversity's benefits. Justices could only voice claims for remedial justice in their dissent. Justice Sonia Sotomayor read from the bench her scathing dissenting opinion, which totaled fifty-eight pages and was joined by Justice Ruth Bader Ginsberg: "Race matters . . . because of persistent racial inequality in society—inequality that cannot be ignored and that has produced stark socioeconomic disparities."[76] She included a direct reproach to the 2006 opinion in *Parents Involved in Community Schools v. Seattle School District No. 1,* written by Roberts, which famously stated: "The way to stop discrimination on the basis of race is to stop discriminating on the basis of race."[77] Sotomayor challenged this color-blind argument by appealing to race-conscious redistributive justice: "The way to stop discrimination on the basis of race is to speak openly and candidly on the subject of race, and to apply the Constitution with eyes open to the unfortunate effects of centuries of racial discrimination."[78]

Given the political conservatism across the branches of the federal government, ongoing activism against affirmative action, and growing enthusiasm for class-based preferences, as advocated by public intellectuals such as Richard Kahlenberg, it seems likely that race-based affirmative action will soon be a relic of the past—another instance in which the legal and policy apparatus erected in the wake of the civil rights movement is being undone.

The Symbolic Politics of Racial Progress in Elite Education

The three cases in this book show tremendous variation in what the diversity movement achieves in relation to the civil rights movement's original mission. The Michigan case, with its central focus on race and policy intervention, exemplifies how that mission has been whittled away. The conservative mobilization, legal doctrine, and ideology of color blindness have cut off the argument that governmental entities should aim to undo the harms of racism. The university administration wanted to defend its affirmative action programs in *Gratz* and *Grutter*, but in the wake of *Bakke*, it could only succeed in court by making a limited argument about the educational benefits of diversity for all students. Given the legal climate, a greater success for progressives is difficult to imagine.

Michigan's extraordinary accomplishment was that it established diversity as a defensible objective under legal doctrine to justify race-targeted policies. This accomplishment was as much political. Its fight for affirmative action helped to cement Michigan's reputation as a major player in the field of higher education. However, it was never as successful at making the campus a supportive, welcoming environment for black, Latino, and Native American students.

The political contention long at the center of this story, entrenched in formal legal processes and focused on discrete policies, excluded the voices of those who wanted to assert radical claims to equality and integration. To interject such claims, some activists organized a savvy strategy of legal intervention that required sophisticated understanding of law, but the obstacles proved to be too great. The debate over affirmative action and the success of the diversity rationale ultimately denigrated a more radical ambition of opening up universities through the equitable redistribution of resources.[79]

Michigan's push for diversity was always selectively inclusive. It adapted racial minority representation to core market demands, institutional logics, and bureaucratic processes, most notably those of competitive admissions. It also helped to facilitate some change in those markets and logics by redefining selectivity as contingent on the presence of a small but significant percentage of students of color. Yet the university's most exclusionary practices—the reliance on standardized test scores and out-of-state students who paid full tuition—remained unchanged. Fundamentally, Michigan's drive for diversity reinforced the hegemony of elite status competition and credentialing. The ideal of merit was continually reified. The administration defined racial progress as racial minorities' success at scaling and staying atop the class hierarchy and as white people's open-mindedness. The university's standing in the competitive markets of admissions and status hierarchy of higher education remained a pinnacle of legitimacy.

Michigan's diversity rationale, translated into polished public relations messaging, provided a language for reaching out to the students that the administration hoped to selectively include. Among those students were students of color who were unaware of Michigan, intimidated by it, or perceived and experienced it as racist. The majority were white people who hoped to attend an elite public college that was more cosmopolitan than their majority-white communities—but not a place where they would feel too out of place or be accused of being racist. Those same students tended to view affirmative action negatively, believing that they would lose resources to students of color. University leaders invoked discourse on diversity's benefits in hopes of minimizing such white stigma. As Lester Monts said at the Pursuit of Excellence symposium, "Everyone in this room represents some branch of diversity." With diversity, everyone seems to win. This rhetoric buffered white privilege. It reinforced white students' sense of entitlement and absolved them of any complicity in racial inequality.

Gratz and *Grutter* redefined the terms of racial progress in higher education. With the success of diversity legal doctrine, administrators of higher education could only discuss race in public venues by imagining the benefits to white people—their acquisition of cross-racial understanding, their disabusing of racial stereotypes, and their preparation for a multicultural workforce. As critical race scholar Derrick Bell observed decades ago, progress toward racial equality for black people is only politically viable when white people see it is as expedient for themselves.[80] For the time being, administrators in higher education had an effective, legally sound policy for repairing some of the damage wrought by racism and social injustice, but only by stressing the advantages that would accrue to white people and by not referencing this country's troubling problem of racism.

PART TWO

Housing Politics in Rogers Park

FOUR

"The Most Diverse Neighborhood in Chicago"

Rogers Park has an emblem: a tree with leaves of different colored hands, with a lakefront shoreline in the background. You see the emblem immediately when you enter the neighborhood from the southeast, on the large brown sign that greets visitors, "Welcome to Rogers Park. Home of Loyola University." As you continue north up the Sheridan Road thoroughfare, you pass it on the banners that hang on streetlight posts (see fig. 4.1). If you turn left onto the commercial strips of Morse Street or Howard Street, the emblem is there again on banners, city fences, and the chipped concrete of the el train underpass. Or, if you continue up Sheridan, you might notice it embossed on the stone wall that runs along Lake Michigan, up to the border of the Evanston suburb. On the official website of Joseph Moore, a white man who represented the neighborhood as the Forty-Ninth Ward alderman on the Chicago City Council, the tree emblem is featured on the headline, along with a photo of African American and white children jumping joyfully and the slogan "Celebrating Diversity in the 49th Ward." It is posted on the neighborhood's Wikipedia entry, too.

While Rogers Park has long between an entry point for immigrants, this symbolism of unity through difference did not become pervasive until the late twentieth century. Between 1970 and 2000, Rogers Park changed from a 99% white neighborhood to a majority-minority one. At the crossroads of a declining manufacturing economy, demographic diversification with persistent segregation, economic disinvestment, and government retrenchment on low-cost housing, the neighborhood became a rare site of racial integration. It became a place where people of color and white people lived in close proximity without the wholesale outmigration of white people. This racial incorporation was inseparable from issues of class, and it played out around development and real estate markets. With these changes,

4.1. Rogers Park neighborhood logo. *Source*: Photo by author

the neighborhood's political leaders, virtually all of whom were white, confronted a new challenge of racial representation: retaining white and middle-class residents.

The push for diversity in Rogers Park emerged in this context. It was not motivated by an obvious shift in the external environment, such as constitutional law or industry trends. Rather, it was both residents' experiential response to local demographic and economic changes and neighborhood leaders' political intervention in those changes. Within and beyond the civic arena, across the political spectrum, and over the decades, locals developed an identity for Rogers Park as a unique model of community pluralism. This identity associated demographic heterogeneity with a good quality of life, civic engagement, and strong property values. It undergirded a strong community norm of tolerance and inclusiveness.

This chapter begins in the 2000s with an introduction to Rogers Park, its identity of diversity, and the political economy and race-class politics of housing. It then looks back to five different points in time to understand how the push for diversity emerged in historical context. Over this time period, predominantly white residents' and decision makers' ideas of diversity symbolically defined the boundaries of the community broadly, although the place of low-income people—especially low-income people of color—was always highly contentious. As political players advocated for and against development strategies and housing policy interventions, the loudest voices were usually those of middle-class, majority-white homeowners.

Welcome to Rogers Park

Rogers Park sits along Lake Michigan on the North Side of Chicago (see fig. 4.2).[1] It is a densely populated, largely residential neighborhood. The tree-lined streets are interspersed with large pre–World War II apartment complexes, condominiums, smaller two- and three-flat buildings, and single-family homes. In the mid-2000s, it was home to twelve schools, Loyola University, a handful of retirement homes, and at least twenty-five churches, temples, and other religious institutions. Train lines provide easy access to downtown Chicago and northern suburbs. The commercial strips are flanked with Mexican taquerias, a Belizean bakery, diners, a kosher deli, and a smattering of upscale restaurants, as well as Laundromats, Afrocentric shops, and liquor stores. African Americans—primarily young men—congregate on Howard Street, the northern commercial corridor. Mexican families and vendors stroll the sidewalks on Clark Street to the west, while cafés on Sheridan Road, to the east, attract predominantly white but racially mixed crowds and students. Dog walkers, tennis players, and a visible population of Eastern Europeans all flock to the popular lakefront beaches.

The people who live in the neighborhood come from many different walks of life. Around the time of this study, in 2000, 32% of the neighborhood's 63,484 residents were white, 30% black, 28% Hispanic, and 6% Asian (see table 4.1). This breakdown mirrored the profile of the city of Chicago. About 34% of the residents were born outside the United States. Over 40% of households spoke a language other than English at home.

The sections of the neighborhood along the lakefront and to the south were visibly wealthier and whiter, while those to the north and west were poorer with more Latinos and African Americans. Still, you could see the

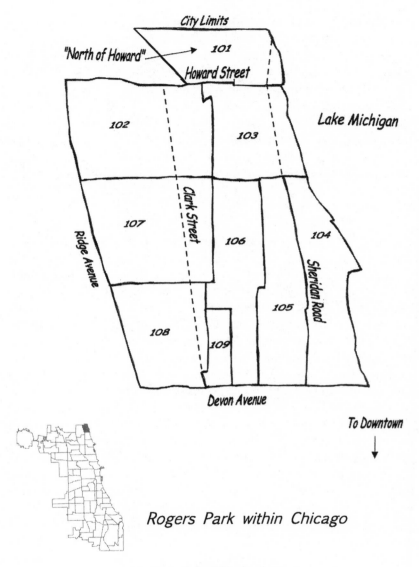

City Limits

"North of Howard" → 101

Howard Street

Lake Michigan

102

103

107

Clark Street

106

104

Ridge Avenue

Sheridan Road

108

109

105

Devon Avenue

To Downtown

Rogers Park within Chicago

4.2. Rogers Park neighborhood maps

community's ethno-racial variation when you walked through the neighborhood, from one block to the next and even within individual apartment buildings. The neighborhood was not just poor or just rich, either, although it was relatively poorer than the city as a whole. In 2000, the median household income was $31,600.[2] Almost half of Rogers Park households had

Table 4.1 Representation of racial groups in Rogers Park, 1980–2010

	White (%)	African American (%)	Latino (%)	Asian American (%)
1980	70	9	12	7
1990	45	26	20	8
2000	32	30	28	6
2010	39	26	24	6

Source: Data from Maly and Leachman (1998), US Census Bureau data reported in tables prepared by Rob Paral and Associates, "Race by Latino Ethnicity, 1990." and Rob Paral and Associates, "Detailed Race, Asian Race and Latino Origin, 2000 and 2010," http://www.robparal.com/ChicagoCommunity AreaData.html, accessed July 8, 2014.

an annual income of less than $30,000, 12% had annual incomes over $75,000, and 41% earned something in between.

Race is always inflected with other social statuses. In Rogers Park's housing market and redevelopment politics, class was the most salient of these. In 2000, the median income for non-Hispanic white households was $36,890, $29,500 for black households, and $31,745 for Hispanic households.[3] The classed dynamics of race were especially evident in residents' housing status. In 2000, 68% of neighborhood homeowners were white, while only 17% were black.[4] The same year, 76% of white households rented their homes, whereas 90% of black households and 89% of Hispanic households did.

For many decades, the public sphere in Rogers Park has had a strong political culture. In the mid-2000s, Rogers Park was home to a wide variety of active community organizations, politically engaged small businesses, and houses of worship. The lively interorganizational politics in Rogers Park constitutes what political scientist Matthew Crenson describes as a neighborhood polity.[5] A polity is a neighborhood-level political regime—one that "carries on the business of governing." Through both formal and informal channels, organizations and residents in a polity shape expressed collective interests and produce public goods. The neighborhood's heterogeneous population has, since the 1950s, included an influential set of socially advantaged residents. For nearly as long, it has also been a home to liberal and progressive activists, bohemians, and artists with both civic and cultural interests. This did not mean that all residents' interests were represented. Disadvantaged residents were comparatively less likely to participate in local politics than their more affluent, property-owning counterparts. One reason was that many neighborhood organizations actively *opposed* the low-income majority.

"The Most Diverse Neighborhood in Chicago"

There is a long American tradition of treating diversity as a defining feature of modern cities. Such treatment is evident from the work of the early Chicago School sociologists to the arguments of activist-journalist Jane Jacobs for neighborhoods with "intricate and close-grained diversity of uses" to the New Urbanism design movement.[6] According to contemporary commentators and city lovers alike, diversity makes cities vibrant, exciting, and welcoming.[7] Some equate neighborhood-level diversity with racial and economic integration.[8] Urbanist Richard Florida associates widespread support for the value of diversity with greater economic prosperity in cities. Neighborhood diversity can be fraught and divisive as well. Sociologist Robert Putnam found that people in ethnically heterogeneous communities "hunker down," with less trust in others, fewer friends, and less engagement in local civic life than their counterparts in more homogeneous communities.[9]

The Rogers Park tree emblem is one expression—an especially well-placed and graphic one—of the community's popular identity as a model of diversity. The same identity was expressed in many other forms, from testimonials by locals to sales pitches by condominium developers. Many residents expressed a deeply felt love for what one homeowner described as the community's "kaleidoscope." They professed their open-mindedness toward people unlike themselves as a badge of honor and a reason for living in Rogers Park.

Residents would often testify to the neighborhood's fine-grained, real-life diversity in interviews, on blogs, at meetings, and during everyday happenings. On a message board discussion of the neighborhood, someone from outside the community posted, "i have a question about RP. Is it TRUE diversity? like door by door you can find a person of a different nationality?"[10] Someone with the username "grapico" replied sarcastically, "what exactly are you expecting? a mexican selling agua fresca to you on their front porch, then knock on the next door and a white guy is smoking a pipe and reading the sunday new york times?" Someone else replied, "You might find just that in Rogers Park." A Rogers Park resident wrote, "What grapico describes dismissively is almost literally my situation. The guy next door to me runs a catering business and pushes an elote/fruit/sno-cone cart for a living. The guy above me is a doctor."[11] Art works throughout the community served as local testimonials, too. A mural in the neighborhood's lakefront park that had been painted by students at a local high school, titled "Power in Diversity," depicted the faces of people of different racial backgrounds, nationalities, and walks of life next to the Statue of Liberty. This is the rainbow nation version of diversity.[12]

The public pronouncements of neighborhood political officials and local political organizations reiterated this same community identity.[13] The 2001 annual report of the Rogers Park Community Council, a large social services and community development organization, stated that "Rogers Park is a place like no other. It's a place where people from every country, religion and walk of life call this neighborhood home. *We are the model of what life can and should be.*" The local real estate industry organization, the Rogers Park Builders Group, made diversity part of its sales pitch. Its twelve-page, full-color brochure for home buyers and investors opened: "Welcome to Rogers Park: The Global Village on Chicago's North Shore." It listed the neighborhood's amenities—the lakefront beaches, commuter rail lines, gracious homes, and "one of the most diverse populations in the metropolitan area"—along with pictures of African musicians, a young white man juggling fire torches, and a Latina girl in dancing shoes. News media, local university researchers, and civic organizations outside the community commonly distinguished Rogers Park for its diversity, too.[14] The curators of a Chicago Historical Society museum exhibit on Rogers Park, themed "Rhythms of Diversity," characterized it as "a microcosm of the world in one neighborhood."[15]

Alderman Moore was the most high-profile diversity enthusiast. He told me during our interview:

> We're a bold experiment . . . whether this whole diversity thing can work and whether our nation can survive as we move forward in the twenty-first century. . . . The issue is, well, are we actually going to be truly diverse or are we going to wall ourselves into various camps—the black neighborhood, the white neighborhood, the Hispanic neighborhood all throughout the city and all throughout the nation.

When Alderman Moore lauded Rogers Park's diversity, he differentiated the neighborhood from the rampant segregation throughout Chicago and its history of racial conflict and from Chicago's white-dominated, economically homogeneous suburbs and social division around the world. His and others' endorsements implied that locals were not like the people in other places, demographically or in spirit. In the drama of urban change, they had made a moral choice to reject segregation and prejudice.

Again and again, he and his chief of staff would cite US Census data on Rogers Park's demographics as evidence of the neighborhood's extraordinary diversity. After the 2000 data were released, these political officials and other allies would echo the census figures on the nearly equal representation of black, white, and Latino residents. A leader of DevCorp North, the neighborhood's economic development corporation, called this "a third, a third, a third." Sociologists Phil Nyden and Michael Maly and their collaborators provided scientific credibility by classifying Rogers Park as one of the country's noteworthy stable, racially and economically mixed neighborhoods— among the 4% of Chicago neighborhoods that stayed racially integrated throughout the 1990s.[16]

These various discourses on the neighborhood and quantitative measures constructed a place-based identity for Rogers Park as a bastion of diversity, growing solid and strong. In symbolism such as the colorful tree emblem, the neighborhood's mix seems organic, beautiful, and essential to neighborhood living—on par with the lakefront and leafy trees. Residents' testimonies and cultural artifacts suggest that Rogers Park's diversity is genuine, not artificially engineered. The formal statements of local organizations signal local leaders' distinctive commitment to diversity. Statistics provide legitimating evidence.

Through this lens, the neighborhood seems a pluralist community that encompasses multiple kinds of people who are culturally unique but in essence the same, with no single group dominating.[17] Race seems a group status and also one of many components of an individual's personal identity—sometimes spotlighted and sometimes included in lists along with ethnicity, class, faith, culture, political views, sexual orientation, educational background, and lifestyle. A variety of racial groups, including white people, are portrayed as essential elements of diversity, equally present (numerically) and equally valued (normatively). Race relations seem utopian. Racism and ethnocentrism seem not to be issues, and social hierarchies seem minimal.[18]

Communities are at once physical and symbolic.[19] Any given place is defined by its tangible, visible, and remarkable features and by people's perceptions of it. These features and perceptions make up a community's identity, which in turn can define people's experiences of that locale. Community identities also are marshaled toward political, economic, and social objectives, becoming part of the symbolic politics of urban life. In the current period of gentrification as urban revival, enthusiastic endorsements of diversity are now a part of efforts to remake cities as tourist destinations and investment opportunities.[20] In US cities such as Boston and Los Angeles and cities abroad from Toronto to Sydney, urban diversity—whether in the form of glamorized ethnic cultures, a gritty and artsy bohemia, or a cosmopolitan multicultural haven—has become emblematic of the contemporary urban order.[21] Mayors extol diversity as a virtuous asset. Bureaucrats attempt to plan for it.[22] Residents take pride in it, while small-business owners and other cultural entrepreneurs cater to their tastes.

Whether as an experiential quality, a commodity, or a political weapon, *diversity* served as a keyword for political participants as they grappled with the racial, economic, and cultural change wrought by housing markets and government intervention therein.

Housing Matters

Housing is the coin of people's access to communities. Where people live matters for the course and quality of their lives. It shapes their schooling, their health, their networks, and other important life outcomes.[23] Housing markets and politics are essential to racial integration because the incorporation of people of color into a white community depends on their ability to access housing. Likewise, maintaining integration depends on maintaining housing access and making the neighborhood desirable to people of color and, especially, white people who have more options to move out.

Racism and classism are fundamental features of housing markets. They shape who lives where.[24] They are the basis of segregation, that fundamental form of urban division that reinforces political and economic inequality.[25] Most US metropolitan regions are characterized by widespread racial segregation between white people and all other groups, with white people the most isolated, although such segregation decreased somewhat across the country between 1980 and 2010.[26] Chicago is at the extreme. Despite modest declines in segregation, in 2010, it was among the five urban regions with the highest rates of black-white segregation, African American isolation, and African American exposure to poverty.[27] Hispanic-white segregation was also high; in the late 2000s, Chicago was the seventh-most segregated in terms of Hispanic and white residents.[28]

Housing in the United States is also stratified by class. To state the obvious, wealthy people usually live in high-end homes in affluent communities. Poor people do not. In Chicago in 2010, 41% of households were either low-income households living in majority-low-income census tracts or upper-income households in majority-upper-income tracts.[29] That year, residential segregation by income was at its highest in at least four decades, with shrinking middle-income neighborhoods and growing isolation of poor and affluent households.[30]

Racism and classism in housing markets operate through prejudiced decisions and the accumulation of centuries of legally sanctioned, socially endorsed marginalization of racial minorities, poor people, and renters and favoritism for white homeowners. Extremes of these dynamics have been evident in the housing market in the Chicago region for decades: mutually reinforcing patterns of profound racial segregation, rising income segregation, and worsening economic inequality.[31] Such conditions contribute to community contexts of durable, deeply entrenched concentrated disadvantage, especially for black neighborhoods, with effects that linger for generations.[32]

Housing markets tend to be decentralized and difficult for any single entity to control. The principle of private property ownership was foundational in the creation of the United States. Private property law shapes housing markets by giving individuals and organizations rights to control and make contracts on real estate they own. The major thrust of the federal government's housing policy has been to promote home ownership. It has never devoted substantial resources to housing for poor people. Its most important and most costly housing policy is to provide tax advantages to homeowners.[33] Subsidies for renters pale in comparison. In 2005, tax expenditures for owner-occupied housing amounted to $147 billion, with more than half of those benefits going toward households in the top 15% of the income distribution. Meanwhile, expenditures by US Department of Housing and Urban Development (HUD), which primarily serves low-income households, totaled $41 billion. Further, as discussed in the next chapter, HUD's budget has been whittled away over the last thirty years. Funding has been redirected away from poor households to subsidize middle-income ones, while oversight of low-income housing has devolved from the federal level to the local level.

Since the 1960s, civil rights law has forbidden discrimination based on race and other statuses in important housing decisions, such as whom a landlord rents to. Title VIII of the Civil Rights Act of 1968 (called the Fair Housing Act), as amended, prohibits discrimination in the sale, rental, and financing of dwellings, and in other housing-related transactions, based on race, color, national origin, religion, sex, familial status, and disability. In addition, Title VI of the Civil Rights Act of 1964 prohibits discrimination in programs and activities receiving federal financial assistance. These interventions have led to declines in the most egregious forms of discrimination, but courts continue to find legal evidence of housing discrimination, and paired housing testing, the sine qua non of documenting housing discrimination, demonstrates that racial minorities continue to be told about and shown fewer homes than their white counterparts.[34]

Government low-cost housing programs and civil rights protections are extremely important for those who are able to take advantage of them. But fundamentally, they are very small-scale remedies to economically and racially skewed capitalist housing markets. In no way do they substantially rectify or systemically transform the sedimented biases of those markets. And most federal housing policy and contemporary laws actually protect and promote class stratification in housing.

Housing can be a source of stability for a community or a locus of community change. Sometimes neighborhoods ascend in their socioeconomic status, with rises in residents' income and housing costs.[35] Ascendency can happen through various processes, among them middle-class in-migration, government intervention, suburbanization, and upgrading by current residents. Neighborhoods decline, too, through harmful exclusionary policies, in-migration of poor residents, and out-migration of employment and businesses, among other processes. The nature of change—its likelihood, direction, and pace—is often uncertain, especially in all but the wealthiest and poorest communities.

Political leaders in cities prioritize growth. As sociologists John Logan and Harvey Molotch argue in their classic treatise, the central imperative of urban politics is profitable economic development, particularly land development.[36] Because Rogers Park has been mostly residential since the beginning of the twentieth century, there is little open land in the neighborhood. Profitable growth happens there, if it happens, through existing housing: by tearing down structures and building new ones, by charging rents but not investing in maintenance (milking), by increasing land value, and by upscaling current properties. As Logan and Molotch explain, profitable urban growth creates revenue for property owners, investors, and other businesses and a hospitable environment for consumers. For political officials, it generates political support and increases the tax base. When there are major disputes in urban politics, they are about growth. Yet the politics of growth are never simply about growth. They are shaped by such factors as the local culture and character of the community, concerns about racial and other demographic changes, and the array of political actors.

How Rogers Park Became Diverse

The economic fortunes of Rogers Park have been in flux for decades. This uncertainty dates at least to the mid-1950s, when the neighborhood—then middle class and all white—began suffering economic decline. It continued through the 1990s and 2000s, when the neighborhood experienced upgrading and modest gentrification. Throughout these vicissitudes of disinvestment and reinvestment, community decision makers remained concerned with encouraging economic growth and appealing to affluent white residents, whereas tenant advocates worked to address the needs of the most disadvantaged residents. At the same time, residents tried to make sense of local racial, class, and social transformations.

As these various actors sought to moderate economic growth and integration and to understand the complicated intergroup relations that ensued, they collectively formulated an identity for the neighborhood as an exemplar of social diversity.[37] This identity became a way for political participants to symbolically define minority representation and the terms of social membership, but with conflicting visions of membership for black, Latino, and low-income residents. Likewise, these groups drew on the neighborhood's identity to make competing claims about housing policies—policies that could influence representation and social inclusion and symbolized very different commitments to race-class inclusion. The diversity advocates with the most political power praised diversity as a uniting value that disavowed racial prejudice, while they largely favored an ambiguous, market-friendly inclusion that disassociated diversity from low-cost housing programs and validated economic development.

Snapshot 1: Before Diversity—a Bridge across Immigrant Groups, 1963

In the 1950s, word got out that developers planned to build to new high-rise residential buildings along the lakefront and that nearby property owners were putting up fences that would block access to the beaches. Community residents were outraged.[38] Although the beaches were not owned by the City of Chicago, locals treated them as public property. Protecting the beaches became the first major campaign of the nascent Rogers Park Community Council. Led primarily by white, Jewish, middle-class homeowners, the community council was an umbrella organization that represented similarly situated residents, other local organizations, and neighborhood businesses. Its goals were community conservation and beautification.

At this time, cities like Chicago had begun to experience the effects of white middle-class suburbanization and the growing population of poor African American residents. The post–World War II population boom had been met with intensive development of single-family homes in Chicago suburbs.[39] Farm jobs in the rural South had dried up, and cities in the North promised well-paying factory work and freedom from Jim Crow exploitation. Black southerners migrated north in massive numbers.[40] There, they were segregated into residential ghettos and employed in the worst jobs.[41] Those ghettos were created by antiblack resistance in white neighborhoods: racist mob violence, landlords who refused to rent to African Americans, and white residents who attached restrictive covenants to the titles of their homes to forbid their sale to black people. Redlining, in particular, was an essential mechanism of racial subjugation and concentrating privilege in white neighborhoods. For decades, the federal government had refused to insure mortgages in black neighborhoods and some other ethnic communities, and lenders refused to offer such loans. In the context of other legal and illegal practices that ghettoized black people, redlining deprived African Americans of the opportunity to buy homes and build equity—the most important basis of middle class wealth.

Simultaneously, there was massive out-migration of whites and white avoidance of majority-black or seemingly transitioning city neighborhoods.[42] These shifts were propelled by white people's prejudice and fears about declining property values and by the federal government, which guaranteed mortgages almost exclusively in white suburbs.

In the 1960s, disinvestment was occurring in Rogers Park, too. The neighborhood had boomed in the 1910s and 1920s, as the population jumped from 6,800 to 57,100, with a mix of immigrants from Germany, Ireland, England, and Russia.[43] By 1960, it was a middle-class neighborhood of white ethnic immigrants, 48% of whom had been born outside the United States.[44] That year, the neighborhood had large percentages of Catholics (40%), Protestants (30%), and Jews (30%)—an unusual neighborhood demographic mix. The leaders of major community groups were Jewish; Reform Jews from Germany had an especially strong presence. Local aldermanic politics were dominated by Irish Catholics.[45] The neighborhood was more affluent than the city as a whole. Of the men in the neighborhood, 66% had white-collar jobs, compared to 37% of male workers across the city. The vast majority of residents, 83%, were renters, and they had very high rates of mobility. This was a transitional neighborhood, but with a solid group of politically engaged homeowners.

The community council soon became the largest organization in Rogers Park as it pushed for planning to prevent building deterioration and an end to haphazard zoning. Its work included publicizing the neighborhood and encouraging positive relationships among the mix of residents. In their community-building efforts, community council leaders cultivated an identity for the neighborhood as a place of "neighbors of many faces."[46] In 1963, it adopted what the leadership called an open door policy, stating that the community "has enjoyed the privilege of a long history as a harmonious community of people representing all races, cultures and religious traditions."[47] According to sociologist Gerald Suttles, such claims were really about nationality: ever concerned about the neighborhood's prestige, the council emphasized census reports to distinguish Rogers Park from the lower-prestige ethnic ghettos where Jewish and Irish immigrants typically first settled.

The community council's characterization of the neighborhood drew from an ideology of cultural pluralism. The identity it constructed valorized the cultures of white ethnics (by this point in history, social boundaries had relaxed enough that Jewish and Irish immigrants were widely viewed as white).[48] It assumed a societal consensus around mainstream American values and affirmed the principle of tolerance toward the cultural practices of different faiths.[49] By promoting this identity, the community council tried to cultivate a sense of we-ness among those who were understood, although not openly acknowledged, as white—a shared cultural connection to each other and the neighborhood, as well as a commitment to supporting the organization's political agenda of conservation.

Snapshot 2: Before Diversity—a Welcome Mat for Black Chicagoans, 1966

In 1966, Dr. Martin Luther King Jr. and civil rights activists with the Southern Christian Leadership Conference turned their sights on Chicago. There, as in many other midwestern and northeastern cities, black people were steered into the ballooning black ghettos on the city's South and West Sides, where they lived in substandard housing and under the threats of white riots and attacks against those who ventured into white communities.[50] Mayor Richard Daley, the Chicago Board of Realtors, and other city leaders refused to meet with the civil rights activists for over a year. Nazis in the white Englewood neighborhood organized a Back to Africa protest march.[51]

But Rogers Park leaders had a different reaction to King's 1966 Freedom Summer campaign. On August 23, leaders of the community council and a group called the Interfaith Clergy of Rogers Park convened on the steps of a neighborhood synagogue. Speaking on behalf of more than one hundred religious and community groups, they declared their support for fair housing. "We support the moral right of all people to live in Rogers Park," they announced. Quoting from the community council's welcoming statement, they continued: "We believe that welcoming all new residents to the community, whatever their diverse backgrounds, is in keeping with American traditions and is basic to the ultimate good of the community."[52] The community council and Interfaith Clergy leaders promised to continue meeting with real estate brokers and property owners to discuss fair housing, as they had been doing for at least a year.

The leaders who made the welcoming statement were signaling to black Chicagoans that the neighborhood was safe. The welcoming statement was part of the community council's broader campaign for open housing. Its emphasis on tolerance countered the reputation that Rogers Park had among black Chicagoans, who viewed it as unreceptive and discriminatory.[53] The statement constructed the ideal community member—the "we" and the "residents"—as open minded and, conceivably, African American. Here, diversity was not yet an ideal but an attribute of people in a tolerant community.

The council's primary audience was white people, especially Jews. In the eyes of community council leaders, the neighborhood was a stable, safe community of middle-income white families, with good schools and high property values.[54] They wanted to keep the economic fortunes of the neighborhood that way.[55] But those families were leaving for the suburbs. The community council leaders believed that the widespread application of open housing laws would help counter that trend. If every neighborhood in the city had to accept black residents, the leadership reasoned, then there would not be an overwhelming influx of poor black people into just a few white neighborhoods, Rogers Park included. The community council issued an open housing resolution to the Chicago City Council in 1968, arguing, "Without the establishment of equal housing opportunities for all citizens, the ghetto conditions now existing in some areas of this city will surely spread to many areas of Chicago."[56]

With its open housing campaign and polite language, the council hoped to encourage white residents to be receptive to black newcomers. They also wanted to assure white resident that their property values would not drop if some black people moved into the neighborhood. These community-based endorsements of integration were motivated by white people's racial and class-based fears about neighborhood deterioration. Such motivations characterized the neighborhood movement for fair housing and racial integration, which was never large in scale but developed in nearly every US city with a swelling black population and transitioning white neighborhoods.[57]

Consider what Rogers Park civic leaders were *not* saying. At the welcoming statement event and other open housing forums, they made no mention of helping low-income black residents who suffered from discrimination and substandard housing. Unlike the spokespeople for King's campaign, they avoided any rationale about remedying racial or economic disadvantage. Instead, they framed racial minority incorporation positively, in terms of the widely shared value of difference, and they posed open housing policy as advantageous for everyone.[58]

Following the 1966 welcoming announcement, Rogers Park was profiled in city papers as safe for black people. In one article, Reverend John Christian, the pastor of Saint Ignatius Catholic Church and the head of Interfaith Clergy, explained, "Our integration has been slow, but very peaceful. We have avoided publicity as much as possible to prevent people from panic-selling."[59] A father of one of the ten new black families that had moved into the neighborhood since the announcement said: "When we heard they were welcoming Negroes here, we took them at their word. We haven't had any trouble." The administrators of local government welfare and housing programs for poor, predominantly black Chicagoans also identified Rogers Park as a receptive neighborhood.[60]

There is no way to verify whether the council's welcoming statement and open housing campaign encouraged the peaceable in-movement of black people that soon followed. Regardless, the council's actions were political interventions. They were attempts by community leaders to prevent economic decline and to embrace—but also contain—racial minority in-migration. Such attempts were forged, in part, through the leaders' promotion of Rogers Park's identity as a place of eclectic, open-minded people.

Snapshot 3: Testimonials to Diversity, 1985

In 1985, Stanley Pukelis, a white police officer, published a *Chicago Sun-Times* column titled "Why I Live Here: East Rogers Park."[61] He wrote, "Our community, as evidenced by our many diverse residents who gather at the beachfront, is positive proof that Rogers Park is a growing, viable community where anyone regardless of race, creed, or ethnic background is welcomed."

The officer was witnessing dramatic changes in Rogers Park's demographics. Starting in the mid-1970s, African Americans migrated to Rogers Park from the extremely segregated South and West Sides of Chicago. Continuing the neighborhood's tradition as an immigrant gateway, new residents arrived from Mexico and Central America as well as from the Caribbean, Africa, Southeast Asia, and Eastern Europe. More Orthodox Jews moved in, too.

The council leaders' fears about racial turnover had proven true, and their open housing policy and advocacy proved ineffective in preventing large-scale turnover. Reform Jews and other middle-class white people moved out and stopped moving in. In the 1970s, the overall population shrunk by 9% (like the rest of the city), and the white population shrunk by 27% (a bit less than the city).[62] In 1965, approximately 85% of the students at Sullivan High School were Jewish. Twelve years later, only 10% were. Between 1970 and 1990, the black population swelled from 1% to 27% and, between 1980 and 1990, the Latino population grew from 5% to 12%.[63] The percentage of families living below the poverty line rose from 5% to 16%, which was a bit below the city rate of 18%.[64] Although the neighborhood never lost all of its white residents, they made up just 45% of the neighborhood population by 1990. The newcomers were, on average, younger, while many remaining white residents were elderly.

These and later demographic transformations were fueled largely by economic and social processes such as changes in immigration law, income inequality, and the decline of feeder neighborhoods—not by the deliberate actions of local government and organizations to promote integration. Because of this, sociologists have labeled Rogers Park a laissez-faire diverse community, or diverse by circumstance.[65] It contrasts with diverse-by-direction communities, such as Oak Park, Illinois, and Shaker Heights, Ohio, which adopted racial maintenance policies and other systematic interventions in the 1970s to encourage racial integration.[66]

In the 1980s, observers, some community spokespeople, and residents such as the police officer quoted above began to reference the neighborhood identity familiar today. Newspapers characterized Rogers Park as a melting pot—multicultural and diverse.[67] Just as this identity became salient for locals, it also became politically important to those community activists who wanted to stop the in-migration of low-income black people.

Snapshot 4: Diversity as a Defense against Subsidized Housing, 1980s

In the 1970s, the Chicago Housing Authority (CHA) selected Rogers Park as one of a few white neighborhoods where it would construct new subsidized housing intended for low-income black people.[68] It proposed a new building with twelve units in the northwestern end of Rogers Park. A few local white residents who lived nearby were so enraged that, in 1980, they tried to halt construction and were arrested.[69] With neighbors, they formed the Pottawattamie Area Committee, staged demonstrations, and requested an injunction from the federal district court to stop construction.

Their protests were indicative of fierce white resistance to government-sponsored integration interventions. With the Housing Act of 1949, in response to the post–World War II housing shortage, Congress took on the goal of supporting "a decent home and a suitable living environment for every American family."[70] Over the subsequent twenty years, it funded public housing developments, some of them very large "projects" with multiple high-rise buildings. Soon the population in those developments was overwhelmingly black and poor. By design, this public housing maintained prevailing patterns of black segregation, further reinforced by government policies of slum clearance and urban renewal.[71] In many Chicago neighborhoods in the 1950s, white aldermen and racist residents protested new developments because they did not want poor African American residents in proximity to their communities.[72] Thus the CHA built new public housing only in black residential areas or next to existing public housing. Underresourced, poorly maintained, and home to extremely disadvantaged households, this housing, especially the massive projects, deteriorated.

Gautreaux v. Chicago Housing Authority was important for this story in Chicago and in Rogers Park. This class action litigation successfully challenged the legality of the CHA's and HUD's practices of concentrating more than ten thousand public housing units in African American city neighborhoods.[73] The litigation led to the creation of the country's largest mobility program, the Gautreaux Assisted Housing Program. The desegregation program provided vouchers to low-income black residents to pay for private-market apartments in predominantly white urban and suburban communities.

When the district court in its 1967 *Gautreaux v. Chicago Housing Authority* ruling found that the CHA had created residential racial segregation, it called on the CHA to also provide low-rise, scattered-site housing in white communities for current public housing residents.[74] Not surprisingly, subsequent attempts by the agency to create such housing were met with violent protests by white people and adamant opposition by politicians.[75] The CHA and the city moved ever so slowly on the new construction because of the political resistance and bureaucratic red tape.

The building proposed for the Pottawattamie area was a response to an order by a 1980 federal judge for the CHA to more rapidly finish its construction of public housing.[76] At that time, about 3% of the housing units in Rogers Park were subsidized, meaning that federal and local housing authorities provided funds to building owners or to individuals to make the units more affordable to low-income households. Of those nine-hundred-odd units, 82% were for seniors.[77] (These numbers paled in comparison to those of the city's African American neighborhoods, where upward of 81% of units were subsidized.)[78]

By this time, the politics of low-income housing and racial transition in Rogers Park had become very contentious. In the 1970s, antipoverty activists started organizing to support low-income people and oppose redlining, which persisted despite being prohibited by the 1968 Fair Housing Act. The Illinois Legislative Investigating Commission received complaints from numerous organizations alleging that Rogers Park had some of the highest incidences of "location discrimination" in the city.[79] The Rogers Park Citizen's Action Program organized a boycott of local financial institutions that refused to give home improvement and mortgage loans in the neighborhood. The activists drew national attention to Rogers Park, and renowned journalist Bill Moyers produced a PBS program on the problem of redlining.[80]

In the meantime, the community council had become a powerful voice of opposition to low-income housing and new minority residents. In the early 1970s, the leadership had approved the CHA's construction of thirty-six public housing units, but then it faced a vehement backlash from property owners. Thereafter, it took the position that low-income housing was a threat. Council leaders voted for a moratorium on additional subsidized housing in Rogers Park, taking a stance similar to that of community organizations in nearby neighborhoods.[81] They did so in a political environment in which the federal government, under President Richard Nixon, was curtailing its involvement in low-income housing policy and cutting funding.[82] The 1980 election of President Ronald Reagan was a watershed; over the next twelve years, his and George H. W. Bush's administrations would oversee an 80% cut in federal funding for subsidized housing and enforcement.

Participants in these political conflicts in Rogers Park drew upon the notion of the neighborhood as racially and economically mixed to justify their opposition to subsidized low-income housing. The Pottawattamie activists used racist language to argue that "the housing project could turn the stably integrated neighborhood into a ghetto."[83] The community council joined a political coalition fighting for a moratorium on new subsidized housing throughout the entire Ninth Congressional District. Those activists couched their stance as support for diversity. The coalition chairman explained,

> The Ninth Congressional District is a multiracial and economically diverse community, which is a fact we all appreciate . . . however, we've seen the

construction of a significant number of additional publicly assisted housing units in our area. . . . Additional subsidized housing at this point could irretrievably overbalance our neighborhoods, destroying all we have worked to achieve. We, therefore, are seeking the moratorium to protect the viability of our multiracial and diverse community.[84]

Loyola University agreed. Just a few years earlier, it had started a walk-to-work program to encourage faculty members and staff to buy homes close by, in hopes of economically anchoring blocks surrounding the university. Arguing against local housing activists who contended that the area was not a dumping ground for the poor, the program administrator told a reporter in 1980, "Diversity is what each of these community groups wants to keep—economic, social, racial diversity. . . . I'm worried that the subsidized housing for the neighborhood will be too concentrated."[85]

The moratoria were unenforceable because the community council and its nonprofit allies did not have legal authority. The CHA eventually built the Pottawattamie-area units. But that conflict deepened the political schism that had developed between the community council, which was firmly oriented to the white homeowners and antagonistic toward low-income Latino and black residents, and the growing number of tenant advocates in Rogers Park. The community council considered low-income and subsidized housing detrimental to the community's economic vitality and property values, while tenant groups considered such housing an important solution to poverty and racial discrimination.[86]

The tenant activists had on their side David Orr, who had been elected as the neighborhood's alderman in 1979. A white man with a thick mustache, Orr was known for his alliance with Chicago's only black mayor, Harold Washington, and his independence from the Democratic machine that dominated Chicago politics. Orr supported local low-income housing activists, sharing office space with the Neighborhood Committee for Better Housing, a progressive organization formed by Rogers Park lawyers to take slumlords to court. In 1981, he told a reporter why government subsidized housing was necessary for the neighborhood: "My key concern is that we have the commitment to find housing for people [in the neighborhood] who live now in overcrowded conditions."[87] Orr was also a supporter of civil rights; throughout his tenure, he sponsored and oversaw the passage of a citywide tenants' rights law.[88] Orr's rhetoric on the neighborhood contrasted sharply with the reactionary diversity talk of the community council. He characterized the community and his office in terms of activism and legal rights. As he told a reporter in 1985, "'I've always been a confirmed political activist and concerned about civil rights."[89] Speaking to the local ethos of community engagement, he said, "I think the spirit of activism in Rogers Park is gaining.'"

The schism between the community council and tenant activists persisted into the 2000s, as did the controversies over low-income subsidized housing. The council's argument—that government and private resources targeted to house poor black residents were *antithetical* to the neighborhood's diversity and stable integration—foreshadowed the arguments that progrowth groups would make about the need for gentrification in the 2000s.

Snapshot 5: A Welcome Mat for Investors, 1988

In December 1988, the *Chicago Tribune* ran a story headlined "Rogers Park Renaissance: Construction, Renovation Set Stage for Comeback."[90] Investors had identified Rogers Park as having potential to gentrify. This was a pivotal turning point in the neighborhood's politics of diversity. Alongside the demographic changes of the 1980s, Rogers Park suffered ongoing economic disinvestment, and social justice–oriented organizations developed more low-income housing. About 5.6% of the neighborhood's units were subsidized, most in the area north of Howard Street at the northern end of the neighborhood.[91] Buildings fell into disrepair from landlord neglect and old age, attracting criminal activity. Rogers Park remained an outpost of progressives, bohemians, and artists, but crime rates got much worse and scared away many who could avoid the neighborhood. In 1994, there were 180 officially recorded robberies and assaults each month.[92] Residents were very concerned with street crime, gangs, and drug trade.[93] The community earned a reputation of being dangerous and rundown.

Just as investors and developers looked to Rogers Park in hopes of capitalizing on inexpensive property, Alderman Orr started to publicly laud the community's diversity.[94] Orr clearly articulated an identity for the neighborhood as uniquely diverse as he praised the new investment dollars. In the aforementioned *Tribune* article, Orr remarked, "Rogers Park [is] . . . among the most legitimately diverse and integrated neighborhoods in any city in this nation. . . . The good news is we've got people who want to invest."[95] His message: Rogers Park is not just deteriorating, not just dangerous, and not just populated by dark-skinned people.

Alderman Orr noted the importance of controlling development in order to protect diversity. Joseph Moore, whom Orr tapped to be his successor, came into office in the early 1990s and elaborated the same themes.

Self-identified as progressive and a Democrat, Alderman Moore acknowledged the importance of low-cost housing, distanced himself from housing activists (after an early affiliation), and did not speak of integration. He made diversity a centerpiece of his political rhetoric on the neighborhood.[96]

The residents engaged in local politics in Rogers Park, the vast majority of whom were white, described the neighborhood's identity in similar terms as did Aldermen Orr and Moore. In a 1993 study by Loyola University sociologists, nearly all of the twenty-two predominantly white community leaders interviewed described Rogers Park's diversity—cultural/ethnic, racial, economic, and religious—as remarkable and a strength.[97] One typical response quoted was that Rogers Park was "one of the most diverse wards in the city."

Local academics provided further support. Phil Nyden, then the chair of the Loyola University Department of Sociology and Anthropology, disseminated his research on Rogers Park and other stable, racially diverse communities in the early 1990s.[98] Nyden, too, saw the term *diversity* as distinct from *integration*. As he explained in a *Chicago Tribune* article featuring his research, "Diversity is seen as more objective, not loaded yet with ideology and values."

The push in Rogers Park to treat race as diversity and to champion the neighborhood as a model of diversity in the late 1980s and early 1990s was reinforced by changes in government housing policy in Chicago and beyond. Low-income and fair housing programs had been politically under attack and left emaciated by funding cuts under the Reagan administration. Some tenant activists beyond Rogers Park had already begun to frame low-income and racial integration programs in terms of diversity. In 1985, Alexander Polikoff, the lead attorney in *Gautreaux*, suggested that he and his allies defend racial integration programs by emphasizing "the positive value of diversity."

The city's large public housing projects had become plagued with serious problems of crime and mismanagement, and popular support for such housing was waning even further. Meanwhile, the death in 1987 of Mayor Washington, an African American man who had challenged the city's Democratic machine, was a major turning point in city politics. It ended a five-year period of progressive reforms, as Washington had promoted people of color and women into the city administration and pushed for economic development in city neighborhoods through local grassroots organizations. What soon followed was the twenty-two-year tenure of Richard M. Daley, who favored neoliberal reforms. The next chapter picks up on these themes in detail.

The Rogers Park emblem—the tree of different-colored hands—was created in this period through a redevelopment effort led by politically active white, middle-class residents, many of them Jewish. The neighborhood's commercial districts had declined precipitously in the 1980s. Sheridan Road, the main commercial thoroughfare, had been targeted by developers for motels and high-rise apartment buildings, strip malls, and fast-food restaurants.[99]

In the late 1980s, advocates enlisted the support of the alderman's office, the city's Department of Planning, and Loyola University, which had begun to make more concerted efforts to spur development in hopes of attracting more residential students.[100] In our interview, Dorothy Gregory, a white woman who helped to spearhead the redevelopment effort, recounted how those involved had thought about the neighborhood's commercial streets: "Clark Street was iffy. Howard Street was iffy, Morse Avenue was a disaster. Let's do Sheridan Road because it's safe and it's also a gateway." They pressed for locally guided planning that would stall economic deterioration and respond to specific community concerns. In particular, they hoped to rationalize zoning on Sheridan and implement streetscaping to retain the street's residential character. Their work was taken up by Alderman Orr's Planning and Zoning Committee, which was made up of about thirty residents, businesspeople, affordable housing advocates, Loyola University, and the community council. Through the activists' prodding and with the help of Alderman Moore, they secured $1.5 million in city funding.[101]

As early as 1986, politically active residents had recognized that the entire neighborhood needed to revamp its image, and the group of architects, real estate consultants, and other urban planning professionals who advised the Sheridan revitalization project agreed.[102] They recommended an intensive beautification effort, including decorative features that would "herald the presence of the community" so that "a definite character [would be] established."[103] Once implemented, a major feature of the project was forty new banners with the neighborhood emblem, which was created by a city designer in consultation with the zoning committee. One journalist called it "a brand-new Rogers Park logo."[104] In 1994, at a ceremony in a neighborhood park to announce the project, Burt Reif, the chairman of the committee, explained that the banners "will give people more of a sense of community. . . . It will express what Rogers Park is about."[105] As Dorothy Gregory recalled, "It's hands helping people—hands and color." It showed the lakefront, she said, and a tree, many of which had been lost with recent development. "It spoke to everybody."

The banners were an example of community-informed development. Since the 1950s, community input had been an important principle in this neighborhood of lively civic politics. Such input was driven by the views of the more affluent, well-resourced white residents who mobilized to pressure the aldermen for support. That input, too, became part of the neighborhood's reputation and was touted by Alderman Moore. He publicly stressed that the Sheridan Road beautification project had been driven by community residents, "not some government bureaucrat."[106]

The silences of the late 1980s and early 1990s—what local political leaders did *not* say publicly—are revealing. When praising diversity, Aldermen Orr and Moore did not talk about remedying disadvantage. No longer did Orr talk about equal rights or government intervention. Likewise, although talk of diversity was the positive spin on demographics of the neighborhood, race-class tensions did not disappear, nor did white leaders retreat from disparaging coded race-class rhetoric. As documented in the 1993 Loyola study, many local leaders saw problems with the greater social distance among residents and with crime, violence, and gangs. They made veiled derogatory references to low-income black and Latino residents. "I sometimes feel myself overwhelmed by the under-class," said one respondent. "Thirteen years ago, welfare people began moving in," said another. In American culture, terms such as "underclass" and "welfare recipients" were negatively associated with low-income African Americans and Latinos presumed to be lazy, drug addicted, culturally deprived, and undeserving of government support.[107]

The term *diversity*, in contrast, indicated a shared buy-in into an unmarked white, middle-class culture of tolerance. Presumably, this culture was made possible by selective inclusion—the incorporation of respectable people of color among white people—but threatened by overwhelming numbers of unrespectable, low-income minorities and the low-cost rental housing they depended upon. Diversity advocates symbolically cast a wide net with their designations of who belonged and who did not. At the same time, they failed to provide a productive conceptual framework for understanding or talking about complicated, undesirable, and problematic social differences.

Reimagining the Boundaries of Urban Community

Over forty years, a political movement for racial and economic justice in American cities gave rise to a fledgling neighborhood movement for racial integration. In Rogers Park, community advocates and residents as well as journalists, researchers, and other observers reimagined the symbolic boundaries of urban community through civic politics and rhetorical and visual renderings. They fostered an identity for the neighborhood as welcoming and distinctively mixed, constructing racial and ethnic differences as a common group interest and commensurate with a good quality of life. This identity was integrated in the popular imagination of the neighborhood and literally made part of the physical infrastructure. It emerged from and spoke to the lived experiences of everyday neighborhood residents. Further, it was taken up in white middle-class politics concerned with community cohesion, control over development, and the retention of white homeowners—and therein legitimized selective inclusion. It was continually up for grabs as well. The relative openness of local civic life enabled different constituents to make claims on the community's symbolic boundaries, redefining it according to their worldviews, interests, and political objectives.

According to sociologist Michael Maly, the construction of a neighborhood image as supportive of diversity is essential for stable integration. "Although image is not everything in a community," he writes, "in the context of white racism, pervasive discrimination, and segregation, it is a key element in maintaining integrated communities."[108] Such an image can help to manage the challenges of minority representation by maintaining and attracting white residents and homeowners and easing intergroup relations. It can counter popular perceptions of racially mixed neighborhoods as unstable and thus prone to problems like crime. It can minimize boundary-heightening practices of racism, xenophobia, and exclusion through a positive recognition of the value of racial and ethnic differences. It is also concept building for a shared sense of belonging and interest. Yet a neighborhood identity of diversity glosses over those elements of neighborhood life that might threaten people with power and privilege—problems of race-class hierarchies, inequality of power and resources, and the racial disparities of economic redevelopment. It goes hand in hand with the valorization of homeownership and the stigmatization of low-income, disproportionately black or Latino renters coping with poverty, housing insecurity, slum landlords, and problems of gangs and drug trade.

The extent to which the civic push for diversity expanded the social terms of membership in Rogers Park in the latter half of the twentieth century was equivocal and mixed. Most economic and demographic change in the neighborhood was outside the control of local political leaders, as were housing conditions. Access to beaches and streetscaping improved the quality of life for all groups, even if those amenities were not pressing priorities for disadvantaged renters who lived in substandard housing. Because of tenant advocates and, in the late 1980s, under Alderman Orr, there were some concerted efforts to include low-income people of color in neighborhood planning and serve their needs. But decision-making bodies in local politics were overwhelmingly dominated by white middle-class homeowners and biased toward their objectives and perspectives. Ongoing political resistance to low-income housing heightened group divisions and minority marginalization. And as the next chapter highlights, the biases of diversity could work much in favor of those seeking profitable investment and high home values in Rogers Park in the 2000s.

FIVE

Gentrification, Displacement, and Color-Blind Opposition to Subsidized Housing

Scene 1: On a cool October morning, the smell of coffee and cinnamon rolls filled No Exit Café, a local institution that opened as a beatnik coffeehouse in the 1950s. About thirty-five people active in local business and social service organizations, nearly all of them white, sat crammed around the small tables. They had come to hear Alderman Moore's 2002 State of Rogers Park address. DevCorp North, the neighborhood's economic development corporation, hosted. Its members received a five-dollar discount on the fifteen-dollar cover charge.

Alderman Moore took the stage, opening with one of his customary groaner jokes. A middle-aged and mild-mannered white man, Moore was a self-identified progressive and Democrat who had a reputation as independent from Mayor Daley, who governed with a rubber-stamping city council. He represented a politically active community where not just homeowners and poor people but also the real estate industry had impassioned advocates, some of whom were in the room. Despite his many vocal detractors and tepid supporters, Moore had been repeatedly reelected to office.

In his State of Rogers Park address, Moore framed recent changes in the community on his terms, lauding the exciting economic growth in the neighborhood, its treasured diversity, and accomplishments achieved during his decade in office, including condominiums "constructed for people of all incomes." Referring to recently released census data, he said:

> We're well on our way to showing that an economically and racially diverse community can be stable and prosperous. . . . The skeptics, who said gentrification would destroy the community's diversity, were wrong. It is possible to maintain diversity and develop.

Moore praised the variety of people in the neighborhood: "It's a place where children can grow up with people from all over. We have decedents of the Mayflower, people who came to the country in chains, people who just recently arrived." There were two reasons the neighborhood remained diverse, he said: the local "commitment to maintaining affordable housing" and the fact that "people here are committed to diversity. . . . [They] don't want to live in a homogeneous community."

DevCorp's executive director, Caroline, a young white woman with a planning background, also spoke. Her comments were upbeat. She praised her organization's contributions to neighborhood improvements and its dedication to the community's racial, ethnic, and economic diversity. "We're leading the effort to revitalize Rogers Park from the inside out," she announced proudly. "Diversity isn't only what we've come to love. We believe it's marketable, and we'll trumpet it around town."

Scene 2: Ben took a deep breath. He was getting ready to disagree with everyone else in the room. A sturdy white man in his mid-sixties, with a white beard and kind eyes, Ben worked as a minister for Good News Partners, a faith-based housing provider in Chicago. He and ten other members of the Community of Opportunity Affordable Housing Coalition sat around a small table on the cramped third floor of a drop-in youth center. The coalition's focus was North of Howard, a poor, majority-minority residential area within Rogers Park targeted by developers for gentrification. Some of the other coalition members were directors of social service agencies. A few were researchers from local universities. Ben was the only one who openly identified with antigentrification activists.

Everyone was rereading a draft of the coalition's vision statement, which they had composed over many meetings:

> The Coalition believes that one of the strengths of the Rogers Park neighborhood lies in its cultural and economic diversity, which is highly valued by our community. The coalition also recognizes that left unchecked, "market forces" often threaten those residents who are least able to compete economically in a neighborhood facing the pressures of gentrification. . . . The coalition works together to create opportunities with information, resources, and support, encouraging all residents to fully participate in the process of preserving the cultural and economic diversity of our community.

In his usual gentle tone, Ben said, "This is nice, but it's not going to get us anywhere."

Ben was used to being a provocateur. A self-described radical civil rights and antiwar activist, he founded Good News Partners in the 1970s to serve what he described as the people at the very bottom of the economic ladder. The organization oversaw rental buildings, a single-room-occupancy building called the Jonquil Hotel, and cooperative housing units. Good News Partners attracted tenants from across the city. Most were African American. Some had been homeless. Many were recovering from drug addiction or struggling with other serious problems.

Ben described the revisions he wanted made to the coalition's vision statement: "We don't just like a diverse neighborhood. We want to support people here. Talk in terms of people, not ideals or a model neighborhood." A white woman from a social service agency suggested that they modify the last sentence to include "*current and low-income* residents." Renee, a white woman from the Rogers Park Community Council, disagreed. Her organization provided social services and had close ties to the alderman and homeowners. "That doesn't help us because there are middle-class and higher people who live in the neighborhood." Then someone changed the topic. The statement was never changed.

Later during the same meeting, Ben asked the coalition members for support in his effort to acquire more properties. The other coalition members seemed sympathetic but very cautious. North of Howard had a troublesome history of nonprofit organizations that poorly managed their low-income rental buildings. Many residents saw Good News Partners as a vestige of that era.

Renee shared her skepticism. "Let me reflect the community perception: There's a band of seven- to nine-year-olds who grab purses, break windows. I can't say they come from the Jonquil Hotel, but they come and go from there. . . . The neighborhood is being terrorized by seven-year-olds." Ben responded, "I always say, if you can identify any of those kids, we'll do what we can. We've got some *deeply* troubled kids." Renee continued, "People drink, pitch pennies. It's very disruptive in a neighborhood that considers itself as residential. . . . People want them out." Ben challenged this sentiment: "Our mission is to help people no one else will help out. . . . When people say they want diversity, do they want already successful people?"

The Twenty-First-Century Push for Diversity in Rogers Park

Construction cranes filled the skyline of Chicago's downtown in the early 2000s. In the surrounding neighborhoods, there were rows of recently built townhouses, fancy gardens, and new wrought-iron fences. The news media buzzed with stories of trendy restaurants and clubs.[1] Across the city, property values were increasing more than inflation, and demand was increasing, too. It was becoming more expensive to buy or rent a home, including in Rogers Park.[2] The assertions made by Alderman David Orr and Alderman Joe Moore in the late 1980s and early 1990s—that investors were interested in Rogers Park—were proving true.

In Rogers Park, the 2000s were a time of demonstrable but uneven gentrification. This raised new local issues of development and diversity, although some issues remained quite the same as they had for decades. There were problems of infrastructure disinvestment, economic decline, neglect, and worsening economic inequality. There also was a new influential constituency: the new homebuyers, most of whom were white and nearly all of whom were middle or upper middle class. The real estate industry was bringing dollars to the community and the alderman's election campaign coffers. Meanwhile, low-income renters, African Americans, and Latinos were being displaced from the neighborhood. Compared to the days of Alderman David Orr, tenant activists had fewer resources to serve them, especially with the retrenchment in philanthropy that followed the 9/11 terrorist attacks.

Normative approval of diversity was very strong among Rogers Park residents active in local civic life, as it had been for decades.[3] The alderman, his allies, and real estate industry advocates tried to engage that approval as they pursued their explicit objectives of fostering economic growth and their unspoken objective of appealing to well-off white residents. Material resources were at stake. They hoped to direct gentrification and the community's shifting race-class demographics in ways that were politically palatable to politically active residents, home buyers, developers, real estate companies, and other campaign contributors.

The push for diversity by progrowth leaders in Rogers Park helped to moderate contentious neighborhood politics, especially the provocations of progressive tenant activists, which got channeled into fights over discrete housing policies and commercial redevelopment initiatives. These dynamics worked mostly but not entirely to the decision makers' advantage. They created a context in which Ben and other radical antigentrification activists had to constantly refute the prevailing discourse on diversity—doing that work of street-level semiotics—and assert their dissident interpretation of diversity as they fought for social justice and the right to the city for poor people, people of color, and renters.

Urban Gentrification and the Loss of Low-Cost Housing

Between the mid-1990s and the economic crisis of 2008, gentrification took place in Rogers Park and many other Chicago neighborhoods, in cities such as Boston and New York, and in some rural areas. This economic growth was fueled by many sources, among them the increasingly powerful finance and real estate sectors, depressed property values in many city neighborhoods, lenders who flooded the housing market with inexpensive home mortgages, and consumers' demand for cosmopolitan city living.

With gentrification and tight rental markets comes a loss of low-cost housing. In Chicago and other large cities, that loss was a systemic problem. It burdened low- and moderate-income people most. At the time of this study, 36% of Chicagoans faced a high rent burden, paying more than 30% of their income toward their rent.[4] These conditions were generated in part by changes in federal and local low-income housing policy. In the 1990s, the US Congress initiated what eventually became the $5.8 billion HOPE VI (Housing Opportunities for People Everywhere) program to overhaul public housing nationwide. Under HOPE VI, the Chicago Housing Authority (CHA) embarked on a massive plan to demolish large-scale public housing projects and create mixed-income communities. The Plan for Transformation entailed the demolition of fifty-one high-rise public housing buildings with eighteen thousand units that had housed extremely poor, predominantly black families. It called for a far smaller number of mixed-income housing developments, with a net loss of fourteen thousand low-cost units.[5]

HUD's budget for other forms of low-income housing remained emaciated. Starting in the 1970s, in its ever more limited capacity of supporting low-cost housing, the federal government had adopted a policy of providing subsidies mostly to very low income people to pay for private-market apartments—then called Section 8 certificates.[6] The Reagan administration's massive cuts to federal low-income housing programs left Section 8 the only large-scale federal housing subsidy for poor households.[7] In the late 1990s and early 2000s, demand for these subsidies far exceeded supply. In 1997, when a lottery was opened to get on the waiting list in Chicago, over one hundred thousand applications were submitted for thirty-five thousand slots. Another lottery was not held until 2006. HUD also had smaller programs providing subsidies to property owners to pay for specific units in rental buildings and giving tax advantages to private investors that funded affordable housing.[8] However, subsidies offered in the 1970s and 1980s were expiring, and many property owners planned to not renew and instead convert their buildings into market-rate units. Community organizers in Chicago declared a housing crisis.

Gentrification and the concurrent dismantling of public housing are centerpieces of the policy shift toward a neoliberal model of urban development, which was being encouraged by the federal government and enthusiastically pursued by the administration of Mayor Daley.[9] Neoliberal strategies combine cuts in public funding for social programs with policies that promote the privatization of public resources, historic preservation, condominium conversions, and subsidies for private investment in disadvantaged communities. Supporters of such policies reason that free-market capitalism is the best mechanism for achieving social goals. They praise the tenets of economic efficiency, privatization, and individual responsibility. This policy orientation had troubling consequences for poor and middle-income people and people of color.

Rogers Park experienced signs of gentrification first in the 1990s and more fully in the early 2000s. Home sales and prices increased, most dramatically for new condominiums and townhouses. From 1993 to 2000, sales of condominiums and townhouses in Rogers Park skyrocketed by 139%, compared to 46% in Chicago, and their average sales price increased 100%, compared to 28% in Chicago.[10] According to a Loyola study, between 1996 and 2000, developers converted at least seventy-nine rental buildings with 1,105 units into condos.[11] Five percent of the rental units in the neighborhood were lost. The pace picked up between 2000 and 2005, when condo conversions reduced the supply of rental housing by 900 to 1,000 units each year.[12] Between 2000 and 2010, the median price of condos and townhouses increased 51%, despite the housing crash in the late 2000s.[13] At the same time, Rogers Park remained troubled by economic disinvestment, particularly in commercial districts, and it never entirely flipped to a wealthy enclave.

Gentrification is racialized and classed, to the benefit of those who are white and affluent.[14] As a columnist for a Washington, DC, paper wrote, "If you're pushed out of somewhere because you have less money than someone else who wants to live where you do, well, those are practically the house rules of capitalism."[15] An audit of properties and mortgage lending showed that condo buyers in Rogers Park were more likely to be white and higher income, while those displaced tended to be lower-income people of color.[16] The neighborhood had no rent control and only a handful of housing cooperatives, both of which can buffer low-income people from the harms of gentrification.[17] Likewise, it had a small supply of

low-income housing subsidized by the government—a conservative esti-
mate was 1,840 buildings units, or 6.7% of the units in the neighborhood,
a third of which were for the elderly.[18] A handful of other buildings had
subsidies from nonprofit agencies and lenders. Most of those buildings,
government subsidized or not, were not permanently protected from economic upscaling.

Although those who support gentrification pitch it as the answer to urban
economic decline, it is an uncertain process. No one can know, at the outset,
exactly how a neighborhood will change or if it will gentrify at all. Analysts
can only verify that gentrification has happened after it has taken place. In
the Rogers Park community politics in the early 2000s, the uncertainty of
gentrification loomed large. Those involved in local housing politics debated, Was the neighborhood gentrifying or not? What should be done,
if anything, to protect diversity? Developers worried about their financial
prospects. Recent home buyers were apprehensive about their home value
dropping. Meantime, activists issued dire warnings about "Condo Mania"
and the displacement of low-income, disproportionately African American
and Latino renters.

At the time of this study, no one knew the extent of the changes that
were taking place. As it turned out, by 2010, the white population would
increase seven percentage points to 39%, and the black and Latino populations would each shrink by four percentage points, to 26% and 24%, respectively (see table 4.1). The percentage of owner-occupied units jumped more
than 40%, from 17% to 26% of all housing units, while the total population declined by 21%, with population growth only among those earning
$75,000 a year or more.[19] The economic circumstances of poor residents
worsened as the poverty rate increased. The percentage of moderate-income
households paying more than 30% of their income toward rent or mortgage
more than doubled. Civil rights groups had been warning that people of
color in Rogers Park were being targeted for exploitative predatory home
loans. However, none of the high-profile decision makers in Rogers Park
publicly predicted that the neighborhood's housing boom was actually a
bubble that would soon burst or that the neighborhood would, by 2009,
become a foreclosure hotspot.[20]

The ongoing condominium conversions and uncertainty about the future created serious hardships for many low-income renters. I spent hours
with renters who had been forced to move from their homes or lived under
fear that they would be shortly. Most of them were very low-income African
American mothers. Patti was one of these women. She became an activist when the government-subsidized building where she lived in North of

Howard was targeted for condominium conversion. One afternoon, with packing boxes stacked throughout her living room and picture frames piled high in the corners, she described for me what was happening on her block: "They just trying to move out everybody, everybody, everybody." Another afternoon, LaKisha, her neighbor and fellow activist, sat surrounded by boxes and wept over and over, "I don't know what we'll do."

The Power Dynamics and Civic Politics of Neighborhood Growth

Four sets of political players were engaged in local redevelopment politics in Rogers Park. The city government was represented most immediately by the alderman's office. It had close allies with DevCorp North and the Rogers Park Community Council, which depended on city funding and worked in lockstep with the alderman. A second camp was the real estate industry, represented politically by the Builders Group. Another set of players included the social service agencies that served poor residents, particularly those involved in the affordable housing coalition. Finally, there were tenant activists, namely, grassroots organizers with the Rogers Park Community Action Network (RPCAN), the Section 8 Tenants Council, and a few allies, Ben included. Aside from the tenant activists, almost all the leaders of these organizations were white homeowners or business owners.

Among the most important players in local development were the alderman's office and the Builders Group. Alderman Moore, who worked out of a storefront office in the middle of the neighborhood, had an office staff of four. He had the complicated role of mediating the neighborhood's various organizations and voting constituents, including progressive and well-educated residents who sympathized with low-income renters, some of them being renters themselves. His chief concern was satisfying voters in the community, especially property owners, and campaign contributors. Moore had a reputation, especially outside the neighborhood, for being receptive to community input.[21] On development issues, this happened through Moore's appointed Zoning and Land Use and Advisory Committee as well as through community meetings at which residents could weigh in on city and private development plans and changes to the zoning code. However, residents routinely criticized such meetings as dog and pony shows. Further, these forums were consistently dominated by white male professionals and property owners. Of the eighteen members of his Zoning and Land Use Advisory Committee, at least five were Moore contributors or a campaign consultant, nine had connections to DevCorp, and five were in the Builders

Group or associated with a major real estate company. Five members represented social service agencies, three with connections to the community council. (The owner of No Exit Café was also on the committee, as were three other unaffiliated individuals.) Moore's office failed to make even token efforts to engage the full range of neighborhood residents. As late as 2006, his office did not print Spanish translations on its fliers about ward events, despite the growing Latino population and written complaints.

The Builders Group, founded in 1993, was a platform for more than one hundred developers, realtors, property owners, investors, and bank representatives (according to the organization's president, about a third of them lived in the neighborhood). Nearly all the leaders and active members were white, and most were men. The organization worked to increase property values and revenue for members through profitable development, much of it upscale. Builders Group members wanted to see brisk sales and booming condo development, but those who made money from high-end housing had differences with large-property owners who invested little in maintaining their buildings.

The alderman and the Builders Group members had an overlapping but not identical interest in profitable growth.[22] Their relationship is best described as symbiotic.[23] Developers were beholden to the alderman because most redevelopment required revisions to zoning codes, which he approved. On the other hand, Moore was beholden to the real estate businesses and organizations for campaign funds. In the months surrounding Moore's 2006 election campaign, the real estate industry was his largest single source of contributions, accounting for 44% of donations.[24]

DevCorp North, the community council, other civic organizations such as block clubs, and other businesspeople and homeowners all had an interest in growth as well, although these groups had varied goals, some of them at odds with each other.[25] The alderman and the allied community council and DevCorp North wanted to reverse decades of disinvestment, improve infrastructure and basic services, and attract private investment. This included establishing a tax increment finance zone around Howard Street to help subsidize a $75 million shopping mall, a $20 million renovation of train and bus stations and streetscaping on Howard, a 120-unit mixed-income building for seniors, and a farmers market. Social service providers, including a few staff members of the community council (but not the board), were troubled by the loss of affordable housing for low- and middle-income renters. Many participants in these groups, along with supporters of the arts, hoped to stabilize the neighborhood and improve the quality of life without the "whitewashing" that so often happens with gentrification.[26] Thus, progrowth interests were at the center of power in neighborhood politics—and I refer to these political players, collectively, as progrowth groups—but there was not a monolithic agenda of upscaling the neighborhood.

There were more stark political divisions between the leadership of these organizations and marginalized residents: poor people, African American and Latino residents, and renters. These groups were underrepresented in decision-making bodies such as the alderman's Zoning and Land Use Advisory Committee. If they were involved in neighborhood housing politics at all, it was usually through RPCAN, a multi-issue social justice activist organization that did grassroots organizing. A large portion of RPCAN's members and some of its leaders were low-income black renters, including Patti and LaKisha. The Section 8 Tenants Council, a small offshoot of RPCAN that represented tenants who received subsidies to pay their rent, was led by mostly very poor African American women. Latino residents were all but absent from redevelopment politics, although a few were involved with RPCAN, and a number with businesses had ties to DevCorp North through its Clark Street networking and revitalization project.

RPCAN activists were very critical of the progrowth groups, whom they saw as championing "low-road" development: rampant and stealth condo conversions, lucrative government subsidies to for-profit developers, and new businesses that paid below a living wage. They argued that the alderman, DevCorp North, and other progrowth groups actively promoted development as usual, which lined the pockets of businesspeople and politicians, displaced low-income people and people of color, and excluded those residents from power. RPCAN activists—whom the alderman, his allies, and many residents considered extremist and obstructionist—sparked fights over development and raised issues of equity, discrimination, and renters' rights. RPCAN was particularly effective at turning the politics of development into a debate rather than a foregone conclusion and putting the alderman on the defensive.

Other individuals active in local politics, some with popular and closely followed blogs, also accused the alderman of catering to developers and DevCorp North of ineptitude and a lack of willingness to take on housing issues. One blogger posted that developers were being permitted to tear down historic homes and then construct "concrete, cookie cutter cracker box" buildings through "a charade of developer friendly rules, regulations, and red tape designed to discourage community dissent and real participation until after the fact."[27]

Progrowth groups often indicated that they could control development, but such claims were in many ways illusory. They could not directly control residents' choices to move in or out of the neighborhood. Only so much property is ever available for sale or development. Further, Moore and his allies often avoided exercising control over development. They never established a broader neighborhood-wide development plan overseen by an elected board or residents through community forums. Rather, they managed development on a piecemeal basis, often one building at a time, and residents engaged on those terms.

Establishing the Terms of Debate over Development

Moore's strategy of managing development politics was to try to appease nearly everyone involved (and to placate RPCAN) while still green-lighting developers' plans. One tactic for appeasing neighborhood critics was to cultivate his reputation as a progressive. Even as affordable housing was being lost in the neighborhood, Moore went out of his way to take high-publicity stances on matters irrelevant to the neighborhood, opposing the war in Iraq, the entry of Walmart into Chicago, and the sale of foie gras by Chicago restaurants on the grounds that it was cruel to geese.

The terms of debate over development were delineated in many ways through the symbolic politics of diversity. Moore, DevCorp North, the community council, and often the Builders Group identified important issues and constituents in reference to the neighborhood's identity of diversity and in ways that legitimated their redevelopment objectives. They did so through four noteworthy processes: by constructing both civic-minded people of color and white homeowners as valuable community members; by championing so-called balanced development and affordable housing; by labeling a poor, majority–African American and Latino section of the neighborhood as undiverse; and by advocating a color-blind diversity policy, mixed-income housing.

Whom Diversity Includes

Leaders of progrowth groups went to great lengths to validate those who, in their view, belonged in a diverse community. The Builders Group, for example, regularly hosted networking events at the Taste of Peru and other local restaurants. These leaders would often recount their meaningful relationships with particular people of color and immigrants in the neighborhood. Often, these romanticized stories were about consumption of the arts and cultural activities—the wonderful service at a restaurant, say, or the great music at the local jazz festival. They framed diversity as a marketplace transaction, revering the novelty or excellence of the products and services as well as the open-minded cosmopolitanism of the patron.

The people they described as models of diversity were invariably civic minded, well presented, industrious, creative, or all of the above. Whenever I went out for lunch with Linda, a friendly white woman who was a vice president of a local bank and a Builders Group leader, we went to an Indian restaurant owned by one of her clients. She would always introduce me to the owner or rave about his family. At one luncheon, she was excited to tell me about a Latino family she was working with. They were poor—they lived in a basement apartment—but when the father decided to start a bicycle shop, the children, who were all in high school or college, donated their savings for his business. "Don't you love those stories?" she gushed.

White decision makers would often tell stories about witnessing or participating in delightful interactions involving people of color. In one issue of the Builders Group's glossy triannual newsletter, the column by the organization's president was titled "Diversity in Rogers Park: A Tale of Hope." In it, he described an experience in which he (white and middle-aged) jogged past two Mexican boys who had accidentally thrown a ball over a fence. He went back to help out, feeling that he "had abandoned the boys," and discovered that an African American family was helping the boys retrieve the ball. "I had witnessed a simple but uplifting example of community. People may do such deeds everywhere, but in Rogers Park our community has an additional element—our diversity. Irrespective of sexual orientation, ethnic background, tax bracket, or color, many incidents occur daily that demonstrate Rogers Park residents' commitment to our unique way of life."

Such portrayals of minority residents and stories of tolerant white people reinforced Rogers Park's identity as a unique model of diversity. They also presented the neighborhood's demographics as compatible with and even beneficial for economic growth. The "Tale of Hope," like the president's columns in all the other newsletter issues, was printed right next to blurbs on condominium conversions and new real estate construction.

On the one hand, the leaders of progrowth groups were quick to characterize the new residents as not just white people. In the Builders Group newsletter, a white developer described who was purchasing condominiums in the neighborhood: "The typical buyers are twenty-five to forty years old, single, professional. . . . Our clients are very diverse, multi-ethnic, and typically Lincoln Park or Lakeview refugees." On the other hand, they insisted that the neighborhood's diversity was inclusive of white residents, including the new, affluent condominium buyers. The Builders Group president's tale of hope conveyed the proper disposition that white people should have toward difference: open-mindedness and generosity. This and their many other depictions of Rogers Park residents suggested that white people have a place in diversity as both appreciators and participants. Marie, a white woman who worked for the Rogers Park Community Development Corporation, an arm of the community council, described the people who attended her organization's training sessions for first-time homeowners and condominium associations:

> The people individually are just wonderful. They really are marvelous folks moving into this community. Many of them had lived here years ago as a student . . . and they really liked the amenities of the community, and they really enjoyed the diversity of the community, and they're coming back for that.

The alderman and his allies made this formulation of the neighborhood's diversity part of their appeal to the new homebuyers. The new, predominantly white owners of high-end condominiums—some of which cost in the range of $300,000 or more—came with expectations of services and amenities, and many felt that the alderman and civic organizations should prioritize their desires. One way that decision makers tried to curry favor with newcomers was by suggesting that these newcomers, too, were valued community members. In an issue of the community council's newsletter, a white professional who was a board member published an article in which she noted that the neighborhood could be "overrun by yuppies." In the next newsletter, the editors published a letter from a new condominium owner who was upset with this statement:

> My wife and I are looking forward to becoming part of the community. We don't wish to be ostracized because of our age and professional status. My advice to you . . . is to welcome ALL members of the community and to NOT bite the hand that feeds you!!!

Alongside his letter, the organization published an apologetic reply by the board member: "Unfortunately, there are some groups in Rogers Park who do believe that gentrification and in-migration of professional households is a danger to Rogers Park's diverse population." Never challenging the letter writer's strong sense of entitlement, she encouraged the couple to get involved in the community council, block clubs, and other local activities:

> "Yuppies" are indeed welcome in Rogers Park because they have skills and energy to make our community a safer and better place to live and work. We should all remember what makes Rogers Park special—it is the mixture and celebration of diversity.

After the 2010 census came out, I had a conversation with Caroline from DevCorp North (which had since been renamed the Rogers Park Business Alliance). Reflecting on the previous decade, she joked, "At the very least, we're encouraging white people who like diversity to move to the neighborhood!"[28]

With such statements, their publicity of the neighborhood's emblem, their sponsorship of diversity murals, and many other activities, the alderman's office and his allies symbolically constructed the very personhood of a model Rogers Park resident: a tolerant member of any background committed to an egalitarian civic community. Such idealized residents are defined by their group membership in a racial group (and sometimes other demographic and social categories), their openness to diversity, and their creative or industrious attributes. They are respectable, civically engaged, and contributors to the public good. This construction of personhood is normatively classed, racialized, and defined by civic orientation. The ideal is not the public housing resident who plays her music loudly, the strident tenant activist who storms out of meetings, or the slumlord who leaves decaying buildings prone to drug dealers and fires.

In local political debates, some participants would mobilize the same ideas of diversity to chastise those who were prejudiced, racist, or classist. When the city announced a proposal to demolish a mall where Latino, African, and Asian vendors sold items like socks and CDs in order to build a much-needed firehouse, a heated community debate broke out over the fate of the site. On an active community LISTSERV, a white male leader of the Builders Group posted that he believed the mall should be demolished: "I'd love to have a place to shop in the neighborhood. I went into the mall once when it first opened. I felt like I was in a third world country." Another homeowner chimed in in favor of better fire services, noting that he paid "a ridiculously large amount of property taxes each and every year." He attributed crime and economic decline in the neighborhood to the people who worked in the mall, shopped there, and politically favored it: "It is the people who [are] crying foul who are forcing the entire community to remain down-trodden, accepting a life of pervasive crime, violent and sense-less gang activity, garbage covering everything, and most importantly, the inability to feel that your neighborhood is your home or that you are safe living there. And is not that most true of the demographic that is supposedly being 'championed' here?"

These sorts of comments infuriated other liberal residents, who wrote in defense of the mall or for an alternative, community-driven solution. A few appealed to the neighborhood's identity of diversity, particularly the norm among residents of appreciating diversity, while they charged their opponents with "classism" and "racism." An openly gay black man who later ran against Moore for alderman wrote:

> My neighbors, I write to you as one of many (A small minority? Are we a silent majority? Who knows?) Rogers Park residents who understand that diversity is an asset and that it makes us great. . . . I believe that there are a few out-of-touch-with-reality folk to whom it has not occurred that their views are extreme and in the minority. . . . Others and I have been concerned about, in reading on these virtual pages, more than one analysis of the issue that contains verbal assaults about immigrants, illegal aliens, and the third world. . . . Alas, I am not surprised. This is America. Institutional racism (and everyday, garden variety, individual bigotry) happens everyday, in every community. . . . Folks, we should forge ahead with debate on the pros and cons of community development proposals. However, we need to stick to the facts and consider their impact on individuals, families, and the community as a whole *without unnecessary and negative references* to the race, ethnicity, class, or culture of the particular individuals, families, or community involved.

Defenders of the mall also framed the mall merchants as model members of a diverse community, describing their "entrepreneurial spirit." Here, diversity rhetoric delineated the terms of acceptable debate in ways that policed or stigmatized boundary-heightening rhetoric and attitudes.

Such verbal sparring notwithstanding, the language of diversity did not provide much of a nuanced vocabulary for making sense of racial inequalities and antagonisms.[29] It was especially inadequate for discussing the existence and behavior of people of color and renters that those politically active white affluent homeowners found objectionable. Instead, such discussions were often couched in racially coded, stigmatizing terms. "Diversity" was far better suited for talking about the sorts of people and behaviors that local decision makers found acceptable.

The Rhetoric of Balanced Development and Affordable Housing

The alderman often repeated a boilerplate statement about the relationship between diversity and growth. One version was "In the face of . . . remarkable development, the census shows that we remain the most racially and economically diverse neighborhood in Chicago." Like the leaders of DevCorp North, the community council, and the Builders Group, he insisted that development was successfully happening and more was needed. But the alderman and his staff, more than the leaders of any of these other organizations, also acknowledged the negative effects of gentrification. During our interview, I asked him to talk about the major issue he confronted. He repeated another of his boilerplate statements:

> I view as the overarching issue, overarching reality that we're trying to preserve in this neighborhood, is its diversity—its racial diversity, its economic diversity. . . . We have development. How do we control that development and make sure that it occurs within the context of maintenance of diversity? So, that's *the* major challenge. Bottom line is my role and I think the role of most of the responsible community organizations in the neighborhood is to try to strike that balance.

Statements such as this one encapsulate the alderman's rhetoric of a unique, enlightened and kinder, gentler sort of community upgrading: balanced development. As he said at the State of Rogers Park event, the neighborhood remained diverse thanks to a local commitment to diversity and affordable housing. He acknowledged that the new condominiums and higher-end businesses posed a threat to diversity, although he downplayed the severity. For the alderman, "balanced development" was an alternative to both the extreme gentrification that some property owners hoped for and the low-road development that RPCAN deplored. DevCorp North was the other major advocate of balanced development in the neighborhood. The organization's mission statement, crafted under Caroline's leadership, stated:

> *Our vision* is to lead the way in showing the City of Chicago and the nation that balanced development is possible. Rogers Park will be the model for an advanced and sophisticated form of community development that *values* diversity, has defined it, planned for it and achieved development projects that serve all constituencies. (emphasis in original)

The alderman did not, in fact, have a specific strategy or protocol for achieving balanced development. His office made some modest efforts, usually under political pressure, to support low-income housing in the neighborhood. Moore was quick to say that his office had created and preserved a thousand affordable housing units, although this was an exaggeration. The alderman commonly took credit for development that he had not driven. Furthermore, affordable housing is not quite what it sounds. The federal government's definition of affordability, which local governments use, does not tie affordability to any particular income bracket. It defines housing as affordable if household members pay no more than 30% of their gross income toward direct housing costs. Under this definition, everyone needs affordable housing regardless of income.

Across the nation, public housing policy has made affordable home ownership a central focus. The city's major housing affordability program, the Chicago Partnership for Affordable Neighborhoods (CPAN), was a voluntary inclusionary zoning program. Developers and aldermen determine how many affordable units, if any, will be set aside in a market-rate development. The program is for home buyers who earned up to 100% of the area's median income (based on the wealthier Chicagoland region, not just the city). In 2004, a Chicago couple earning $60,300 could participate in CPAN. Under CPAN, Moore established that residential housing developers working in the ward had to set aside at least 10% of their units as affordable if they were developing buildings that required a change of zoning. In city council, Moore also voted for citywide inclusionary zoning, which requires large residential developments that involve city financing or property financial assistance to include some affordable units.

Housing programs of this sort have some important strengths. They provide moderate-income households the opportunity to build equity and enjoy the satisfactions of home ownership. They provide substantial incentives to developers, including waivers of the permit fees required for construction. They do not normally rile opponents of public housing. Unfortunately, they are an insufficient an answer to the low-income housing shortage. They are very small in scale, serve only those who are equipped to purchase a home, and depend on political officials' willingness to participate. As of 2006, Moore had overseen the creation of just nine CPAN units.[30]

For Moore, the political appeal of balanced development and affordable housing was more important than their implementation. This rhetoric enabled him to juggle his objective of encouraging profitable development and the normative pressures to nod to the value of diversity and community input. His rhetoric of balanced development portrayed his office, his allies, and civic-minded residents as effective stewards of the neighborhood's fate—motivated by tolerance, the civic good, and pragmatism.

DevCorp did in fact try to implement this notion of balanced development through some of its formal planning. When creating the 2006 Commercial Corridor Plan for Howard Street and Morse Street, the organization incorporated ideas of diversity and balance into its work by stressing the input of multiple stakeholders. With the University of Illinois and the Northeastern Illinois Planning Commission, DevCorp organized a twenty-member community steering committee composed of non–DevCorp North directors and members to identify community assets that could be built upon. It garnered input from the residents of Rogers Park and so-called community stakeholders by conducting interviews and surveys with 150-odd customers and residents and by organizing three community meetings, attended by almost 200 individuals. The goal was to solicit ideas and "create consensus around a shared vision for what the two commercial corridors could and should become."[31] The final recommendations in the written plan included goals to "celebrate the diversity of Rogers Park through a broad mix of businesses and services, varying in size and type and catering to a range of incomes, races and ethnicities" and "enhance the safety of the streets for everyone at all hours of the day through preventative and responsive measures."

Such statements and activities construed balanced development as the outcome of a cutting-edge, forward-thinking, and community-sensitive planning process. They minimized negative consequences of growth, focusing instead on the problems of a lack of growth—empty and unattractive shop fronts and stores that serve only poor people, especially. DevCorp's 2008 progress report highlighted the decrease in commercial vacancies and the new development around Morse and Howard, including improvement in "retail variety" on Morse, where a high-end bar, an upscale restaurant, and a new coffee shop had opened. It noted that "opportunities for youth on Howard" had improved but the number of workshops for adults needed to be expanded. With official documents such as the commercial corridor plan and community input meetings, the organization insinuated that it could be trusted to guide a special sort of development that was profitable for investors and also fostered diversity.

The Problem of North of Howard: The Antithesis of Diversity

Another way that progrowth decision makers delineated the terms of debate over development was by designating the North of Howard area undiverse. North of Howard is a nine-square-block area that includes the commercial strip on Howard and is somewhat cut off from the rest of the neighborhood, as it borders an Evanston cemetery to the north, a train yard to the west, and the lakefront to the east. Prior to the 1970s, it became known as Juneway Jungle because the bars attracted military members and party seekers from the suburbs.[32] This nickname took on racist connotations when poor African Americans and Latinos moved in. In 1970, in the census tract that primarily includes North of Howard, just 5.6% of the residents were black, another 3.3% identified as nonwhite, and 9.4% were Spanish-speaking.[33] By 1990, 51% were black and 34% reported Hispanic origins.[34] The poverty rate had nearly quadrupled to 27%. According to some activists, poor African Americans were discriminatorily steered to North of Howard after being displaced by urban renewal projects and public housing demolition. Many of the new low-income social service and low-income housing providers were located in North of Howard. In 2002, almost half of the units in the neighborhood with some kind of direct government subsidy were there. With youth gangs, a very active and visible illegal drug trade, high rates of crime, especially poor management of many buildings, and a commercial strip with liquor shops and empty storefronts, North of Howard anchored Rogers Park's bad reputation.

Developers aggressively targeted North of Howard for gentrification. As the Builders Group leadership saw it, Rogers Park could not gentrify if North of Howard did not, too. The organization commissioned a scoping study in 1998 that found that it was too dense and too poor and profiled the investment happening there in its newsletter. Condominium sales picked up pace in the late 1990s and early 2000s. In the census tract that included North of Howard and a few wealthy blocks on the lakefront, 11% of the rental units were removed from the rental market between 1996 and 2000.[35] The same census tract experienced a 25% increase in median household income between 1990 and 2000, which was by far the greatest increase in the neighborhood. However, developers wanted to see far more upscale redevelopment of that area, as did many new condo owners.

The alderman, his allies, and the Builders Group all depicted North of Howard as an aberration from the neighborhood's diversity. The Builders Group's scoping study characterized North of Howard as having "distinct demographics in terms of density and income levels as compared to other community areas near or adjacent to it."[36] The leaders of these various groups agreed that North of Howard was segregated. As a white woman active with the community council and community policing in North of Howard told a reporter, "Our ward brags about how heterogeneous it is, but what's happened is we've developed pockets that are culturally and economically segregated. . . . We have gangs you've never even heard of, one for each ethnic group."[37]

North of Howard, they said, was troubled by a disturbing concentration of poverty. The director of the Rogers Park Community Development Corporation, which was an arm of the community council, told me that low-income housing providers in the neighborhood had "created a concentration of low-income housing. . . . There was no balance at all in that community." The HUD liaison to the neighborhood explained for me the history of North of Howard: "The problem was, of course, the concentration of poverty." Often, people spoke of the area in other racially coded language, referring to "the Jungle," the overabundance of "Section 8," "problem renters," and, as did Renee at the affordable housing coalition meeting, criminal children.[38] Put this way, North of Howard was the antithesis of diversity and Rogers Park's civic culture.

While the alderman and his staff would allow that some affordable housing and affordable home ownership was necessary in North of Howard, Builders Group members took the position that North of Howard was not diverse enough. They would candidly claim that more condominium conversions and more middle-tier and high-end stores were needed. Mark, the president, told me in an interview, "I will view this community as having made progress when I could walk up Howard Street and enjoy it." I asked what that would mean. He said, "To enjoy it would mean that there is diversity, that I would want to take my daughter and not have to worry. I wouldn't have to park my car and leave my dog in it, just to make sure I don't get busted. That I don't see people hanging out in front of storefronts."

Stigmatizing North of Howard was central to the Builders Group's objectives of increasing property values and home sales and eliminating housing for poor people. As in the debates over the fire station, white affluent pro-growth leaders premised their agendas for change based on their desires, interests, and worldviews, which were biased in favor of similarly situated residents but not acknowledged as such. Good development was synonymous with development that satisfied their tastes.

These political leaders' terminology of affordable housing and concentrated poverty was not original. They were borrowing from the playbook of national and local public housing policy. The notion of "concentrated poverty" is derived from scholarship by the well-known sociologist William Julius Wilson and has been taken up by the government and policy analysts as a justification for the massive overhaul in public housing policy and demolition of public housing.[39] However, as critics observe, the notion is frequently stigmatizing and degrading.[40] It is grounded in the stereotype that poor people are pathological, and it is associated with black people.

Participants in Rogers Park housing politics advocated another policy option that was also directly from new public housing policy: mixed-income housing.

Diversity Goes Color-Blind

While the alderman, his allies, and the Builders Group rhetorically praised diversity of all sorts, when they spoke of *preserving* or *promoting* diversity, they usually spoke of housing. And when they got into the specifics of housing policy, diversity became color-blind. No longer did they speak explicitly of race. These leaders would only specify economic class—individuals' income range, individuals' status as renters or homeowners, or types of units (government subsidized, rentals, or owner occupied). They criticized low-income and subsidized housing, and they championed the new home buyers. Their discourse on economic diversity euphemized race with seemingly neutral but racially coded, pejorative language. Only political progressives in Rogers Park, some of them discussed below, emphasized the racial inequalities of condominium conversions and residents' housing status.

Thus diversity, when operationalized in housing politics and policy, became economic diversity, and the policy prescription du jour was "mixed-income" housing. This language and policy agenda echoed the mandate of the federal HOPE VI program, which was to deliberately encourage residents of different incomes and working statuses to live near one another. The reasoning was that income mixing can facilitate the upward mobility of poor people by encouraging them to interact with affluent, working neighbors.[41] Such mixing is meant to be an antidote to the concentration of poverty and other attendant ills of public housing: unemployment, crime, single motherhood, and drug abuse.

The rhetoric of economic diversity narrowed the political debate over redevelopment. With diversity as an ideal, concentrated poverty as the problem, and mixed-income housing as the stated policy objective, debates over redevelopment and diversity quickly turned into debates over the proper mix of different sorts of housing or units within a development. The Builders Group, alderman's office, and community council all called for mixed-income housing as a solution to North of Howard's troubles. Builders Group members drew on this rhetoric to lobby on behalf of affluent home buyers. Mark told me in the same interview, "The way to get to my vision of Howard Street . . . what I'm striving for—and I've told you this before—is a stable mixed-income community. Without a doubt in my mind, the way to obtain that is to bring more ownership into the community."

As Mark and others put it, low-cost housing interventions were *not* diverse and *not* conducive to market development. High-end development would actually enhance Rogers Park's economic diversity. Likewise, their message was that a model diverse community not only makes room for affluent white residents—it also conforms to their tastes and proclivities.

The rhetoric and strategies of these political players are elements of the neoliberal processes that are currently reshaping cities. Federal and local governments have been retreating from efforts to remedy problems of economic and racial inequality in cities. Urban political officials and the private sector have dismantled and privatized welfare provisions and promoted gentrification in ways that abet their political and economic goals, typically at the expense of poor people and people of color. In Rogers Park, a colorblind notion of diversity facilitated those neoliberal processes. Progrowth decision makers used this notion to justify the dismantling of subsidized housing and to rationalize very limited new programs of housing support for the middle class.

The politics of economic diversity allowed for dissent. Activists, progressives, and even the alderman invoked notions of economic diversity to advocate for low- and moderate-income housing. Again, the alderman politically needed to show some support for low-income housing, and this infuriated Builders Group members and more conservative participants in neighborhood politics, who believed the alderman caved in to tenant activists or was simply negligent and ineffectual. In turn, gentrification advocates were sometimes cornered into making a defensive argument about how low-cost housing fit into a mixed-income community undergoing rapid condo conversions.

By and large, the political objective and rhetoric of economic diversity buffered against outright racist antagonism while it papered over structural racism. It reinforced a progrowth agenda in which growth advocates' class- and race-biased interests and worldviews were the standard against which housing development should be judged. These dynamics played out in the protracted political conflicts over a few subsidized buildings in North of Howard.

Economic Diversity and the Fight over Subsidized Housing in North of Howard

One summer evening, twenty-one RPCAN housing activists gathered in the dining room of a soup kitchen to discuss the problems with two federally subsidized buildings up the street where most of them lived. The large room was sparse, with folding chairs and, at the other end of the room, a table piled with bags of bread, which a few people took at the end of the meeting. Almost all the attendees were African American mothers, and all had very low incomes. Some of the families had lived in the subsidized buildings since the 1970s. Like the other leaseholders, they paid $200 or less a month in rent. Some paid nothing at all.

The buildings were changing ownership, and everyone had to move. LaKisha introduced herself. "I'm stressed out," she said, frowning and scrunching her brow. Her building, called Juneway Commons, was slated to become affordable condominiums for middle-class buyers. These were the condominiums "constructed for people of all incomes" about which Alderman Moore had boasted in his State of Rogers Park speech. Nelly, a white woman with mental health problems, squirmed in her seat and echoed, "I'm stressed out!" The fate of her building, Jonquil Terrace, was unclear, but it had been slated to become a parking lot for the condominium owners. Patti, who lived in Juneway Commons, recalled what the alderman had recently told them:

> "You should be proud. Your building gonna be the first low-income housing condominium in Chicago, maybe in Illinois, maybe in the United States! The first low-income condominium for people who have been strugglin' and could never afford it. But you got thirty days to move. Make sure you hurry up and get out of here." This is how he came to us.

As the meeting wrapped up, another Juneway Commons resident remarked, "I know I couldn't afford no condo. It wouldn't be us." One of her neighbors added sarcastically, "Oh yeah, there's gonna be diversity."

In the 1990s, the buildings had been owned by Peoples Housing, a nonprofit low-income housing provider with a social justice mission. Between 1987 and 1995, the organization attracted at least $12.8 million in private investment through syndicated tax credits for North of Howard alone.[42] It had at least seventeen buildings, with thirteen in North of Howard. It proved to be a very poorly run organization. It could not sustain its pyramid financing structure. The buildings fell into disrepair. Dealers sold drugs out of some of them. Peoples Housing went bankrupt in the mid-1990s, and its buildings went into receivership. HUD took over Juneway Commons and Jonquil Terrace and kept them subsidized for a few years. Then, in the late 1990s, HUD announced it would sell the two buildings to the city. Alderman Moore, responsible for soliciting developers, had over-seen the plan to create the affordable condominiums and a parking lot (or else a community garden or children's play lot).

That Juneway Commons and Jonquil Terrace had been owned by Peoples Housing made the redevelopment of the buildings even more contentious. In the eyes of many political leaders, Peoples Housing represented some of the worst of low-income housing provision. Meanwhile, tenant activists saw the collapse of Peoples Housing as a tragic contribution to the dwindling supply of long-term low-cost housing. A number of the organization's other former buildings were being purchased by developers and converted into market-rate condominiums.

Normally, activists have little recourse when trying to stop a condominium conversion, but because the federal government owned Juneway Commons and Jonquil Terrace, some legal protections accompanied the ownership changes. That gave community activists legal leverage. RPCAN organized ten tenants as plaintiffs and, with the Legal Assistance Foundation of Chicago and other allies, filed a civil lawsuit to stop the sale. The suit charged that HUD was violating fair housing law. The activists had political leverage, too, because the alderman had a great deal of power in the sales. RPCAN activists and their allies proposed to the alderman that both buildings be made into low-income cooperatives, while other advocates in the community spoke out against the possible loss of green space.

Economic Diversity as Defense

By creating political turmoil over the buildings, the RPCAN activists put the alderman on the defensive. After much stalling, the alderman's office eventually settled on a compromise—what he and his staff called mixed-income housing—and defended that position in the name of economic diversity. He backed off of the plans to turn Jonquil Terrace into a parking lot. Because of a HUD decree pursuant to RPCAN's lawsuit, all units in that building would be for very low-income renters and protected by a twenty-year contract. The alderman brought in Chicago Metropolitan Housing

Development Corporation (CMHDC), an arm of the CHA that financed primarily low-income apartments, to rehabilitate the building into fifteen rental units. Priority would be given to existing residents.

The alderman did keep the plan to redevelop Juneway Commons—which would be renamed Vista North—into "affordable condominiums." The redevelopment was subsidized by a city government home owner-ship program related to CPAN, called New Homes for Chicago. The New Homes program reduced the purchase price of condominiums for first-time middle- and working-class home buyers. Between 1990 and the early 2000s, the program financed the construction of less than 550 homes citywide; among them were the twenty-one condos in Vista North and thirty con-dos in Birchwood Court, another former Peoples Housing building around the block. Residents displaced from either Jonquil Terrace or Juneway Commons could qualify for a Section 8 voucher.

In their public statements on the buildings, the alderman and his chief of staff spoke effusively of Vista North and Birchwood Court, while down-playing the CMHDC plans. They framed their involvement as a noble, pro-active defense of economic diversity. The alderman's chief of staff described for me the community deliberations over the fate of Juneway Commons: "A lot of people said, 'That building's a hellhole. We want you to take it down.'" I asked him who had said that. "Oh, it was a lot of, you know, up-per middle class who want to bring the neighborhood up. The other side was, 'We don't want to displace people.' Which was [our position], we don't want to displace people either. That would've been the least appealing of all the options, of course." He and the alderman characterized Vista North and Birchwood Court as for "the working poor" and "a way to maintain diversity and . . . still improve the neighborhood by giving those people an ownership stake."

As the alderman and his staff presented it, mixed-income housing policy altruistically helped deserving working-class residents, maintained balance, and protected economic diversity. By associating mixed-income housing with diversity, they imbued it with positive normative associations. The af-fordable condominiums were emblematic of selective inclusion in the com-munity; they were for the deserving poor and middle class and for the reified purposes of home ownership. The alderman defended his effort to put in a parking lot as an effort to look out for the working class. In a letter to the editor of a local paper, he quoted someone at a planning workshop who said, "'If yuppie condo owners can have off-street parking, why can't we?'"[43]

The technical design of the New Homes program lent legitimacy to the alderman's political claims of defending economic diversity. Moore wrote to the local paper that the new Vista North condominiums would be for families earning between $25,000 and $40,000 a year. He and others originally announced that the condo prices would range from $42,000 to $82,500 for Vista North and $54,000 to $109,000 for Birchwood Court. Such income requirements and price points make income mixing seem rigorously designed and real. Those criteria are symbolically significant, especially because the scale of the program is so small. They designate who matters for community diversity (working and middle-class homeowners) and the status basis of their inclusion (their income and home values). They reify homeowners as the valued class of residents.

With programs such as New Homes, early promises of local benefits and affordability can be misleading. Although the alderman claimed that "many, if not most, of those new homeowners will come from the immediate neighborhood," there were no mechanisms to ensure this. The final list prices turned out to be much higher than the prices initially announced, ranging from $109,000 to $139,000. After the subsidies, buyers paid between $60,000 and $119,000. Vista North and Birchwood Court were not accessible to most Rogers Park residents and certainly not to the buildings' former tenants. Moreover, the condos could be sold at market rate five years after purchase, making them a potential boon for individual buyers but not ensuring long-term affordability.

While the alderman's public position reinforced a political climate that validated tolerance and inclusion, it was a symbolic gesture, not a serious intervention into the housing market. Concessions to state affordable housing interventions such as this one actually legitimize the routine operation of capitalist housing markets by failing to take on the central dynamics of those markets. His list of over a thousand units of affordable housing that he had saved also left unnoted the fundamental market dynamics of the neighborhood: the high rate of renter-occupied units (which might scare off new home buyers) and the incomes of those buying market-rate condominiums or the price points of those condos (which would provide fodder to gentrification opponents). It was a political strategy that the alderman hoped would generate the cooperation of different constituents in the form of home purchases and would diffuse opposition from residents wary of gentrification. And race is, of course, made irrelevant by law. This sort of policy could not exist if it were based on race; it would be even more politically controversial and under most circumstances illegal.

Tragically, after the housing crash of 2008, the Vista North condos proved a burdensome liability for new owners, at least some of whom had tremendous difficulty selling them. Like so many of the condominium developments that took place during this rush-to-redevelopment period, there were fundamental problems with negligent management, the physical foundation, and the governance structure as well as the fallout of a housing market in which homebuyers were encouraged to take out mortgages they could not afford. Residents experienced problems of shoddy construction, a dysfunctional and apparently corrupt board, absentee condominium owners, and foreclosures.[44] Nearby crime and lack of parking remained major complaints as well.

But before that played out, the alderman's plans for the buildings remained controversial among progentrification constituents. The Builders Group wanted input but got involved late in the process. The two private developers that were rehabbing Vista North and Birchwood Court—respectively, Hispanic Housing and Chicago Equity Fund—both belonged to the Builders Group. Representatives from each were invited to speak at the Builders Group's monthly board meeting, after which the board voted unanimously in favor of the affordable condominium plans (it was a symbolic vote). Members said they were supportive because the developers had terrific reputations, and the condos would only be locked in as affordable for five years. To make a case against the Jonquil Terrace redevelopment, the organization's leadership drew upon the color-blind rhetoric of mixed-income housing and economic diversity as well as maps, market research, and social scientific authority that designated North of Howard as problematically homogeneous.

Disputing the Proper Economic Mix

On a windy weekday afternoon, I walked with Mark and a CMHDC official, Ricardo, from CMHDC's office to a classy restaurant in downtown Chicago. At the alderman's suggestion, the Builders Group had invited Ricardo and the alderman to speak at an upcoming board meeting. Mark wanted to get a better sense of CMHDC and hoped to convince the organization not to develop the Jonquil Terrace building into low-income rental units. As we approached the restaurant, he told Ricardo that the Builders Group was focusing on North of Howard because "that area has to be fixed up for the neighborhood to really thrive." When developers marketed high-end condominiums on the lakefront blocks, he said, they found that prospective buyers were turned off as soon as they saw Howard Street. Ricardo, a light-skinned Latino man, looked uninterested and slightly annoyed.

Over lunch, Mark quizzed Ricardo about Peoples Housing, proper management techniques, and how long he had "been here." He then pulled out a series of seven maps that the Builders Group had created to document former Peoples Housing buildings, other tax-credit housing, and project-based Section 8 buildings in North of Howard. That small area, Mark said, "is oversaturated" with low-income housing. He alternately appealed to the need for gentrification, the problem of concentrated poverty, and the importance that development be done by neighborhood insiders. Ricardo remained unmoved: "The tenants have been there for a long time. They should be able to stay in the community."

The following week, about fifty people, nearly all of them white men, gathered for the Builders Group's board meeting in the conference room of a branch of a national bank. As it unfolded, the theme of the meeting was a contest over the proper mix of housing in North of Howard—what was the proper mix of low-income and market-rate housing—and the definition of affordable housing, with each side marshaling maps and statistics to support its position. The Builders Group distributed packets that included the maps and an excerpt from the scoping study that began, "The North of Howard Neighborhood has distinct demographics in terms of density and income levels as compared to other community areas near or adjacent to it" as well as RPCAN's "Stop Condo Mania" flyer and an article about the buildings of interest written by the community council director, called "Building a Mixed Income Community."

Mark opened the meeting by saying that there was a lot of debate about the affordable housing in the neighborhood, noting RPCAN's claims that gentrification was displacing people. Mark said that the Builders Group had commissioned the scoping study and was creating the maps "to understand the facts about the situation because it gets so emotional."

Then Alderman Moore spoke in defense of the plans for Juneway Commons and Jonquil Terrace, framing them as a policy success he had orchestrated and a way to protect economic diversity:

> There is an overabundance of rentals and there has been a recent wave of condo conversions. . . . I have the goal of a stable, mixed-income community, so there should be ownership opportunities, too. But not everyone is able to become an owner, so we still need to have rental options. . . . [These buildings are] good for efforts to maintain economic diversity.

He passed around copies of a list of "affordable rental units lost" in North of Howard because of Vista North and the expansion of a local elementary school—a total of 139 units. Ricardo spoke next, describing his organization's deep pockets and reiterating, "We're not public housing." All the units in the building would be for very low-income renters.

Almost immediately, the Builders Group members, the alderman, and Ricardo got into a disagreement about how to define affordable housing, never coming to an agreement. The Builders Group members interrupted Ricardo, asking rapid-fire questions, and the alderman kept jumping in. The exchange centered on what should be the proper mix of types of housing and whether the fifteen units in CMHDC's building conformed. Brenda, a white Builders Group officer and private developer, told the alderman, "The Builders Group has always recognized the need for supporting mixed-income [housing]. But it also wants to diversify. There's already too much low-income housing there." Referring to the maps, Mark noted, "We're trying to figure out the real numbers, so we can understand if the 'great gentrifiers' are coming in."

The alderman got angry about one map that underestimated the number of market-rate units: "This [map] must include single family homes! You're screwing the numbers." Quiet laughter broke out in the back of the room. Brenda responded, "Builders Group has always recommended mixed-income. I don't want to see more housing tied up for twenty years!" The snickers grew louder. "Not *more*," the alderman replied. "This isn't new. This is just preserving fifteen units." Brenda snapped, "How can we expect to diversify if it's tied up for twenty years!" "Fifteen units!" exclaimed the exasperated alderman. "This week!" she shot back.

After the board meeting, some Builders Group members gathered at a nearby bar to debrief. They had a heated conversation about why low-income housing was so detrimental to North of Howard's economic mix. Carl, a white Builders Group officer and property developer, explained that it was not the number or percentage of low-income units that mattered. "The real issue," he announced, "is income." The others nodded over their drinks. Brenda asked the others, "How do we diversify economically?" Carl responded, with an eye toward me, "There's someone named . . . um, Julius Wilson William? He wrote about the importance of mixed-income neighborhoods, that people need to have other opportunities and a concentration of poor people is bad. He said that this shouldn't happen. I completely agree with that." The others nodded again.

In these disputes, the alderman, Mark, and these other political leaders appropriated Rogers Park's identity to make upscale development seem important and justifiable. They racialized and classed particular geographic areas and assigned different values to those areas and people within them. As they framed it, the strength of the neighborhood *writ large* was its colorful diversity (understood as including ample but not only white and middle-class homeowners). The problem was the aberration of North of Howard's homogeneity (described in color-blind rhetoric but understood as black, brown, and poor renters).[45] Subsidized housing such as CMHDC's project, progrowth leaders said, was an affront to the neighborhood's exemplary diversity. The terms of discourse—a debate over the proper economic mix—papered over inequality and flattened hierarchical power relations. The debate became a claims-making contest over who should belong in the mix.

Although Builders Group members did not succeed in stopping the plans for Jonquil Terrace, the organization was nonetheless engaged in a coordinated effort at a land grab in North of Howard.[46] That land grab was conveyed in terms of diversity and public housing policy priorities and legitimized with seemingly scientific authority. Mapping practices are exercises of power, not simply mirrors of social reality.[47] They are discursive objects that normalize social relationships according to the interests and worldviews of those who have resources to create them. Much like the criteria for the affordable condos, the maps operationalized diversity's meanings. They represented diversity as a principle that should exist on small scale in the housing market (a nine-square-block area) and defined diversity narrowly, in terms of income and housing status.

Although some community leaders who were openly hostile toward people of color, especially in their complaints about crime, the high-profile leaders did not normally disparage people of color in explicitly racial language. Instead, they criticized low-income and subsidized housing, or they championed the new home buyers. Overt racism was not acceptable. Classism was. Their discourse on economic diversity euphemized race with seemingly neutral but racially coded pejorative language.

As evident in the exchanges at the board meeting and the bar, Builders Group members appropriated ideas from federal policy to disparage remedial government and private intervention targeted to poor people. For these members, the incorporation of poor people in North of Howard was an affront to market-rate redevelopment. Government intervention on behalf of poor renters was distorting the workings of the free market. Even Ricardo distanced his organization's work from public housing.

The alderman's concession to the redevelopment of one building with low-cost rental units was a major victory for the tenant activists and of great importance to the tenants who lived there. His support for mixed-income housing affirmed the legitimacy of inclusiveness in the community. But in the scheme of neighborhood gentrification, it was tokenistic. Indeed, this concession and the new affordable condos the alderman preferred to speak of reified capitalist housing markets by leaving them largely unquestioned and focusing instead on the small-scale incorporation of groups deemed marginal—namely, low- and middle-income home buyers.

Because RPCAN activists were involved, the contests over Juneway Commons and Jonquil Terrace were not resolved entirely in the favor of developers. The activists kept the issue controversial and were able to take advantage of the legal protections that accompany government-subsidized low-cost housing, even as that very housing was being dismantled. To do this work and voice their dissent, the activists tried to subvert and reframe the debate over gentrification.

Progressive Activists Talk Back

According to the two tenant activist organizations in Rogers Park, RPCAN and the Section 8 Tenants Council, ongoing redevelopment was unjust: it was pricing out the neighborhood's low- and moderate-income, dispropor-tionately black and Latino renters, and creating ever more burdens and in-securities in those residents' lives. The leaders of those two organizations believed that redevelopment, left unchecked as it was, would altogether transform the neighborhood into an enclave for affluent, mostly white homeowners. Yet these were two different sorts of organizations, with some-what different bases of power, objectives, and rhetoric.

RPCAN: "Diversity without Displacement"

On a hot, overcast summer morning, a dozen members of the Rogers Park Community Action Network gathered in front of a large red brick build-ing on a street corner in North of Howard to protest. RPCAN leaders had chosen this spot as paradigmatic of condo mania. With the city's assistance, the building, once owned by Peoples Housing, was sold to a well-known for-profit developer who was converting the apartments into luxury con-dominiums. As potential condo buyers trudged past the protesters for a re-altor's open house, the activists—most middle aged and white or African American—chanted, "One, two, three, four, diversity's worth fighting for! Five, six, seven, eight, mix us in, it's not too late!" A white activist initiated a call and response: "I don't know but I've been told, lots of buildings being sold. Condos may look kind of nice, but we cannot afford that price." A few African American women paused to swap stories about the problems they faced with rising rents and landlord discrimination, one of them speaking to a documentary filmmaker holding a large camera. The other activists kept marching and chanting: "Diversity is under attack. What do we do? Stand up! Fight back!"

RPCAN was a multi-issue, multiracial group that organized tenants and pressured political officials to preserve low-cost housing. Following in a thirty-year history of tenant organizing in the neighborhood, RPCAN activists had the formidable task of intervening in local growth politics. This included the challenge of persuading other Rogers Park residents that they should be wary of, not thankful for, redevelopment projects like this condominium building, despite the decades-long economic troubles of the area. With just a few full-time staff members at most, the organization's mostly white but racially and economically mixed leadership also had the challenge of building bridges across the organization's 250-odd members, who came from all walks of life but tended to be female, low income, and African American.

The organization managed these challenges and pursued its goals by framing diversity as a social justice mandate: an objective in the battle against racial and economic injustice.[48] Diversity, they argued, was in danger, and they, not politicians or developers, were its genuine defenders. The organization's T-shirt had the slogan "Diversity/Affordability" on the front, with an image of different types of people holding hands, their fists raised in a triumphant pose (see fig. 5.1). On the back, the T-shirt read: "Join the campaign for Diversity, Affordability & Justice."

RPCAN activists' version of diversity conveyed their understanding of race and class as intersecting group statuses defined, foremost, by structural conditions that put unfair burdens on marginalized groups.[49] As Bill, the white man who was executive director of the organization, wrote in an "action alert" e-mail sent a few weeks after that Saturday protest: "Nearly everyone being displaced in all these condo projects are people of color. The people making the decisions and making money out of the deals are almost all white." For RPCAN, race was not simply a cultural attribute expressed in interesting social interactions (and certainly not an appropriate grounds for accusing young black men of being criminals), as progrowth groups so often suggested.

Through its claims about diversity being at risk, RPCAN contested decision makers' praise of economic progress. They also cast doubts on the romanticized popular image of the neighborhood, which denied racism and hierarchy. As these activists saw it, preserving diversity required government policies that proactively protected low-income housing.

5.1. Rogers Park Community Action Network T-shirt. *Source*: Photo by author

To make these claims, RPCAN activists needed to debunk the rhetoric favored by the alderman and his allies. At one RPCAN meeting, activists from
a few local groups discussed their plans for an upcoming RPCAN-led march,
debating for at least half an hour whether they should invite the alderman
to speak. Frank, a white RPCAN board member, made a prediction about
the alderman: "He'll get up there and say, 'I support diversity.' And someone
will say, 'Why didn't you support . . . ?'" Frank implied there was a litany
of diversity-related projects that the alderman had not backed. Later in the
meeting, Frank waved his arms dramatically and exclaimed, "Look at diversity on his projects. His committees don't look like the neighborhood. The
most diverse neighborhood in Chicago?! Not even cosmetic! Like the Morse
Street Task Force. It's all wealthy white people except [an African American

woman] who used to work for him, and a Latino business owner." The other activists at the meeting rolled their eyes and grimaced in agreement.

Through such use of street-level semiotics, RPCAN activists claimed that local decision makers' talk of diversity hid malicious motives and favoritism for affluent residents and for-profit developers. With such critiques, they portrayed their opponents as untrustworthy and themselves as savvy political operators. The organization's leaders trained members to do the same. At its many workshops and training sessions, RPCAN politicized participants by teaching them skills of critical analysis and encouraging open, critical discussion.[50] At one workshop in a series on Development and Diversity, Bill began by asking attendees to brainstorm their personal definitions of *diversity*. Building on this exercise, he shifted the conversation to the best balance between home ownership and rental units. As the workshop progressed, some participants began to pose critical comments and questions about diversity. A white man asked, "We can take a position to maintain our current diversity. Or is diversity something you're working for?" An elderly white man remarked, "Diversity may not always be the goal. Inclusiveness . . . may be."

Thus, just as the alderman and his allies invoked diversity and balanced development as rhetorical coverage for inaction and biases, their detractors invoked the same notions as a standard of evaluation. RPCAN and critics throughout the neighborhood referenced diversity and balanced development as their barometers of credible political action, whether they were charging the alderman with hypocrisy or accusing DevCorp North of overlooking local talent when it commissioned artists from outside the neighborhood to paint a blocks-long mural.[51]

As the case of RPCAN demonstrates, some challenger activists may find the term *diversity* helpful for communicating their political platforms. To keep diversity from becoming a liability, as was Ben's experience in the coalition meeting, these activists denounced their opponents for using the term and reclaimed it. But engaging in street-level semiotics is not always easy or desirable. Sociologist Kristina Smock observes that discussions such as the one at the diversity and development workshop depend on "a culture of interaction rooted in a middle class tradition of individualism that assumes a certain level of cultural capital."[52] Middle-class, white, and well-educated activists may be more willing to take on the post–civil rights politics of diversity this way than would their less advantaged counterparts, and they may find it easier to do so. In other words, there is a class bias not only in decision makers' push for diversity but also in the work of *challenging* those diversity efforts.

This is not to say that low-income and minority individuals and those with less formal education are incapable of participating in critical discussions of diversity. Rather, for those individuals, workshops about words can seem like a diversion from their pressing basic needs. That much was true for Georgia, an African American RPCAN activist and member of the Section 8 Tenants Council. When Georgia sat in on a meeting of the steering committee for the development and diversity workshop, she raised objections to their goals. Looking at everyone around the table through her oversized glasses, she proclaimed: "We've been talking about diversity for a long time in Rogers Park and across Chicago. Trying to get people to come in and talk about their ideas—it will be hard. . . . How are we going to keep people here? How [are] we going to teach people to keep fighting?!" No one responded. She and another Section 8 activist soon left and did not participate in subsequent planning meetings or the workshops.

The Section 8 Tenants Council: "We Have to Fight for Our Rights!"

Tenants rights were one of RPCAN's core causes, but they were *the* cause pursued by the Section 8 Tenants Council. The Section 8 Tenants Council represented residents in Rogers Park who had government-subsidized vouchers. In 2002, those residents lived in 3.7% of the neighborhood's renter-occupied housing units.[53] Like the majority of voucher holders, most members of the Section 8 Tenants Council were African American and poor.[54]

RPCAN had convened a Section 8 committee in the late 1990s. A few years later, the committee split off from RPCAN following a funder's requirement that they have their own separate 501c(3) nonprofit organization in order to receive a grant, but it maintained ties with RPCAN. The Section 8 Tenants Council leaders worked to educate themselves and other voucher holders about their legal rights. In Chicago, landlords cannot legally refuse vouchers for a qualifying apartment. This is because the Chicago Fair Housing Ordinance and the Cook County Human Rights Ordinance prohibit landlord discrimination on the basis of source of income, in addition to local, state, and federal prohibitions on discrimination against people based on their race, sex, and other protected classes.

The Section 8 activists almost never spoke of diversity. Instead, they framed their objectives as a fight for legal rights, affordable housing, and tenant empowerment. They drew on an ideology of group-based civil rights. This was evident at a large community forum that the council hosted in 2002 with CHAC, Inc., the private agency that administered the voucher program. Approximately seventy-five people attended, sitting on old folding chairs and mingling over coffee in the cavernous meeting hall of a Rogers Park church. Most were African American. About a third had vouchers, and another third were on the voucher waiting list.

Ruby, an outspoken African American woman who was the president of the Section 8 council and an RPCAN board member, opened the event. She began with a poignant story about trying to find a new apartment after she learned that her building was being converted into condominiums:

> I looked all around the neighborhood for a building that looked good, but . . . they were going condo. To make things worse, the landlord told me, "Oh, we don't take Section 8." And I was stuck. Then one day, I got a flyer from RPCAN—Rogers Park Community Action Network—about a workshop. When I went to the workshop, I learned that I was being discriminated against and didn't know it. When I heard the stories of other tenants, I knew it was happening to all the Section 8 tenants and all the Section 8 tenants would need to get together to fight back.

Ruby urged the audience members to join the Section 8 council and RPCAN—in the fight for their rights. "I ask you today if you'll come together with us and we can fight and win. . . . We will not be displaced! We have a right to be here just like anyone else!" While the CHAC administrators watched attentively from the sidelines, the audience cheered.

Not one of the many Section 8 activists and audience members who spoke at that CHAC forum mentioned diversity. In fact, never in my two years of on-the-ground research studying this group of Section 8 activists— first as an RPCAN committee, then as a separate organization—did I hear these activists describe their organization's goals in terms of diversity. Although they often wore RPCAN T-shirts and participated in RPCAN chants, they did not characterize the neighborhood as a model community. Georgia's interjection at the meeting about the diversity and development workshop was one of the few moments in which I heard a Section 8 activist criticize anything about diversity discourse. Likewise, during the many private conversations I had with the Section 8 activists about their political values, personal struggles, and perceptions of the neighborhood, only one of them (also an RPCAN activist) discussed her love of Rogers Park's diversity.

Conceivably, the Section 8 activists could have claimed that voucher holders were a critical stripe in Rogers Park's rainbow. Instead, they spoke of themselves as voucher holders, renters, black, and disabled, all of which are group identities upon which they could make rights-based claims. The activists' understanding of race rested on a vision of personhood in which individuals are rights-bearing citizens, not model diverse residents.

The activists' focus on rights makes sense in a pluralist political system predicated on the distribution of rights and responsibilities to discernible, competing interest groups.[55] Such a focus was strategic, given their organization's single-issue agenda and its narrowly defined constituency. The discourse on rights served as a savvy means of reaching voucher holders because it appealed to voucher holders' basic needs and referenced a mechanism that potentially could be used to solve their housing problems. The Section 8 council faced many obstacles to organizing voucher holders, who are very disadvantaged and face numerous constraints and stresses in their daily lives, from physical disabilities to a lack of transportation. Voucher holders are also dispersed throughout a city or region. A premise of the program is that voucher holders can live anywhere in the city and blend into a community, avoiding the stigma and segregation of public housing.

The notion of rights also gave meaning to and defined the Section 8 council's cause. It designated the issues to care about, the reasons to act, the types of people who should act, and the appropriate strategies for social change. On numerous occasions, I witnessed new members of the Section 8 council start to speak of their housing troubles in terms of rights. The idea of rights resonated with the activists so much so that they often claimed a right to housing as poor people, even though law provides no protection against most economic discrimination.[56]

The Section 8 activists' orientation to rights follows from the historical legacy of African American activism in the United States. Much of the fight for black equality has been a struggle for equal rights under law. Legal rights are one of the few powerful mechanisms by which disadvantaged minority groups can collectively exercise power in capitalist housing markets, as long as they know their rights and have access to law. National legislation and local ordinances enable individuals to file legal complaints of housing discrimination. Such litigation can be burdensome and stressful for those who pursue it, who have slim chances of winning. Nonetheless, *Gautreaux* and other class action suits have successfully challenged public housing segregation and the denial of credit for residents in black neighborhoods.[57]

Few Section 8 activists ever filed a lawsuit charging discrimination in housing, but as law and society scholars would say, these activists mobilized rights in other ways.[58] They took the pragmatic steps of educating themselves and other renters about their rights. They found inspiration in the knowledge that they had such rights and in their ability to name unfair treatment as discrimination. At the CHAC forum, Ruby described the empowerment she felt by learning about her rights. As they pressured CHAC and landlords to act in their interest, these activists publicized that they *knew* their rights.

The Section 8 activists were far outside the neighborhood debates over redevelopment. In part, this was because of their internal problems. The council foundered after it split from RPCAN, mired in infighting. Even under the best of circumstances, though, its goals were difficult to pursue, as urban politics do not prioritize rights-based protections and often violate them. The council leaders pressed CHAC to be more responsive to voucher holders' needs. But they could not be too confrontational because they depended on CHAC to gain access to their constituents' mailing addresses. The activists' distance from the heart of local politics, however, did not stop the alderman from enlisting them as token supporters to publicize his sensitivity toward diverse neighborhood constituents. He secured Ruby's endorsement for reelection (according to one RPCAN leader, he did so by giving the Section 8 council a free printer). His campaign mailer included a photograph of him with Ruby. As a civically engaged, smart, well-spoken low-income black woman (and with a visible disability, supported by a cane), she embodied an archetype of diversity that Moore could appropriate.

The fact that *diversity* was not in the Section 8 activists' vocabulary is instructive for understanding the racial and class biases of neighborhood politics in the post–civil rights period. Very low-income, predominantly African American renters were clearly marginalized from the local politics of redevelopment. A neighborhood identity or community value of diversity fails to fully represent their priority. When race and redevelopment are framed in terms of diversity, the issue of discrimination quickly becomes invisible.[59] Calls for diversity may fail to speak to the narrow class interests of marginalized groups, their political goals, or their spirit of racial and class solidarity.

In the years following this study, the tenant activists suffered political setbacks. RPCAN faltered, hampered by internal problems and lack of funding, and then joined with a similar organization to form Northside Action for Justice, which spanned more neighborhoods. Because of infighting, the Section 8 Tenants Council split into two smaller organizations, one of which then went defunct.

The Symbolic Politics of Racial Progress in Neighborhood Life

The Rogers Park case illustrates another variation in how the drive for diversity relates to the civil rights movement's early aims. In this case, the outcome is indeterminate and contradictory. *Diversity* is appropriated by political officials and developers to drive out long-term, low-income residents from prime real estate. At the same time, it has social justice–grassroots connotations that never totally disappear, especially as connected to affordable housing and the arts. The neighborhood's vibrant civic politics create some opportunities for marginalized groups to exercise power, but these are loudest-voice-wins politics, which works against those very groups. With the loss of low-cost housing and escalating inequality, people of color, poor people, and immigrants are ever less likely to be politically engaged.

In debates over low-income housing and high-end condominiums, neighborhood leaders' symbolic politics of racial progress centered on low-stakes cultural affirmation and concept building of mutual obligations. These politics animated leaders' pursuit of a top-down, color-blind agenda of economic growth conducive to prodevelopment interests. Such politics legitimated the involvement of some members of the neighborhood polity—those who fit acceptable archetypes of diversity as minority groups with an inoffensive culture to share, homeowners of different economic brackets, open-minded white young professionals, and eclectic types. They were made to seem more scientific through the authority of statistics, mapping, and neoliberal government housing policy.

Decision makers' agenda for diversity was selectively inclusive. For developers, diversity was acceptable so long as it was superficial and culturally pleasing, and therein compatible with consumerism and market capitalism. For them, diversity needed to prioritize affluent homeowners. The alderman posed diversity similarly but paid more lip service to the needs of poor people and, under pressure, conceded to remedial state intervention. The fundamental workings of housing markets—the largely unchecked profitable land development—stayed in place. These political actors' drive for diversity left unquestioned the hegemony of for-profit urban growth and the American dream of home ownership. But neighborhood diversity politics enabled contestation against those priorities. As decision makers in Rogers Park pushed a progrowth agenda, there was push back from civic activists who understood community input and the political and economic representation of poor people and people of color as crucial elements of a community progress.

All told, the push for diversity in Rogers Park was a politicized contest with odds in favor of developers but subject to housing markets and political dissent. At stake, then and now, is whether race-class integration will continue to be biased toward selective inclusion and consumer choice at the top of the class hierarchy or can be broad-based incorporation that also attends to the needs of the most disadvantaged residents.

PART THREE

Human Resource Management in Starr Corporation

SIX

"Diversity Is a Strength of Starr Corporation"

The ballroom filled with three hundred female executives, senior managers, and professionals—the most powerful women in Starr Corporation's US offices—buzzed as if a rock star were about to appear. The women were gathered for Starr's Women's Summit, a two-day conference in a ritzy suburban hotel. Plush red and gold carpet lay beneath their feet. Ornamental chandeliers hung above their heads. When Ron, the company's CEO, finally walked on stage for his headlining presentation, the attendees jumped up from their cushioned seats and clapped enthusiastically. Iva, an Asian American senior vice president, introduced him, noting his business degree from an elite university and his twenty-eight years with the company. She was cheerful and confident: "Ron is a huge proponent of diversity. Yes, gender diversity. Yes, ethnic diversity. . . . It's about experiential diversity. It's about style diversity. It's about thought diversity."

Ron, a white middle-aged man with a reputation for being demanding and aloof, remarked that it had been "a very exciting week." He had just been to Washington, DC, for US president George W. Bush's signing of the Central American Free Trade Agreement, which Starr supported. The audience cheered. Then he turned to the topic of diversity management: "Iva actually stole some of my thoughts. I take a very broad view of diversity." He recounted growing up in different parts of the world. He spent his early years in California, "which was very open, lots of Asians. I lived in Berkeley in 1967." Someone in the audience called out, "The summer of love!" From there, he had moved to racially segregated Tennessee. "When did the Voting Rights bill pass?" A few people responded, "1964!" "Right. This was 1967. They still had white and colored signs in restaurants." After that, he lived in Zurich and Paris and then different major US cities. He commented on how this background had influenced his understanding of diversity:

> My view of diversity has been shaped by this. It is gender. It is race. It is any overt culture or nationality. It's as much educational background. I got concerned that Starr was taking too many students from [a nearby university]. Nothing against that university, but you need different perspectives. . . . Style—I think that's the most important.

Ron went on to make the business case for diversity: "Sure, diversity is good for business. Importantly, we're a consumer goods company. So we need to reflect the consumers we sell to." He outlined strategies for transforming the company through diversity management: "We need to avoid stereotypes about leadership styles. We want diverse styles. The diversity of styles is what allows the diversity of thought to occur." Later, referring to a PowerPoint slide behind him, he spoke about the composition of his executive team: "We're four women out of 14. If you want to know, I think that's not enough. . . . We only have one non-American and also one person of color. We don't have enough." A question and answer session followed. He left the stage to a standing ovation.

Fifty years earlier, there was no such thing as a women's summit. No one made any such mention of "diversity," be it of gender, race, style, or level of education. In 1960, white men held nearly all of the company's managerial positions and made up the vast majority of its employees overall, and company leaders treated this as entirely appropriate. The company's leaders showed absolutely no interest in increasing the numeric representation of people of color and women in management. Nothing about inclusion was part of the company's public image. By 2005, people of color and white women had made considerable headway into all tiers of the workforce. In the intervening years, Starr adopted the goal of hiring substantial numbers people of color and women and easing their social integration into a corporate workplace. The company needed to indicate its compliance with federal antidiscrimination law and industry trends and appeal to these so-called diverse employees, but without turning off investors or unduly aggravating the majority-white male workforce.

The push for diversity at Starr, in name, dates specifically to the early 1990s. It was a top-down managerial move to demonstrate concern for the representation of employees of color and female employees. A key component of that move was executives' construction of the company's identity:

a profitable corporate titan that proactively made diversity a strength of its workforce, products, and production processes. That identity defined diversity ambiguously but associated it with people of color and framed diversity management as not only a nondiscrimination intervention but also conducive to the company's core objective of profit making.

This chapter introduces the company and explains the importance of employment decisions such as hiring and firing, corporate politics of diversity management, and market dynamics of shareholder capitalism. It details Starr's contemporary identity as a corporate supporter of diversity and tracks the historical evolution of that identity and diversity programming at the company over three points of time, starting in 1973. That history illustrates how decision makers drew on the discourse and social relations of diversity to symbolically expand the boundaries of the business class. In some very modest respects, their diversity efforts also helped to break glass ceilings and create greater access to positions of economic power and authority, which have been so completely monopolized by white men.

To tell Starr's history, the chapter draws heavily on the research of Frank Dobbin, Alexandra Kalev, Lauren Edelman, and their collaborators. This body of neoinstitutionalist scholarship identifies the organizational, legal, and professional motivations that drove the nationwide creation of diversity management in the 1980s and 1990s.[1] It captures the influence of human resource professionals as an occupational group (influence that is not detectable in the available historical sources on Starr) and industry-wide trends (which are beyond the bounds of a single case study).

What this and the following chapter add to that scholarship is a contextualized explanation of the implementation of diversity management. It explains how industry-wide notions and practices of diversity were incorporated into everyday organizational practices, in relation to the on-the-ground power plays of managerial authority and the workplace pressures of neoliberal capitalism. The analysis is in step with the current revival of organizational ethnographies that investigate how organizational participants draw on discourse and construct appropriate lines of action as they make sense of and negotiate the official rules, normative concerns, and pragmatic demands that govern their activities.[2] Of the many insights gained by looking at diversity management in its everyday context, one is especially significant: the push for diversity at Starr reinforced the class-stratified division of labor. Diversity personnel drew on ideas of diversity in an effort to support people of color and women—but only those at the top of the class hierarchy.

Welcome to the Company

Starr is a multinational public company that produces consumer goods. In 2005, it was one of the largest companies in its industry in the world, with annual revenue of $35 billion. It employed approximately 100,000 people in more than 80 countries and sold products in 140 countries. Its products are widely available, and its brands are well known. The company had multiple headquarters. The global headquarters is a four-story sprawling office complex on a manicured suburban campus surrounded by a small lake, trees, and a large parking lot.

In 2004, Starr had approximately fifty thousand US employees. About 33% of those employees were exempt—meaning they received annual salaries over $23,600 (in 2005), were neither unionized nor paid hourly, and had administrative, professional, managerial, or executive responsibilities.[3] This study is of exempt employees (whom I alternately refer to as business professionals and businesspeople). Another 30% of Starr's US employees were unionized. The rest were nonunionized and paid hourly.

Starr's overall US workforce was 26% people of color and 36% women.[4] As a point of contrast, the overall US labor force around this time was 30% people of color and 46% women.[5] People of color and women were represented in the top third of Starr's workforce as well. Of the company's exempt employees, 17% were people of color and 25% were women. One (7%) of the fourteen members of the senior executive team was a person of color, and four (29%) were women; these figures approximated the average representation of women in top executive positions nationwide and were higher than average among Fortune 500 companies.[6]

"Large." "Bureaucratic." "Slow to change." "Great for career development." "Good pay." "Lots of talent here." "No work/life balance." "Fun environment, but you have to run hard." "It's corporate America." This was how the company's business professionals commonly described the culture of the company in interviews and on popular career websites such as Glassdoor.com. Jobs at Starr were in high demand, and the company hired people out of top business schools and universities. Exempt employees often spent long careers at the company. The compensation was very competitive and benefits good. One major business publication deemed Starr excellent at facilitating businesspeople's career progression.

However, the company was not ranked among *Fortune*'s hundred best companies to work for, and in the late 2000s, it received low marks in other external ratings of good employers.[7] In the corporate headquarters, the workplace environment was fairly formal, intense, and political. There, business professionals were routinely expected to work ten to twelve hours a day. Many employees considered Starr a ruthless employer because of the overwhelming demands on their time and foremost priority of increasing shareholder value.

Hiring and Firing Matter

Whether someone is employed or not and the types of jobs people hold are vital for their basic financial stability and sustenance, health, relationships, and emotional well-being. In the contemporary United States, people need to be included in the mainstream economy to fully participate in society.[8] The incorporation of people of color into predominantly white workplaces hinges on how employers recruit, select, train, assess, and treat employees—in other words, on their employment decision making and other human resources practices. HR management matters for the representation and integration of white women and other minorities in the workplace as well. Decisions such as hiring and firing fundamentally determine who works in an organization and their positions.

Workplaces are rife with racial and gender inequality. Foremost, there are extensive disparities in the types of jobs people hold.[9] Prior to the passage of the Civil Rights Act of 1964, employers in the United States could legally discriminate against applicants and employees based on their race, color, religion, national origin, and sex. People of color and white women had minimal or no access to well-paid, stable, upper-level jobs or (especially for people of color) employment in powerful organizations.[10] Title VII of the Civil Rights Act prohibited such discrimination. Since the mid-1960s, people of color and white women across the country, abetted by civil rights activists pushing for workplace integration and pragmatic government bureaucrats, have advanced into craft, managerial, and professional positions.[11] Yet these groups remain underrepresented (sometimes shockingly so) in comparison to their white male counterparts.[12] Such trends are not solely the outcome of unequal schooling or inequality in society at large. Employers' practices actually generate and sustain inequality.[13] People of color and white women are tracked into positions with lower pay, lower status, and less autonomy. Their jobs are less secure. They receive less respect at work.[14] They also encounter glass ceilings: artificial, discriminatory barriers that keep them from advancing into the highest levels within the organization.[15] Those people of color and women who reach the status of executive or professional still find that they do not have the same informal social power that their white male counterparts enjoy.[16] For instance, their

colleagues do not necessarily presume that they are competent. These disparities are overlaid by inequalities of class as well as sexual orientation, age,
disability, weight, and other status distinctions.

Many racial inequalities in the workplace are visibly obvious. We can
observe who serves coffee in a restaurant and who supervises that waitress.
Employers commonly leave those inequalities unacknowledged. Worse yet,
employers make them seem valid.[17] For example, popular recruitment and
screening methods, such as finding new employees through current employees' personal networks, appear neutral and reasonable but actually disadvantage racial minorities.[18]

Race, Gender, and Diversity Management

Diversity management is one of many possible responses to racial and gender disparities in the workplace. It consists of identity-conscious personnel
policies, offices, programs, and initiatives such as training, mission statements, and task forces that personnel professionals characterize as relevant
to diversity.[19] Diversity management strategies vary widely. They might include targeted recruitment at career fairs, work/life balance programs such
as flexible work hours, measures to ensure pay equity, and performance
bonuses. The impulse of diversity management is to make workplaces
more egalitarian, especially for racial minorities and women—to minimize
the boundary-heightening tendencies of so much organizational activity,
particularly employment decisions.[20] Melissa, the cool-tempered African
American woman who was Starr's director of diversity, summed up the
goal of diversity management as "helping this organization become more
inclusive."

In 1998, 75% of Fortune 500 companies reported having a diversity
program, Starr included.[21] In 2008, a survey of eighty-nine companies with
more than ten thousand employees found that only 11% did not have a diversity management strategy.[22] Starr was among those few medium and large
private employers—11% nationwide—that had the most effective forms of
diversity management: offices and staff positions that oversee diversity management, affirmative action, or equal employment opportunity.[23]

There are many obstacles to making workplaces equal. Fundamentally,
those in management, who are more likely than not white and male, do not
have an interest in dramatically overhauling employment practices to better accommodate underrepresented employees. A racialized and gendered
workplace hierarchy works in many ways to their advantage. In addition,
inertia is powerful. Established routines and corporate culture are difficult

to change. There is more interpersonal tension and conflict in a heterogeneous workforce, which management might like to avoid. Many employees, most evidently white men, are resentful of identity-conscious interventions that they (inaccurately) believe unfairly deprive them of jobs, resources, and advancement opportunities. "I did not get that job because of a black man," is a common refrain—an expression of what critical sociologists identify as color-blind racism.[24]

Those who wish to create organizational change do not have many effective legal or HR tools. Title VII and subsequent civil rights legislation forbid employers from discriminating based on race, sex, age, disability, and a few other protected statuses. Those protections have helped to eliminate some of the most egregious discrimination. Nonetheless, enforcement is weak, discrimination persists, and many of the harms that employees experience at work are not legally prohibited.[25] Pursuing litigation places tremendous burdens on employees who believe that they have experienced discrimination.[26]

The creation of government-regulated affirmative action programs in the late 1960s and early 1970s was, at the time, a major intervention. It called attention to the white prejudices and institutional biases that thwart racial minority mobility. Such programs can effectively move racial minorities and women into management.[27] Many analysts attribute the significant increase in black employment in middle- and upper-tier jobs in the 1970s and 1980s directly to affirmative action.[28] However, those programs have been politically attacked since their inception. Enforcement is underfunded and anemic, and black progress has stalled since the 1980s. Likewise, both litigation and affirmative action fail to address the ubiquitous problems that legal scholar Susan Sturm calls second-generation employment discrimination: discrimination that takes place in subtle, implicit, and nondeliberate ways.[29] And none of these interventions, diversity management included, recognizes class and economic inequality as workplace obstacles.

Diversity management interventions, like civil rights protections and affirmative action programs, are addenda to the overwhelming inegalitarian structure of employment decisions. Many diversity interventions—including the most popular one, diversity training—are ineffective or untested. Nonetheless, a subset of these interventions has been proven to make workplaces more equitable.[30] Diversity task forces and offices, mentoring programs, and tailored recruitment can bring women and people of color into management.[31] Affinity groups—formalized networks that connect racial minority, female, or lesbian, gay, bisexual, and transgender employees to each other—can provide participants with supportive relationships, giving them a sense of community and connectedness.[32] Mentoring programs can enable participants to expand their networks to include people who are unlike themselves and who have more power within the organization. In sum, diversity management can support racial minority and female employees in ways that translate into access to more powerful jobs and greater job satisfaction but largely do not disrupt fundamental workplace hierarchies.

Symbolic politics are a defining feature of corporate diversity management. Since the 1960s, there have been strong pressures on companies to show an altruistic concern for people of color and women. Employers have responded by showing far more interest in symbolizing their social responsibility than in ensuring the effectiveness of their programs.[33] In many companies, diversity rhetoric and diversity management structures, such as policies, offices, and training, have become essential organizational forms. The existence of a diversity management program stands in as a positive sign of corporate concern.[34] As neoinstitutionalist scholarship crucially points out, such offices and policies are not accurate reflections of organizational realities but rather part of the myths that organizations invent to suggest that effective action is being taken.[35] Those myths have been promulgated by human resource managers and by companies hoping to convince courts of their compliance with civil rights law.[36]

But while diversity rhetoric and structures are routinely decoupled from the core technical functions of a company and, under many circumstances, irrelevant to consequential employment decisions, they still play important roles in the social life within a company such as Starr. They do the symbolic and, sometimes, social work of designating who belongs and who does not. At Starr, much of this work was done through claims about the company's identity.

"Diversity Is a Strength of Starr Corporation"

In 2005, someone looking for job postings on Starr's website would quickly see that the company featured diversity—alongside compensation, benefits, professional development, and work/life balance—as a cornerstone of a career at Starr. According to the site, Starr strove to become a top US corporation by means of its diversity management, with "strategies and actions that effectively attract, develop and retain the highest caliber talent and the full utilization of that talent to achieve undisputed leadership in [our] industry." A similar boilerplate phrase was repeated at the bottom of company job postings. Another version of this formulaic business case for diversity was available to those who already worked for the company as well, in

Starr's diversity management policy. That policy was posted on the diversity department's intranet site, titled "Diversity Works at Starr" and illustrated with a logo of white, beige, and brown hands holding the earth. The policy, presented as a letter from the CEO, stated: "Diversity is a strength of Starr Corporation. . . . Diversity drives better business results."

Through public relations and the publicized existence of its extensive diversity management interventions, Starr leaders constructed an image of Starr as a successful, profitable company with leadership that pragmatically supported diversity. On the company's public website, job seekers would see the business case rhetoric—here, Starr's "Diversity Vision"—spelling out how Starr would leverage employees' talent to achieve "superior business results." As the public website also stated, Starr put "Diversity in Action," particularly through its diversity management programming. Ten employee affinity groups were listed on the website, including Women in Operations, the African American Group, the Hispanic/Asian Sales Group, and the Rainbow Group, which represented employees who were gay, lesbian, bisexual, and transgender (in diversity managers' lingo, "GLBT").

Other diversity management activities included recruiting, mentoring programs, conferences, and professional development training targeted to African American, Latino, Asian American, and female business professionals. At work, the company provided mandatory diversity training and hosted heritage celebrations. Diversity personnel pointed to the company's departments of talent acquisition, multicultural marketing, supplier diversity, and charitable contributions as relevant to diversity management, too. Many of these activities, such as the company's affinity groups, are deemed by the diversity management industry to be "best practices." Diversity management personnel frequently characterized those groups as "the drivers of diversity" at Starr.

In the public image that the company projected, diversity management was a prerogative of the top leadership and engaged people at all levels of the company. On the Starr website, job seekers could see who was charged to "take responsibility for diversity." The top management committee was "responsible for leading." Managers strove to meet diversity objectives. The entire workforce was expected to maintain "an inclusive and supportive work environment." Quotes from unnamed employees praised the company's and its leadership's dedication to diversity. A member of the African American Affinity Group said: "We've gotten full commitment from the organization to sponsor educational programs, networking sessions and other activities. It's great to work for a company that really cares." Someone else stated, "As an Asian American, I am very proud of our initiatives." Another proclaimed, "When we say that diversity is a business imperative, we're not just repeating buzzwords. We really mean it."

Such rhetoric was paired with statistics on the numerical representation of people of color and women as well as images of business professionals who were African American, Latino, Asian American, white females, or based outside the US. Further legitimating evidence came in the form of industry-wide approvals. The website showcased Starr's high marks in trade industry rankings of companies with strong diversity management: a slot near the top of DiversityInc.com's Top 50 list, one of the one hundred best companies for working mothers, a vice president listed on *Fortune*'s Most Powerful Black Executives list, and other accolades.

Stock photographs in the company's HR promotional materials depicted young, attractive men and women of different racial backgrounds in formal business attire, staged as working collaboratively in teams or singled out individually, in sharp focus. Such imagery paints the company's workforce as a unified, productive, heterogeneous group of high-status individuals. Here, employees seem energetic, driven, multicultural individuals who are equal participants in a goal-oriented corporate organization. People of color, white women, and minorities from outside the US are portrayed as if they are just like their white, male, US counterparts, aside from their visible marks of ethno-racial, gender, or national identity. According to such depictions, Starr employees are not the old white boys club—that chummy network that monopolizes the best jobs and most coveted information. The people of color and women portrayed are not isolated, encumbered, or disillusioned. Nor are they undeserving recipients of unfair preferences, promoted just for their race or gender. This construction of employees' subjective personhood valorizes those employees who succeed in the competitive markets of corporate hiring, who facilitate the pursuit of profit, and who have meritoriously earned their places near the top of the corporate hierarchy. These subjects are exemplars of racial minority representation and racial integration—people who are easy to manage and symbols of the company's success at proactively promoting diversity.

In the company's image making, diversity had many, malleable meanings. According to one HR pamphlet, "The Wealth of Diversity" at Starr was possible because the company had employees "in 68 countries bringing a broad array of backgrounds, ethnicities, education, lifestyles, and cultural orientation to the company." The business case rhetoric, with its instrumentalist reasoning of win-win, bottom-line diversity, framed the representation of all sorts of talented people as good for everyone involved and, above all, good for business. The CEO's remarks at the Women's Summit invoked this rhetoric when he described a range of identities, "style" included, as conducive to corporate objectives of fostering talented leadership and, ultimately, economic competitiveness. Others in top management characterized the official purpose of diversity management as, ultimately, treating race, gender, and other status characteristics as somehow irrelevant. I heard as much when I asked the Starr executive vice president of global human resources—a white man who was nearing retirement—what diversity meant. He said, "It's just making sure that you're giving everybody an equal opportunity, irrespective of their background or individual styles . . . irrespective of either those direct things such as race, gender, religion, things that you see, and those that you don't see, how they think, how they behave, their culture."

Yet Starr's diversity management programming clearly operationalized diversity as applying to a few minority groups: people of color, women, and (much less consistently) those who are GLBT. The CEO, in his speech at the Women's Summit, reiterated the company's primary definition of diversity: numerical demographic composition of the workforce, especially the upper management. In practice, diversity also had a fuzzier operational meaning: the interactional norms of the workplace culture.

Further, diversity management—the programming, the numbers, the culture—was for and about *exempt* employees. This was taken for granted among diversity personnel in the company headquarters, so much so that it was almost never mentioned. When diversity personnel or other Starr executives and managers mentioned "diverse employees" at the company, they normally meant exempt women and people of color. They spoke and acted as if the exempt workforce *was* the workforce, or at least the workforce that mattered. The design and scope of the company's diversity initiatives, events, and affinity group activities relied on the same definition of diversity. The Women's Summit and Starr's other large internal diversity conferences were for exempt employees of color and women. The employee affinity groups met and hosted events during work hours, when most hourly and unionized workers were not able to attend. Only exempt employees were required to attend the company's introductory diversity training. In some plants and field offices, nonexempt employees participated in diversity training and affinity groups, but this was not consistent; it varied depending on the local supervisors. Starr's diversity programming did not target nonexempt, nonunionized employees.

Starr's identity as a corporate citizen responsible for the social good of its professional workforce was not original, as other research has shown. The company's management did not concoct the business case or invent diversity management programs wholesale.[37] The leaders of many Fortune 500 companies presented their firms in much the same way. The executive vice president echoed corporate managers and diversity consultants across the country when he referred to people of color and women as well as perspective, lifestyle, and other expressions of identity irrelevant to workplace discrimination, as defined by civil rights law.[38] In some form or another, Starr was emulating those firms and industry organizations, and some were likely emulating Starr.[39] And Starr's image making was not just to entice applicants to work there. Like other companies, Starr was signaling to current and potential employees, peer companies, and the government that the company abided by both industry standards and civil rights laws regarding nondiscrimination.[40]

All this said, Starr's corporate identity was, foremost, as a large consumer products firm. The company's public communications highlighted its product brand identity much more prominently than its diversity management. In its commercials, website, and packaging, Starr's brand was depicted as so trustworthy, essential, and quintessentially American that it might be a member of someone's family. In the annual reports for shareholders—those polished documents created every year to educate and persuade investors, regulators, and other audiences—the company appears oriented toward profit. Its products seem superior in quality and tailored for niche markets around the world. In only some years did the annual reports laud the company's practices as an employer, but they always boasted of its highly skilled, driven management.

How Starr Corporation Became Diverse

Starr's push for diversity, in name, dates to the early 1990s, but its active recruitment of people of color and women dates to the late 1960s. In the intervening years, new challenges of racial representation and integration emerged, particularly stemming from new regulatory requirements and legal constraints. Company leaders faced heightened demands for profitability and industry-wide pressures to look diverse. Human resource managers emerged as an occupational group with vested interests in race- and gender-conscious programs. Managers' interests in hiring and firing changed as well, as did their understanding of workforce relations.

In this context, Starr leaders cultivated an identity for the company as altruistically responsible and financially hardheaded. They drew on this identity to discursively frame the company's race- and gender-sensitive policies as commensurate with good corporate practice. The company's publicly available annual reports, along with documents from its private archive and retrospective interviews with a few senior managers, tell this story.

Snapshot 1: Before Diversity—a Responsibility for Minority Opportunity, 1973

Through the first half of the twentieth century, Starr's executive leadership was exclusively white and male. The company openly condoned discriminatory policies and exclusionary practices. Photographs from the company's early annual reports reveal just how unproblematic the company's racial, gender, and class hierarchy was. A 1960 photograph portrays about 250 Starr employees standing outside a large factory, arranged according to their job position, race, and gender. Six white men in business suits—the managers—stand shoulder to shoulder in the front row. Behind them, most of the employees—line workers, presumably—are white men in uniforms and caps, although approximately thirty-five are white women. To their right is another cluster of employees. White women in skirts stand in the first two rows; they are secretaries or administrators, perhaps. Behind them are about twenty black men, black women, and white women dressed in white uniforms and caps. The photograph communicates a distinct identity for the company: an efficient bureaucratic operation with an uncomplicated racial and gender hierarchy predominated by white men.

After the 1960s, white men continued to make up the vast majority of the company's leadership, but the company's PR materials no longer so blatantly displayed their homogeneity or their authority over people of color and white women. Starr's 1973 annual report includes an image that had not been printed in any prior annual report: a black person in management. The man stands at the front of a room wearing a hard hat and a white button-down dress shirt, explaining a diagram to two white male colleagues who are seated. The photograph is in a two-page special section that singles out equal opportunity as one of six areas of corporate social responsibility. It explains Starr's ongoing affirmative action program as "a basic responsibility of local management . . . to promote further progress and effective use of corporate resources."

The period between the mid-1960s and early 1970s was a watershed for employment discrimination law. The federal government's capacity to mandate equality of opportunity expanded dramatically.[41] Title VII of the Civil Rights Act of 1964 and Executive Order 11246 were the most important reforms. They ushered in new pressures on Starr company leaders to hire more people of color and women and to appear to be doing as much. The company needed to show that it complied with law.

Starr voluntarily began practicing affirmative action in 1965 under a short-lived federal program, the Plan for Progress. In 1966, the Equal Employment Opportunity Commission began to require large employers and government contractors to complete reports on employees' race and sex.[42] Starr fit both of these categories and complied. Executive Order 11246, issued by President Lyndon B. Johnson in 1965, prohibited employment discrimination based on race, creed, color, or national origin by large government contractors and by the US government. Starr, as one such contractor, was required to submit affirmative action plans to show progress toward hiring and promoting racial minorities and women. The order also obliged contractors to ensure fair treatment by acting preemptively to "take affirmative action" by aggressively recruiting minorities into the applicant pool.[43] Soon thereafter, the Labor Department required Starr and other federal contractors to submit affirmative action plans with numerical goals and timetables for improving minority opportunity and increasing their proportional representation.

Companies such as Starr were in the midst of a massively changing, uncertain political and legal environment. Meanwhile, activists working for black civil rights were pushing for jobs and racial justice. White women, Mexican Americans, and other activists had begun to follow a similar path.[44] Starr leaders worried about civil unrest in cities. The new laws gave employers ambiguous directions, though.[45] This context created tremendous uncertainty and potentially serious risks. Employers faced the threat of new discrimination claims, and their failure to comply with affirmative action regulations could have serious repercussions, such as large fines and exclusion from future federal contracts. To signal their legal compliance, companies adopted organizational structures such as offices and new specialists, and they echoed the rhetoric of federal lawmakers and similarly situated companies.[46] Affirmative action personnel played a central role in institutionalizing equal employment opportunity and affirmative action (EEO/AA) structures, stressing in their professional literature that demonstrating good faith was essential to compliance (perhaps more so than establishing quotas) and that formalizing EEO/AA would aid managers' priorities of efficiency and productivity.[47]

In this period, Starr created an affirmative action program with policies and initiatives guided by directives such as "Employment advertisements will include the 'equal opportunity employer line.'" It began setting numerical goals for employing minorities and women. By 1971, the company was among the approximately 21% of large private-sector employers that had affirmative action plans.[48] By the time it published the photo of the black manager, the company had created a new centralized Department of Urban Affairs. The department oversaw a Plant City initiative, which convened joint corporate-community task forces in different cities to work on recruitment, educational programming, and minority contracting. It established the "Pipeline" initiative to advance racial minorities (which at that time meant black people) into higher-level positions. According to company leaders, the purpose of these and other programs was to bring minorities into the company, help them adjust to their jobs, and train supervisors to recognize their distinct needs. It used salary classifications, job postings, and other bureaucratic hiring and promotion practices that were becoming increasingly common among employers across the country.[49]

In the 1970s and early 1980s, the numeric proportional representation of people of color and women at Starr increased. Company managers considered these changes noteworthy enough to announce them in annual reports, and they attributed the changes in minority representation to Starr's affirmative action interventions. In 1973, racial minority employees made up 6% of Starr's US employees in higher-status office, clerical, and management positions, up from to 2% in 1965. At that time they made up 12% of Starr's US workforce overall, which was nearly double their representation in 1965. That figure reached 14% by 1984. In 1973, women made up over 2% of officials and managers, 12.5% of professionals, 13% of technical personnel, and 1% of the sales force. By 1984, white women made up 29% of Starr's US workforce. Other notable changes at the company were not announced in the report but were visible in its photographs. In 1972, a white woman and a black man joined Starr's board of directors. That year, the company hired a female vice president of public relations, its first female corporate officer. By 1978, four of the company's thirty-five officers were women.

In the 1970s and early 1980s, Starr's management hoped to project the image of a socially conscientious corporate citizen. Using the popular rhetoric of the times, the company framed its actions in terms of affirmative action and creating opportunities for minorities. Nearly every Starr annual report produced between 1968 and 1989 references the topics of equal opportunity, affirmative action, or opportunity for the disadvantaged. According to the 1973 report, the company had "obligations" of "providing opportunities for personal growth, job enrichment and security and . . . continuing to increase our participation in the solutions of social problems." Company leaders characterized EEO/AA policies as good for people of color, women, and racial minority communities and businesses. According to a 1982 company newsletter, one purpose of these policies was to "identify and support organizations and programs in minority communities that will improve the status of residents." In twelve of the nineteen years between 1971 and 1989, the reports mentioned the numerically proportional representation of women and people of color, usually with statistics on upward change. They also made numerous references to the accomplishments of its Minority Purchasing Program, ranging from four contracts with minority construction firms in 1973 to investments of $25.7 million in minority-owned firms and $5.5 million in firms owned by women in 1985.

The company's leaders equated EEO/AA policies with good personnel management, which was also standard practice in the professional management literature at this time.[50] Further, they suggested that the company pursued such policies out of goodwill, not for legal purposes. None of the annual reports mention federal EEO/AA requirements.

The new corporate image that Starr leaders publicized in the 1970s rested on an ideology of pursuing equity through corporate benevolence. As management portrayed it, Starr was a successful business that altruistically took responsibility for supporting the career opportunities of racial minorities and women. Invoking this image, they tried to minimize political and legal uncertainties, act in step with similarly situated companies, hire some people of color and women, and—to shareholders, regulators, employees, civil rights groups, and other stakeholders—explain what they were doing. This newfound identity as a supporter of minority opportunities contrasted markedly with the company's identity in prior decades.

Snapshot 2: Before Diversity—the Benefits of Corporate Diversification, 1979

"Another year of record sales and earnings," declared the Starr chair of the board and CEO, a white middle-aged man, in his 1979 letter to shareholders. According to the annual report that year, the company's financial achievements were outstanding. Its management was excellent. Its reputation was trustworthy. The chair's letter states, "Our building strategy is based in part on the concept of diversification, both within our present business and into different fields of endeavor." He also announced a new "plan of 'diversification through acquisition.'" Following a common strategy among US companies at the time, Starr planned to acquire and merge with a consumer products firm outside of its industry.[51] The result, according to the chair, would be a wider range of product lines and areas of business.

Three years later, in their annual letter, the president and the chair and CEO applauded the results of the merger to shareholders: "The company is a well-balanced mix of comparatively recession-resistant businesses and others more directly affected by economic conditions. This diversity provides steady growth in periods of cautious consumer spending . . . and should provide more dynamic progress when the marketplace is robust." The diversification was increasing revenue and saving costs, they declared. Over the next few years, the executives' letters continued to credit the company's performance to the diversification plan, making economic diversification central to Starr's corporate identity and image. They had strong incentives to claim that the acquisition was bringing greater competitiveness and cost-efficiency, even if that was not true. Acquisitions are extremely complex business transactions in which shareholders and top management have much to gain financially if all goes well. As it turned out, Starr executives' claims proved to be overstated. In the mid-1980s the top management decided to split up the two firms because the acquired business was not as profitable as Starr.

Although the executives' massive diversification effort failed, it illustrates how company leaders construed Starr's identity in terms of economic diversification. For decades, Starr leaders had been expanding the company's product lines and introducing more variation. Product and market differentiation in the United States dates to the 1920s, when more companies began to sell goods to consumers rather than to other producers. In the post–World War II boom, when consumers had more discretionary income and demanded more choices, companies faced even greater pressures to create variety, and the appearance of variety, within their product lines.

Starr executives characterized those practices of diversification as advantageous for consumers and the bottom line. The 1961 letter from Starr's president, an elderly white man with black browline glasses, trumpeted the company's "record established in world-wide sales" and "the wide variety of the product lines" that "offer a wide choice" to shoppers. In the 1970s and 1980s, the company further diversified its products to align with changes in consumer and workforce demographics, in order to reach growing niche and international markets. In the 1978 annual report, a two-page spread featured a confident white woman, dressed in a suit jacket and skirt and holding a briefcase, using Starr products: "She doesn't look like a revolutionary but the working woman's lifestyle is crafting new markets and changing others." Along with "the emergence of the working women," the annual report took note of the decline of the traditional family, a rise of young people living alone, and other demographic shifts. "These social trends . . . have presented unprecedented changes to [our] industry," the reported asserted. The 1982 report noted that increasingly, households are "Black, Asian, or Hispanic." Those households were new profitable niches—distinctive in relation to white households yet desirable. "While each of these ethnic groups retains a strong sense of identification, they typify other households in most respects."

At the end of the 1980s, company executives confidently announced, "Our large scale and varied product mix helps us generate growing returns for investors and bring the benefits of diversity and quality to customers and consumers, as well as opportunity to our employees, in all our markets and communities." Such claims about diversification reinforced their image of Starr as a high-functioning, successful company—one that was advancing "in profitability and toward our goal of being the best consumer products company in the world."

At this point in time, company leaders' rhetoric on organizational diversification had nothing to do with the workforce. Within a few years, though, they applied their long-standing ideas about diversification to employees. Diversity, they would claim, was a desirable trait not just of Starr's business operations, products, and marketing but also of its people. Their rationale for diversification—that greater variety improves economic growth, competitiveness, and consumer choice—became their rationale for pursuing racial minority representation and workplace integration.[52] It became the business case for workforce diversity.

Snapshot 3: A Competitive Advantage and Social Responsibility, 1992

If corporate diversity management has a birth date, it is 1987.[53] The conservative Hudson Institute issued a report, *Workforce 2000*, that advised companies to update workforce policies designed primarily for white male employees.[54] The authors predicted (inaccurately) that women, racial minorities, immigrants, and older workers would imminently make up the majority of the workforce.[55] A multimillion dollar diversity management consulting industry quickly developed to offer training, manuals, and advice. In the 1980s, a small percentage of medium and large US companies had some type of diversity program, many of which were part of companies' antidiscrimination efforts.[56] By the early 1990s, many more large US corporations began to institutionalize such programs as well as new policies and training on cultural awareness, sexual harassment, and accommodations for people with disabilities.[57]

Starr's 1992 annual report announced "The Year of Diversity." The top executives, both of them older white men, wrote in their annual letter, "We launched a formal diversity program to help us understand and serve our diverse worldwide markets better, and to ensure that we can attract and retain the best quality of people—all people." The diversity program included celebratory diversity events, a Diversity Policy Council, and employee affinity groups for women, blacks, and Hispanics in sales. By 1993, more than six thousand employees had participated in the new two-day diversity training session called Diversity at Work. The company soon received external awards for these efforts, including one from the US Department of Labor.

In the 1980s, company executives were ever more concerned about discrimination law, which was expanding to cover more groups. Meanwhile, affirmative action regulations had come under attack by New Right activists and hostile political officials. As Dobbin demonstrates, human resource personnel were at the forefront of the corporate push for diversity.[58] Concerned with their job security and professional status, these personnel offered companies strategies to show compliance with ambiguous federal mandates of nondiscrimination. Many of their new diversity management initiatives were actually repurposed affirmative action programs with new names.[59] In 1992, Starr's Equal Employment Opportunity and Urban Affairs Department was renamed the Diversity Management Department. Its Minority Purchasing Program became the Diversity Supplier Program.

But at Starr and elsewhere, *diversity* meant more than race or gender. Across the country, a new managerial rhetoric on diversity became enormously popular in the early 1990s, apparent both in the professional management literature and in companies' diversity mission statements.[60] This business case rhetoric added nonlegal categories of diversity, such as attitudes and communication styles, to protected classes of race and gender, and it emphasized profitability and productivity. It posed human attributes that were the basis of disenfranchisement as equivalent with attributes that managers deemed necessary for workforce effectiveness. In doing so, it minimized problems of inequality and divorced them from civil rights law. Such rhetoric was indicative of a business culture, popularized by management trendsetters, that appropriated and transformed legal ideals to serve managerial objectives, not egalitarian ideals.

Starr's 1992 annual report stated that diversity management would enable the company to reach global markets and retain top talent. This was an early iteration of the business case for diversity: "Our most important assets are the Starr employees who add value to our products and processes every day. We are creating and maintaining a talented, productive, and diverse workforce focused on meeting—and exceeding—our business objectives." According to the report, the new diversity training would help employees develop so they could "learn, work, and be rewarded up to their full potential." Although Starr's diversity management programs were justified with this expansive rhetoric, the content of its diversity activities centered on people of color and other minority groups. Further, only diversity training and celebratory events were for all employees. Otherwise, a program title that included the term *diversity* was, presumably, for people of color and women.

Starr's annual reports had long characterized upper management as talented and dedicated. Now upper management was also diverse. Throughout the 1990s, nearly every one of Starr's annual reports showcases diversity, sometimes very prominently, as a desirable attribute of the company's upper-level workforce.[61] Photographs include businesspeople who are racial minority, non-US natives, ethnically ambiguous, or white and female. One report spotlights a black male vice president and an Asian American (or Asian) female director of business development. Another captures the managerial theme that people of different backgrounds could collaborate productively. One photograph portrays a group of senior managers in a special international leadership development training session: a white woman, a Latino man, a black woman, and a few others in business suits are gathered around a table, deep in conversation. In these depictions, the subjective personhood of the racial minority and white female employees embodies the company's notions of diversity: they are successful, talented, and engaged toward business goals. White people, when depicted among people of color, are portrayed as cooperative participants in egalitarian relationships and generative interactions that cut across racial groups, gender, and national identity.

The company took credit for generating minority representation and cooperative intergroup relations at work. The 1992 annual report described Starr's "Strategies to Be the Best," which included the new diversity management programs that would "help our people develop, so that all our employees can learn, work, and be rewarded up to their full potential."

In the 1990s, the company also presented diversity as a social responsibility—just as it had framed its affirmative action programs. Text of the 1997 annual report describes diversity as a value that reflects the company's "belief in helping others in need." The report highlights Starr's funding of "a wide range of women's and minority groups," such as a grant of almost $1 million to support a teacher training program. But the corporate responsibility theme disappeared from the annual reports in the late 1990s. By

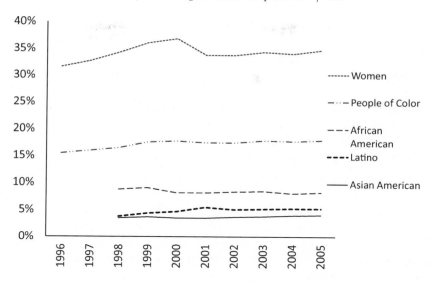

6.1. Representation of people of color and women in Starr US exempt workforce. *Sources:* Data for 1989–1996 are from the Starr corporate archives. Data for 1997–2004 are from Starr annual Key Human Resource Statistics reports. Data for 2005 are from Starr 2nd Quarter Diversity Results report. On file with author.

2000, diversity was no longer the right thing to do. The report that year and subsequent ones through the mid-2000s refer to diversity only in relation to the company's financial performance: a feature of the product lines and an attribute of upper-level employees that enabled the company to reach global markets. By this time, the company's imagery, rhetoric, and programmatic reach of diversity management was only about racial and gender representation in professional, managerial, and executive positions.

The implementation of diversity programs at Starr corresponded with increases in the representation of people of color and women in the company's exempt workforce. Between 1989 and 1996, coinciding with the implementation of diversity management programming at Starr, the exempt workforce changed from 10.1% to 15.5% black, Hispanic, and Asian (see fig. 6.1).[62] The percentage of exempt women increased from 24.7% to 31.6%. In the subsequent nine years, that representation changed much more modestly, up to 18% people of color and 35% female in 2005. There is no way to know whether the increases in the 1990s can be attributed to the company's diversity management platform, although the parallel changes are noteworthy.

Thus, Starr's initial adoption of a regime of affirmative action in the 1970s and its initial adoption of diversity management programming in the 1990s corresponded with increases in the representation of people of color and women in the workplace. However, racial and gender representation at Starr remained little changed in the intervening years. Some of these patterns are similar to those seen in the US workforce overall.[63] African Americans and Latinos, especially males, made notable gains in managerial and professional jobs in the 1970s through the early 1980s. After that, those men's advancement largely stagnated, and gains were evident for women of color and Asian men and women. Between 1966 and 2001, managerial and professional jobs became much more accessible to white women, relative to the overall employment of white women in the labor force, and these increases were steady over time. For all these groups (with the exception of white female professionals), their representation in managerial and professional jobs remained dramatically below their representation in the national workforce. Meanwhile, white men were dramatically overrepresented in these jobs throughout the entire period. Company data suggest that the same was true at Starr.

The company's intermittent reporting on the proportional representation of racial minority and female employees through the 1970s and mid-1980s and again in the early and late 1990s is ideological, as is my own reliance on that data. The numbers provide a necessary measure of racial and gender progress. They are concrete evidence in a cloud of lofty rhetoric. However, they are poor substitutes for evidence of the actual effectiveness of affirmative action and diversity interventions, which companies such as Starr and diversity management industry experts have shown little interest in demonstrating empirically.[64] Reported as such, these numbers lend an aura of objectivity to an organizational reality in which diversity is the identity-conscious "other" in relation to the unmarked status quo. No reference is made to the representation of white people or men or to the white, male favoritism enabled by routine organizational practices.

Reimagining the Boundaries of the Corporate Workforce

Over a forty-year period, an antiracist, antisexist political movement to open up good jobs had been thoroughly managerialized, only partially empowered, and in many ways watered down.[65] At Starr, company executives and managers drew on managerial practices, logics, and symbolism to redefine the symbolic boundaries of the corporate workforce.

Company leaders negotiated the challenges of a rapidly shifting, uncertain legal and economic environment by crafting an organizational identity for Starr as a profitable company with a proactive diversity strategy. According to this identity, Starr's HR strategies ultimately worked to the benefit of people of color and women *and* white people and men and to the competitive advantage of the company at large. Their push for affirmative action and antidiscrimination, and then diversity, was mostly reactionary and defensive, motivated by a corporate interest in avoiding lawsuits and federal scrutiny, maintaining legitimacy among peer companies, and economically succeeding in competitive global and niche markets.

With this identity, the company professionalized the goal of bringing some black people into the predominantly white company, framed first in the legal terms of minority opportunity in the 1970s and 1980s and then in private-sector terms of leveraging diversity in the 1990s. The company's new rhetoric of workforce diversity sounded much like its long-standing rhetoric on the diversification of products and businesses. In Starr's annual corporate reports, the imagery and text distinguish African Americans and white women—and, over time, Latinos, Asian Americans, and employees from outside the United States—and intimate that the company's actions to support these employees were driven by concern. Its reporting of statistics on racial minority and female representation signals the effectiveness of such actions and create an objective appearance of substantive change. The symbolic boundaries of the corporate workforce appear to be broad and inclusive and determined by benevolence and meritocracy, not bigotry or favoritism. With its diversity identity, the firm recast integration as the inclusion of racial minority and female businesspeople who shared the dispositions and desires of upper management—as compatible with corporate interests.

Corporate annual reports do not simply summarize a company's activities and financial performance. They are public relations material. They serve as an authoritative statement on who and what is within the scope of corporate concern. They preclude any alternative rendition of racial and female movement into the business class, including the very likely reality of white male antagonism toward the new employees and white men's ongoing monopoly on the best jobs.

SEVEN

Diversity Management, Shareholder Capitalism, and the Biases of Meritocracy

When I asked diversity management personnel at Starr about the issues they confronted in their jobs, they typically responded by talking instead about the opportunities. They largely agreed that the company was, in their positive spin, committed to diversity. As a black woman who was a senior vice president of HR explained, "There is this . . . broad recognition that, yes, you want a diverse group of people within this company and, yes, you want a diverse group of people in your leadership team." They would add that the company's well-developed diversity management programming needed updating and renewed attention. Some focused on outcomes. As a white woman who led the Women's Sales Group put it, "There is support for diversity. We're doing some good things. But I don't know that our programs are moving the needle." Others were concerned with the company's diversity practices outside the United States. "Figuring out global diversity . . . probably is our biggest opportunity and our biggest challenge to be a viable global organization," said Jack, a black man who was a sales director and the previous director of diversity.

On the minds of all these personnel was the major restructuring that company executives were pursuing. In the early 2000s, a portion of Starr's stock became publicly traded on the stock market. With these changes, corporate leaders became acutely concerned with the company's short-term stock value. They oversaw a major global reorganization that integrated the company's North American and overseas units, and they eliminated sixteen thousand positions. In 2004, the company laid off an additional six thousand workers. In 2005 and 2006, during my study, the company earned a profit, but the price of its stock continued to drop. Executives implemented yet another wave of restructuring. Small packs of consultants who were auditing the company—mostly white men in dark business suits—occasionally marched through the hallways of the corporate head-quarters, making office employees nervous. In early 2006, company leaders announced that another eight thousand positions would be cut.

In the current era of neoliberal corporate capitalism, companies treat employees as costs to be minimized.[1] Dramatic changes have taken place in corporate ownership and accountability: institutional investors now hold a far greater share of corporate equity—57% in the early 2000s, compared to 17% in the 1960s—but are underregulated, and so they have tremendous influence over corporate strategy.[2] Executives, too, have an incentive to focus on stock value, as their compensation is now linked to stock performance.[3] Corporate leaders have shrunken the ranks of both low-wage and white-collar employees by eliminating positions, increasing workloads, deunionizing, outsourcing work, and hiring less expensive temporary workers.[4] They have justified this ideological and strategic shift with a managerial discourse that valorizes profitability, high stock prices, and executive compensation. Under such a regime, the assumption is that the priority of profits supersedes the priority of employee well-being or employee equity. Simultaneously, the US government has backed off from long-standing commitments to providing a safety net to protect the health and economic well-being of most Americans. With these institutional changes, workers suffer greater insecurity and economic risk. Political scientist Jacob Hacker calls this restructuring the great risk shift.[5]

At Starr, the pressures to reduce employee costs and fears about job security cast a dark shadow over diversity management. From the perspective of the company's diversity personnel, recruiting and retaining high-status people of color and women was challenging under the best of conditions. The company, they believed, generally did a great job recruiting exempt people of color and women but an inadequate job of developing, promoting, and retaining those employees. Now, the company's financial status and the broader context of corporate retrenchment posed even more formidable barriers. The restructuring appeared to be disproportionately hurting people of color. In late 2005, the annualized turnover rate for exempt employees of color—meaning the projected net loss of those employees in the upcoming year—was 13.4%, compared to 10.5% for the overall exempt workforce.

In the face of the restructuring, in a context in which their managerial power was already circumscribed, diversity personnel at Starr's headquarters—the majority of whom were African Americans or white women—were continuously compelled to justify their work of diversity management. The Global Department of Diversity Management was at the forefront of this drive. Motivated to keep their jobs and also ideologically concerned about problems of exclusion, these personnel focused their energies on normatively changing the corporate culture. However, they shied away from questioning biased employment decision-making practices—the practices that sociologists have identified as core mechanisms of workplace inequality.[6] Moreover, they were ever wary that executives and supervising managers viewed diversity management as a diversion from the core profit motives of the company. So they focused their attentions on reiterating the good that would come from diversity.

The Dynamics of Managerial Power

In companies, executives and managers exercise power to control employees, decision making, resources, information, and workplace procedures. They do so materially and instrumentally, through the formal bureaucracy of salary grades, job hierarchies, employee evaluations, and other standardized systems and procedures.[7] They allocate power to make decisions and affect others' actions. Executives and managers also control employees normatively and ideologically through practices that influence an organization's culture, employees' identities, and their deeper thoughts and emotions.[8] The structure of the organization enables this.[9] Employees are subject to control. To stay employed, they cannot simply perform their work responsibilities. They must participate appropriately in a company's bureaucratic procedures and conform in some measure to the organizational culture. Critical organizational scholars call this process co-optation.

Diversity managers at Starr hoped to exercise managerial authority over others in the company. Three sets of diversity management personnel worked on HR matters in the company's US offices.[10] There was the diversity department, which was an HR department centralized in the company's headquarters and overseen by corporate executives. The department included a director, an associate director, two managers, and an administrative assistant. There were diversity advisers: senior managers, directors, and vice presidents who had HR positions with formal responsibilities involving diversity and staffing. These advisers were employed in different businesses and functions across the company, such as marketing, research and development, and finance, so through their positions, oversight of diversity initiatives and relevant employment decisions was decentralized. And there were the leaders of the employee affinity groups, whose activities were overseen by the diversity department. The leaders of those groups were administrators, managers, or directors, but not necessarily in HR. Their involvement in diversity management was volunteer work.

For all these personnel, the pretext of their diversity management work was that they supported exempt people of color, women, and less consistently GLBT employees—so-called diverse employees—especially those who were high-achieving and in positions just below the most elite senior management positions. The personnel had pragmatic reasons for endorsing diversity management, above and beyond any normative commitments they had regarding equality or opportunity. For those in HR, diversity management was their livelihood and brought rewards and career opportunities.[11] The affinity groups' leaders work was unpaid, but they viewed their participation as helpful for their personal career goals and professional needs by, for example, creating opportunities to interact with executives. One told me about the group he ran, "You can take much more risk in the group. You can be a little more out there. . . . It's a great leadership, character-building experience." According to him and other diversity personnel, diversity management provided them and the employees they represented with cognitive and emotional benefits, including information about the organization, knowledge of other groups, feelings of empowerment, and socialization into the company's norms and networks.

Although the company provided these diversity managers with some material resources to do their work—far more than most large companies did—these managers tended to be stretched thin, and their authority had real limits. The diversity department staff did not directly make hiring and promotion decisions. They had a programming budget of $500,000 for 2005. Diversity advisers had some influence over employment decisions, but their reach depended on the senior managers and vice presidents who oversaw them. For example, diversity and staffing for sales was overseen by Nadine, a white woman who was an associate HR director and a diversity adviser. It was difficult, Nadine told me anxiously, for her to develop programs from headquarters and then implement them in the decentralized field offices. The division had at least eight thousand employees and a new vice president who was unsympathetic to diversity issues. She and her assistant administrator were the only staff dedicated to overseeing the work. "There are not enough resources we can deploy for diversity," she said.

Diversity personnel could not influence what many considered the most important diversity management practice: holding managers and executives accountable for racial minority and female representation.[12] Each of the company's senior executives set goals for the representation, hiring, and promotion of racial minorities and women within his or her organization. The company publicly claimed that it held managers accountable for those goals, but this was not true. It was far more important for supervising managers and other businesspeople to devote their energies to producing what they called business results. Faith, a white woman who was the diversity adviser for global supply chain, described "the reward piece" as the greatest shortcoming of diversity management at Starr. She described how the executive vice president of global supply chain was evaluated. "We put [diversity] goals out, but if we miss them, for the most part it's not reflected in compensation. . . . So if he misses his diversity numbers but his business just bangs out of the house, he is still going to get an 'exceeds' [highest employee evaluation] right now." Given the rigid hierarchical authority structure of the company and their relatively low status, diversity managers mostly endured such problems of resource allocation and organizational strategy.[13]

Just as diversity personnel tried to exercise managerial power, they were subject to it. Their work assignments were determined by their superiors, who evaluated them formally and informally. Darnell, an African American man who was the company's associate director of diversity, pointed to the workload of the diversity department staff: "The senior leaders have high expectations, and those trickle down. . . . They're expecting a lot out of [the director of diversity], so we're feeling the heat." This evaluative pressure that diversity personnel experienced reinforced their apprehensions about their job security. Their heightened sense of fear was apparent in our interactions. One, who lost her job near the end of this study, would barely answer my interview questions. Those individuals likely wondered if I had some kind of affiliation with the dark suits combing the company for ways to cut costs. For diversity advisers and, especially, the affinity group leaders, diversity management was usually secondary to their already overloaded work responsibilities.

However much the diversity personnel quietly grumbled about the intense pressure to perform, they also internalized that pressure as acceptable. They spoke of it as a matter-of-fact demand of "corporate America" and, as long as employees took personal initiative, "an opportunity for career growth." Like the managers sociologist Robert Jackall studied, these personnel would analyze themselves according to the logic of functional rationality common to their workplace environment; each treated him- or herself as an object to be scrutinized, adjusted, and promoted.[14] Darnell shared his reasoning about staying at Starr. He could work at another company, he said, for "eight hours a day and that's my life. But I made a conscious choice, and I want to grow."

Diversity personnel were further disempowered because they held HR positions, which are generally lower status in corporate offices and not paths to more powerful positions. Corporate executives typically prioritize those functions most directly relevant to profit and growth, not HR. There are popular perceptions that HR personnel are less competent than other professionals.[15] HR personnel tend to be disproportionately racial minorities and females; these groups are tracked into HR, where they are segregated and marginalized.[16] This was true at Starr. At the end of 2005, people of color made up 22.6% of the exempt Starr employees working in HR positions in the United States, and women filled 63.1% of those HR positions. These figures were noticeably higher than the representation of either group in the company's overall exempt US workforce (18% and 35%, respectively), especially the representation of women. These dynamics of occupational prestige, hierarchy, and segregation were not openly acknowledged by the diversity personnel but surely limited their ability to influence anyone else at the company.

Implementing Diversity Management

Diversity personnel recognized that the real power over hiring and firing rested with executives and supervising managers, over whom they had little sway. With the corporate restructuring, the problems of managerial inattention and limited resources had only worsened, according to diversity personnel. They saw the new CEO and some of his executive team members as at best indifferent toward diversity management. An affinity group leader said in an interview, "With the current leadership, it feels like diversity's completely off the radar screen." Diversity personnel could not openly oppose the restructuring. They would lose credibility and put their jobs in jeopardy. Further, they were constrained by the limits of their own offices within the corporate hierarchy. They also lacked legal recourse and did not have support from outside their workplace. Neither the company's unions nor civil rights activists were pushing hard for workforce integration, much less challenging the racial and gender consequences of corporate restructuring.

Given these dynamics of managerial power, diversity personnel had to constantly engage in symbolic workplace politics in order to legitimate their work of diversity management. They fashioned themselves as change agents who could motivate change in others toward the company's profitability. As evident in the quotes that open this chapter, they were constantly making claims about the change needed, and they did so in constructive, fairly positive terms—citing not issues but opportunities. They characterized Starr's diversity management platform as successful but stagnating, and they presented egalitarian workplace relationships—between white people and people of color and between women and men—as not yet a reality but vital and within reach. Many of these claims rested on what they called "the numbers."

The Numbers: Who Counts and Who Doesn't

While Starr's public relations materials implied that everyone at Starr contributed to diversity, the raison d'être of diversity management programs was to support exempt employees of color and female employees. This was technically operationalized in the company's diversity metrics, which reported the proportional numeric representation of exempt employees of color and female employees.

Starr tracked information about employees based on their race and gender. This is a management practice that most companies do not engage in, even though industry specialists consider it one of the best ways to manage diversity. The company's diversity advisers analyzed these data for their functions. The diversity department staff compiled that data to produce quarterly and annual diversity reports on the metrics. The reports showed the representation of exempt racial minority and female US employees as well as trends in their hiring, promotions, and annual turnover.[17] The company's senior executives primarily cared about the metrics, more so than any other aspect of diversity management programming. When the director of diversity, Melissa, met with them, their meetings centered on the diversity reports. The metrics were important for the company's rankings in the diversity management indexes produced by industry groups.

The company's focus on the metrics—much like its focus on shareholder value—was always short term, from quarter to quarter or year to year. If executives were ever held accountable, it was for short-term changes. At the end of this study, I created a final report for the company in the form of a PowerPoint presentation. For that report, I created a graph of changes in the metrics between 1989 and 2005 (the data reported in fig. 6.1). When I presented the report to diversity personnel, many gasped under their breath, looking deeply dismayed. They had never seen the quantitative data tracked over time. A few noted that this graph was the most striking part of my report.

Diversity personnel relied on the diversity metrics to define basic issues of diversity management. In their internal meetings, they would identify patterns in the numerical representation and brainstorm the employment decisions that affected these patterns. This was a theme of a two-day meeting of diversity personnel in sales. The meeting was for the Diversity Sales Group, which had recently been created by merging the affinity groups representing women, blacks, Hispanics, and Asians in sales. The purpose of the meeting was to develop a strategic plan for the combined affinity group. The attendees included an outside diversity consultant, nine leaders of the sales affinity groups, a few diversity department staff, a few upper-level managers, and, adding gravitas to the event, the senior vice president of sales.

Nadine, the sales diversity adviser, first presented the "Situational Analysis." Referring to a few large pieces of butcher paper taped to the wall, she said, "During our last conference call in August, you asked for numbers." In the second quarter of 2005, people of color made up 14% of the exempt sales workforce and women 26%. Compared to other functions at Starr, sales had the second-lowest representation of people of color and the lowest representation of exempt women. Nadine provided a fine-tuned review of the statistics on the representation, hiring, promotions, terminations and turnover of those sales employees by various categories—all of sales, divisions within it, geographic regions, and salary grade.

Overall, the figures showed that sales was losing more exempt racial minority and female employees than were hired. Nadine advised, "We need to think about what external and internal things contribute to them." The meeting participants pointed out a few patterns they considered important, though not surprising. The representation of people of color and women had "remained flat" for three years. Those employees were fairly well represented at the lowest exempt salary grades but dismally underrepresented at the highest levels. In the tiers in between, much of the low representation of women could be pinpointed to a division of sales that required heavy lifting and had physically uncomfortable work conditions. Darnell from the diversity department remarked, "There is endless opportunity for sales when it comes to diversity."

The company's diversity reporting also measured disparity at the company. It compared the percentage of people of color or women in exempt positions to those in the banded positions. Banded employees were the most elite employees: vice presidents, directors, and senior executives, all of whom received stock options as part of their compensation. They were categorized from I to A; the most powerful executives were in the bands F through A. The disparity measure encapsulated, quantitatively, the glass ceiling. Within sales, there was noticeable disparity (see table 7.1). For example, people of color made up 17% of employees in salary grades 3 to 9, which included sales representatives in the field. They made up just over 12% of

Table 7.1 **Representation of people of color and women in Starr US exempt sales workforce, by band or salary grade, 2005**

	People of Color (%)	Women (%)
Bands:		
A–F	2.0	0
G–I	7.3	18.0
Salary grades:		
10–13	12.2	26.3
3–9	17.0	27.0

Source: Author field notes from Starr Diversity Sales Council strategic planning meeting.

sales employees in salary grades 10 to 13, which included senior managers. And they were just 2% of the employees in top executive sales positions.

Diversity personnel used these metrics and measures of disparity to establish priorities and guide their work, or they intimated that they were doing as much. During Nadine's presentation, Christina, a white woman who led the Women's Sales Group, remarked that women in sales in salary grades 6 to 9 were terminated at a higher rate than women in lower and higher salary grades. She added that the Women's Sales Group had done exit interviews with women who had stopped working for the company to understand this sort of issue: "Most are leaving for other companies, not to be stay-at-home moms."

Nadine's presentation was followed by a brainstorming session about follow-up actions. Curt, the senior vice president of sales, was an energetic white man with balding brown hair who described himself as a "wall breaker downer." He remarked, "This is a classic challenge: do we wait ten years to move up those people [at lower salary grades], or do we move to external hiring? That's part of the culture change that's within our scope." Van, Nadine's supervising manager, noted, "We could focus on 10 to 13 or 3 to 9 for training." Unlike Curt and Van, who actually oversaw hiring and firing, the affinity group leaders could only suggest areas of focus. Bernie, a leader of the Hispanic/Asian Affinity Group, noted, "We can influence hires but not fires. Maybe we can influence retention."

These discussions reveal how diversity managers developed a sophisticated analysis of the status of racial minority and female businesspeople in the company, according to their occupational attainment. They were using this analysis to understand and, they hoped, open up the most powerful jobs in the company to groups who had long been excluded. In so doing, they reified the occupational hierarchy. Starr's diversity metrics focused diversity personnel's attention, and they defined who mattered for diversity management (exempt employees) and the reasons they mattered (numerical representation). They codified the business class of employees as the important class. Their measures of disparity reinforced the division of labor, too, by turning inequality into a measure of the racial and gender composition of the almost-elite in relation to the elite.

Notably, the diversity reports did not track majority groups: men and white people. Further, they did not include the bottom two-thirds of the occupational hierarchy—the nonexempt employees who were either unionized (about a third of the workforce) or paid hourly (the remainder of employees). Diverse employees were not those who drove trucks, packed boxes on the factory floor, or cleaned bathrooms.

The Culture: Creating a Feeling of Inclusion

The numbers cannot tell you everything about a workplace, diversity managers would often say. Not only is not everyone counted—not gays and lesbians, not people of color outside the United States. The numbers also failed to capture what these managers called "the culture." Alisha, a senior director of marketing and a leader of the African American Affinity Group explained, "We still talk about numbers, which is a first step in it, but it's really more about feeling respected, feeling like you do have equal intelligence of the next person."

Starr had formal public relations statements on the importance of an inclusive workplace culture: "bring your whole self to work." The sentiment was that employees should be able to express their personal identities and individuality in the workplace, regardless of race, gender, or any other idiosyncratic difference. The vice president of global human resources, a charismatic black man named Kalim who was much admired by the diversity management personnel, described the culture that diversity management should create: "Diversity is the attempt to humanize the workplace. . . . It says to people, you don't have to be a cookie-cutter personality. . . . I always say, we're not all born equal, we're all born equally different. And that's the beauty." When I asked him if he had seen changes at the company with the implementation of diversity management, he replied emphatically, "Well, I think it allowed for people to bring their whole selves to work."

Adia Harvey Wingfield and Renée Skeete Alston's theory of racial tasks helps to explain Kalim's statements and popularity. The highest-level executives involved in diversity management, such as Kalim, had ideological tasks: extolling the effectiveness of diversity management (and calling for more of it) while reinforcing an image of the corporate environment as fair and equal and leaving unquestioned white privilege.[18] Below the executive level, diversity personnel and the employees they represented had the task of conforming to this top-down organizational culture, which required that they couch the challenges they faced in terms of the available appropriate language. The notion of bringing one's whole self to work resonated with Alisha and other affinity group leaders, and they in turn believed it resonated with the racial minority, female, and GLBT employees they spoke for. These employees felt pressured by the corporate culture to fit into a narrow mold best suited to white, male, and heterosexual counterparts. Julie, a white woman who co-led the Rainbow Group, described her experience in her first position in the company: "Everybody that I was talking to were mothers with children. I didn't fit. . . . Where I was in procurement, it's rather conservative. They are not really saying, 'Hey, you're gay, great.'" Of the twenty Rainbow Group members who replied to an internet survey by the group's leadership, only seven were out to their manager.

In an office environment replete with catchy corporate sayings, there were no slogans to describe the conditions that prevented minority and female employees from being fully included and respected. Diversity personnel saw people of color and women at the company (and themselves) treated and evaluated differently than their white male counterparts. Melissa did in fact have a well-developed vocabulary for talking about these issues as problems of cognitive bias, as described below, but the other diversity managers did not. They did not talk about what they observed as discrimination. Further, they lacked the terminology developed by sociologists and social psychologists to describe the subtle processes of nondeliberate discrimination and microaggressions or the diffuse structural dynamics of segregated social relationships, power differences, and formal processes that limit the advancement of employees who are not white men.

Diversity personnel's lack of terminology about workplace exclusion exacerbated their feelings of isolation, frustration, and distrust in the workplace. It compounded the racialized labor they already were doing to manage the power dynamics at work. Alisha told me about her experiences with bias at Starr:

> I don't think people are overt. It's to the point that most people, if they are treating people differently, they're not even aware of it, so that's tougher. That's tougher. It does happen. I don't think I would be exaggerating if I said

I question people's actions probably on a weekly basis. Like, "Is this happening?" or "Why is this happening?" I do think people try to really think first that it's not because of race or anything like that. So you try to rationalize it, but when you don't really know, sometimes you throw up your hands and say, "I have no idea." Often it's not, but sometimes it probably is, and you just never really know.

She described the stressful uncertainty these circumstances created for her and other African American professionals, as they asked themselves and each other: "How do you deal with it? . . . How much of yourself do you change to fit in? How much of yourself to you keep? And the answer is no simple answer. It kind of all depends." Like the slogan of bringing your whole self to work, the problem was individualized, and the onus was put on the less privileged employee to make sense of what to do.

There was one critical slogan that some diversity personnel used for a brief period to characterize people of color, women, and GLBT employees and the challenges those groups encountered in their workplace environment: the "canary in the coal mine," a concept elaborated in a 2002 book by critical race scholars Lani Guinier and Gerald Torres. Kalim had spoken about the miner's canary at a meeting of the affinity group leaders, and Melissa later repeated it (Melissa attributed it to Kalim, and then others attributed it to Melissa). As Melissa once explained, "Canaries die when there are noxious gases. They are very sensitive to them. Miners would use them to determine if it is safe to go into a mine. If they see the canary die, they have time to get out quickly." The analogy provides a way to explain the importance of rectifying the exclusion experienced by people of color. It characterizes that exclusion as pernicious in its own right and also as indicative of systemic organizational and social problems.

Out of that meeting with Kalim, diversity department personnel spearheaded an effort with the affinity group leaders to formulate a few pithy statements about the critical issues that affinity group members faced. They worked on the statements for nine months, intending to present them to the Starr executive team. In the first months of those meetings, Melissa called the affinity group leaders' messages "canary issues." To explain what the leaders were doing, she said, "The affinity groups' issues are canary issues. They feel it first. . . . Bad policies are enough to annihilate them, but they will eventually affect everyone. We asked the affinity groups to highlight the major canary issues and the impacts on them. For them, the impacts may be immediate, but they will affect everyone in the long term." Guinier and

Torres's concept provided a language for talking about bias in the workplace environment, although Melissa and others primarily used it in a way that deemphasized the problem of white male privilege (nor did they reference Guinier and Torres's radical agenda of cross-race coalition building to reform democratic processes). Instead they invoked it to underscore the instrumental good that could be gained for all employees by addressing the issues that stymied the workplace experiences of minorities.

The diversity personnel's use of the canary slogan proved to be short lived. For the final version of the statements, the diversity department staff dropped the language of "canary messages," calling them instead "key messages." The leaders of the affinity groups continued to struggle with how to inoffensively characterize the problems their members confronted. When the affinity group leaders met to review that final version, many raised objections and were confused because they had missed the prior meeting. One message on "Employee Retention" was unusually provocative, and this made some of the group leaders wary. It stated, "Eliminate double standards for Advancement:—Women & people of color vs. majority." Victor, the leader of the Hispanic Affinity Group, asked, "What are double standards?" Darnell responded, "People feel that there's a double standard for women, people of color, and the gay/lesbian group."

The people sitting around the table debated how to phrase the message. Bernie, representing the Hispanic/Asian Sales Group, said, "I'm wordsmithing here, but personally, I don't like 'double standards.' Because it can have serious legal implications. I'm not sure if it is a double standard. . . . Double standards sounds premeditated." Victor agreed: "I don't think it's double standards. It's a level of comfort with gender or whatever color." Darnell encouraged them to consider another way to phrase it: "Take the legal part out. Think about how your constituency would communicate this." Jill, a white representative from Women in Manufacturing, was blunt: "Managers use different eyes with men and women. For example, a man is a great candidate for leadership because he's assertive, while a woman is a bitch." Victor disagreed, "It's comfort."

The affinity group leaders' entire effort to communicate with the company's leadership was futile. After that last discussion with affinity leaders, while we walked back to the diversity department, I asked Darnell about revising the statements. He told me that the meeting with Starr executives had been canceled and would likely never happen. Before he had walked into the room earlier that day, Melissa handed him the chart and told him not to change anything. The opinions of the affinity group leaders were not a priority of the executive team. The entire effort to articulate systemic problems of inequity devolved from a critical rhetoric on toxicity to silencing.

Are GLBT Employees Diverse?

The distinctive experience of GLBT diversity managers highlights the limitations of the numbers and boilerplate corporate slogans for expressing GLBT employees' marginalization at work. Two years before this study, in 2003, a small group of GLBT employees had formed the Rainbow Affinity Group. The number of large companies with GLBT employee networks had grown modestly since the 1980s, and at this time, they were represented in just under 10% of Fortune 500 companies.[19] Appropriating the company's rhetoric about being your true self in the workplace, the Rainbow Group pushed for changes to Starr's HR policies. In step with other large firms, the company leaders soon began offering health insurance coverage and other benefits to employees' same-sex partners, and they amended the company's nondiscrimination policy to prohibit discrimination based on sexual orientation and gender identity. By 2005, the Rainbow Group had 109 members and a budget of just over $14,000. It held celebratory and networking events and regularly participated in a local pride parade. The company sponsored prominent gay and lesbian events, and a few Starr executives openly supported such causes.

Yet, even with some resources and protections, the members of the Rainbow Group had a marginalized role within diversity management activities. Most of the other diversity personnel seemed uninterested in or outright uncomfortable with GLBT employees' concerns. During their meetings, diversity personnel almost never mentioned GLBT employees unless a Rainbow Group leader was present and reminded them to do so. When personnel did speak of GLBT issues, they would refer to the "Rainbow Group" or the "gay/lesbian group" rather than saying "gay and lesbian" or "GLBT" employees; Darnell said just this when he met with the affinity group leaders to discuss the canary messages.

The absence of GLBT metrics exacerbated that marginalization. Again, the numbers were the priority for senior executives, and when diversity personnel met among themselves to discuss their activities, they spent much of their time reporting on the metrics for their functions. But the company would not ask employees to report their sexual orientation. That was considered intrusive. This meant that GLBT employees who wished to improve the climate and protections lacked a key basis of legitimacy within diversity management: evidence of numerical representation. Not having metrics presented bureaucratic problems for the Rainbow Group, too. The leaders struggled with how they could identify potential members, target their communications, and assess the concerns of GLBT employees.

Frustrated, the leaders of the Rainbow Group decided that they needed to emphasize the economic power of the GLBT consumers, and they alit on the business case to make that pitch. By formulating a business case for GLBT diversity, they hoped to represent GLBT employees as uniquely valuable and the Rainbow Group as distinctly useful for the company. Matt, a white gay man who worked as a professional in marketing resources and was a coleader of the Rainbow Group, pointed out that the company did little niche marketing to gay and lesbian consumers, even though that consumer population could be quantified. "We have data. We know we have gay and lesbian consumers. We know we can ballpark how many, we know what kinds of products they like." For Matt, that could provide a purpose for his group, besides giving support directly to GLBT employees—a purpose that hewed truer to the objective of corporate profits. "We can definitely help them," he argued, "help Starr to market toward them, to understand that group of people."

As organizational sociologists have observed, the business case for diversity presents difference as a resource for the business, and it poses the financial value of diversity as its primary value.[20] While scholars have documented the ubiquity of this rhetoric, especially its use by diversity management personnel and industry groups, little is known about how people mobilize it as source of meaning in the workplace and in relation to specific issues of inclusion. At Starr, one way that company spokespeople used the business case was to publicly explain the company's support for GLBT issues. When antigay conservative family values organizations threatened to boycott Starr for sponsoring GLBT community events, a senior executive wrote a letter to Starr employees defending the company's sponsorship. The company's commitment to diversity was long standing, he wrote. He defined diversity as "inclusive," stating that the company considered gender, ethnicity, and personal style as well sexual orientation and gender identity all forms of diversity. Diversity made Starr "a stronger company" and better able to serve its consumers. The letter was e-mailed to all employees and was soon circulated on blogs and websites outside the company.

Matt explained how the Rainbow Group used the executive's letter as a resource as well. The organizations protesting Starr had urged their members to call the company's toll-free number to complain that the company's sponsorship was immoral. In response, the Rainbow Group gave the call centers a version of the letter "so that when people called in, they had a script that said . . . basically the same thing." Matt described the letter in glowing language: "[It] says, 'We're not wavering. We understand that not everyone agrees with certain issues but, you know, diversity is part of our company and, you know, we value the diversity of our employees.' . . . It was a great memo." The letter clearly made him feel good about working for the company and made him identify more strongly with the organization.

The executive's letter also paid off pragmatically for the Rainbow Group. The group's membership skyrocketed after the letter was released. Matt thought that, more than anything, it heightened people's awareness of the group. "And then I guess," he added, "for others, maybe it just triggered a little sense of pride that we [the company] would not only support it, but defend it." Here, the executive's instrumental work of defending the company and signaling to employees that the company valued diversity was communicated through normative statements, with means-end rationales, that legitimated the company as well intended.

The Rainbow Group's struggle to gain credibility with company executives is indicative of a broader issue the diversity managers grappled with: who should change to make the company more inclusive?

How to Push at Glass Ceilings

To fulfill their assumed role as change agents, diversity personnel needed to identify *who* should change. They had in mind a few different sets of actors: senior executives, white male supervising managers, the exempt workforce at large, racial minority and female businesspeople, and diversity personnel themselves. These groups were essential to breaking glass ceilings. They were the lynchpins to selective inclusion—to addressing problems of representation and exclusion that hampered the careers of upwardly mobile racial minorities and women.

Diversity personnel's perceptions of these actors and access to resources for influencing them varied tremendously. They remained ever alert that their efforts to influence should not appear to interfere with the company's pursuit of profit. Often the best these personnel could do was to normatively assert their knowledge of the experiences of racial minority, female, and GLBT employees, expressing it as an important source of authority. They had relatively few opportunities to actually compel other people to act in ways that were sensitive to diversity. The personnel had had the least sway over those they believed had the most power over diversity management: the senior executives.

Hands-Off Executives

Starr's senior leaders did not prioritize diversity management. The CEO of Starr and other top executives would sometimes speak out publically on diversity issues, and one black female executive was quite vocal about them, but overall the corporate structure kept the senior leadership extremely insulated, both physically and socially, from diversity managers and other lower-status personnel.[21] The company's website noted that Starr had a Diversity Steering Team overseen by the company's executive committee, but this was not true. That team, which would have been led by Starr's CEO, was inactive in the mid-2000s. Executives signaled their indifference toward diversity management in the annual reports produced between 2001 and 2006. Those reports showcased diversity in the company's consumer base and products, showing multicultural-appearing consumers from different countries and displays of Starr's varied product lines and brands. If the reports referenced the topic of employee diversity, it was only mentioned in passing as a desirable personal trait of the company's leaders and only visually represented with photographs of executives. Starr leaders were no longer trying to sell stockholders on the company's responsibility to employee diversity—or any other responsibility to the workforce, for that matter.

Likewise, many diversity personnel believed that the company's senior executives, especially the CEO, were neglecting diversity management, although they would usually only raise this criticism outside of formal meetings or behind closed doors. With the company's new emphasis on short-term profitability, diversity had been "dropped," they would say, and the senior leadership no longer saw diversity and the business as "intertwined." A Latino sales manager noted that the involvement of top executives in the past had infused the Hispanic Council with energy and excitement:

> I went to [a meeting of] the Hispanic Council here. It was like you can't even get in the meeting room because there were so many people, standing room only. A hundred people, one hundred thirty, one hundred forty, I mean a lot of Hispanic employees. We had this great atmosphere. You could see the leaders up there, and you could see they were trying to put forth an agenda of things to do. And then it, it stayed like that for years. . . . People at the top in the organization, the [names of executives]'s of the world, they were leading the charge. . . . And then all of a sudden in the last two to three years, we've seen a decline where the focus [is] from an organizational perspective.

Diversity personnel wished to revive executive involvement. One of the affinity group's key messages had been "Management Support for Diversity."

The integration of Starr's US and non-US businesses also meant that many new executives working in the United States were not US citizens or had accrued most of their work experience in international regions. Thus they had not been schooled in the importance of valuing diversity. At a meeting of the diversity advisers, someone who worked under a German executive vice president explained diplomatically, "Our leadership is cross-cultural. People are both here and abroad. So people were thinking about diversity as Irish, Italian, and German. The perception outside the US is that diversity is quotas and laws."

Under Melissa, the diversity department took some cautious steps to encourage the company's executives to direct more attention to diversity management. During our interview, Melissa relayed to me strategies that she said she was using to reach Starr executives. Repeating a creed in the diversity management industry, she said, "You need to start working at the top levels and getting them to send the right messages and hold people accountable." She explained her own actions: "I've been impressing as I've been meeting with the Starr executive team members, how important it is for them to role model, because so much of what they do and who they are is emulated by everyone else in the organization."

To illustrate this point about executive influence, Melissa would tell a story about the new CEO of another large corporation where she had once worked. That company had a very formal culture—"the blue suits, the red ties, the white shirts."

> One day [the CEO] came down, just walked down to the marketing department. . . . He had on a pair of light gray [suit] pants . . . and a white shirt, but he had on a pale paisley yellow tie. And yellow braces. And he just looked quite stunning. The word went around, "You have to see [the CEO] today. He looks great." By the end of the next week, guess what half of the marketing men had on? I mean, it was hysterical. We laughed about it so many times. But later in life, I realized, just what [executives] eat for breakfast, everything about them becomes a significant point of influence.

Melissa described how she and her staff were trying to change the behaviors of Starr executives by changing how they understood diversity issues: "One of our goals is to influence their thinking and help provide the spotlight, or the analysis, or the data, so they can look at their organizations from a conscious diversity view." Her message was that executives' role was primarily symbolic. They should indicate to supervisors and other diversity personnel that they recognized the importance of viewing their organizations in terms of diversity.

Nonetheless, Melissa and other diversity personnel were intimidated by the CEO and other top executives. Melissa had little authority to tell executives how to act, and the e-mail messages, face-to-face discussions, and other communications between her office and the company's executives were not open to diversity personnel (or to me). If nothing else, she sought to *appear* as if she were putting pressure on executives—to give the impression of exercising influence.

The issue of hands-off executives was, at its heart, an issue of executive authority and white male privilege. Starr senior executives were widely revered, largely out of reach, and treated as almost untouchable. They were buffered by their offices and unquestioned authority. Few diversity personnel openly questioned whether those executives deserved the power they had, although they wished the executives would exercise that power differently. There also was a sense that the company executives believed that they were above diversity management—that their talents and acumen need not be spent on such affairs. At one meeting about the diversity messages, the affinity group leaders discussed what they needed from the senior executives. Jack, the previous director of diversity, observed, "Upper management isn't doing a good job at pushing this down to middle managers." Darnell nodded, commenting, "I agree completely. Part is middle management. But part of our message is that upper management needs to drill this down." Linda, who represented the African Americans in Manufacturing Group, both explained and excused upper management as color- and gender-blind: "The Starr executive team members were assembled because they are great leaders. They don't care about gender, color."

Through their offices and ideological influence, executives created and reinforced a corporate culture in which being white and male is treated as standard, with diversity management a compartmentalized, mostly performative, and normatively charged set of activities.[22] Likewise, these executives created a corporate culture that treated the occupational/class hierarchy as the unquestionable measure of worth, meritocracy, and success.

My own experience in the field confirmed the constraints that diversity personnel faced around influencing executives. After I prepared my final report for the diversity department, I presented it at different meetings of diversity personnel. Afterward, a number of them told me that the most important element of the report, in addition to the chart on long-term trends in representation, was the statement that diversity programming needed greater "visibility and support from senior leaders." Many appreciated that the report noted their desire for greater accountability for diversity goals among senior executives and managers. These personnel would say, emphatically, that they appreciated my forthrightness. Melissa and Darnell hoped that I could present my findings to the CEO and his team. "You're the only one who can give this presentation," Darnell told me.

I never presented my report to senior executives. As my field research was officially ending, Melissa was replaced with a diversity director who was more ingratiated to senior managers and less inclined to challenge them. My understanding is that my report was not circulated beyond diversity personnel, because it was no longer of interest or perhaps because it was provocative. According to one diversity manager, it was "buried."

The Problem of Middle Managers

There was widespread consensus among Starr diversity personnel that "middle managers"—the predominantly white male managers with supervising authority to make hiring, promotion, and firing decisions—were a problem. They viewed middle managers as too busy, centrally focused on the business, and in need of stronger skills at developing racial minority and female employees. Susan, an African American associate director of HR who was the diversity adviser for finance, explained that the hiring managers in finance were willing to hear from her but did not prioritize diversity issues. "It's a one-off. It's not daily work. If they're hiring, they just want things done." A few diversity personnel implied that some middle managers resisted diversity management outright.

The topic of problematic middle managers surfaced many times at the two-day Diversity Sales Group meeting. From the perspective of diversity personnel at that meeting, senior executives who at least spoke of the importance of diversity management were stronger allies than were middle managers. During a brainstorm about the group's long-term goals, someone suggested "changing the middle manager mindset." Jack agreed. He had recently heard a senior executive describe a woman who had left the company because her manager would not let her work from home, despite the company's work/life balance policy. "That's a perfect example." A leader of the Hispanic/Asian Sales Group, remarked: "The Consumer Development [sales] Leadership Team gets it. Maybe one or two layers down get it." Someone from the Black Sales Group finished his thought: "Managers don't get it."

According to diversity personnel, the middle managers remained within a narrowly circumscribed comfort zone and were not open minded or flexible, favoring insiders and excluding outsiders instead of fostering workplace inclusion. Speaking about resistance from middle managers, Melissa once said, "That's where the real power is, and it's whether they execute on a day-to-day basis." Melissa told me that, at another company she once worked for, she had scrutinized the list of employees who had been positively evaluated by their supervisors and deemed promotable. She identified people on the list that had been in the same positions for six years or more, and discovered that they were disproportionately people of color and women. The list indicated to her that the company's succession planning was inadvertently biased and that this was the doing of supervising managers.

Rarely did diversity managers talk about this as a problem of "white men" or of bias or discrimination. While there was an unspoken understanding that the problem of middle managers had to do with the fact that most were white and male, diversity managers did not question managerial privilege per se. As with the senior executives, diversity personnel did not explicitly contest the power that these managers wielded. They treated the problem as one of ignorance, inattention, and lack of accountability—enabled by managers' privilege and the failure of senior executives to "drill down," all to the detriment of people of color and women.

Again, the problem of middle managers was frequently characterized as one of "comfort." Melissa drew on the language of cognitive bias and organizational development—the use of behavioral sciences to improve organizational and individual performance—to talk about this. This reflected her own professional background; unlike the other diversity personnel in this study, she had her own diversity consulting firm. Her conception of the challenges to diversity management emphasized the unconscious preferences that motivate behavior, skill building, and assessment—which, as Victor had said at the affinity group meeting, she characterized not as bias but as comfort and affiliation.[23] In her opinion, the first step of changing managers' behaviors was to make them aware of their own subtle preferences and their impact on other people. As she explained, a person's unconscious preferences will manifest in seemingly benign ways, but the effects can be pernicious for people of color and women: "You are socialized to be more comfortable with some people than others." She described how a person, over his or her lifetime, learned behavioral cues from their role models, religious leaders, neighbors, and classmates about how to feel around other people. "So if you have people you are most comfortable with and you bond with, it's a natural inclination to help them. Sometimes it is so natural that you can't see it." Combined with a lack of accountability, this lack of comfort could disadvantage groups that supervisors considered not as smart, less capable of leadership, or too emotional.

As most of the diversity personnel lacked any bureaucratic power over middle managers, they were uncertain about how they could encourage those managers to change. Some used the business case for diversity to make an appeal for including supervising managers in leadership roles in diversity initiatives. At the Diversity Sales Group meeting, during a discussion of the group's short-term priorities, Jack asked, "How critical do we view inclusion? If we look at our group, we've not included the largest group—middle managers. In my opinion, we left out a big piece. That piece needs to come together to make diversity travel . . . [so] no one feels excluded." Curt, the senior executive, noted, "Jack, you bring up the classic question: where are the middle managers? . . . But those middle managers won't help us with these [short-term] priorities." Bernie, from the Hispanic/Asian Sales Group, shared Jack's position, "They should've been on the train from the get-go." He believed that diversity should encompass everyone, not just minority groups. He added a line from the business case: "Diversity as a business imperative takes into account thoughts, perspectives." A woman with the Black Sales Group nodded her head in agreement.

Curt advocated a different approach, one of strategic management that focused on efficiency: disregard those managers who were most resistant. "Anytime you go through a change model, 20% of the people are with you, 50% aren't sure and are going to step back and watch, [and] 30% will never be on board. Don't waste a minute on that 30%. . . . We need to focus on that 50%." From this perspective, intractable white men were a lost cause. The discussion circled back to the importance of getting support from senior executives. Van concluded, "Well, we need to find the white male champions."

Melissa once told me that diversity training had become a "road block" with managerial resistance, as people learned "the right things to say" and "the intellectual arguments," but it did not provide "motivation to change" or "consequences." Still, diversity training was the primary diversity management initiative that involved middle managers.

For Middle Managers and Other Exempt Employees: Lessons in Thinking and Talking

The broader exempt employee population, including and beyond middle managers, was another part of the workforce that Starr diversity personnel hoped to influence. This was a large swath of Starr's US workforce—approximately one-third—and predominantly white and male. The diversity department had the opportunity to engage these employees through the company's mandatory diversity training, which each exempt employee had to attend once.

For human resource personnel, training programs are an organizational structure that is relatively easy to deploy. HR training is one of those "solutions looking for issues to which they might be an answer," as the authors of an important sociological statement on organizational problem solving would put it.[24] In diversity management, training is the most popular initiative. In their study of private-sector employers, sociologists Alexandra Kalev, Frank Dobbin, and Erin Kelly found that 39% of employers were using diversity training by 2002.[25] The same study showed that such training efforts are especially ineffective and even counterproductive because they breed resentment and do not translate into long-term change. They do not move white women or most people of color into management and—when offered in the absence of a diversity office or another mechanism of accountability—can actually *depress* black women's representation in managerial positions.[26]

Starr's half-day introductory diversity training, Power of Difference, was a didactic lesson. The lectures and each of the participatory small group exercises instructed participants in the proper ways of speaking about different types of people—especially people of color—and interacting in small group settings. The training, which was normally facilitated by an HR manager, began with a few icebreaking activities. In one exercise, the participants identified themselves as daytime or nighttime people and had a brief discussion about their working styles. The take-away message, summed up by the facilitators, was that everyone should be aware of the time of day that a person prefers to work because it can make a real difference in how people get their work done.

Another group exercise was on collusion. At one training session, the facilitator—a white manager named Stella who introduced herself as "100% Greek"—began the exercise by defining collusion: undesirable behaviors that passively go along with inappropriate comments, reinforce such comments, or deny something inappropriate had happened. She passed out a fictional case study for everyone to read. In the case, peer employees are at a meeting, and one of them, Susan, tells another, Yi, to "lighten up" and mocks his accent. Stella asked the trainees to identify "the comments which are generally inappropriate in the work environment (or questionable at best)." One young white woman remarked that Susan had made fun of

Yi's "racial" Asian act. Stella agreed that the teasing was unacceptable but then corrected the woman, saying that Yi's accent was not racial—it was "cultural."

Diversity training methods such as this one are attempts to exercise normative influence. Power of Difference is a method of cultivating the disposition of the ideal Starr employee: someone who is open minded, cosmopolitan, and savvy in cross-cultural interactions. As sociologist Andrea Voyer writes, diversity training instructs participants to "acquire competence in the use of a particular multicultural vocabulary and rules of interaction."[27] It has the effect not of improving mindsets or undoing inequality, she argues, but of fostering a multicultural self that is modern, moral, and psychologically sound.

In Starr's diversity training, the problem of racial and gender inequality at work was framed in terms of insults and other behaviors that denigrated a member of a minority group and made the employee feel uncomfortable. Neither white people nor men nor heterosexual people were explicitly identified as common offenders (nor were they identified as having a culture). The training also presented a solution to such situations—a pathway to racial equality, so to speak. The answer was a culturally sensitive employee.[28] In their office conservations and interpersonal dealings, businesspeople at Starr were supposed to exhibit a polite tolerance of others' cultural attributes (and disapprobation of people who were not tolerant), an awareness of racial background and other factors that might shape an individual's life and identity, and the ability to collaborate with team members across salient social boundaries. This approach to managing diversity leaves whiteness unnamed while constructing a role for white people as participants in cordial, productive, workplace relationships.

For Middle Managers and Other Exempt Employees: Diversity Awareness as a Leadership Skill

Another way diversity personnel tried to influence middle managers and other exempt employees was through diversity-themed events and meetings. Some of these were heritage celebrations featuring ethnic food or music. The kickoff event for the Hispanic Month was announced by a voice mail message sent to exempt employees' phones from a vice president who said, "Buenos días and good morning everyone," and the event itself, attended by eighty people, was officiated by the CEO and honored a respected Latino filmmaker from the region. Events such as these are forms of what diversity consultants have called "floppy disk diversity" or, more recently, "flash drive diversity."[29] Diversity themes are plugged in for a brief period of time, but the dominant defining culture of the company and its normative favoritism for white people—the hard drive—remain fundamentally the same.

Less frequently, the company hosted diversity-themed meetings at which diversity personnel gave substantive presentations. One of these meetings, hosted by Grueber & Co., a subsidiary of Starr headquartered in another state, centered on the theme of the business case for diversity. William, a tall, dignified African American man and a senior HR manager, co-organized Grueber's midyear meeting on the theme of diversity and community engagement, in collaboration with the Grueber affinity groups. The objective, he said to me, was "keeping [diversity] in front of folks." The organizers had invited Melissa to speak because they hoped she would instruct Grueber business professionals in the business case. The company had conducted an internal employee survey that included a question about the business case for diversity, and, he said, "The employees wrote a lot of verbiage. This was a sign to me that people weren't really clear about what the business case was, and we needed to get people on board."

More than six hundred exempt employees attended the Grueber conference, held in a cavernous meeting room in a hotel convention center. Rows of tables were festively covered in a rainbow of tablecloths. About 85% of the attendees were white. Aside from Melissa, all the company spokespeople were white men.

Melissa's presentation began with the business case. Dressed in a peach business suit with her short dark hair slicked back, she strode confidently across the stage. She quoted a recent statement by the CEO: "'Everything that we do should reflect the diversity of the society that we are. . . . Consumer markets, customers, even psychodynamics.' I thought that was the best articulation of the business case." Then she suggested that Grueber had solid diversity management programs in place but that those programs needed improvement. She referred to a recent diversity meeting at Starr that had been themed "Building a House of Diversity." That theme was relevant to Grueber, she said. "The house is here. We just need to renovate." Up until this point, which was about midway through her speech, she had not said that anything was especially unique about people of color and women. Any employee, she indicated, might feel left out of the house.

But then she shifted gears, to reiterate an instrumentalist argument about why middle managers and other presumably white exempt employees should be motivated to learn diversity management skills. "We need to gain a critical mass of women and people of color 'in the house' to achieve business success." She told a story about another company to illustrate the experiences that people of color and women had at work that made diversity management so necessary. A black employee at that company had told his mentor that he was resigning. The employee said to the executive, "You did wonderful things for me, but other than that I never felt I was 'in the house.' I was a guest." Melissa said that she wanted everyone in the room to both feel "in the house" and to make sure that others feel that way, too. "This doesn't mean there are no rules. We need to give feedback and allow [people] to overcome mistakes. . . . This also means opportunities for failed experiences and coaching to overcome them."

Melissa framed the issue in terms of win-win outcomes. Starr's already impressive diversity initiatives would be improved by exempt employees who voluntary exercise leadership skills in diversity management. This skill development would not only be a way to help diverse employees; it would help all employees (she did not refer to the coal miner's canary, but it was the same idea). Moreover, developing diversity management skills would improve one's own career. Melissa's concluding exercise made this point visceral. She led the audience in an exercise in which all the participants closed their eyes. Then she walked quickly throughout the crowd, repeating over and over, "If someone touches your arm, stand with your eyes closed. If someone touches your shoulder, stand and open your eyes. If someone touches your head, stand and do whatever you want." If someone was not touched, he or she was to remain seated. After Melissa had made her rounds, most people were still seated with their eyes closed. Some stood with their eyes closed. Just a few stood with their eyes open.

Melissa directed everyone to open their eyes. She asked, "The people who were sitting—how did you feel?" People called out answers like, "Left out!" She asked the people who had been tapped on the arm and stood with eyes closed how they felt. "Disappointed!" said a black woman. And the people who had been tapped on the head and could act freely? People exclaimed: "Chosen!" "Empowered!" "Opportunity!" Melissa remarked, "Those of you sitting, many of you may resent me for not selecting you. Same for those who were tapped on the arm. But I never said that *I* had to tap you!" Many audience members laughed loudly. Her message: each person in the room could take initiative as leaders on diversity; they should not wait to be told. "Each of you is empowered to pursue and create an atmosphere of diversity."

Melissa was exercising normative influence, in hopes of persuading the audience of majority-white businesspeople in the room that they would derive an instrumental benefit from encouraging the development of the people of color and women they supervised. She conveyed this message by downplaying race and gender altogether. To be a good leader, according to Melissa, Starr businesspeople would need to shift their cognitive orientation and their interpersonal behavior. The message was not that supervising managers were unmeritocratic in their treatment of their supervisees but that these managers had the potential to lead on diversity and could personally gain from doing so.[30]

Even these nonconfrontational formulations of workplace problems and solutions had detractors. A number of Starr businesspeople complained quietly at work and vociferously on websites such as vault.com, where they could be anonymous. Some accused the company of hiring any person of color over a white person. Some were resentful or took offense. Some were unmoved by the company's lessons in talking and thinking about diversity. At the Grueber conference, near the end of Melissa's talk, a pregnant white woman at my table smiled and said, "She's good!" A red-haired and bearded white man sitting next to her—who had rolled his eyes when Melissa began the exercise—sat with a blank, bored expression on his face, saying nothing in response.

For Diverse Employees: A Model of Individual Empowerment for Promotables

Of all the people that diversity personnel hoped to influence within the company, racial minority and female businesspeople were most clearly within their purview. These employees were among the easiest to reach. They were most likely to seek out diversity management resources, and diversity personnel were far less constrained in interactions with them than they were with executives or middle managers. And by focusing on these employees, the diversity personnel could avoid confronting the company's biased employment practices directly.

In general, Starr had extensive resources for employee professional development and was recognized internationally as a great employer for career management. Most of the company's diversity management initiatives applied Starr's ideology of career development to assist exempt people of color and women. Most were designed for those racial minority and female businesspeople who took personal initiative to improve their experience at work and further their career.

African American, Latino, Asian American, white female, and GLBT businesspeople at Starr could get involved in one of the company's employee diversity affinity groups. Through an affinity group, they could attend monthly receptions and social mixers, receive e-mail updates with professionalization tips, and attend events such as a power breakfast or "lunch-n-learn" with other affinity group members. They also might take on a leadership role in the affinity group as, say, treasurer. The goal of the affinity groups, according to diversity personnel, was to provide diverse employees with career coaching and mentoring, a sense of community, and resources for developing their leadership skills. One affinity group leader told me that her group, the Women's Sales Group, schooled its members on "How do you play the game that's called Starr Corporation?"

The affinity groups organized activities centered on self-help themes. The Asian American Employee Group, for example, held a two-day class on "Successful Communication." The first day of activities covered obstacles that Asian Americans confront when trying to communicate: their upbringing, religion, values, customs, and stereotypes that they themselves and others may have adopted. On the second day, participants were video- and audiotaped, and then they analyzed their own performance. According to Greg, a leader of that diversity affinity group, the goal of successful communication was to help Asian American employees counter popular stereotypes about their abilities:

> I sit in meetings where I know that if I am quiet too long, people will marginalize my role in the meeting. So as a male, as an Asian male . . . sometimes you almost just have to just overcompensate. I kind of walk in and just say, "Hey, you know I'm a player in this room. Let me give my opinion." Otherwise you're pushed aside pretty quickly.

The diversity department also organized Global Diversity Learning and Growth seminars, which were specialized professionalization training sessions for women and employees of color. Most of the internal seminars were run by outside firms, and they varied in cost from no charge to over $3,000. Both the affinity groups and the functional units identified seminar participants and paid some portion of the cost.

The understood objective of these professionalization activities was to help employees find greater satisfaction in their jobs, make desirable lateral moves, and advance to positions with more power and higher compensation. The activities were supposed to provide employees with tools to better understand their own strengths and limitations in order to grow and perform better.

One especially popular seminar series at Starr, run by a consulting firm, was called Efficacy. There were two versions, Efficacy for Women and Efficacy for Professionals of Color, and both focused on themes of individual empowerment and self-actualization. At the Women's Summit, a consultant named Donna—a large African American woman with a gruff voice and dark circles under her eyes—described Efficacy. Soon after she began speaking, a white woman from Starr who was a senior manager jumped in to praise the seminar: "The most important thing you learn in Efficacy is what holds yourself back. It's a chance to be frank. Different cultures have different learning styles, but those can become an obstacle." The main message, she said, is "It's not the stimulus, it's the response." Donna agreed, "That's exactly it." She showed a slide with the same slogan: "It's not the stimulus, it's the response." Donna explained, "You can decide whether you're going to be reactive or angry . . . or clear-headed and proactive . . . and figure out which way will serve you better." At other meetings and in interviews, diversity personnel at Starr praised Efficacy and repeated this phrase.

According to Starr diversity personnel, workshops organized around self-empowerment themes were popular among so-called diverse employees. The chair of the African American Affinity Group recounted what African American employees had told her about the affinity group events they liked best:

> "Can I go to something where I'm going to learn to make me a better person?" "Can I go to something that's going to help me figure out this big and complex organization?" or "It's going to let me in on a secret that everybody else knows, on how to be successful, because I must be missing one." I do think African Americans like myself sometimes feel like there's this secret communication going on between everybody else and I'm kind of left out of it, so can I meet with other African Americans to learn, you know, what's going on behind the closed doors and the secret communications that I might not be a part of? It's those types of sessions that will draw the most people.

The Successful Communication workshop, Efficacy seminars, and other professionalization initiatives attempted to counter exclusion that results from bias in patterns of interaction, norms, networking, and evaluation.

The diversity personnel acknowledged openly that the workplace problems face by women and people of color could not be solved simply by teaching members of these groups to adjust their attitudes and behaviors. At one meeting of diversity personnel, Melissa noted the limits of an individual empowerment approach: "Efficacy emphasizes the theme of effecting positive change and taking control. . . . People may come out of that feeling very empowered, but they still feel they do not get their managers' support." At the end of my study, the diversity department announced it was adding new Efficacy seminars—Efficacy for Men and Efficacy for Management and

Reinforcement. (Based on public documents, the company did eventually adopt Efficacy for Men as well as Efficacy for GLBT employees.)

Nonetheless, the company put a premium on its professionalization initiatives tailored to people of color and women. Through these initiatives, the company supports a managerial model of individual empowerment. In this model, diversity personnel facilitate the career success of so-called diverse employees by exposing them to resources, knowledge, tools of self-understanding, and relationships. This strategy focuses on the self-actualization of the individual member of a marginalized group rather than, say, the modification of hiring managers' behaviors or legal penalties. It poses the empowerment of individuals through skill development and savvy know-how as a critical strategy for overcoming workplace obstacles. And it treats the corporate hierarchy as the utmost standard of racial and gender progress, with the greatest achievement being attainment of a position near or at the top.

For Diversity Personnel: Becoming Agents of Organizational Change

The diversity department staff believed that diversity business advisers and affinity group leaders, especially, needed to change in order to achieve successful diversity management. Melissa hoped to demonstrate to executives and supervisors that diversity management was a professional, effective, well-oiled operation. As she saw it, one way to convey that image and to court those who were resistant was to ensure that diversity personnel used consistent, clear messaging. Before an affinity group could post a message about diversity on its website, the diversity department had to review and approve it. Further, when it came to the business case, she believed that diversity personnel were not adequately on message. She stated at one meeting that they should be "singing from the same page."

Her perception that diversity personnel did not, in fact, know Starr's business case for diversity was correct. During interviews and at meetings, these personnel did not articulate a consistent understanding of it. Some spoke of the need to reflect consumers. Others said employees needed to feel accepted at work. Few knew specific examples of ways that having employees who were racial minority, female, GLBT, or otherwise diverse had positively changed the company. Some recognized that they were not on message and needed more direction from the diversity department. At meetings, they would ask the diversity department staff for a clearer statement of what they should say. Near the end of this study, the diversity department announced that it would develop a new website with the business case and distribute a CD with appropriate messages. Here, Melissa was mobilizing this instrumental rhetoric about bottom-line payoffs in an attempt to exercise normative influence over personnel and, she hoped, her higher-ups.

With the company's restructuring plan, Melissa also mounted an effort to enlist diversity personnel in becoming agents of organizational change. In fall 2005, Starr executives announced a new Business Process Improvement and Simplification Initiative to further cut costs and streamline practices. A senior vice president sent a letter about it to Starr employees stating that the company's competitors were growing faster, so the company needed to refocus and move nimbly to gain competitive advantage. Diversity personnel were worried about what some called "the abatement." They swapped rumors of what would happen next. One said to me, "That's the biggest story around here right now." Another spoke of already feeling the effects in sales: "The East Coast region lost four Customer Category Managers in a week. The CCMs are up to here [with work]. Work/life balance is out the window." Company leaders cut funding for some internal diversity conferences, and the threat of more cuts loomed. The affinity groups especially were under scrutiny. Personnel had heard that some senior managers believed the affinity groups spent too much money on networking and "goodwill" events such as heritage months.

Melissa was tasked with making recommendations to her supervisors and the company's senior executives on how to reposition diversity management. She created a PowerPoint presentation that she showed when she met with company executives, diversity advisers, and affinity group leaders. Adopting the language of strategic management, she counseled that diversity management required leadership, which meant embracing the simplification initiative and rethinking the affinity groups. She cautioned, "You all saw the letter." Her advice was to reframe and reengineer diversity management activities as efficient and useful for the bottom line. She advised the diversity business advisers and especially the affinity group leaders to lead strategically and produce results if they wanted to survive.

Melissa's PowerPoint slides framed diversity management according to the language and concepts of the simplification initiative: speed, flexibility, focus, simplicity, and success achieved through strategies such as decomplexity and systems harmonization. She had created a series of charts, each with two columns. The first column listed ways that the simplification initiative concepts were being applied to the company's business. The second column, titled "Opportunities for Affinity Groups," listed ways that the same concepts could be applied to the affinity groups. The company was trying to "reduce activities that drive a lot of work," so the parallel opportunity for the affinity groups was to "reduce 'nice to do' activities that drive work." Because the company would "close manufacturing facilities," the affinity groups should "eliminate low value initiatives." The premise of her charts was that the affinity groups should become more productive.

At a meeting of the affinity group leaders, Melissa explained, "What I really want to do is shift people's thinking to align with the process of business simplification." She warned them: "This train is rolling forward with you or without you. This is an opportunity for every affinity group to make its strategic change now."

Most of the diversity personnel seemed to agree with her that they needed to change. A leader from sales remarked, "We're guilty of doing a lot of low-value initiatives." The diversity personnel from Operations talked about how they had formed an umbrella affinity group to more efficiently coordinate women and African Americans and would "subcontract" various initiatives to that umbrella group. Other diversity personnel were fiercely skeptical about Melissa's presentation. Victor worried that the organizational restructuring was hitting hardest African Americans, Hispanics, Asian Americans, and women, who were already sorely underrepresented among supervising plant managers in his division. He was upset: "I'd rather be talking about what skills do our people need to be ready for next year. Major changes are coming." Melissa replied curtly, "I can't help you with that. . . . I can say it emotionless because if we're going to be viable, we have to think like the business. This is strategic mode." Many in the room nodded in agreement. She added, "It's an opportunity to be leaders or victims."

Melissa's advice to the diversity personnel is indicative of the narrowing of the discursive frame of diversity management. It represents the extreme appropriation of racial minority inclusion. Rhetorically, she was constructing racial and gender inclusion according to a corporate logic of retrenchment. According to that reasoning, diversity management activities were acceptable only if they seemed to directly support the company's short-term goals of cost cutting and profit maximization. That her advice was pitched at the affinity groups—the company's best-mobilized racial minority, female, and GLBT employees and an unmistakably difference-conscious intervention—was striking, as was her message that that the social networking and socializing practices of these groups was of low value. Thus, at a moment when Melissa and other diversity personnel were least in control, a truncated rhetoric on the business case seemed the only viable rationale for their existence.

Just as Starr diversity personnel struggled to establish their authority and influence different groups of employees in the workplace (or appear to be doing as much), they were resolutely clear on what they were *not* doing to improve diversity at the company.

What's Not Diversity?

The unwritten but official line on diversity management at Starr was that diversity issues were not legal issues. The diversity department was entirely separate from the legal department. The company had separate training and policies on discrimination or "zero tolerance." Diversity personnel avoided calling unequal treatment of racial minority and female employees "discrimination," and they said that any cases of discrimination would be referred to the legal department.

Diversity managers even more ardently distinguished diversity management from the company's affirmative action programs. Starr was still required by the federal government to practice affirmative action, and the affirmative action plans for the company's various US work sites were overseen by two diversity department staff members. One afternoon, I asked Darnell to explain the difference between affirmative action and diversity management. He leaped up from his desk, taped a large piece of paper to his office wall, and drew a line down the middle. Turning to me, he said emphatically, "Starr treats affirmative action plans and diversity as two totally separate things." The US government required Starr, as a federal contractor, to practice affirmative action. Affirmative action was organized and driven by government protocols. The company faced the threat of material consequences for not passing affirmative action audits: fines, loss of government contracts, bad publicity. "Diversity is your own business," Darnell told me, echoing a theme popularized by the diversity management industry and other HR personnel. The consequences, he said, depended on the prerogative of the CEO and vice presidents.

At face value, affirmative action and diversity management share important similarities: both are supposed to improve representation, hiring, promotions, and terminations of people of color and women. Although Starr used two separate data systems to track metrics for affirmative action and diversity, both programs operationalized gender and race as the US federal government has defined them for equal employee opportunity purposes since the 1970s: the numerical representation of anonymous minorities.[31] In the company's reports for each program, women and racial minorities were treated as distinct. Individuals were categorized into one of three major racial groups—African Americans, Hispanics, and Asians—and aggregated as people of color.

As Darnell noted, Starr's affirmative action programs and its diversity management programs had significant structural differences. Although the federal government had curtailed affirmative action enforcement and penalties were uncommon, the company faced the threat of legal and monetary penalties for failing to comply. This contrasted to the company's self-regulation of diversity management, with its elective, inconsequential diversity objectives. In addition, affirmative action applied to all employees and was organized by company location. Diversity management was selective. At Starr, it applied only to the top third of the workforce and was structured according to the company's organizations and functions nationwide.

Starr diversity personnel almost never brought up the topic of affirmative action of their own volition. I had to ask about it. The company's website did not list affirmative action as one of the many highlighted features of its diversity management platform. Personnel seemed to think it was not especially important for their work, although they were not entirely dismissive of affirmative action either. When asked about it, many told me that they thought affirmative action was still "the right thing to do." They sometimes referred to affirmative action as part of a historical evolution within the company, framing it as an early diversity initiative. Both these tropes are standard in the diversity management industry.

Like their industry counterparts, Starr personnel insisted that the company could be trusted to achieve inclusion without much government meddling and that diversity management was far more effective than regulation. They were not interested in whether or not affirmative action was actually effective at moving people of color and women into management (it is).[32] They commonly described affirmative action as outdated, imposed by the government, and not tailored to the company's business needs. When Darnell detailed the differences between affirmative action and diversity management for me, he waved a thick white binder with the affirmative action plan for one plant and said gravely, "This is like doing your taxes." With these sorts of statements, the Starr managers were echoing the well-worn story told by diversity consultants and human resource professionals: affirmative action had outlived its usefulness, or at least it was of limited utility.[33] Corporate leaders, they argued, needed better tools to manage differences among employees, especially on teams. Such rhetoric and practices discredit affirmative action, presenting it as burdensome and irrelevant.

Another issue was usually outside the official purview of diversity management, although diversity personnel did not boast of it openly: unionized employees and hourly paid employees, all of whom were nonexempt.

Not Lower-Level Workers

While I was doing field research, I tried to learn more about nonexempt workers' experiences of diversity management, or lack thereof. I made many efforts through the diversity department to reach those employees. Every attempt failed. My simple initial request dumbfounded diversity personnel because the lower-status workers were so far outside their managerial purview.

There were many bureaucratic obstacles that exemplified (and surely exacerbated) the distance between the diversity department and nonexempt employees. The staff members did not oversee nonexempt employees that they could easily refer me to. Darnell eventually put me in contact with a nonunionized hourly employee. Then I encountered a technological hurdle. With exempt employees, I could easily schedule appointments through the shared calendar system on the company's intranet using the ID, password, e-mail address, cubicle, and desktop computer the company had provided me. But the person to whom Darnell referred me did not have an online calendar, which was a convenient technology that businesspeople at Starr routinely used (as did I). I played phone tag with that person a number of times—mostly me calling him—and eventually I gave up. Darnell never found a unionized employee for me to interview. He explained to me that such an interview would be difficult to set up, anyway, because of the union rules—who would cover that person's shift or pay for lost time? I gradually realized that I would need to conduct an entirely separate study to understand nonexempt workers.

Diversity personnel understood the exclusion of lower-level workers as unremarkable, practical, and altogether acceptable. When I asked why diversity management did not consistently reach lower-level workers, some managers explained that the needs of those workers were fundamentally the same as the needs of higher-status workers. A leader of the Hispanic Employee Group explained about nonexempt employees, "As far as what they would like to see done, it's the same thing: to be seen, to be recognized." Other diversity personnel believed that diversity management efforts targeted to higher-status workers would trickle down to benefit lower-status ones. Jack, speaking from his expertise in diversity management, told me,

[Exempt positions are] positions of power and influence in the organization and also decision making about hiring, promotion. . . . [Exempt women
and people of color] bring a different perspective, which allows what? More
women and color, you would assume, to be hired. It certainly increases retention because women and people of color at a lower level see there is a possibility. . . . So you create this upward spiral of success.

Still others saw the company's focus on exempt employees as strategic
and efficient. Faith told me why global supply chain did not provide advanced training to nonexempt workers. "If you are looking at the blue-collar
employees—and this is a total general statement—but, for the most part,
those are folks who do not have advanced degrees and are not looking to
move up to be a very senior-level person within the organization."

That lower-level workers were deemed not diverse and not productive
raises deeper questions about structural problems of class inequality and
hierarchy. Could diversity management add focus further down the workforce? For example, would management really want unionized people of
color employees to feel a greater sense of efficacy, which might strengthen
union solidarity? Would management want to invest resources to help female cafeteria workers to move up the ranks, and if so, where would they
move? These issues extend beyond firms. Like civil rights mandates, corporate diversity management does not recognize class as a status of disadvantage. But both civil rights of nondiscrimination and government-mandated
affirmative action have the often unnoted advantage of applying to an organization's entire workforce. With weak and diminishing state protections
for workers and the rise of diversity management, with its facade of helping
all employees, we see further retrenchment of a neoliberal order that deval-
ues labor.

The Symbolic Politics of Racial Progress in Corporate America

The Starr case is the capstone of this book and provides another vantage
point on the diversity movement's achievements with regard to civil rights
activists' ambitions of full equality. This case exemplifies how those ambitions have mostly been derailed. The managers who are officially at the
forefront of integrating the workplace have little bureaucratic power, fear
for their job security, and face unrelenting pressure to increase shareholder
value. Company executives show little interest in the substantive needs of
diverse employees, much less in figuring out how to effectively serve them.
The movement for diversity at Starr seems to have helped some people of

color and women push through glass ceilings and cope with the stress of those white- and male-dominated environments. Ultimately, though, it is complicit in the neoliberal market forces that degrade low-level workers and demean the moral significance of substantive equality.

In Starr's regime of diversity management, the symbolic politics of racial progress played out around a bureaucratic infrastructure of difference-conscious initiatives and normative affirmations that formulated common interests. The company's diversity management practices were organized according to a corporate logic. The firm's market position was regarded as the utmost basis of legitimacy, and managerial authority was glorified. The goal of corporate profits was reified. Diversity management was mostly cordoned off from core decision making, though, and treated as secondary to the company's market success.

Diversity advocates at Starr equated racial and gender progress with scaling the top rungs of the corporate ladder. More than in the other cases in this book, inclusion at Starr was extremely selective. Diversity statistics, programming, and the business case reiterated the acceptable archetypes of corporate diversity: high-achieving, high-status racial minority and female individuals to be empowered and white male supervisors and managers with the leadership skills of sensitivity to diversity. Ramping up the pressure, the director of the department called on those she worked with to more zealously incorporate the tenets of efficiency, cost reduction, and profitability in service of those employees.

At Starr, diversity management posed some challenges to long-standing hierarchies of race, gender, and sexual orientation by making disparities in representation and feelings of discomfort known, contested, and undesirable. Their race- and gender-conscious rhetoric provided an alternative to the difference-blind language of meritocracy, Yet, in many other ways, their prioritization of selective inclusion legitimated hierarchies of class, race, gender, and sexual orientation. By design, diversity management discounted the class disadvantages of lower-level workers and overlooked the company's exploitative labor practices. Also by design, the company's push for diversity minimized problems of white favoritism. Diversity by and large meant people of color and women, who were implicitly framed as aberrations from the norm. Diversity management did not problematize whiteness, masculinity, or the accumulation of privilege.

Through their myriad activities, diversity proponents at Starr tried to linked minority representation and workplace integration to the company's stature as a transnational, publicly traded consumer goods firm. Their vision of racial and gender progress was the most expedient, viable framework available to them. It was oriented toward a difficult-to-achieve, laudable objective: breaking glass ceilings. This vision was also complicit in the glorification of corporate power. Here, progress toward integration was acceptable so long as it was part and parcel of a neoliberal economic order—compatible with profitability; the insulation of executives; a deregulated workplace; and the interests and worldviews of the elite, majority-white, and majority-male workforce.

Neoliberalism, Color Blindness, and Inequality in the Age of Diversity

In his acclaimed 2006 book, *The Trouble with Diversity: How We Learned to Love Identity and Ignore Inequality*, Walter Benn Michaels, a professor of English and leftist iconoclast, argues that diversity is an accomplice to neoliberalism. According to Michaels, "our current notion of cultural diversity" and "the American love affair with race" obscure the real problem: the gap between rich and poor.[1] Liberalism's preoccupation with racial identity and getting rid of racism, sexism, and homophobia make no difference in combating the ravages of economic inequality. Economic diversity is "ridiculous" as well, because poverty is not something to celebrate but rather something poor people hope to escape by going to an elite college.[2] And, he claims, liberals have gotten comfortable with easy, feel-good fixes—like corporate diversity training and language policing—leaving market supremacy unquestioned.

Is Michaels right? Before I answer, a few disclaimers are in order. *The Trouble with Diversity* is political critique and cultural commentary, not rigorous social scientific research. Polemical and provocative, it rests on many analytic and empirical fallacies: that social inequality is rooted in a single principle (the distribution of wealth), that there is a zero-sum game between fighting racism and fighting capitalist exploitation, and that the change that has taken place in the wake of the civil rights movement has been insignificant.[3] *The Trouble with Diversity* deserves a groan of disbelief: Yet another white man saying that the obstacles people of color and women confront are not important? Another white leftist with a bullhorn who thinks only class really matters? Another color-blind argument that paying attention to race impedes other social goals?

But it is worth holding up Michaels claims, which so many commentators find persuasive, to empirical realities of the internal organizational processes and interorganizational politics of diversity documented in this book.

Neoliberal Diversity

The Michigan, Rogers Park, and Starr cases provide some empirical support and add nuance to the argument that organizations' focus on diversity facilitates the efficient operations of a neoliberal economy. Neoliberalism, to be clear, is a theory of political economy. It joins abstract liberalism's commitment to individual liberty with a model of neoclassical economics that prescribes free markets over state intervention.[4] According to its critics, in practice it is characterized by economic polarization, concentration of wealth and resources among the most powerful, political demobilization of anyone other than the elite, and market triumphalism.[5]

In the cases studied, the organizational drive for diversity compliments neoliberalism in that it is primarily a drive for minorities who are high status or otherwise desirable for those in the majority. It is selectively inclusive. At the university and the company, racial progress is about people of color who are striving hard for the top rungs of the economic ladder or are already there. In the neighborhood, local leaders put a premium on homeowners of whatever racial background and people of color who purvey art, food, or some other consumable culture that middle-class, predominantly white people can experience. The drive for diversity commonly idolizes or leaves unquestioned the elite status of the affluent and their achievement of their status. This was evident, for example, in the reification of the class hierarchy at Starr.[6]

In the university and neighborhood cases, there were some circumstances in which decision makers who were concerned with diversity also recognized class-based inequalities—contrary to Michaels's claims that concern with economic diversity is a complete farce. The community council had educational programs for new homeowners, many of whom were not wealthy. Likewise, the objective of addressing the economic needs of people of color was not inherently antithetical to an objective of economic equality. For example, some college administrators understood that creating racial diversity on campus required enrollment of low-income students of color and thoughtful attention to those students' needs.

But by and large, the diversity efforts in these cases largely favored resource distribution to well-off people or did not disrupt the processes by which the well-off could hoard resources and opportunities. They also did not prioritize the problems of the poor or widening class disparities. At

Michigan, admissions criteria and merit scholarships remained to-ward affluent white students. The raison d'être of the university remained the creation of a powerful, credentialed political and economic class. In Rogers Park, political leaders minimized the issue of poverty, particularly its racialized dimensions. At Starr, the problems of the lower two-thirds of the workforce were not even visible to diversity managers in corporate headquarters.

The analysis in this book also illustrates how organizations' diversity activities can reify market success. Two different sorts of market competition are relevant: the markets that determine institutional access through admissions, housing, and labor and consumer markets. Decision makers very much want to successfully compete in markets of access by, say, attracting investment to the neighborhood for high-end condominiums. Those same markets also systematically marginalize people of color, bring unearned advantages to white people, and, particularly in labor markets, reinforce gender inequalities.

Many decision makers acknowledged boundary-heightening tendencies of such markets. As one diversity manager at Starr noted, managers in the finance division just wanted to expediently hire great employees; they did not want to bother seeking out a diverse slate of candidates. She and other diversity personnel presented diversity interventions as the key to moderating such tendencies. However, the diversity interventions that organizations put into place tend to be small in scale and decoupled from consequential decision making, so they do not dramatically alter such markets or the inequalities they sustain.[7] At Michigan, affirmative action is an add-on policy that effectively brings students of color into the university. Yet it mostly leaves untouched an admissions process that advantages affluent, predominantly white students and is essential for the university's prominent standing in the field of higher education. The university can claim a concern with minority representation while retaining its elite status. The interventions that come closest to changing those competitive markets are most likely to be politically resisted. Affirmative action in admissions is an obvious example.

The push for diversity also is commensurate with niche consumer markets. Sanitized images and consumer experiences of diversity are leveraged to sell products and places. The Rogers Park Builders Group's promotion of local eateries owned by immigrants and the glossy college booklets that Michigan produced are illustrative. At Starr, the discourse of market and product diversification preceded, and seemed to be a template for, its discourse on human diversity.

Modest changes in both markets of access and consumer markets can be driven by a demand for diversity as well. These changes may be motivated by appreciation, taste, fears of scrutiny, social justice concerns, or pragmatism. On several occasions, African American and Latino diversity managers at Starr offhandedly referred to the headhunters who persistently tried to lure them and their colleagues of color to other companies.

The neoliberal proclivities of the diversity movement are noticeably evident in what decision makers designate as *antithetical* to diversity: federal oversight of admissions, government subsidies for low-income housing, or government mandates for workplace affirmative action. From the perspective of many diversity boosters, especially in the neighborhood and at the company, government measures intended to redistribute resources downward are unnecessary or insufficient for fostering diversity. Diversity, in so many words, should be managed by the light touch of limited, elective policy intervention. This runs contrary to conservative criticisms of the diversity movement. Sociologist Nathan Glazer and law scholar Peter Schuck both characterize the imperative of managing diversity as a heavy-handed, largely misguided attempt by the government to do social engineering.[8] Decision makers documented in this book preferred interventions that were voluntary, semiprivatized, or altogether privatized.

Michigan is, in some ways, an exception. It *is* a state entity. However, an argument against federal intrusion in admissions policies was an undercurrent of the administration's legal defense and has origins in the early years of the push of diversity. The amicus brief submitted by Harvard and other elite universities in *Bakke*—the brief that was a template for Powell's statement on diversity—was not foremost an argument for diversity. The schools mobilized to urge the court to exercise "judicial restraint."[9] The court, they wrote, should not "substitute its judgment for that of educators" because "the guiding principle of freedom under which American colleges and universities have grown to greatness is that these institutions are expected to assume and exercise responsibility for the shaping of academic policy." Across these cases, the drive for diversity was routinely informed by an ideology that racial progress is best accomplished through organizations' elective independent efforts, not through government intervention (nor through political agitation or radical restructuring). This overlaps with the antiregulatory stance of neoliberal reforms and of the conservative movement.

Thus, by favoring high-status people of color, reinforcing market dynamics, rejecting federal intervention, and buffering the powerful, organizational diversity politics indeed facilitate neoliberalism. Even with these limitations, though, there is little evidence in the cases studied that, as

Michaels implies, society would be more economically equal if diversity advocates gave up their cause. If Starr eliminates its diversity management budget, it will not reallocate those funds to prounion organizing. As feminist critic Katha Pollitt writes, "Diversity can be cringe-making, arbitrary, insincere and sappy. But take it away and you won't get more equality—you'll only get more privilege."[10]

The simplistic master narrative of diversity put forth by Michaels and other armchair critics glosses over a troubling, fascinating, and complex double-edged reality that becomes apparent by scrutinizing real-life organizational contexts: just as the drive for diversity legitimates some hierarchies, it upends others.[11] Critics overlook this reality because they misunderstand the diversity movement and its power dynamics. They characterize it as one thing (liberalism) when its proponents' aims are varied and not necessarily to end racism and sexism. Promoting diversity often means photoshopping, but not all is smoke and mirrors. Power operates in more complicated ways. RPCAN activists argued for "high-road" urban development as a means of sustaining diversity. This book, with its attention to the gray areas and counterintuitive politics of diversity, is meant to highlight these complexities and provoke not only readers' ambivalence but their indignation.

The Fluidity of Cultural Meaning in Practice

Missing from Michaels work, and from much critical scholarship on racial discourse and ideology, is sensitivity to the fluidity of cultural meaning. Cultural meanings shift relative to organizational framing, political and power dynamics, social stratification, and institutional practices. While diversity is associated with positive recognition of cultural differences, the meaning of diversity is not absolute. Organizational and political actors combine it with other ideas, ideologies, and symbols toward a range of objectives. Contingency and agency matter, as well, for meaning making and the exercise of power. Discourses do not have power independent of their mobilization. Discourses do not *do* things; they facilitate or impede people's ability to do things, and, even more fundamentally, they bring those very things into being.

Law is an important example. Law grants diversity's meanings tremendous authority in organizational and political settings. The *Bakke* and *Grutter* decisions created an impetus for universities practicing affirmative action to adopt justifying rationales based on the diversity rationale. At the same time, meanings have an iterative relationship with practice, as people define and redefine law in relation to structural constraints such as legal doctrine, organizational interests, resources such as professional expertise, and legitimated strategies of knowledge production.[12] This is particularly evident in the ways the university made law. University lawyers, administrators, and educators formulated the diversity rationale by drawing on core practices, logics, and ideologies of higher education. Their legal defense in *Gratz* and *Grutter* defined the legal concept of diversity's educational benefits using social scientific measures; Patricia Gurin's analysis of individual students' learning and democracy outcomes was a centerpiece of their case. The court's decision in *Grutter* further codified diversity's educational benefits in that social scientific language of outcomes.

University administrators also made law in much more subtle, less instrumental ways. They conveyed their organizational conceptions of law through their selection of spokespeople, their design of the lawsuits gallery exhibit, their website with court filings and analysis, and their other public representations of the litigation. Through such practices, administrators intersubjectively constructed reality and gave law power.[13] They constituted law's meaning. Their interpretations of law were grounded in (necessarily) biased knowledge traditions and communicative practices. Furthermore, they presented and symbolically amplified their particular interpretations of law as universal and authoritative.

In other words, meanings are not overdetermined by structural constraints such as law. Organizations improvise on them. The fluidity of cultural meaning is especially evident in the political contests over diversity. When movement activists effectively mobilized to battle with high-level bureaucrats, they could turn ideals into controversies. The activists at Michigan and in Rogers Park rarely attained the outcomes they fought for, but they sometimes effectively changed the terms of debate through their provocative political actions and their demands for rights and remedies to injustice.

Color Blindness and Diversity

This analysis of the push for diversity sheds insight on the contemporary phenomenon of color blindness. Like neoliberalism, colorblindness gained currency alongside diversity. Is diversity a radically different vision of racial progress compared to color blindness? Or could it be an accomplice to color blindness too? There is no simple answer. The relationship between these cultural systems varies. Table C.1 summarizes five different orientations to color blindness and diversity in legal doctrine, policy paradigms, organizational and political normative cultures, social psychology, organizational structures and processes, or racial discourses.

Table C.1 Orientations to color blindness and diversity

Orientations	Examples
Oppositional legal doctrines and policy paradigms	University of Michigan: *Grutter v. Bollinger* (2003)
Distinct normative cultures and psychological beliefs	Mission statements that either make no reference to racial/social differences or that reference the value of difference
Unmarked or marked structures, activities, and processes	Starr Corporation: human resource management or diversity management
A false binary/irrelevant	College and community activists advocating equality, integration, justice, or civil rights
Distinguishable yet overlapping ideologies	Overlap: Disavowal of racism Rejection of need for race-based redistribution Valorization of liberal ideals, esp. merit Reification of class hierarchy and/or whiteness Cultural interpretation of race Insistence on fundamental sameness

Comparing color blindness and diversity sheds light on the symbolic politics of racial progress. Such comparisons, however, are complicated by the fact that color blindness and diversity are different cultural forms. Color blindness is an ideological formation that social scientists and critical race scholars have identified, labeled, and critiqued as racism and institutional discrimination. While the ideology varies with context, the central theme is that racial differences are of minimal or no importance and should be irrelevant in organizational decision making. In contemporary law and politics, those who espouse such ideas sometimes use the term *color-blind* but may prefer vocabulary such as individual rights or constitutional protections against discrimination. Meanwhile, *diversity* is a keyword that is also a buzzword, not a coherent ideology. It commonly conveys the ideological messages that there are meaningful differences in the social experiences of different racial groups and these differences should be recognized and positively valued by organizations. But it can convey other, even divergent ideological messages as well.

The relationship between color blindness and diversity is easiest to discern in legal doctrine and philosophical debates regarding race-conscious admissions. Therein, color blindness and diversity are explicitly articulated oppositional positions. They are shorthand terms for rival bodies of legal doctrine that political actors marshal to take positions for or against a governmental policy: *color blindness versus diversity*. In court decisions, one or the other prevails. Color-blind doctrine is the idea that equal protection law prohibits the government's use of race, whether to promote or remedy racism, and that the US Constitution only allows remedies to what is legally defined as intentional discrimination.[14] The diversity rationale is the argument that a government entity can take race into account in university and college admissions decisions for the purposes of achieving the educational benefits of diversity. *Grutter* is the consummate example. By a five to four vote, the diversity rationale won. The *Grutter* case exemplifies another crucial aspect of the oppositional relationship between diversity and color-blind doctrines: it sidelines or altogether silences arguments for civil rights justice or proactive integration in higher education.

While color blindness is relevant in many legal cases and has a long legal history of application to a variety of institutional contexts, the comparatively short-lived diversity rationale applies only to higher education, as was made explicit in the Supreme Court's decision in *Parents Involved in Community Schools v. Seattle School District No. 1* (2007). In *City of Richmond v. Croson* (1989), *Ricci v. DeStefano* (2009), and other cases, color-blind legal doctrine has been mobilized to contest governmental workplace affirmative action and set-aside programs. Those contested policies, like affirmative admissions, have long-standing roots in a civil rights agenda of proactively promoting integration, offsetting discrimination, and remedying racial inequality. In those legal cases, the defenses have been based not on argument about diversity but on an argument about remedying discrimination under the equal protection clause or disparate impact theory under Title VII.[15]

In public policy, diversity and color blindness can also be explicit, politicized oppositional paradigms regarding race, although outside the courts, their meanings and uses are more flexible and more variable. A color-blind policy paradigm is based on the premise that recognition of race should be removed from policy because civil rights reforms have triumphantly eradicated racism.[16] It reasons that racism has dissipated, lingering on only in bigots' attitudes; ongoing inequities are due to black people's cultural deficiencies. A diversity policy paradigm may recognize ongoing inequities and the structural and historical reasons for segregation, although supporters tend to advocate policies that positively recognize racial, gender, and perhaps other minority group differences and promote inclusion along those lines. The opposition between such paradigms is evident in state referenda such as Michigan's Proposal 2.

There have not been major color-blind challenges to corporate diversity management policy. The reasons are unclear. It may be because diversity management tends to focus on softer decisions that organize work, such as recruitment to select members of a hiring committee, so that the harms to majority groups are less easily identified.[17] When he testified before the EEOC to oppose its new E-RACE initiative (Eradicating Racism and Colorism from Employment), Roger Clegg of the Center for Equality Opportunity called for a color-blind offensive against corporate diversity programs under Title VII of the Civil Rights Act. He threatened to confront companies with prodiversity policies favoring applicants and employees according to their race, national origin, or gender, and he urged the commission to file such legal cases.[18] He claimed that workplace discrimination was much reduced, and although it was not extinct, "the solution is not to overlay a system of preferences on top of it." Likewise, in the context of housing policy, there continues to be fervent resistance to racial and economic integration efforts. However, this resistance is not explicitly framed as a fight for color blindness, in name, nor are the efforts opposed formalized as a wide-scale, coherent diversity policy paradigm.

In institutional contexts further afield from jurisprudence and policy platforms, the relationship between color blindness and diversity changes. It is less likely to be adversarial, but whether someone or something is oriented to color blindness or diversity has important consequences. Social psychologists have operationalized people's perceptions on race and ethnic differences according to these categories. They distinguish between the belief that such differences should be ignored (color blindness) from a belief that racial and ethnic group differences should be valued (diversity).[19] Each belief has some opposite effects and is associated with different policy preferences. A contrast between recognition of diversity and color-blind denial of difference is evident in the normative culture of an organizational or community environment as well. The cases in this book were selected because of the explicitly marked prodiversity normative culture, which is apparent in organizations' mission and vision statements, among other places.

Distinctions between color blindness and diversity exist in organizational and political structures, activities, and decision making. Structures may be discursively unmarked or marked as identity-conscious. It is up to the analyst to determine what has been unmarked, and is thus color-blind, and the implications. When a practice is marked as diversity-relevant, it signals that the distinct experiences and needs of people of color, women, low-income people, GLBT people, or other minorities are somehow relevant. Those groups will be the participants, the subjects, or both. This marking is in relation to the normative, hegemonic experiences and needs of white people, men, the affluent, and straight people—which may be explicitly identified and critiqued but more often go unnamed and unquestioned. In the university, neighborhood, and corporate cases, marked diversity policies were selectively inclusive, designed to modify the composition and perhaps the culture of an environment but not to fundamentally change basic logics and wide-scale patterns of interaction.

For some, the distinction between color blindness and diversity is irrelevant or a false binary. This was true for BAMN, RPCAN, and the Section 8 Tenants Council. BAMN leaders, who explicitly criticized both color-blind legal doctrine and the diversity rationale, argued for race-based affirmative action as a proactive means of furthering equality and integration. In Rogers Park, RPCAN activists did not challenge color blindness in name, but they persistently stressed that policy makers needed to be difference-conscious and that social policies needed to be socially just, or else people of color and poor people would be hurt. The Section 8 activists argued for a color-blind policy—they wanted their housing civil rights protected through the state's enforcement of nondiscrimination—but in the civil rights movement tradition, they paired that with claims for the political power of low-income people and African Americans.

The distinctions between color blindness and diversity can get quite blurry. For instance, many adherents to diversity describe color blindness or sameness as their ultimate aim. In his written statement on his personal view of diversity, Kalim, Starr's vice president of global human resources, described it as being "where extraneous attributes of race, religion, ethnicity, and gender do not influence how the person is perceived." And he definitely believed that diversity management was necessary to achieve such an aim.

There are a number of overlapping themes in color blindness and diversity. These points of similarity are most evident when we examine them as legal doctrine or as ideologies expressed through rhetoric. One point of commonality is the disavowal of racism. Neither adherents of color blindness nor adherents of diversity argue that racist hate is a positive aspect of social life that should be actively promoted.

Another striking point of similarity is the fundamental position on inequality. As legal scholar Kimberlé Crenshaw persuasively argues, color blindness erases the very notion of race-based redistribution.[20] Diversity often does the same when it is the vocabulary for talking about and conceptualizing racial progress. Legal doctrine on the diversity rationale and organizations' public relations rhetoric on diversity in these cases largely deny the ongoing manifestations of racial inequality and the need for transformative, structural intervention. In litigation, those who defend race-conscious admissions policies *weaken* their case if they argue for both promoting diversity and remedying inequality. Hence, Michigan did not share its time for oral arguments before the Supreme Court with the *Grutter* interveners. Similarly, in Rogers Park, political officials denied racial inequality by not acknowledging the racial consequences of housing redevelopment and through their token programs of "economic diversity" for working- and middle-class home buyers, whom they described as deserving recipients of government subsidies and public sympathy. When diversity advocates ignore racial inequities or reject remedial racial justice, they abet color blindness. They give power to the claim that historical racial discrimination no longer affects people's lives.

Color blindness and diversity doctrine and ideology both relieve white people of responsibility for racism and excuse white complicity. Sociologists Wendy Leo Moore and Joyce Bell describe this as the protection of white privilege through the assertion of white innocence. The diversity rationale, they argue, normalizes white superiority without invoking overtly bigoted claims, and it creates a coercive environment for students of color, who must defend their right to inhabit white-dominated spaces. I return to this topic of white privilege below.

A final point of ideological convergence between color blindness and diversity is around ideals of liberalism. As expressed in individuals' spoken discourse, color blindness interprets race in terms of abstract American ideals such as meritocracy, individuality, assimilation, and choice.[21] In the cases studied, decision makers treat diversity as a color-conscious, difference-sensitive objective in the service of many of the same ideals.[22] Michigan treated the pursuit of diversity through race-conscious admissions as an addendum to a meritocratic admissions system, the legitimacy of which it did not publicly question. In Rogers Park, community norms of endorsing diversity assumed some assimilation into the cultural mores of civically engaged, majority-white homeowners. Starr's professional development workshops were predicated on a model of individual empowerment, designed to enable female and racial minority participants to better scale the corporate ladder.

The schema presented in table C.1 provides a springboard for future research on the relationship between color blindness and diversity. This book leaves much ground uncovered. It was not designed to systematically document how organizational participants personally interpreted diversity or color blindness or how they perceived local leaders' diversity interventions. Moreover, it does not try to capture the range of ways that color blindness manifests in organizational and political practice, nor does it examine the nuanced ways in which color blindness and diversity are simultaneously present in organizational practices or social policy.[23] These are topics well suited for historically grounded ethnographic research.

The rise of postracialism and its relationship to the push for diversity merits further treatment as well. The postracial sentiment that racial problems have been transcended could be a not-so-subtle undermining of diversity objectives or it could be diversity's ultimate realization. President Obama—the ubersymbol of postracialism—did not campaign as a diversity candidate. To the dismay of many supporters, he largely avoided the topic of race and sidestepped issues of pressing concern for people of color (as of the writing of this book, he was on track to deporting more immigrants than any previous president). Yet he was elected after decades of prodiversity organizational advocacy. He very well may have been the beneficiary of affirmative action. It seems quite likely that his political achievements and popularity were facilitated by a prodiversity culture, particularly the valorization of people of color in elite occupations. To understand the organizational and political relationship between diversity and postracialism, historical analysis would be instructive. For instance, millennial postracial humor pokes fun at race in ways that can be interpreted as enlightened, clever, irreverent, or simply racist. It seems likely that the antecedent of postracial humor is the conservative mockery of political correctness and diversity interventions, which became popular in the early 1990s.

Boundary Minimization and Dynamics of Destigmatization

The push for diversity minimizes symbolic and social boundaries by validating *inclusiveness*. Organizational and community-based identities valorize difference. Decision makers' aspirational diversity rhetoric provides a language for characterizing the morality of inclusiveness and the good that comes of it. Archetypically diverse spokespeople and poster children serve as visual and embodied signs of minorities' representation. Statistics serve as legitimating evidence. Many diversity initiatives are framed and technically designed such that they appear to support the upward mobility of already desirable people of color, women, and GLBT people. Other initiatives seem to create an interactional order—an institutional culture of norms and expectations—in which expression of cultural difference is met with respect and honor. Processes of selective inclusion, when implemented in consequential decision making, increase the representation some people of color and other marginalized groups.

Organizational and political actors who are striving to attain and preserve voluntary cohesiveness may gravitate toward a conceptual or mythical ideal of diversity because it asserts a collective objective and collective obligations. In a neighborhood such as Rogers Park, a community identity of diversity is part of political leaders' strategy of maintaining and managing integration. An ideal of diversity provides a basis for group making—of defining who "we" are—in which the boundaries of social membership are quite expansive. Diversity symbolically broadens who belongs (who is a valued student, resident, or employee) and provides explanations of why that belonging is valuable (for learning, for quality of life, for productivity and innovation). This is diversity as a totem that binds members based not on obligation or penalizing rules but on intentional allegiance—even allegiance to that very word, *diversity*.[24]

When decision makers project an identity for their organizations or communities as models of diversity, they give new meaning to the racial order. They reimagine the racial order as a peaceful, productive mosaic—not an exploitative hierarchy or a color-blind democracy. They reframe racial integration as an accomplishment in which all parties benefit—not a zero-sum game or a moral imperative to help black people. From this perspective, racial inclusion, especially the integration of black people into predominantly white settings, appears to be a fairly uncomplicated, universally positive process. These identities of diversity also give new meaning to American pluralism. Pluralism is not imagined as a regime of inequality (as some sociologists characterize it) or as divisive group making (as claimed by some critics of multiculturalism) but as an emergent social order in which cultural difference is as a social good and competitive advantage, to be honored and appropriately managed.

The push for diversity legitimizes inclusiveness by *destigmatizing minorities in high-status and culturally desirable positions*. It designates certain minorities as deserving, and it validates their numbers, visibility, and voices. This ideological move can help to lessen oppressive hierarchies. In his historical-sociological study of how Irish and southern and eastern Europeans assimilated into the white mainstream in the United States, Richard Alba finds that the advancement of immigrants was possible because their upward mobility stopped impinging on the prospects of those groups that already enjoyed advantage.[25] Their mobility was no longer threatening. It was "non-zero-sum." Ideologically, majority groups came to see these minorities as worthy of higher status. Put differently, immigrants' minority status was destigmatized and became less of an obstacle for their life experiences.

The destigmatization of minorities is valuable when it counters well-entrenched mechanisms of inequality—when it stops white people from monopolizing credentials or when it creates an institutional culture free of microaggressions and degrading stereotypes. The push for diversity has been particularly successful at validating minority group members' claims to representation and respect. Being an archetype of diversity can be a basis of claims making. The Students Supporting Affirmative Action activists carefully created substantive diversity in their coalition through their organizational and leadership structure, and they staged that diversity in the media spotlight to collectively claim an entitlement to the rewards that accrue through affirmative admissions. These claims have credibility in diversity politics, as there commonly is an expectation that people of color and maybe other minority groups will somehow have input into the issues that involve them.

Minority group claims are only successful when decision makers actually respond by directing resources, respect, and rewards accordingly.[26] The extent to which this happened in the cases studied varied tremendously, from Michigan's supplemental yet effective (and now dismantled) race-based admissions policies to Starr's relatively miniscule budget for diversity management programming (in 2005, 0.000016% of the company's annual revenue). Decision makers—some of whom themselves are black, female, or of another minority status—may allow or advocate minority representation, visibility, and voice. They often try to stage it. And they sometimes just photoshop it. Public relations is a driving concern, as minority representation and palpable involvement symbolize decision makers' own sensitivity.

In some limited ways, the diversity movement proactively *delegitimizes stratification by questioning privilege*. Proponents minimized boundaries by identifying and critiquing them. One of the most powerful ways this happens is when decision makers and participants ideologically mark—make identity-conscious—practices that at face value seem neutral but, in fact, favor high-status groups. When someone complains that a panel of speakers or an organization's leadership team is not diverse because everyone involved is a white man, that is critique of hierarchy. It draws attention to who monopolizes power.

But in this study, the mainstream diversity advocates by and large seek to minimize the stigma attached to minority groups, not to stigmatize majority groups. They tend not to speak critically of the demographics of those who enjoy privilege. Although some outsider activists do, those at the center of power do not.

Critique of privilege is foundational to claims for remedial and redistributive racial justice, because to call for remedy, one must make reference to the problems that need redress. The leaders studied tended not to acknowledge or take seriously such claims. The activists who voiced those claims at Michigan and in Rogers Park were not well liked. Decision makers tried to silence them, avoided them, and co-opted their images. For decision makers, such claims were not credible, given the institutional constraints they confronted and their political priorities, positions, worldviews, and desires. Redistributive justice was not compatible with decision makers' political-economic objectives of maintaining an elite organizational status, garnering political power, pursuing profitable business ventures, and ensuring their own favored status.

The activists discussed in this book who called for redistributive justice and proactive integration needed to rely on provocative political actions. Although they had some limited but important successes at securing resources for the people of color and poor people, these activists, and their claims, were marginalized within the formal channels of contestation and decision making. The lack of oppositional activism at Starr is evidence of, and contributes to, the hegemonic prioritization of corporate power and class hierarchy over equity goals. As insider interest groups, the affinity groups were best positioned to criticize dynamics of privilege in the company. But they avoided provocation, as when they renamed their "canary messages." And not even they could get a meeting with the CEO.

Rather than challenging privilege, the diversity advocates preferred to assert the *worth* of majority groups. They legitimize inclusion by *destigmatizing white people*. The desirable white person is one who opts into racially integrated environments and has the taste, vocabulary, and disposition to engage in generative cross-cultural interactions. This frames white people as contributors to diversity, beneficiaries of it, and part of the proverbial solution. Legitimation of white people's authority and normativity can happen in a number of ways: when diversity is an evaluative standard (judged against whiteness), numeric proportional representation (in reference to white representation), the experiences of marginalized groups (but not those of their privileged counterparts), a consumer experience (stuff white people like), low-stakes affirmation of cultural differences (more stuff white people like), or superficial window dressing (the appearance of change within an unfair, unequal status quo).

The destigmatization of whiteness may help to disarm potential resistance from white people, whose buy-in is an essential ingredient of racial integration. It provides white people with a comfortable, positive role—something other than a villainous racist or a victim of reverse racism. Social psychological research intimates that when organizations explicitly include white people in their definitions of diversity, white people will feel a stronger sense of belonging and be more supportive of organizational inclusion.[27] However, such a strategy of minimizing boundaries ignores the problem of white advantage or, subversively, turns white racial identity into a claim to resources and respect. In downplaying the fortunes that white people enjoy, it disconnects those fortunes from the obstacles that people of color encounter.

The destigmatization of selective minorities and of whiteness also can buffer decision makers' authority. Through their advocacy of diversity, decision makers define a role for themselves as compassionate facilitators of inclusion. They project responsibility and, to some extent, shield their organizations, their offices, and themselves from charges of discrimination.

None of this means that people of color actually experience the diversity movement as inclusive, that the movement effectively enlists white people, or that decision makers are inoculated. The empirical evidence on this is very mixed, and more is needed. The acceptable roles for people of color can be stereotypical and constraining, and obstacles to their substantive, meaningful inclusion remain largely intact.[28] White people report lower support for diversity efforts in colleges, communities, and workplaces and commonly feel excluded from organizations' definitions of diversity.[29] By and large, affirmative action is not surviving legal challenge.

The Organizational Legitimation of Inequality

This book sheds light on the role of culture in inequality by showing the constitutive role of culture in organizational and political practice. Using analogical theorizing, it highlights commonalities in meaning making, as well as variability and contingency, across organizational contexts and at different levels of analysis.

As the analysis reveals, the push for diversity simultaneously delegitimates and legitimates inequality. Those legitimacy processes are apparent in decision makers' practices of boundary minimization. They designate particular objectives, social statuses, hierarchies, resource inequities, and strategies of redress as undesirable. They label those things as in need of change. They leave other statuses, hierarchies, inequities, and redress unquestioned. Sometimes, they disrupt practices of exploitation and opportunity hoarding when they validate new claims—such as a claim to representation—and when they change the interaction order to be less oppressive. But, again, the trick of the diversity movement is that it is far easier to symbolize inclusion than to socially dismantle inequality.

Moreover, and most pertinent for the study of organizational culture, scholars can better understand the organizational legitimation and delegitimation of inequality by identifying mechanisms by which decision makers associate ideological meanings with organizational practice. This requires that we differentiate among cultural forms and meanings and their role in social life.

As this book shows, the cultural meanings of diversity become associated with formal organizational and political activities.[30] More specifically, organizations have different bureaucratic conceptualizations of race and diversity, and those conceptualizations are salient in different tasks, for different purposes.[31] For instance, decision makers' aspirational rhetoric on diversity constitutes social reality differently and facilitates different claims to resources, in comparison to their diversity statistics. Their aspirational rhetoric typically conceptualizes human diversity as distinctive cultural identities possessed by all sorts of people. Leaders mobilize such rhetoric to assert, explain, and persuade audiences that everyone has a common interest in inclusion.

Statistics, in contrast, operationalize human diversity as quantifiable populations of people of color and maybe women. They define referent groups and provide benchmarks for progress.[32] Diversity advocates mobilize those statistics as they try to signify their commitments to inclusion and persuade others to prioritize proportional representation. In their everyday practices, decision makers do not use aspirational rhetoric as a standard for evaluating any given diversity program. This is one of the many distinctions that is lost in scholarship that focuses exclusively on organizations' official diversity rhetoric. By making this distinction, analysts can better specify the relevance and consequences of culture.

One important mechanism by which organizational culture can delegitimate and legitimate inequality is through the patterned associations of certain meanings with certain organizational activities. In the cases in this book, organizational actors tether *particular* conceptualizations of diversity to *particular* practices in patterned ways. This tethering is especially legible when diversity's meanings are ideological and overt—as is so characteristic of much organizational the drive for diversity. (It is less legible when diversity's meanings are unspoken and implicit, in the form of interactional norms or individuals' self-understanding.)

Some patterns in tethering stand out. At Michigan, in Rogers Park, and at

Starr, there is *officially codified organizational symbolism of diversity that becomes the object of organizational work.* Examples include the boilerplate text pasted into a PowerPoint slide and the logos that hang on community banners. These are readily observable expressions of discourse. They usually take the form of aspirational, justifying rhetoric and visual symbols. Diversity advocates spend considerable time writing, revising, practicing, and disseminating these meanings.

Diversity's meanings get tethered to organizational practices in the form of the *social material that decision makers invoke as evidence of diversity and their commitment thereto.* As neoinstitutionalists have long observed, organizational and political actors reference diversity offices and policies as evidence of organizational commitment and successful action.[33] The cases in this book reveal even more. The leaders studied frequently cited statistics on demographic representation as evidence of real diversity. They treated individuals, experiences, and interactions that exemplify acceptable archetypes of diversity as such evidence as well. This is a reason why the choice of spokespeople becomes so important in diversity politics. Most decision makers, as well as activists, need their organizations to look diverse (as those parties define it and according to the audience's expectations).

And diversity's ideological meanings get attached to certain organizational practices through *the stated purposes and technical design of diversity intervention.* The stated purpose and technical design of a given intervention reifies a strategy of racial progress, with assumptions about hierarchies, obstacles, and resolution. One such example is that Starr managers' professionalization seminars for people of color and women are organized around the presumption that racial progress is the upward mobility of highly skilled, exempt people of color. Meanwhile, Starr's affinity groups are characterized and designed as a strategy of giving voice to a marginalized group—that, too, is a strategy of racial progress. Likewise, the criterion for participating in a professionalization seminar, affinity group, or any other diversity intervention designates who is worthy of resources—typically, those deemed appropriately diverse and meritorious.[34] This form of tethering, between meaning making and technical design, is crucial for the legitimacy of selective inclusion.

The tethering of diversity' meanings to organizational and political practices takes place in a range of activities, from mundane routines to spectacular protests to well-oiled public relations campaigns. It is possible because diversity's meanings are imposed and officially sanctioned but still malleable and wide ranging. Tethering is an important process by which the diversity movement constitutes hegemonic social realities. When certain meanings "stick" to certain organizational tasks and activities, they become consequential dimensions of social action. These are institutionalized, embedded in everyday practice, and symbolically amplified. They seem more normal and more desirable.

Finally, processes of legitimation and delegitimation also characterize the contests between decision makers and their detractors. Not everyone who hears diversity rhetoric or participates in a diversity program agrees with the meanings decision makers favor and the associations they make. There is negotiation, resistance, and push back. This is most evident in activists' challenges. Oppositional activists question decision makers' designations of appropriate objectives and strategies of change. They cast doubts on the efficacy of decision makers' actions. They define as important objectives, hierarchies, and strategies that decision makers have ignored or reified as normal. Although decision makers resist these challenges, activists have a significant claim: they represent the diversity that decision makers laud.

Activists face many challenges to political engagement. They are marginalized in formal processes of political contestation. In the cases studied, activists routinely had little option but to take sides in for-and-against contests over isolated policies, which detracted from the transformative political aims that so many aspired to. Their rhetorical gymnastics around diversity, including their technique of street-level semiotics, illustrate the linguistic and analytic skills that outsider activists need to challenge racial inequality at a time when decision makers' public relations cast race in wooly, plastic, and seemingly positive terms.

While social movement scholars have attended to some such contestation, those who study framing contests have paid less attention to the interactive dynamics between challengers and those they target. Further, they have not adequately excavated the work of public relations. This an aspect of the symbolic racial politics that has been all but overlooked by race scholars and that organizational sociologists have not thoroughly examined from the ground.[35] As sociologist Eric Klinenberg puts it, organizational and political elites now govern by public relations.[36] Public relations is part of the organizational machinery that maintains official commitments to equality in the face of enduring racial stratification and white privilege. It is also a mechanism by which organizations adopt and adapt scripts from their organizational fields and project inclusion. Understanding it requires analytic attention to the situations in which public relations are employed and how people actually do public relations, such as their consultations with policy experts and the work of practicing scripts and staging ideas. Activists must contend with public relations as well, deploying it in their own communications and managing the public relations of those they challenge.

Containing Racial Justice

There is no precedent for the racial integration that now exists in many universities, communities, workplaces, and other domains of life, including in some of the most elite circles and the most sought-out environments. The issue of racial representation has assumed a newfound importance in the United States. There are widespread expectations that major institutions will not be outright dominated only by white men. And yet the structure of politics, the economy, competitive markets, and social relations all still largely reinforce the privileged status enjoyed by white people, especially men, and the subordination of people of color. Popular hostility to race-conscious interventions and legal restrictions by the courts make it all the more difficult to directly address inequality.

The drive for diversity emerged in this historical moment as an organizational-political attempt to adapt racial representation, minority inclusion, and social pluralism to the institutional needs and priorities of those in power. Despite what its detractors might say about radical liberals and unconstitutional quotas, it has some strong conservative tendencies. The push for diversity is usually about insulating people with power. The polyvocality of the very term prevents critique because it co-opts and deflects contrary positions.

And still ideas of diversity can be concept building for a shared, collective interest that supersedes racist, nativist, and other bigoted tendencies. It can constitute people's self-conceptions and their social relations in ways that can undergird meaningful, boundary-reducing, and more egalitarian relationships. Likewise, because diversity is so plastic and broadly appealing, it can justify effective policy interventions such as affirmative admissions, and it can animate progressive political action to redistribute resources to the disadvantaged, too.

All told, the drive for diversity has contained the struggle for racial equality. It is hopeful, yet its promises always come with pitfalls. Diversity is a term that can make people feel good about inclusion and invested in that objective. This can heighten a sense of belonging and diminish restrictions on some minorities' opportunities, but by minimizing problems of deep-seated racial inequalities and cutting off language about the need to redistribute resources. Some of diversity's ideological sentiments seem to resonate with white people, yet those very sentiments relieve white people of responsibility. Diversity rationales can provide cover for effective policies, such as affirmative action. However, they also provide cover for ineffective action. Most diversity interventions fail to acknowledge and redress formalized organizational biases, nor do they monitor (much less effectively sanction) persistent discrimination and harassment. Diversity's proponents have accentuated numeric proportional representation as a standard for progress, but to the neglect of substantive diversity in the form of everyday interaction and meaningful integration. Selective inclusion can facilitate some important social change, including the mobility of people of color, women, and GLBT people into positions long monopolized by white men and their cultural acceptance. Yet it is complicit with larger political-economic forces that prevent deep structural transformation. Ultimately, the drive for diversity serves as a partial but insufficient answer to the unfinished project of racial justice.

ACKNOWLEDGMENTS

I owe thanks, first, to the many people at the University of Michigan, in Rogers Park, and at Starr Corporation who made this research possible by welcoming me into their organizations, offices, and homes. My ability to write this book depended foremost on your openness and cooperation. A few important individuals became friends and colleagues, provided checks on my findings, and read my work.

This research was possible thanks to the generous funding of the American Bar Foundation (ABF), Law and Social Science Program of the National Science Foundation (Grant No. 0418547), John D. and Catherine T. MacArthur Foundation, Chicago Community Trust, University at Buffalo–SUNY Julian Park Fund, and the Law School's Baldy Center on Law and Social Policy, as well as Northwestern University's Center for Legal Studies, Department of Sociology, and Graduate School. Fellowships from the ABF and through Northwestern University's Institute for Policy Research and Joint Center for Poverty Research supported data collection, analysis, and writing.

I was very fortunate to launch this project in the Department of Sociology at Northwestern University, which was an extraordinary environment for learning to do theoretically engaged ethnography. Wendy Griswold's kind and critical advice shaped this project and helped me to prioritize. Mary Pattillo shared her time, resources, keen eye for detail, and enthusiasm, giving meticulous feedback on multiple drafts and talks. Eric Klinenberg, who supported my vision of this project from the start, asked tough questions and encouraged me to think creatively about the research design. Wendy Espeland's detailed comments identified essential revisions for the book. Micaela di Leonardo was a welcome thorn in my side, pushing me to consider political economy and neoliberalism in ways I would not have pursued otherwise.

It is difficult to put into words how much Robert Nelson and Laura Beth Nielsen have influenced my intellectual development and all-around happiness. You have been thoughtful advisors, caring friends, and genuine supporters. Writing this book would have been a much lonelier, more difficult experience if not for you.

I have been embedded in wonderful intellectual communities throughout this project's many stages. The Northwestern University Culture Workshop, under Wendy Griswold, provided a supportive home where fellow participants gave deeply engaged, brutally honest feedback. The Ethnography Workshop and Ethnography Support Group, under Gary Alan Fine, were valuable sounding boards. The enriching culture of the ABF anchored this project while I did the analysis and wrote the dissertation. At the University at Buffalo–SUNY, I am deeply appreciative of Michael Farrell and Robert Granfield for ongoing enthusiasm and support. My colleagues in the sociology department thoughtfully protected my time as I finished it.

The Baldy Center, under Errol Meidinger, hosted a manuscript workshop that was enormously helpful in my rethinking of core elements of the book. I am especially grateful to Khiara Bridges, Doug Hartmann, and Nancy Maclean. Your intellectual acumen, practical suggestions, and generous spirit have influenced every chapter. Thank you, also, to the workshop participants. Notably, Erin Hatton and Camilo Trumper gave important, detailed feedback. I am indebted to Lynn Mather for her astute comments and crucial involvement.

During academic talks and in memorable personal exchanges, I gained valuable insight from Robert Adelman, Nicki Beisel, Lauren Edelman, Penney Edgell, Joe Gerteis, Angela Harris, Steve Hoffman, Robert Kagan, Athena Mutua, Christopher Mele, Cal Morrill, Aldon Morris, Christopher Schmidt, Susan Silbey, Sudhir Venkatesh, and Kim Weeden. The book benefited from helpful feedback and encouragement from Mitch Berbrier, Jomillls Braddock, John Comaroff, Robert Emerson, Stephen Engel, Angela Harris, Amanda Lewis, Bonnie Lindstrom, Daniel Lipson, Carl Nightingale, Mitchell Stevens, Chris Tomlins, Mariana Valverde, and Eric Walker. Thank you to graduate students in my Race and Racism seminar, as well, notably Kiera Duckworth, Tory Ervin, Wanda Garcia, Sarah Glann, Ryan Graham, Matthew Perry, Watoii Rabii, and Paul Durlak, who also provided research assistance.

Japonica Brown-Saracino, Tristin Green, and John Skrentny provided instructive comments at key junctures in the process of writing this book.

Heather Schoenfeld and Micaela Desoucey, who each read multiple drafts of my work, were more than generous with their time and insight.

A very special shout out goes to the inimitable Amin Ghaziani, who has been an intellectual companion, confidante, coach, and—above all else—dear friend from start to finish. You have kept me sassy and sane. I am ever appreciative of Page Knolker, whose sage wisdom has counseled me on the fine points and opened my mind to the big ones. Long conversations with Michelle Boyd grounded my thinking and inspired me through rough spots, thanks to her smart advice and clarity. Late night marathon sessions with Corey Fields fueled revisions to the book's core argument. Dan Hirschman and Fiona Rose-Greenland brought much-appreciated enthusiasm and input on historical details. Anna Lappé and Adam Berrey improved this book with wordsmithing and wit.

Kevin Berrey, Poppy Burke, Gabrielle Ferrales, Emily Meyer-Siegel, Wenona Rymond-Richmond, Shana Kuhn-Siegel, Amanda Margulies, and Jean Stark sustained me through this research with love and laughter. Rachel Ablow, Ana Mariella Bacigalupo, Des Curran, Laura Duquette, Jaume Francesca, Jordan Geiger, David Herzberg, Dalia Mueller, Ali Newman, Miriam Paeslack, Sarah Robert, and Marion Werner cheered me over the finish line.

Numerous individuals helped me gain access to a company to study, including Gary Gebhardt, who provided helpful advice and document templates. My ability to do fieldwork in Michigan depended on the kindness of two strangers, Noelle Goodin and Wroksie Jackson, who gave me a place to sleep. Thanks to Murielle Harris, Julia Harris-Sacony, Diane Holfelner, Lucinda Underwood, and Laura Wirth for administrative support, to the transcriptionists at DataShop, Inc., and to Dotti Hydue for copyediting.

Portions of chapters 2 and 3 appeared in earlier form in Ellen C. Berrey (2011), "Why Diversity Became Orthodox in Higher Education, and How It Changed the Meaning of Race on Campus," *Critical Sociology* 37 (5): 573–96. Portions of chapter 5 appeared in earlier form in Ellen C. Berrey (2005), "Divided over Diversity: Political Discourse in a Chicago Neighborhood," *City and Community* 4 (2): 143–70. Portions of chapter 7 appeared in earlier form in Ellen Berrey (2014), "Breaking Glass Ceilings, Ignoring Dirty Floors: The Culture and Class Bias of Corporate Diversity Management," *American Behavioral Scientist* 59 (2): 347–70.

Vinnie Roscigno and anonymous reviewers for the University of Chicago Press sharpened this book with thoughtful input that was both complimentary and critical. At the Press, Doug Mitchell saw the value of this book in its fledgling state. His intellectual enthusiasm and optimism buoyed me to the end. Tim McGovern helped with technical advice. George Roupe provided excellent copyediting.

I have been so fortune to have Robert and Becky Berrey's love and support, which have enabled me to focus on my work in good conscience. Thank you, Dad, for your ongoing intellectual involvement and for pushing me, quietly and kindly, to achieve. My mom, Betsy Berrey, was a best friend, around-the-clock cheerleader, and careful copyeditor. If she were here, she would be smiling her sunshine smile.

To my beautiful children, Eli and Adela: thank you for tolerating your mom's distraction and long days glued to the computer. A few years ago, Eli announced joyfully (but incorrectly) that a box that had just arrived from Amazon contained my book. That is how much you wanted this finished. Well, now we really can celebrate. And my deepest appreciation goes to my husband and life partner, Steve Hoffman, who held my hand and kept my back covered at each step of this journey. I am so grateful we are in this together.

This book is based on three ethnographic-historical case studies. To document the contemporary dynamics of the push for diversity in each case in the mid-2000s, I relied on participant observation, interviews, and organizational texts and images as well as legal documents, media coverage, and secondary statistics. I collected these ethnographic data over a period of more than six years. I did more intensive fieldwork during four of those years, meaning that I did observations or interviews at least multiple times a month and often multiple times a week. On a few occasions, I spent all day following an individual or group, doing what ethnographers call shoe-leather fieldwork.[1] More often, I did strategic observations of formal events. I conducted hundreds of hours of participant observation of meetings, panels, large forums, public presentations, and training sessions as well as marches, press conferences, and other political events. When appropriate, I took handwritten field notes.

I conducted a total of eighty-five semistructured, open-ended interviews that lasted, on average, one hour each. I tailored the questions to the participant's organizational position and the relevant social problems. The interviews were tape-recorded, transcribed, and analyzed with my field notes. I conducted numerous informal interviews as well. The organizational documents analyzed range from promotional materials like admissions brochures to policy and mission statements to Internet and intranet documents.

To document the histories of the three cases, I relied on archival sources, secondary sources such as organizational newsletters, and news media. I selected a primary document source for each case that revealed the topics of interest, such as minority admissions, and was produced consistently over the last thirty-five or forty-five years (the *Chicago Tribune*, Michigan's undergraduate viewbooks, and Starr's annual reports). I examined these sources retrospectively to understand the historical development of important themes and issues I had identified through fieldwork. I also inductively identified themes and issues in the historical sources, letting the texts speak for themselves. To track changes in organizational discourse on websites in the 2000s and to find information that organizations had once posted and then took off line, I relied on the Internet Archive (archive.org), which is a wonderful source for that sort of research. By triangulating my contemporary data sources with historical ones, I developed the analysis and argument of this book.

Below, I detail the specific methods, unique challenges, and noteworthy fieldwork travails for each case, presented in the chronological order that I did the fieldwork.

Rogers Park

I conducted fieldwork on Rogers Park redevelopment politics between summer 2000 and late 2002. I observed or participated in organizations' internal meetings, coalition meetings, and public forums; political activities like marches, door knocking with a tenant organizer, and an anticrime sit out; community events like a playground-building day; social activities; and casual conversations in parks, stores, and people's homes. I conducted twenty-five semistructured interviews (one of which was a group interview) with a total of twenty-nine organizational leaders, participants, and some nonparticipants. I followed print and electronic media such as community LISTSERVs and the weekly newspaper covering Chicago's Far North Side. I identified organizations for study and research participants based on local media sources, secondary literature, and my initial observations and through snowball sampling (recommendations from people I had already contacted).

I lived in the neighborhood while conducting this research. For two years of this study, I was employed as a research assistant for a study of reception of public housing residents in Chicago, led by Northwestern University professors Mary Pattillo and Dan Lewis. (Thank you, Mary!)

To analyze Rogers Park's history, I examined *Chicago Tribune* coverage from 1960 to 2005. I searched digital records of the newspaper for articles and editorials that referred to (East) Rogers Park and included the words *diverse, diversity, housing, integration,* (Alderman David) *Orr, tenants' rights,* and *Rogers Park Community Council.* Other sources included online newspapers and magazines that covered more limited time frames, such as the *Chicago Defender* (1849–1985, 1989–present), the *Chicago Sun-Times* (1985–present), and *Crain's Chicago* (1986–present); the Chicago *Community Fact Book*; the Internet Archive; and various brochures and reports about the neighborhood, a number of which were produced by Loyola University researchers. Sources came from the Northwestern University Library, the Chicago Historical Museum, and the Rogers Park / West Ridge Historical Society. I use first-name pseudonyms for all individuals in the Rogers Park case study except elected officials, but I use the real names of community organizations.[2]

Doing fieldwork in a politically divided neighborhood was sometimes challenging. At least some members of any given organization suspected that I was siding with their adversaries, especially with the tenant activists. I began my study with RPCAN, and I certainly sympathized with the activists' political causes. These activists and I share certain sociological precepts: that broader structural problems shape local issues and that discourse analysis can reveal how people use language to frame social problems. At one meeting, an RPCAN leader critiqued how local developers used the word *diversity*, referring to his analysis as Sociology 101. My association with tenant activists was not the only cause for suspicion and tension. Some activists and social service providers questioned my relationship with the real estate industry organization, the Builders Group. I also got caught in the middle of conflict between university researchers and some service providers involved in the affordable housing coalition.

Community leaders frequently asked me to take on leadership roles or assumed that I would do so. The Builders Group assigned me a role without my knowledge. One day, I discovered that I was listed as an advisor on their website. I promptly asked that they remove my name, and they did. I avoided taking these positions as best I could, wary that it would compromise my ability to cross over political battle lines. Instead, I offered technical or research support when it seemed appropriate, such as teaching computer classes or creating charts of demographic data. Four years after I finished my fieldwork on the neighborhood, I became an advisor to the Section 8 Tenants Council and served in that capacity for about a year.

University of Michigan

My study of contemporary dynamics at Michigan was, essentially, an ethnography of the *Gratz* and *Grutter* lawsuits and their immediate aftermath. It was conducted over the course of almost three years, from spring 2002 to winter 2005. I collected data about key individual actors, bureaucratic units of the university, and activist organizations that were immediately involved in the lawsuits, directly impacted by the lawsuits, or concerned with educating the student body about the lawsuits. I identified organizations and individuals for study based on local media and Internet sources, secondary literature, my initial observations, and snowball sampling.

I did fieldwork primarily on Michigan's Ann Arbor campus and in the university's satellite undergraduate admissions office in Detroit, although I conducted some ethnographic research in Chicago and made two trips to Washington, DC. I did not live in Ann Arbor during this study. Between November 2002 and January 2005, I traveled to Ann Arbor and Detroit an average of once or twice a month for three to five days per visit to collect data.

The data collection was divided into two distinct phases. Between spring 2002 and the US Supreme Court's decision in June 2003, I investigated the university's public activities and the political activism around the lawsuits. I did observations or participant observations of events such as educational panels, marches, rallies, and a bus trip from Ann Arbor to Washington the night before the Supreme Court oral arguments.

Between July 2003 and winter 2005, I focused intensively on changes in the Office of Undergraduate Admissions (OUA). I attended OUA campus recruitment sessions, high school student outreach in different cities, training for OUA application reviewers, and meetings in which reviewers made decisions about applicants. Throughout the study, particularly in the last year, I also collected evidence about campus diversity programming, such as the opening of the film *Campus Diversity, Student Voices*, pedagogical theater productions concerning diversity, and a large planning conference for Michigan's proposed Center for Institutional Diversity. I obtained and transcribed video and audio recordings of some of these events. My closest repeated contact was with administrators in the undergraduate admissions office and with activists in Students Supporting Affirmative Action and BAMN. I suspect that I gained such terrific access to the undergraduate admissions office because administrators there hoped to demonstrate that they had nothing to hide from the public eye.

I interviewed a cross-section of organizational participants, ranging from upper-level deans to student activists. I conducted thirty formal interviews with student and nonstudent activists, a Center for Individual Rights spokesperson, upper-level administrators such as deans and a university lawyer, the directors of admissions for the law school and undergraduate program, OUA officers, faculty members, and staff in various diversity programs as well as innumerable informal interviews during events like marches.

Texts analyzed included the legal filings, court decisions, and promotional materials for undergraduate admissions. I drew upon the vast range of scholarship and policy analysis about affirmative action and racial preferences as scholarly sources when appropriate, but I also tried to treat these sources as primary data to better understand the contours of the debates over the legal cases.

Campus media sources included the *Michigan Daily*, the *Michigan Record*, the *University Record*, press releases from Michigan News and Information Services, and Michigan's extensive website devoted to the cases.[3] I also followed some coverage of the cases in regional and national media and popular culture sources, such as the *Detroit Free Press* and *Chronicle of Higher Education*.

I use the real names of organizations in this case study and the real names of individuals who have public identities that I could not conceal (such as the university president), made comments on the public record, or gave me written permission to use their real names (almost all interviewees consented). I use first-name pseudonyms for any other individuals in the study.

My primary historical source was the application viewbook that the OUA produced and distributed to potential applicants from 1971 to 2005. I reviewed the entire viewbook but focused on the introductory description of the university, the description of Michigan students, the letter from the university president or other university officer, and descriptions of race-targeted programs. I analyzed terms such as *disadvantaged, opportunity, diversity, diverse, race,* and *minority* throughout the text. I coded for depictions of race-targeted programs (particularly the Opportunity Awards Program), the university, the student body, and the general tone of the text.

I also analyzed the online archives of the minutes of the university's Board of Regents, focusing on the period between 1966 and 1995 and on the terms *diverse, diversity, Opportunity Program, minority recruitment, minority report, Bakke,* and *Michigan Mandate.* Other historical sources included admissions materials produced by the OUA prior to 1960, OUA newsletters for guidance counselors, pamphlets and other historical admissions materials from the Michigan Bentley Historical Library, major university documents related to minority inclusion such as strategic plans, and secondary sources about the university. I collected the archival sources from the University of Michigan Bentley Library, OUA, the university's website and the Internet Archive as well as some retrospective interview accounts.

This case study posed many challenges, particularly the contemporary data collection. It was difficult to define the parameters of this case study.

The legal issues and media spotlight made many university leaders more difficult to accessible. I was entering a field with many wise, well-educated, and seasoned analysts, reporters, and scholars. What was more, many of these individuals were my research subjects. More than one person I interviewed at the university asked me what my research question was.

When I was spending time with SSAA activists, I found myself most acutely aware of my racial identity and age. Social relationships among students on campus are shaped by color lines and cohort affiliations, which affected my access to students. I encountered some of the color lines the evening before the march on Washington, when I tried unsuccessfully to get a seat on a bus that was carrying almost only black students.[4] I witnessed white students blunder when they interacted with black students (some of whom were quick to point out the blunders), and I certainly made a few of my own. On the day before the march on Washington, SSAA organized a day of silence. Students of colors and their allies wore thick, black gags over their mouths to symbolize their silencing and oppression in the absence of affirmative action. After participating in and observing two frantic days of campus organizing by SSAA, I was exhausted. I walked into a quiet office of the student government where two black female SSAA activists were making posters, and remarked on how nice and quiet it was. The women glared at me. Then I saw that one of them still had a gag hanging around her neck. For a moment, it felt as if I had said her voice should not be heard.

Excruciatingly uncomfortable fieldwork experiences are part of doing ethnographic research. These experiences are even more freighted and more likely to be harmful when the ethnographer is a member of a majority group doing research on those of a minority group. Once we recover from the embarrassment or horror and do our best to repair any damage, we may hope that these experiences make our analyses stronger.

Through such experiences, I came to appreciate on a deeper level the university administration's legal arguments that valuable learning happens in racially mixed contexts. I came to agree much more emphatically that universities should teach students to think critically and reflectively about their relationships with people of other racial backgrounds. I also could see shortcomings in the legal diversity rationale more clearly. On campus, cross-racial interactions (or lack thereof) happen in the social context of college students' friendship networks. The acute anxieties that many college students feel about having friends and being included can exacerbate the tensions between racial groups. Those anxieties surely contribute to white students' (mis)perceptions that students of color are socially exclusive. Even more important, the diversity rationale does not acknowledge some important realities of much cross-racial interaction: the blinders of privilege that so many white students bring to campus; the insults, frustrations, and hostility commonly experienced by students of color in their interpersonal interactions with white students (and administrators and faculty members); and the unfair burden put on students of color to respond to those indignities by, say, educating white students on race and racial etiquette or remaining silent.

Starr Corporation

My fieldwork and interviews at Starr examined diversity management activities within the company over the course of almost a year, from spring 2005 to winter 2006. Data collection focused on key managers, executives, and bureaucratic units active in diversity programming. Data sources included participant observations, interviews, internal intranet and externally available Internet website content, and media reporting. In the field, I obtained access to limited internal quantitative data as well. I conducted thirty-one interviews with staff from the diversity management department, diversity advisors, leaders of the affinity groups, senior executives, and staff from other departments such as multicultural marketing. I conducted observations of diversity training; internal organizational meetings of diversity management staff, diversity advisors, and affinity group leaders; company-wide celebratory diversity events in the corporate headquarters; and larger events such as the Women's Summit. Texts analyzed range from managers' PowerPoint presentations to the intranet website content for the nine employee affinity groups and the diversity department.

To construct the history of Starr Corporation, my primary historical source was the annual reports produced by Starr or its parent company between 1960 and 2005. Most of the reports are held in the Northwestern University library. My analysis focused on the introductory letter, the opening pages of the reports, and any sections on social responsibility and employees. I looked for terms such as *minority*, *disadvantaged*, *diversity*, and *diverse* and coded for general depictions of the company, employees, race, gender, diversity, consumers, and marketing strategies.

I supplemented the annual reports with a small set of newsletter articles, brochures, policy documents, and other materials related to affirmative action and diversity released by Starr's private corporate archives. I also relied on a few retrospective interviews with corporate leaders, older documents posted on the company's private intranet, the Internet Archive, industry websites, and materials available at the Chicago Historical Museum archives.

Conducting empirical sociological and historical research about a corporation is a challenging task. Perhaps the greatest obstacle is secrecy. Companies limit outsiders' knowledge by restricting public access to employees, company facilities and events, and print documents. Companies do not normally release to the public their internal documentary materials. In-depth news reporting on internal human resource practices is rare. The size of the company is another obstacle. Ethnographic research can only cover a miniscule and geographically circumscribed area of the organization.

Telling a coherent, accurate modern history of a company is complicated. One issue concerns how to define the corporation as an object of study. Starr went through numerous mergers, acquisitions, and changes in ownership structures during the 1980s, 1990s, and 2000s. Some of these were small. A few were major and very consequential. The name of the company that I refer to as Starr actually was modified more than seven times between 1960 and 2006. Notably, between the late 1980s and the early 2000s, when Starr was one of a few major businesses within an even larger corporation, Starr did not produce its own annual reports, so I use that corporation's reports instead. I rely on internal Starr documents from the 1980s and especially the 1990s to triangulate my findings from the annual reports and to provide details on programs that were specific to Starr but not necessarily used throughout the larger corporation.

By far the most time-consuming aspect of this case study was gaining initial access to a company. I began contacting potential companies for study in August 2004, while I was still collecting data about Michigan. I carefully crafted a research proposal that looked somewhat like a business plan. Printed on paper with Northwestern insignia, the proposal was full of white space, bulleted points, a chart, and text that—as much as possible—sounded like corporate language. I tailored the proposal to specific companies, proposed various deliverables, and detailed my credentials. I packaged it in a glossy purple Northwestern folder along with a cover letter, a letter from my dissertation chair, and my Northwestern business card.

I submitted the research proposal to four companies between fall 2004 and January 2005. Starr was one of the two companies that agreed to participate. Starr's legal department, the diversity department, and I spent a number of months negotiating a letter of agreement that outlined the terms of my study and setting up a research plan. I later learned that the diversity department was supposed to do an internal review of its programs around this same time, and the director of diversity planned to use my final report for this purpose. One manager privately joked to me that I was free labor.

In contrast to my data collection in the neighborhood or the university, the company had control over whom I could speak to and what events I could attend. I had a primary contact person in the diversity department. I identified interviewees in conjunction with him, and he was present at most of the events I attended but not at the interviews. I enjoyed the benefits of a parking pass, a company visitor's ID, a cubicle with a desk and ergonomic chair, a company phone number and e-mail address, and an ID I could use to access the company's intranet and calendar system for setting up interview appointments.

I use pseudonyms to disguise the identity of the company and all research participants in this case study in accordance with my agreement with the company. I also do not provide some specific details about the company to protect anonymity. I have checked to ensure that quotes from company documents are not searchable on Google.com. Publicly available search technology will surely become more sophisticated in the future. For now, I am confident that the quotes and other detailed material in this book cannot be traced specifically to the company I call Starr. These measures to protect the anonymity of the company somewhat comprised my ability to discuss its financial status and power.

In the final two months of the study, I gave numerous presentations of my final report to company managers. I consider these presentations and the feedback I received to be data and analyze them as such. They provide what qualitative researchers call a member check. Many Starr managers told me that my report accurately reflected the strengths and weaknesses of the company's programs. At the end of my study, a few people holding key positions in human resource and diversity management changed. My understanding is that my report was too controversial for the new leaders, and they ignored it.

Ethnographers commonly experience a crucial turning point in their fieldwork when local subjects begin to accept them. My turning point at Starr was defined by my gender and familial status. A few months into my fieldwork, I announced that I was three months pregnant. Before that, my casual interactions with most research participants were a bit awkward. They were not used to strangers hanging around, and they were that much more wary because of the ongoing audit by consultants that led to the Business Simplification Initiative. With my announcement, I suddenly had fodder for water-cooler talk and a basis for bonding. I went shopping for maternity clothes with one woman who was also pregnant. I talked about baseball and summer camp with other parents. I felt less self-conscious of small things, like driving my small, dented Honda Civic through a parking lot of expensive SUVs. I watched people's faces light up when they saw my growing belly—a common reaction to women who fit the American ideal of a mother as white, affluent, married to a man, and insured.[5] I got a small glimpse into the socially conformist, heterosexist pressures that GLBT employees encountered at work. Most research, like social life, is much easier when you seem more like the dominant group.

NOTES

INTRODUCTION

1. On managerial trade publications, see also Edelman, Fuller, and Mara-Drita (2001).
2. Hartmann, Edgell, and Gerteis (2005). See also Gerteis, Hartmann, and Edgell (2007).
3. Bartelt (2009), Berrey (2005), Berrey (2011), Dobbin (2009), Edgell (1998), D. Green (2004b), Lipson (2007), Lynch (1997).
4. *Regents of the University of California v. Bakke* 438 US 265 (1978).
5. Morris (1984), MacLean (2006).
6. Skrentny (1996), Stulberg and Chen (2014).
7. Brown et al. (2003), Haney-López (2006).
8. Cited in Maly (2005), p. 6.
9. Friedland and Mohr (2004), Geertz (1973), Sewell (1999).
10. Friedland and Alford (1991), Stryker (2000).
11. Ellen (2000), Espenshade and Radford (2009), Farley (2010), Stainback and Tomaskovic-Devey (2012).
12. Hochschild, Weaver, and Burch (2012). On the movement to make multiracialism an option on the US Census, see K. Williams (2006).
13. US Bureau of Labor Statistics (2013).
14. Zweigenhaft and Domhoff (2006).
15. Fischer and Hout (2008), Hout, Fischer, and Chaves (2013).
16. For example, M. Alexander (2010), Krysan (2011).
17. Bonilla-Silva (1997).
18. Tomaskovic-Devey and Stainback (2007).
19. Bonilla-Silva (2003), Brown et al. (2003), Haney-López (2006), Lewis (2004), Royster (2003).
20. Alba (2009), Bonilla-Silva (2003), Collins (1983), Hochschild, Weaver, and Burch (2012).
21. Bonilla-Silva (2003), DiTomaso (2013).
22. Collins (2011b), p. 519.
23. M. Edelman (1974), M. Edelman ([1964] 1985).
24. On power, see Weber (1946). On cultural forms and the exercise of power, see Fairclough (1989), Foucault (1972), Thompson (1984).

25. On organizational identities, see Albert and Whetten (1985), Martin (2001). On community identities, see Gioia, Schultz, and Corley (2000), Suttles (1972).
26. Gioia, Schultz, and Corley (2000).
27. Bielby (2008).
28. Institutional logics are higher orders of values and norms that legitimize by providing a collective explanation of interests, relations, roles, and actions. See DiMaggio (1997), Thornton (2002), Thornton, Ocasio, and Lounsbury (2012), Friedland and Alford (1991), p. 248. See also Stryker (2000), p. 184.
29. See Bell and Hartmann (2007).
30. See chapter 3 and Alon and Tienda (2007).
31. *Gratz v. Bollinger* 539 US 244 (2003), *Grutter v. Bollinger* 539 US 306 (2003).
32. This bias stems from universities' admissions criteria, including their reliance on standardized test scores (affluent students score highest) and steep tuition rates. See chapter 4.
33. On the early rhetoric of remedying disadvantage, see Stulberg and Chen (2014). On discourses of diversity and excellence in higher education, see Urciuoli (2003), Lipson (2007), Stevens (2007).
34. See, e.g., Brown-Saracino (2010), Zukin (2010).
35. On this trend beyond Starr, see Dobbin (2009), Edelman, Fuller, and Mara-Drita (2001), Kelly and Dobbin (1998).
36. For reviews of the constraints that challenger activists face and the ways in which they might respond, see McAdam (1982), McAdam, Tarrow, and Tilly (2001).
37. See also Billig (1995), Tarrow (1998).
38. On the necessity that activists develop sophisticated rhetorical skills to engage in frame alignment, see Snow et al. (2014). See M. Edelman (1977), Gaventa (1980), Gramsci (1971) on the ways in which political officials and business leaders rely on some similar methods of replacing commonsense terms. See also Lakoff (2002).
39. On social movement framing, Benford and Snow (2000). On critical pedagogy, see Friere (1970), Shor (1992).
40. Hochschild, Weaver, and Burch (2012).
41. On exploitation and opportunity hoarding see Tilly (1999). See also Massey (2008). Tomaskovic-Devey (2014) elaborates Tilly's foundational work for organizational contexts by adding the resource-pooling, claims-making, cognitive-biases, and interaction orders.
42. Agenda-setting work by Acker (2006) identifies inequality regimes as characteristics of organizations. I am appropriating the concept to loosely apply to other institutional settings.
43. Omi and Winant (1987).
44. Bourdieu (1984), Lamont (1999), Tilly (1999).
45. Lamont and Molnár (2002), p. 168, Lamont (2000), Lamont and Molnár (2002). Also see Bourdieu (1984).
46. Fredrickson (2002), Hacking (2005).
47. Fredrickson (2002), Omi and Winant (1987).
48. Blau (1977) in Tomaskovic-Devey (2014).
49. Tomaskovic-Devey (2014).
50. Hochschild, Weaver, and Burch (2012).
51. On the changing racial order, see Hochschild, Weaver, and Burch (2012), chaps. 6 and 7, Gans (1999), Gold (2004), Twine and Warren (2000), Bonilla-Silva and Dietrich (2009).

52. Zhou (2004).
53. Bonilla-Silva (2002).
54. For example, Conley (1999), Espenshade and Radford (2009), Pager (2003), Tomaskovic-Devey and Stainback (2007).
55. Tomaskovic-Devey (2014).
56. See Wimmer (2008) on boundary expansion. With the assimilation of certain immigrant groups, notions of the nation and citizenship expand. See, e.g., Wimmer (2009).
57. See Vallas and Cummins (2014), n. 7, on diversity management as a human resources function that seeks to prevent boundary-heightening workplace practices.
58. On identity-conscious organizational structures, see Konrad and Linnehan (1995).
59. Lukes (2004), Roscigno (2011).
60. For a classic statement on symbolic politics, see M. Edelman ([1964] 1985). For an instructive review of Murray Edelman's work, see Ewick and Sarat (2004).
61. Swidler (2001), p. 3064. Also see Fairclough (1989).
62. Foucault (1972).
63. Blommaert and Verschueren (1998), Mumby (2004), p. 26.
64. I. Reed (2013).
65. On ideology, see Geertz (1973), Mannheim (1936), Thompson (1990). On discourse as ideological expression, see Fairclough (1989).
66. Kertzer (1988), p. 5.
67. See also Ewick and Sarat (2004).
68. Emirbayer (1997), Mische (2011), Vaughan (1992), Vaughan (2004).
69. Kunda (1992), Morrill and Fine (1997), Perrow (1986), Selznick (1949).
70. Desmond and Emirbayer (2009), Roscigno (2011).
71. On the sociological philosophy of diversity, see Alexander and Smelser (1999), Glazer (1997), Hartmann and Gerteis (2005). For critical assessments, see Duggan (2003), Lynch (1997), Michaels (2006), Wood (2003). For analysis of law and legal doctrine, see Schuck (2003). See also Bowen (2011).
72. For one overview of these debates, see Sterba (2009). For examples of endorsements of diversity, see Gurin, Lehman, and Lewis (2004), Gurin, Nagda, and Zuniga (2013). For opponents, see American Enterprise Institute (2002), Lynch (1997).
73. For example, Kalev, Dobbin, and Kelly (2006), Herring (2009), Thomas and Ely (2001).
74. Page (2007) exemplifies an ideologically driven, instrumentalist argument for diversity.
75. Dobbin (2009), Edelman, Fuller, and Mara-Drita (2001), Edelman, Uggen, and Erlanger (1999), Kalev, Dobbin, and Kelly (2006), Kelly and Dobbin (1998).
76. For analysis that bridges neoinstitutionalist theory on organizational legitimacy and cultural theory on organizational identity, see Pederson and Dobbin (2006).
77. Emirbayer (1997), Mische (2011), Vaughan (1992), Vaughan (2004).
78. See Griswold (1987).
79. For example, Ragin (1994).
80. Analogical comparison extends grounded theory beyond single-case analysis and accounts for structural and political economic context. Vaughan (2004). See also Vaughan (1992).
81. On transferable concepts, see Auerbach and Silverstein (2003).
82. Stinchcombe (2005).
83. On Michigan's initial adoption of affirmative admissions, see Greenland, Chen, and Stulberg (2010), Stulberg and Chen (2014).

84. Lewis Mumford Center, University of New York at Albany (2001), Sandoval and Li (2004).
85. Small (2009).
86. While social scientists who study cities often attend to schools and workplaces, those who study higher education and employment pay far less attention to the importance of place.
87. On fieldwork methods, see Becker (1998), Emerson (1983), Emerson, Fretz, and Shaw (1995).
88. McCann (1996), Obasogie (2014).
89. For overviews and theoretical statements, see Roscigno (2011), Roscigno and Wilson (2014a), Tomaskovic-Devey (2014).

CHAPTER ONE
1. Rochon (1998). See also M. Edelman ([1964] 1985).
2. Rochon (1998), p. 15.
3. See Glazer (2005).
4. Berrey, Hoffman, and Nielsen (2012).
5. Some conservative commentators are exceptions. See, e.g., Coulter (2009).
6. Schuck (2003), p. 12.
7. Glazer (2005), Schuck (2003).
8. Bell and Hartmann (2007), Marvasti and McKinney (2011).
9. Truitt (2011).
10. Simon (2010).
11. *Regents of University of California v. Bakke*, 438 US 265 (1978), *Grutter v. Bollinger*, 539 US 306 (2003).
12. Swan (2010).
13. Schuck (2003).
14. On keywords, see R. Williams (1983). On their usage, see Ghaziani and Ventresca (2005).
15. Urciuoli (2003) characterizes diversity as a strategically deployable shifter. Following the work of Murray Edelman, Boxenbaum (2006) and Downey (1999), describe it as a condensation symbol with a multivalence and indefiniteness that enables different constituencies to attach different meanings to it.
16. Ghaziani and Ventresca (2005). See also Swidler (1986).
17. On equality, see Condit and Lucaites (1993). On revolution, see Sewell (1996). On the American Way, see Wall (2008).
18. Morris (1984).
19. Notably, civil rights leader Dr. Martin Luther King Jr.'s stance became more radical over time. By the end of his life, he believed that civil rights were insufficient for upending the economic and cultural oppression created through white supremacy. See Singh (2005).
20. *Brown v. Board of Education*, 347 US 483 (1954).
21. Schmidt (2008).
22. Skrentny (2002).
23. See Skrentny (2014) for a synopsis.
24. Ghaziani (2008), MacLean (2006).
25. Skrentny (2002).
26. Skrentny (1996).

27. Skrentny (2014).
28. Bonastia (2004).
29. Stulberg and Chen (2014).
30. The US government has formally engaged in racial classification and enumeration since the inception of the US Census, but as a method and consequence of the government's explicit policy of discriminating against people of color. See Morning and Sabbagh (2005).
31. Skrentny (2002).
32. Hollinger (2000).
33. Feagin (2006), Harper and Reskin (2005). Skrentny (1996) characterizes affirmative action by the US federal government as a race-conscious approach that actually downplays discrimination while prioritizing the numerical representation of racial minorities.
34. A. Freeman (1998). *Griggs v. Duke Power Co.*, 401 US 424 (1971).
35. Schuck (2003). *Gautreaux v. Chicago Housing Authority*, 296 F. Supp. 907 (N.D. Ill. 1969), *United States v. Yonkers Board of Education*, 518 F. Supp. 191 (D.C.N.Y. 1981).
36. Karabel (2005).
37. Lemann (1999).
38. Karabel (2005).
39. Karabel (2005), pp. 407–8.
40. Goodwin (1979), Maly (2005), Molotch (1972).
41. Molotch (1972), p. 77, Goodwin (1979), p. 127.
42. MacLean (2006).
43. *Regents of University of California v. Bakke*, 438 US 265 (1978).
44. Shuck (2003).
45. MacLean (2006), p. 223.
46. 2009, p. 7.
47. Gleason (1984). Political pluralism has a different legacy. James Madison introduced one of the initial arguments for it in the 1780s when he proposed that factions would prevent any single group from dominating American politics.
48. Kallen (1915).
49. Gleason (1984), Spillman (1997). For an empirical analysis of assimilation and pluralism as idealizations of American life, see Berbrier (2004).
50. Rojas (2007).
51. Di Leonardo (1998), Glazer (1997), Singh (2005).
52. For a cogent analysis, see Haney-López (2006).
53. Haney-López (2006).
54. On anti–affirmative action activists, MacLean (2006). On administrative pragmatism, Skrentny (1996).
55. Nelson, Berrey, and Nielsen (2008). For example, *Wards Cove Packing Co. v. Atonio*, 490 US 642 (1989), *City of Richmond v. J. A. Croson Co.*, 488 US 469 (1989), *Washington v. Davis*, 426 US 229 (1976).
56. Haney-López (2000).
57. For example, *United States v. Starrett City Associates*, 840 F.2d 1096 (2d Cir. 1988).
58. Polikoff (1985).
59. 467 US 547 (1990).
60. Dobbin (2009).

61. Kelly and Dobbin (1998).

62. Dobbin (2009), Edelman, Fuller, and Mara-Drita (2001).

63. For example, L. Edelman (1992), Edelman et al. (2011). On the impact of diversity management structures on managerial representation, see Kalev, Dobbin, and Kelly (2006).

64. L. Edelman (1990).

65. L. Edelman (1992), Meyer and Rowan (1977).

66. On isomorphism, see DiMaggio and Powell (1983).

67. Dobbin (2009), Duany, Plater-Zyberk, and Speck (2000), Kelly and Dobbin (1998), Lipson (2007).

68. Lipson (2007).

69. Shiao (2005).

70. Collins (1983), Tomaskovic-Devey and Stainback (2007), Landry and Marsh (2011).

71. Portes and Rumbaut (2006).

72. For example, Wilson (1996).

73. Menand (1995). In the United States, grassroots groups trying to achieve racial reconstruction through local public schools were the initial advocates for multiculturalism. See Newfield and Gordon (1996). Around the same time, governments in Canada and Australia were establishing official policies of multiculturalism. See Kymlicka (1995).

74. Binder (2004).

75. J. Alexander (2001).

76. Collins (2011b), Menand (1995).

77. On multiculturalism and incorporation, see J. Alexander (2001), J. Alexander (2006). On sociological theories of multiculturalism, see Hartmann and Gerteis (2005).

78. Di Leonardo (1998), Gitlin (1995).

79. Randolph (2012), p. 18.

80. On productive diversity, see also Berrey (2011), Davis (1996), Randolph (2012).

81. Harvey (2005).

82. Sassen (2001).

83. Harvey (2005).

84. Fligstein (1990), Harvey (2005).

85. Krugman (2002), Smith (2001).

86. Di Leonardo (2008). See MacLean (2008) on the historic and regional roots of US neoliberalism, which she locates in the labor-repressive, racialized political economy of the conservative South.

87. Downey (1999), Zukin (1995).

88. Simon (2010), Zukin (1995), United Colors of Benetton, press information, "Colors," http://www.benetton.com/food/press/pressinfo/colors/, accessed June 21, 2013.

89. On the commodification of race, see Boyd (2008), Pattillo (2007), Zukin (1995). On racial realism in employment, see Skrentny (2014).

90. Schuck (2003), Glazer (2005).

91. Kalev, Dobbin, and Kelly (2006).

92. Bowen and Bok (1998).

93. Herring (2009).

94. Green and Kalev (2008).

95. For example, Thomas and Ely (2001).

96. Page (2007).
97. Plaut, Thomas, and Goren (2009).
98. Bonilla-Silva (1997).
99. For a formulation of this paradox, see Winant (2000), p. 180.
100. Bonilla-Silva (2003), Bonilla-Silva, Lewis, and Embrick (2004)
101. Bell and Hartmann (2007).
102. Edelman, Fuller, and Mara-Drita (2001).
103. On ideology and exploitation, see Jackman (1994), Marx and Engels (1947).
104. Wacquant (1997), p. 228.
105. For a related critique, see Loveman (1999).
106. For similar observations, see Wimmer (2009).
107. For example, Almaguer (1993).
108. For example, Lewis (2003).
109. Dobbin (2009), Edelman, Fuller, and Mara-Drita (2001), Edelman, Uggen, and Erlanger (1999), Kalev, Dobbin, and Kelly (2006), Kelly and Dobbin (1998). But see Dobbin and Kalev (2008).
110. On symbolic amplification and vilification as legitimacy processes, see Roscigno (2011).
111. On contrasts as an essential element of symbolic systems, see Saussure (1966).
112. Stevens (2007).
113. Political scientist Anthony Marx (1998) observes that in the United States, Brazil, and South Africa, there was a period of political reform driven by a conception of racial discrimination rooted in structural conditions. Subsequently, in each of these countries projects of racial reconstruction emerged that had in common a conception of race as culture.
114. Berrey (2011).
115. See also Edelman, Fuller, and Mara-Drita (2001).
116. On models of multiculturalism, see Hartmann and Gerteis (2005). See also J. Alexander (2001). On rhetoric that conflates diversity and cultural pluralism, see Marvasti and McKinney (2011).
117. See also Frymer and Skrentny (2004) on instrumental arguments for affirmative action and Skrentny (2014) on racial realism. See also Berrey (2011), Randolph (2012).
118. Valverde (2012).
119. Norton and Sommers (2011).
120. Plaut et al. (2011).
121. Pippert, Essenburg, and Matchett (2013).
122. On the doctored photo and fallout, see Lisa Wade, "Doctoring Diversity: Race and Photoshop," The Society Pages, Sept. 2, 2009. http://thesocietypages.org/socimages/2009/09/02/doctoring-diversity-race-and-photoshop/, accessed Jan. 10, 2014.
123. For example, American Enterprise Institute (2002), Wood (2003).
124. For example, Bell and Hartmann (2007), Downey (1999), Edelman, Fuller, and Mara-Drita (2001).
125. For example, Moore and Bell (2011).
126. Michaels (2006).
127. Simon (2010).
128. See, e.g., http://100percentmen.tumblr.com/, accessed Mar. 15, 2014.
129. "Diversity," Stuff White People Like (blog), Jan. 19, 2008, http://stuffwhitepeoplelike.com/2008/01/19/7-diversity/, accessed Jan. 10, 2014.

130. Konrad and Linnehan (1995).
131. On the decoupling of diversity programs and consequential decision making, see also Collins (2011a), L. Edelman (1992), Kalev, Dobbin, and Kelly (2006). On the symbolism of organizational structures, decoupling, and legitimacy pressures, see DiMaggio and Powell (1983), Meyer and Rowan (1977).
132. Thompson (1990).
133. Acker (2006), Tomaskovic-Devey (2014).
134. On cognitive bias, see Ridgeway (1997). On discrimination in hiring, see Nielsen, Nelson, and Berrey (2013), Roscigno (2007), Skrentny (2014). On mortgage lending, see Newman (2009).
135. For example, Alon and Tienda (2007), Reskin and McBrier (2000), Valverde (2012).
136. For theoretical statements and overviews see Roscigno (2011), Roscigno and Wilson (2014a), Roscigno and Wilson (2014b), Tomaskovic-Devey (2014).
137. Roscigno (2011). See also Roscigno and Wilson (2014a), Vallas and Cummins (2014). For examples of such empirical work, see Vallas (2001), Wingfield and Alston (2014).
138. See Lukes (2004) on the three faces of power.
139. On color-coded "feeling rules," see Wingfield (2010). See also Elijah Anderson (1999). On gendered, racialized, and classed bureaucratic structures, see Acker (1990), Acker (2006). On efficiency and affirmative admissions policy, see Hirschman, Berrey, and Rose-Greenland (2012).
140. For examples see Berrey (2005), Collins (2011b), Embrick (2011), D. Green (2004b), Litvin (2002), Urciuoli (2003).
141. On the impact of diversity management structures on managerial representation, see Kalev, Dobbin, and Kelly (2006). On courts' responses, Edelman et al. (2011).
142. Light, Roscigno, and Kalev (2011), Roscigno (2011). For additional relational perspectives on discrimination, see also Berrey, Hoffman, and Nielsen (2012), Nielsen, Nelson, and Berrey (2013). On racial tasks that ideologically idealize whiteness, see Wingfield and Alston (2014).
143. Martin (2001). On the interaction order in organizations, see Tomaskovic-Devey (2014).
144. Geertz (1973), Sewell (1999).
145. Martin (2001). For example, Kunda (1992).
146. Sewell (1996).
147. Griswold (1987), Rochon (1998).
148. Schudson (1989).
149. Ghaziani (2009).
150. There is a rich tradition of organizational ethnography that shows the processes by which organizations construct meaning and inculcate power relations. See, e.g., Kunda (1992).

CHAPTER TWO
1. University of Michigan, Undergraduate Admissions, Oct. 14, 2004, http://web.archive.org/web/20041014063805/http://www.admissions.umich.edu/index.html.
2. University of Michigan, Office of the Registrar (2013b). The representation and support of racial minority faculty members, staff, and graduate students have been important issues at the university as well but are not covered in depth in this study.
3. University of Michigan, Mar. 21, 2005, http://www.umich.edu/~oapainfo/TABLES/PDF/UM_Research.pdf, accessed July 10, 2013.
4. U.S. News and World Report (2005).

5. Reardon, Baker, and Klasik (2012).
6. University of Michigan, Office of Budget and Planning (2006b).
7. University of Michigan, Office of the Registrar (2013b). These and other figures in the chapter are based on the US/Puerto Rican undergraduate student body and do not include nonresident alien (foreign) students, following the university's reporting conventions.
8. University of Michigan, Office of the Registrar (2005a), University of Michigan, Office of the Registrar (2005b).
9. The university releases very little data about the socioeconomic status of its students. See Matney (2003) for students' self-reports of income.
10. Seguine (2006).
11. College Board (2006), University of Michigan, Office of Budget and Planning (2006a).
12. University of Michigan, Office of Budget and Planning (2006a), University of Michigan, Office of Budget and Planning (2006b).
13. University of Michigan, Office of Academic and Multicultural Initiatives (n.d.).
14. Waeraas and Solbakk (2009).
15. Bok (2003), Hoffman (2012), Slaughter and Rhoades (2004).
16. Bok (2003).
17. See also Stevens (2007), Urciuoli (2003).
18. Rivera (2011), US Department of Education (2011).
19. Haskins (2008), US Department of Education (2011).
20. US Department of Education (2012) on racial minorities. Heller (2005) on low-income students.
21. Reardon, Baker, and Klasik (2012).
22. Humes (2006).
23. Lemann (1999).
24. Espenshade and Radford (2009), p. 259. On social closure and educational credentials from superelite universities, see Rivera (2011).
25. Sauder and Espeland (2009), Stevens (2007).
26. Espenshade and Radford (2009).
27. On wealth preferences, see Sturm and Guinier (1996), p. 953.
28. Espenshade and Radford (2009). In 2004, only 6% of high school graduates students headed for highly selective institutions came from families with annual incomes below $25,000, while 58% came from families with incomes over $75,000. See Reardon, Baker, and Klasik (2012). These institutions gave some admissions preferences to low-income students, regardless of race, but thus far those efforts have not much changed the composition of their student bodies. See also Stevens (2007).
29. On the effects of racially biased standardized test scores, see Alon and Tienda (2007).
30. Sauder and Espeland (2009).
31. See University of Michigan, Office of the Vice President for Communications, Public Affairs, "Understanding Tuition," June 2014, http://www.vpcomm.umich.edu/pa/key/understandingtuition.html, accessed July 25, 2014.
32. Harper and Reskin (2005).
33. Skrentny (2002).
34. Grodsky (2007), Lipson (2007).
35. Reardon, Baker, and Klasik (2012).
36. Espenshade and Radford (2009) and Bowen and Bok (1998) find that although black and Latino students at selective institutions have lower GPAs and are less likely

to graduate than their white and Asian peers, the long-term gains made possible by attending a more selective school outweigh the downsides. For a contrary argument that some racial minorities are hurt by their "mismatch" into selective institutions, see Sander and Taylor (2012).

37. Alon and Tienda (2007), Reardon, Baker, and Klasik (2012), Saez and Piketty (2003).

38. Private colleges and universities are not subject to the Fourteenth Amendment's ban on discriminatory government action. The vast majority of these institutions receive federal funds, though, so they are held to the same prohibitions on racial discrimination as are public universities under the equal protection clause.

39. Killgore (2009). See also Hirschman, Berrey, and Rose-Greenland (2012), Stevens (2007).

40. On administrators' diversity consensus, see Lipson (2007).

41. Sauder and Espeland (2009).

42. Quoted in Stulberg and Chen (2014).

43. Stulberg and Chen (2014), Greenland, Chen, and Stulberg (2010).

44. Peckham (1994).

45. For an analysis of the role of university leaders in origins of affirmative admissions in the United States, see Stulberg and Chen (2014).

46. Peckham (1994).

47. University of Michigan, Office of Undergraduate Admissions (1974), p. 2.

48. Hirschman, Berrey, and Rose-Greenland (2012).

49. Greenland, Chen, and Stulberg (2010).

50. University of Michigan Regents' communication, Apr. 14, 1970, by Stephen H. Spurr, University of Michigan Office of Budget and Planning, "Minority Enrollment Info Circa 1970 and Earlier," in Hirschman, Berrey and Rose-Greenland (2012).

51. Peckham (1994), Rojas (2007).

52. J. Anderson (2007).

53. For example, University of Michigan, Board of Regents (1979), p. 192, and Peckham (1994).

54. For example, University of Michigan, Board of Regents (1970), pp. 391–94.

55. Biondi (2003), MacLean (2006), Skrentny (1996).

56. University of Michigan, "Newcomer's Guide" (1961).

57. Nelson (1967).

58. Schuck (2003).

59. Letter from Robbin Fleming to Robert Manning of *Atlantic Monthly*, Oct. 31, 1977, University of Michigan, Office of the President Papers, Bentley Historical Library, University of Michigan.

60. Hirschman, Berrey, and Rose-Greenland (2012).

61. Hirschman, Berrey, and Rose-Greenland (2012).

62. On the legitimizing effects of court decisions, Clawson, Kegler, and Waltenburg (2001). On law "on the street," Ewick and Silbey (1998), Nielsen (2004).

63. On black student enrollment, Peckham (1994), p. 346. See also University of Michigan, Office of Undergraduate Admissions publications, box 1, Bentley Historical Library, University of Michigan.

64. Peckham (1994).

65. Hirschman, Berrey, and Rose-Greenland (2012).

66. Stevens and Roksa (2011).

67. See Stulberg and Chen (2011) for a discussion of this phenomenon at other universities.

68. *Michigan Daily,* Feb. 2, 1987.
69. Bachman (1987), p. 16.
70. University of Michigan, Board of Regents, (1987), p. 1058.
71. University of Michigan, Office of the President (1990), p. 3.
72. Lynch (1997).
73. University of Michigan, Office of the President (1990), p. 7. In the 1989 *Croson* case, the court found that "remedying past societal discrimination" was *not* an acceptable rationale for a race-conscious governmental program. For further discussion, see chapter 3.
74. E.g. University of Michigan, Board of Regents (1993), pp. 218–21.
75. University of Michigan, Board of Regents (1988), pp. 36–37, University of Michigan, Office of the Registrar (2013b).
76. University of Michigan, Office of the Registrar (2013b).
77. Quoted in Stohr (2004), p. 15.
78. Lipson (2007).
79. University of Michigan, Board of Regents (1993), p. 222.
80. Matlock, Gurin, and Wade-Golden (2003).
81. University of Michigan, Board of Regents (1994), p. 266.

CHAPTER THREE
1. Hochschild (2002).
2. Haney-López (2006).
3. *Hopwood v. Texas* 78 F.3d 932 (5th Cir. 1996).
4. If a university or college receives federal funds, it is subject to the Fourteenth Amendment, so law circumscribes how it can treat race in decision making.
5. Brief for the petitioners in *Gratz et al. v. Bollinger et al.,* p. 17.
6. Brief for the petitioners in *Gratz et al. v. Bollinger et al.,* pp. 17, 12.
7. Hirschman, Berrey, and Rose-Greenland (2012).
8. Skrentny (2002).
9. *City of Richmond v. J. A. Croson Co.,* 488 US 469 (1989).
10. Justice Scalia, concurring opinion, *Croson,* p. 528.
11. Justice Marshall, dissenting, *Fullilove v. Klutznick,* 448 US 448 (1980), p. 519.
12. I thank Khiara Bridges, personal correspondence, for clarification.
13. Brief for the respondents in *Gratz et al. v. Bollinger et al.,* p. 2.
14. Stohr (2004).
15. For a detailed account of the activities of the major players in the cases, see Stohr (2004).
16. D. Green (2004a), Stohr (2004).
17. D. Green (2004a), D. Green (2004b).
18. For example, Gurin et al. (2002).
19. Expert Report of Patricia Gurin, in *The Compelling Need for Diversity in Education,* http://www.umich.edu/~urel/admissions/legal/expert/gurintoc.html, accessed Mar. 24, 2014.
20. D. Green (2004a), D. Green (2004b), Stohr (2004).
21. Ford (1999).
22. Brief for *Amici Curiae,* sixty-five leading American businesses, *Grutter v. Bollinger* 539 US 306 (2003), pp. 5–6.
23. *Grutter v. Bollinger,* 539 US 306 (2003), pp. 3–4.
24. *Gratz v. Bollinger,* 539 US 244 (2003), p. 4.

25. Gamson and Modigliani (1988), Richardson and Lancendorfer (2004).
26. For example, Miller (2003).
27. See University of Michigan, Information on Admissions Lawsuits, http://www
    .vpcomm.umich.edu/admissions/.
28. Gurin, Lehman, and Lewis (2004).
29. Llewellyn (1930).
30. On contract disputes, Macaulay (1963). On media representations of the legal
    system, Haltom and McCann (2004). On legal consciousness, Ewick and Silbey
    (1998), Nielsen (2004).
31. Office of the Press Secretary (2003).
32. The Ford Foundation, whose philanthropic giving had been driving the develop-
    ment of diversity initiatives across the country for decades (Shiao [2005]), donated
    at least $600,000 to help the university defend its policies. University of Michigan
    (2001).
33. Waeraas and Solbakk (2009).
34. See, e.g., Elizabeth Anderson (2002).
35. Matlock, Gurin, and Wade-Golden (2003), p. 29. On the absence of discussions of
    diversity in Michigan's law school classrooms, Deo (2011).
36. See, e.g., Fears (2003).
37. This analysis identifies each activist organization's distinctive orientation to diver-
    sity and explains how that orientation follows from the organization's legal position-
    ing and political objectives. Departing from the standard sociological approach to
    social movements, it does not try to demonstrate whether diversity helps or impedes
    activists' efforts to mobilize. For a justification, see Walder (2009).
38. Shanta's racial identity was unclear. It was a topic of speculation among people out-
    side of BAMN and was never mentioned in news coverage of her. A BAMN orga-
    nizer told me she was biracial, with one African American parent and one Indian
    parent.
39. Edney (2002).
40. BAMN leaders were pleased when they heard that I was a sociologist. As they pointed
    out to me personally, the amicus brief submitted by the American Sociological
    Association, Law and Society Association, and Association of Black Sociologists
    made a similar argument about racial bias in standardized test scores. At the time of
    this writing, I am a member of two of these organizations.
41. Brief for Respondent James (Certiorari), *Grutter v. Bollinger*, 123 S. Ct. 617, 17, 30
    (2002).
42. On politics of claiming to represent a racial minority group, especially African
    Americans, see, e.g., Fields (2013).
43. Stohr (2004).
44. For an analysis and critique of BAMN's legal intervention along these lines, see
    Brown-Nagin (2005).
45. There are some parallels between SSAA's mobilization and the mobilization of col-
    lege students to participate in the 1964 Freedom Summer campaign organized by the
    Student Nonviolent Coordinating Committee. See McAdam (1990).
46. See also Berrey (2004).
47. These findings are based on text searches of all major English-language newspapers
    for the year 2003 using the Lexis-Nexis search engine. The search engine does not
    include small local newspapers or other nonmajor news sources.
48. See also Berrey (2004).

49. See Rob Goodspeed, "BAM-N Launches Organizing Drive in DC," *Goodspeed Update* (blog), June 24, 2006, http://goodspeedupdate.com/category/university-of-michigan/bam-n, accessed July 9, 2013.

50. Wang (2002).

51. Conservative activists would challenge such claims, asserting that right-wing funders are vastly outspent compared to the money given to "the Left" by federal, charitable, community, corporate, and foundational support and that funding for conservative journalism is dwarfed by that available for liberal journalism. For examples, see discoverthenetworks.org: A Guide to the Political Left, http://www.discoverthenetworks.org/, accessed Dec. 12, 2011, or K. Daniel Glover, "The Future of Conservative Journalism," June 15, 2009, http://www.aim.org/aim-column/the-future-of-conservative-journalism/, accessed Mar. 13, 2012.

52. The Collegiate Network supports students through conferences, journalism courses, fellowships, manuals with public relations talking points, and strategic advice about staging campus events. See Colapinto (2003), Miller (2004).

53. SourceWatch, "Echo Chamber," http://www.sourcewatch.org/index.php?title=Echo_chamber, accessed Mar. 13, 2012.

54. For example, *Michigan Review* (2002).

55. Brief for the petitioners in *Gratz et al. v. Bollinger et al.*, p. 17.

56. For example, American Enterprise Institute (2002), American Enterprise Institute (2003).

57. Students for Academic Freedom, http://www.studentsforacademicfreedom.org/documents/1925/abor.html/, accessed July 8, 2014. See also Hebel (2004). Versions of this document were introduced in nineteen state legislatures and the US House of Representatives. That legislative campaign was largely unsuccessful.

58. Kim (2002).

59. On the lack of transparency of the new policy, see Hirschman, Berrey, and Rose-Greenland (2012).

60. Kirkland and Hanson (2011).

61. University of Michigan, Office of the Registrar (1999b).

62. University of Michigan, Office of the Registrar (1999b), University of Michigan, Office of the Registrar (2004a). Between 1993 and 2004, the number of first-year Asian students in CSP increased from zero to ten.

63. Wade-Golden and Matlock (2010).

64. University of Michigan, Office of Financial Aid, "Miscellaneous (Other) Scholarships," http://web.archive.org/web/20030802044942/www.finaid.umich.edu/otherschols.htm, accessed July 8, 2014.

65. University of Michigan, Office of Financial Aid, http://web.archive.org/web/20031204115919/http://www.finaid.umich.edu/Types_of_Financial_Aid/Scholarships/Entering_Undergraduates/otherschols.asp, accessed July 8, 2014.

66. University of Michigan, Office of the Registrar (2004b), University of Michigan, Office of the Registrar (2006).

67. Lipson (2008).

68. Lipson (2008), p. 698.

69. University of Michigan, Office of the Registrar (2013a).

70. University of Michigan, Office of the Registrar (2003), University of Michigan, Office of the Registrar (2013b). Some, but not all, of the drop in underrepresented minority first-year enrollment may be accounted for by the addition of the "Two or

More" racial category in 2010. The drop is less likely to be explained by changes in the percentage of first-year students reporting "Unknown" race, which increased between 2003 and 2013 but dropped and rose throughout the intervening years. See University of Michigan, Office of the Registrar (2013a).

71. University of Michigan, Office of the Registrar (1999a).

72. On cost of attendance, University of Michigan, Office of Financial Aid, "Cost to Attend U-M," http://www.finaid.umich.edu/TopNav/AboutUMFinancialAid/Costof Attendance.aspx, accessed Mar. 19, 2014. On enrollment, University of Michigan (2013).

73. Ratchet is an ambiguous derogatory slang term typically used to characterize black women as low class and inappropriately behaved in public, or "ghetto."

74. *Fischer v. University of Texas at Austin et al.* For a summary by the respected Supreme Court blog, see Howe (2013).

75. *Schuette v. BAMN*, 572 US ____ (2014).

76. Justice Sotomayor, dissenting, *Schuette v. BAMN*, 572 US ____ (2014), p. 45.

77. *Parents Involved in Community Schools v. Seattle School District No. 1*, 551 US 701 (2007), pp. 40–41.

78. Justice Sotomayor, dissenting, *Schuette v. BAMN*, 572 US ____ (2014), p. 46.

79. See also Moore and Bell (2011).

80. Bell (1980).

CHAPTER FOUR

1. Locally, this community is called East Rogers Park, to distinguish it from the adjacent West Rogers Park/West Ridge neighborhood.

2. Center for Urban Research and Learning (2002).

3. US Census 2000, Summary File 3, Sample Data. Income reported for black households regardless of racial group.

4. US Census 2000, Summary File 3, Sample Data. Home ownership rates and rental rates are for white-only households and black-only households (meaning, regardless of Hispanic origin) and Hispanic households of any racial group.

5. Crenson (1983).

6. Fischer (1975), Jacobs (1961), p. 19. Sociologists associated with the Chicago School viewed diversity in terms of interethnic conflicts, often pejoratively. Wirth (1938). Urban analysts subsequently challenged these assertions. Jacobs's ideas were taken up by New Urbanism, which arose in the early 1980s and made diversity a central principle of urban planning.

7. Fischer (1999).

8. For example, Farley and Frey (1994), Wilson (1987).

9. Putnam (2007).

10. Comments on "Is Roger's Park Truly Diverse," City-Data Forum, June 12, 2010, http://www.city-data.com/forum/chicago/1003207-rogers-park-truly-diverse.html, accessed Dec. 12, 2012. Grammar and syntax have not been modified.

11. Eloté is Mexican corn on the cob.

12. Valverde (2012).

13. See also Berrey (2005), Burke (2012).

14. For example, Elejalde (2006).

15. Searcey (1996).

16. Nyden, Maly, and Lukehart (1997) use census tract data and interviews to identify

stable, diverse neighborhoods in the ten largest US cities and twelve midsize or small cities. On changes in the 1990s, see Maly (2005). According to Ellen (2000), by 1990 about 20% of US neighborhoods had between 10% and 50% black residents and had not experienced massive out-migration of white people.

17. See also Grams (2010).
18. See also Burke (2012).
19. Hunter (1974), Suttles (1972).
20. Berrey (2005), Brown-Saracino (2010), Goode (2001), Horton (1995), Pattillo (2007), Tissot (2011), Valverde (2012).
21. On diversity and "urban canopies," see Elijah Anderson (2011). On the commercialization of ethnic cultures, see Zukin (1995). On neobohemia, see Lloyd (2002).
22. Valverde (2012).
23. Sampson (2012).
24. Schuck (2003).
25. Nightingale (2012).
26. Ellen (2000), Farley (2010).
27. These data are based on the fifty urban areas with the largest respective minority populations. See Logan (2011a), Logan (2011b).
28. Logan (2011b).
29. Taylor and Fry (2012).
30. Reardon and Bischoff (2011).
31. Massey and Denton (1993), Reardon and Bischoff (2011).
32. Sampson (2012), Sharkey (2013), Wilson (1987).
33. Quigley (2006).
34. On legal cases, see Roscigno, Karafin, and Tester (2009). On testing, see Turner et al. (2013).
35. For an analysis and typology, see Owens (2012).
36. Logan and Molotch (1987).
37. See Mele (2000) for a historical analysis of how the real estate industry and political officials in New York City constructed the identity of the Lower East Side and mobilized toward their economic objectives.
38. *Chicago Tribune* (1956).
39. Hirsch (1983).
40. Lemann (1991).
41. On occupational status, see Adelman and Tolnay (2003). On mechanisms of segregation, see Hirsch (1983), Nightingale (2012).
42. For a discussion of white avoidance, see Ellen (2000).
43. Chicago Fact Book Consortium (1995).
44. Welter (1982).
45. Suttles (1990).
46. Suttles (1990), Welter (1982).
47. Welter (1982).
48. On the racialization of immigrants as white, see, e.g., Alba (2009).
49. On faith tolerance in the neighborhood, see Grams (2010).
50. Hirsch (1983), Massey and Denton (1993), Sugrue (1996).
51. *Chicago Daily Defender* (1966b).
52. *Chicago Daily Defender* (1966a).
53. For example, *Chicago Daily Defender* (1963).

54. For example, Sullivan (1962).
55. For example, *Chicago Tribune* (1957), *Chicago Tribune* (1964). On the importance of stabilizing a neighborhood's white population for maintaining integration, see Ellen (2000).
56. *Chicago Tribune* (1968).
57. Graham (2000), Maly (2005). See also Saltman (1990).
58. Many fair housing and civil rights activists framed their claims about integration in terms of the benefits to whites. Lau (2004).
59. Yackley (1967).
60. Buck (1972), Getz (1967). For the racial demographics of the welfare population, see Moynihan (1960).
61. Pukelis (1985).
62. Welter (1982).
63. Welter (1982).
64. Chicago Fact Book Consortium (1984), Chicago Fact Book Consortium (1995), Maly and Leachman (1998).
65. Maly (2005), Nyden, Maly, and Lukehart (1997).
66. Maly (2005).
67. For example, Ansley (1981).
68. Buck (1972).
69. McCabe (1980).
70. Orlebeke (2000), p. 489.
71. Hirsch (1983).
72. Rubinowitz and Rosenbaum (2000).
73. Rubinowitz and Rosenbaum (2000).
74. *Gautreaux v. Chicago Housing Authority*, 265 F. Supp. 582 (N.D. Ill. 1967).
75. Jorvasky (1992).
76. Branegan (1980).
77. Yates (1971).
78. Swanson (1980b).
79. Darrow (1973), Lowe (1973).
80. Welter (1982).
81. Swanson (1980a). People involved in Rogers Park politics sometimes also used the term "subsidized" to refer to private housing for poor people financed with tools such as tax credits, or they confused such private housing with subsidized housing.
82. Bonastia (2004).
83. Branegan (1980).
84. Ziemba (1980).
85. Swanson (1980b), Swanson (1980c).
86. For example, Swanson (1981b).
87. Swanson (1981a).
88. Swanson (1981c).
89. Munson (1985).
90. Hopp-Peters (1988).
91. City of Chicago, Department of Planning (1988).
92. Skogan and Hartnett (1997).
93. Skogan and Hartnett (1997).
94. A 1988 *Tribune* article stated that Alderman Orr often boasted of Rogers Park's diversity, but I could not find other such statements prior to 1988 in newspaper

reporting or archival materials in the Chicago Public Library or the Chicago Historical Society.
95. Rutstein (1988).
96. For example, Steele (1996).
97. Gronbjerg et al. (1993).
98. Allen (1993).
99. City of Chicago, Department of Planning (1988), Hartstein (1994).
100. City of Chicago, Department of Planning (1986).
101. City of Chicago, City Council (1994).
102. City of Chicago, Department of Planning (1986).
103. City of Chicago, Department of Planning (1988).
104. Hartstein (1994).
105. Hartstein (1994).
106. Hartstein (1994).
107. Di Leonardo (1998), A. Reed (1999).
108. Maly (2005), p. 19.

CHAPTER FIVE
1. For example, *Chicago Sun-Times* (2000).
2. Metropolitan Planning Council (1999).
3. See also Burke (2012) on the approval of diversity among Rogers Park community activists.
4. Metropolitan Planning Council (1999).
5. Chicago Housing Authority (2000).
6. Voucher holds must find a landlord who will participate in the voucher program and whose building meets HUD's quality standards. The landlord is paid directly by HUD for the difference between the fair-market rent for the surrounding area and 30% of the household's income. In 1999, the fair-market rent for a two-bedroom unit in Chicago was $737. See Metropolitan Planning Council (1999).
7. Daye (2000).
8. Orlebeke (2000).
9. A. Reed (1999), Zukin (1987).
10. Center for Urban Research and Learning (2002).
11. Center for Urban Research and Learning (2002).
12. Lakeside Community Development Corporation (2006).
13. City of Chicago, Department of Community Development (2010).
14. On the intraracial dynamics of gentrification in black Chicago neighborhoods, see Boyd (2008), Pattillo (2007).
15. Sommer (2012).
16. Lakeside Community Development Corporation (2006).
17. L. Freeman (2005), Kennedy and Leonard (2001).
18. Center for Urban Research and Learning (2002).
19. Chicago Rehab Network (2013), 2010 dollars.
20. National People's Action (2010).
21. Following this study, Moore adopted participatory budgeting, a democratic approach to planning that enables residents to make decisions about the ward's capital budget. The Forty-Ninth Ward was the first US community to adopt it. He also oversaw a two-year planning process to solicit community input to revise the Forty-Ninth Ward zoning map.

22. Logan and Molotch (1987).
23. On the symbiotic relationship between government and bankers who profit from mortgage markets, see Fligstein and Goldstein (2010).
24. Developing Government Accountability to the People (2006). Data are for Jan. 2005–June 2006. The election was held in Feb. 2006.
25. For an analysis of the power dynamics of progrowth groups, see Logan, Whaley, and Crowder (1999).
26. Grams (2010), p. 155.
27. "Stop the Development: We Need a Plan," 24/7 North of Howard Watchers, Jan. 31, 2006, http://howardwatchers.blogspot.com/2006_01_01_archive.html, accessed July 17, 2013.
28. On the growing proportion of young white adults who opt for racially integrated neighborhoods, see Wagmiller (2012).
29. Bell and Hartmann (2007).
30. Developing Government Accountability to the People (2006).
31. DevCorp North (2006), p. 12.
32. Comment on "The Jungle Area in Rogers Park," Forgotten Chicago Forum, Apr. 17, 2011, http://forgottenchicago.com/forum/5/5649/the_jungle_area_in_rogers_park_, accessed July 10, 2014.
33. Chicago Fact Book Consortium (1984).
34. Chicago Fact Book Consortium (1995).
35. Center for Urban Research and Learning (2002).
36. "North of Howard Scoping Study," prepared for the Rogers Park Builders Group, prepared by Siemon, Larsen & Marsh, Jan. 13, 1998 (on file with author), 5.
37. Ihejirika (1995).
38. See also Burke (2012).
39. Wilson (1987).
40. Bennett and Reed (1999).
41. Bennett, Smith, and Wright (2006), Pattillo (2007).
42. Crain's Chicago Business (1995).
43. "Reader Forum: Ald. Moore Defends Condo Plan," News-Star Booster, Oct. 13, 1999.
44. "Pipes Bursting at Vista North Condominiums," Vista North Owner's Blog Group, Dec. 13, 2013, http://vistanorthownersgroup.blogspot.com/, accessed July 9, 2014.
45. On wealthy white people who see diversity as both physical proximity to "others" and distance from them, see Tissot (2011).
46. Bennett and Reed (1999).
47. Harley (1989). See also Foucault (1972).
48. Berrey (2005).
49. The RPCAN activists' analysis of race and racism shares many similarities with sociological analyses of institutional, systemic, or social structural racism, e.g., Bonilla-Silva (1997), Feagin (2006). In fact, some scholars identified RPCAN as an exemplary activist organization. It was awarded a Social Action Award by the Society for the Study of Social Problems in 1999. See Society for the Study of Social Problems, http://www.sssp1.org/index.cfm/pageId/1254, accessed Mar. 12, 2012.
50. On this organizing strategy, see Smock (2004).
51. For example, "Morse Mural," The Living Room in Rogers Park (blog), June 27, 2006, http://thelivingroom.blogspot.com/2007/06/morse-mural.html, accessed July 17, 2013.

52. Smock (2004), p. 138.
53. By this time, the program was called the Housing Choice Voucher Program, but activists still referred to it as Section 8. On representation of voucher holders, see CHAC, "Housing Choice Voucher Families by Community Area, Mar. 2002," based on data from CHAC's EmPHAsis Computer Systems Database (on file with author).
54. In 1999, 92% of the participants in Chicago's Section 8 program were African American, and about 65% had annual household incomes under $10,000. Popkin and Cunningham (1999).
55. McAdam (1982), p. 5.
56. On the right to the city—the notion that people should have a common, collective right to transform cities—see, e.g., Harvey (2012).
57. Massey and Denton (1993).
58. Albiston (2005), McCann (1994).
59. For an analysis of the eclipsing of rights in corporate rhetoric on diversity, see Edelman, Fuller, and Mara-Drita (2001).

CHAPTER SIX

1. Dobbin (2009), Edelman, Fuller, and Mara-Drita (2001), Edelman, Uggen, and Erlanger (1999), Kalev, Dobbin, and Kelly (2006), Kelly and Dobbin (1998).
2. For example, Binder (2007), Hallett (2010), Hoffman (2011).
3. According to the federal government, an employee who is "FLSA exempt" is not covered by the Fair Labor Standards Act's minimum wage and overtime pay. Starr also used the categories of exempt and nonexempt to determine eligibility for benefits such as health care coverage.
4. Data on Starr's workforce are derived from information that the company submitted to Diversity, Inc., and internal human resource reports. They correspond with figures posted on the company's internal website. They do not match the figures posted on its public website around this same time, which stated that 18% of the company's US employees were people of color and 42% were women.
5. Figures for 2005. On women, Hatton (2011), US Bureau of Labor Statistics (2007). On people of color, Population Reference Bureau (2008).
6. On the national average, see Caiazza, Shaw, and Werschkul (2004). On the Fortune 500, see Catalyst (2006).
7. In 2013, as an employer, Starr was rated 3.4 out of 5 stars on Glassdoor.com (accessed July 24, 2013) and was not recognized as a good employer in the Good Company Index (goodcompanyindex.com, accessed July 24, 2013).
8. MacLean (2006).
9. Stainback, Tomaskovic-Devey, and Skaggs (2010).
10. Acker (2006).
11. MacLean (2006), Skrentny (2002), Tomaskovic-Devey and Stainback (2007).
12. Tomaskovic-Devey and Stainback (2007).
13. Nelson, Berrey, and Nielsen (2008), Nelson and Bridges (1999).
14. Acker (2006).
15. Cotter et al. (2001), Kanter (1993).
16. Elijah Anderson (1999).
17. Wingfield (2010). See also Nkomo (1992).
18. Moss and Tilly (2001), Royster (2003).

19. Konrad and Linnehan (1995).
20. Vallas and Cummins (2014).
21. Ryan, Hawdon, and Branick (2002).
22. Reported in Collins (2011b).
23. Kalev, Dobbin, and Kelly (2006).
24. Bonilla-Silva, Lewis, and Embrick (2004).
25. Berrey, Hoffman, and Nielsen (2012), Nielsen et al. (2008), Pager (2003), Trautner and Kwan (2010).
26. Nielsen, Nelson, and Berrey (2013).
27. Kelly and Dobbin (1998).
28. Collins (1983), Tomaskovic-Devey and Stainback (2007).
29. Sturm (2001).
30. For reviews, see Kim, Kalev, and Dobbin (2012), Kulik and Roberson (2008a), Kulik and Roberson (2008b).
31. Dobbin, Kalev, and Kelly (2007), Kalev, Dobbin and Kelly (2006).
32. Kulik and Roberson (2008a), Kulik and Roberson (2008b).
33. L. Edelman (1992). See also Friedland and Alford (1991).
34. Collins (2011b).
35. Meyer and Rowan (1977).
36. Dobbin (2009), Edelman, Fuller, and Mara-Drita (2001), Edelman et al. (2011).
37. Dobbin (2009).
38. See also Edelman, Fuller, and Mara-Drita (2001).
39. DiMaggio and Powell (1983).
40. L. Edelman (1992), Edelman et al. (2011).
41. L. Edelman (1992), Pedriana and Stryker (2004).
42. Graham (1990), Skrentny (1996).
43. Graham (1992).
44. Biondi (2003), MacLean (2006).
45. On competing ideologies, see Skrentny (1996). On legal ambiguity, see L. Edelman (1992).
46. L. Edelman (1992), Kelly and Dobbin (1998).
47. L. Edelman (1992).
48. Kalev, Dobbin, and Kelly (2006).
49. Dobbin and Kalev (2013).
50. Edelman, Fuller, and Mara-Drita (2001).
51. Sobel (1993).
52. In the 1960s and 1970s, black management consultants pitched affirmative action and new black employees as a good business strategy. See Collins (1997a).
53. Kelly and Dobbin (1998), Lynch (1997).
54. Johnston and Packer (1987).
55. On the inaccuracies, see Edelman, Fuller, and Mara-Drita (2001).
56. Dobbin and Kalev (2013).
57. Riccucci (1997).
58. Dobbin (2009).
59. Dobbin (2009), Kelly and Dobbin (1998).
60. See, e.g., Thomas (1994). On management literature, see Edelman, Fuller, and Mara-Drita (2001). On mission statements, see Dobbin and Kalev (2013).
61. On this division, see Lynch (1997).

62. Data on the racial and gender representation of the workforce of an individual firm are not readily publicly available. The data here are based on internal sources. Data for 1996 through 2001 are from August. Data for 2002 through 2004 are year-end. Data for 2005 are from the second quarter. If there were discrepancies between key HR statistical reports, data from the most recent report were used.
63. Tomaskovic-Devey and Stainback (2007).
64. Kalev, Dobbin, and Kelly (2006). For an example of industry resistance, see *Diversity Inc.* (2006).
65. See also MacLean (2006).

CHAPTER SEVEN
1. Fligstein (2001).
2. Ryan and Schneider (2002).
3. Fligstein (1990), Harvey (2005).
4. Brockner (1988), Fligstein (2001), Hatton (2011).
5. Hacker (2008).
6. Bielby (2012), Wilson and McBrier (2005).
7. Mintzberg (1983).
8. Kärreman and Alvesson (2004), Kunda (1992).
9. Perrow (1986).
10. Non-HR diversity management at Starr, such as charitable contributions and minority contracting, were not the primary focus of this study.
11. Dobbin (2009).
12. On the importance of accountability structures for moving people of color and women into management, see Kalev, Dobbin, and Kelly (2006).
13. On conflict management strategies, see Perrow (1986).
14. Jackall (1988).
15. For example, Fast Company staff (2005).
16. For example, Collins (1997b).
17. For further discussion, see Berrey (2013).
18. Wingfield and Alston (2014).
19. Briscoe and Safford (2008), Raeburn (2004).
20. Edelman, Fuller, and Mara-Drita (2001), Litvin (2006).
21. On executive insularity, see, e.g., Perrow (1986).
22. Wingfield and Alston (2014). See also Collins (1997a).
23. See, e.g., Krieger (1995).
24. Cohen, March, and Olsen (1972).
25. Kalev, Dobbin, and Kelly (2006).
26. On resentment, see also Lynch (1997).
27. Voyer (2011), p. 1.
28. On employers' cultivation of employees' self, see Kunda (1992), Sharone (2004).
29. TalentTrumps!, "Flash Drive Diversity," Feb. 2, 2013, http://talenttrumps.blogspot.com /2013/02/flash-drive-diversity.html, accessed Jan. 22, 2014.
30. Dobbin and Kalev (2013) argue that diversity management is more successful when managers are treated as part of the solution, not the problem.
31. Skrentny (2002).
32. Kalev, Dobbin, and Kelly (2006).
33. Konrad and Linnehan (1999).

CONCLUSION

1. Michaels (2006), p. 7.
2. Michaels (2006), p. 89.
3. See also Pollitt (2006) for an excellent critique.
4. Harvey (2005).
5. For example, di Leonardo (2008).
6. See, e.g., Office of University Partnerships, *Diversity Works*, http://archives.huduser
   .org/oup/files/pubs/newsletter/Diversity1-1.pdf, accessed Mar. 22, 2104.
7. On the decoupling of programs and consequential decision making, see also Collins
   (2011a), Kalev, Dobbin, and Kelly (2006).
8. Glazer (2005), Schuck (2003).
9. Brief for Columbia et al., *Bakke v. Regents*, pp. 314, 336–37, in Karabel (2005),
   pp. 492–93.
10. Pollitt (2006).
11. For example, Wood (2003).
12. For example, Hoffman (2011).
13. McCann (1996).
14. Haney-López (2006).
15. *Ricci v. DeStefano*, 129 S. Ct. 2658.
16. Brown et al. (2003).
17. T. Green, personal correspondence. See also T. Green (2010), Skrentny (2014).
18. Clegg (2007).
19. For example, Plaut et al. (2011).
20. Crenshaw (2007).
21. Bonilla-Silva (2003).
22. See also Marvasti and McKinney (2011).
23. For an interesting analysis, see Mele (2013).
24. Durkheim ([1912] 1995).
25. Alba (2009).
26. Avent-Holt and Tomaskovic-Devey (2014).
27. Plaut et al. (2011).
28. For example, Goode (2001), Wingfield (2010).
29. Plaut et al. (2011).
30. On organizational tasks as cultural carriers, see Ghaziani (2008).
31. On individuals' racial conceptualizations, see Morning (2011).
32. On statistics, see also M. Edelman (1977).
33. For example, L. Edelman (1992). Organizations do not adopt or maintain organiza-
    tional structures such as policies simply for utilitarian purposes; they do so for sym-
    bolic reasons, especially to signal their legitimacy to outside audiences. DiMaggio
    and Powell (1983), Meyer and Rowan (1977).
34. There are many ways that organizational actors associate diversity's meanings with
    practices that are not explored here. Crucially, decision makers may make identity-
    conscious decisions that determine access to resources, such as the acceptance of
    college applicants, decisions about whom to rent to, or firing choices. Because those
    decision-making processes were largely out of the purview of this research project, I
    do not single them out for analysis.
35. But see Dávila (2001).
36. Klinenberg (2002).

METHODOLOGICAL APPENDIX

1. Duneier (2004).
2. This is a departure from an earlier article I wrote about Rogers Park, in which I disguised the names of community organizations. Berrey (2005).
3. University of Michigan, "Information on Admissions Lawsuits," http://www.vpcomm.umich.edu/admissions/, accessed Mar. 27, 2013.
4. Berrey (2004).
5. For example, Bridges (2011).

REFERENCES

Acker, Joan. 1990. "Hierarchies, Jobs, Bodies: A Theory of Gendered Organizations." *Gender and Society* 4 (2): 139–58.

———. 2006. "Inequality Regimes: Gender, Class, and Race in Organizations." *Gender and Society* 20 (4): 441–64.

Adelman, Robert M., and Stewart E. Tolnay. 2003. "Occupational Status of Immigrants and African Americans at the Beginning and End of the Great Migration." *Sociological Perspectives* 46 (2): 179–206.

Alba, Richard. 2009. *Blurring the Color Line: The New Chance for a More Integrated America.* Cambridge, MA: Harvard University Press.

Albert, Stuart, and David Whetten. 1985. "Organizational Identity." In *Research in Organizational Behavior,* edited by Larry L. Cummings and Barry M. Staw, 7: 263–95. Greenwich, CT: JAI.

Albiston, Catherine. 2005. "Mobilizing Employment Rights in the Workplace." In *Handbook of Employment Discrimination Research: Rights and Realities,* edited by Laura Beth Nielsen and Robert Nelson, 301–24. Dordrecht: Springer.

Alexander, Jeffrey C. 2001. "Theorizing the 'Modes of Incorporation': Assimilation, Hyphenation, and Multiculturalism as Varieties of Civil Participation." *Sociological Theory* 19 (3): 237–49.

———. 2006. *The Civil Sphere.* Oxford: Oxford University Press.

Alexander, Jeffrey C., and Neil J. Smelser. 1999. "Introduction: The Ideological Discourse of Cultural Discontent." In *Diversity and Its Discontents: Cultural Conflict and Common Ground in Contemporary American Society,* edited by Neil J. Smelser and Jeffrey C. Alexander, 3–18. Princeton, NJ: Princeton University Press.

Alexander, Michelle. 2010. *The New Jim Crow: Mass Incarceration in the Age of Colorblindness.* New York: New Press.

Allen, J. Linn. 1993. "Rare Blend: Achieving, Maintaining Diversity Is No Easy Task." *Chicago Tribune,* Nov. 28, p. 1.

Almaguer, Tomás. 1993. *Racial Fault Lines: The Historical Origins of White Supremacy in California.* Berkeley: University of California Press.

Alon, Sigal, and Marta Tienda. 2007. "Diversity, Opportunity, and the Shifting Meritocracy in Higher Education." *American Sociological Review* 72 (4): 487–511.

American Enterprise Institute. 2002. *American Enterprise Online: Diversity.* Washington, DC. Sept.

———. 2003. *American Enterprise Online: Race, Broken Schools, and Affirmative Action.* Washington, DC. Apr.–May.

Anderson, Elijah. 1999. "The Social Situation of the Black Executive." In *The Cultural Territories of Race: Black and White Boundaries*, edited by Michèle Lamont, 3–28. Chicago: University of Chicago Press.

———. 2011. *The Cosmopolitan Canopy: Race and Civility in Everyday Life.* New York: W. W. Norton.

Anderson, Elizabeth. 2002. "Integration, Affirmative Action, and Strict Scrutiny." *New York University Law Review* 77:1195–271.

Anderson, James D. 2007. "Past Discrimination and Diversity: A Historical Context for Understanding Race and Affirmative Action." *Journal of Negro Education* 76 (3): 204–15.

Ansley, Mary Holm. 1981. "Residents, Housing Varied: Rogers Park—a Diverse Community." *Chicago Tribune*, Feb. 1, p. W_B2C.

Auerbach, Carl F., and Louise B. Silverstein. 2003. *Qualitative Data: An Introduction to Coding and Analysis.* New York: New York University Press.

Avent-Holt, Dustin, and Donald Tomaskovic-Devey. 2014. "A Relational Theory of Earnings Inequality." *American Behavioral Scientist* 58 (3): 379–99.

Bachman, Carrie. 1987. "Racism on Campus: Conflict and Challenges." *Michigan Alumnus*, May–June, 14–21.

Bartelt, Eric S. 2009. "Army Unveils Diversity Policy at West Point Conference." Official Homepage of the United States Army. April 7. http://www.army.mil/article/19371 /Army_unveils_diversity_policy_at_West_Point_conference/. Accessed Oct. 13, 2011.

Becker, Howard. 1998. *Tricks of the Trade: How to Think about Your Research While You're Doing It.* Chicago: University of Chicago Press.

Bell, Derrick A., Jr. 1980. "*Brown v. Board of Education* and the Interest-Convergence Dilemma." *Harvard Law Review* 93:518–33.

Bell, Joyce M., and Douglas Hartmann. 2007. "Diversity in Everyday Discourse: The Cultural Ambiguities and Consequences of 'Happy Talk.'" *American Sociological Review* 72 (December): 895–914.

Benford, Robert D., and David A. Snow. 2000. "Framing Processes and Social Movements: An Overview and Assessment." *Annual Review of Sociology* 26:611–39.

Bennett, Larry, and Adolph Reed Jr. 1999. "The New Face of Urban Renewal: The Near North Redevelopment Initiative and the Cabrini-Green Neighborhood." In *Without Justice for All: The New Liberalism and Our Retreat from Racial Equality*, edited by Adolph Reed Jr., 175–211. Boulder, CO: Westview.

Bennett, Larry, Janet L. Smith, and Patricia A. Wright. 2006. *Where Are Poor People to Live? Transforming Public Housing Communities.* Armonk, NY: M. E. Sharpe.

Berbrier, Mitch. 2004. "Assimilationism and Pluralism as Cultural Tools." *Sociological Forum* 19 (1): 29–61.

Berrey, Ellen C. 2004. "Field Note: The Drive for Diversity." *Contexts* 4 (1): 60–61.

———. 2005. "Divided over Diversity: Political Discourse in a Chicago Neighborhood." *City and Community* 4 (2): 143–70.

———. 2011. "Why Diversity Became Orthodox in Higher Education, and How It Changed the Meaning of Race on Campus." *Critical Sociology* 37 (5): 573–96.

———. 2014. "Breaking Glass Ceilings, Ignoring Dirty Floors: The Culture and Class Bias of Corporate Diversity Management." *American Behavioral Scientist* 58 (2): 347–70.

Berrey, Ellen C., Steve G. Hoffman, and Laura Beth Nielsen. 2012. "Situated Justice: A

Contextual Analysis of Fairness and Inequality in Employment Discrimination Litigation." *Law and Society Review* 46 (1): 1–36.

Bielby, William T. 2008. "Promoting Racial Diversity at Work: Challenges and Solutions." In *Diversity at Work*, edited by Arthur P. Brief, 53–86. Cambridge: Cambridge University Press.

———. 2012. "Minority Vulnerability in Privileged Occupations: Why Do African American Financial Advisers Earn Less Than Whites in a Large Financial Services Firm?" *Annals of the American Academy of Political and Social Science* 639:13–32.

Billig, Michael. 1995. "Rhetorical Psychology, Ideological Thinking, and Imagining Nationhood." In *Social Movements and Culture*, edited by Hank Johnston and Bert Klandermans, 64–81. Minneapolis: University of Minnesota Press.

Binder, Amy. 2004. *Contentious Curricula: Afrocentrism and Creationism in American Public Schools*. Princeton, NJ: Princeton University Press.

———. 2007. "For Love and Money: Organizations' Creative Responses to Multiple Environmental Logics." *Theory and Society* 36: 547–71.

Biondi, Martha. 2003. *To Stand and Fight: The Struggle for Civil Rights in Postwar New York City*. Cambridge, MA: Harvard University Press.

Blau, Peter. 1977. *Inequality and Heterogeneity: A Primitive Theory of Social Structure*. New York: Free Press.

Blommaert, Jan, and Jef Verschueren. 1998. *Debating Diversity: Analysing the Discourse of Tolerance*. London: Routledge.

Bok, Derrick. 2003. *Universities in the Marketplace: The Commercialization of Higher Education*. Princeton, NJ: Princeton University Press.

Bonastia, Chris. 2004. "Hedging His Bets: Why Nixon Killed HUD's Desegregation Efforts." *Social Science History* 28 (1): 19.

Bonilla-Silva, Eduardo. 1997. "Rethinking Racism: Toward a Structural Interpretation." *American Sociological Review* 62 (4): 465–80.

———. 2002. "We Are All Americans! The Latin Americanization of Racial Stratification in the USA." *Race and Society* 5:3–16.

———. 2003. *Racism without Racists: Color-Blind Racism and the Persistence of Racial Inequality in the United States*. Lanham, MD: Rowman and Littlefield.

Bonilla-Silva, Eduardo, and David R. Dietrich. 2009. "The Latin Americanization of U.S. Race Relations: A New Pigmentocracy." In *Shades of Difference: Why Skin Color Matters*, edited by Evelyn Nakano Glenn, 40–60. Stanford, CA: Stanford University Press.

Bonilla-Silva, Eduardo, Amanda E. Lewis, and David G. Embrick. 2004. "'I Did Not Get That Job Because of a Black Man . . .': The Story Lines and Personal Stories of Color-Blind Racism." *Sociological Forum* 19 (4): 555–81.

Bourdieu, Pierre. 1984. *Distinction: A Social Critique of the Judgement of Taste*. Cambridge, MA: Harvard University Press.

Bowen, Deirdre. 2011. "*Grutter's* Regrets: An Empirical Investigation of How Affirmative Action Is(n't) Working." *University of Pittsburgh Law Review* 73:339–98.

Bowen, William G., and Derrick Bok. 1998. *The Shape of the River: Long-Term Consequences of Considering Race in College and University Admissions*. Princeton, NJ: Princeton University Press.

Boxenbaum, Eva. 2006. "Lost in Translation: The Making of Danish Diversity Management." *American Behavioral Scientist* 49 (7): 939–48.

Boyd, Michelle. 2008. *Jim Crow Nostalgia: Reconstructing Race in Bronzeville*. Minneapolis: University of Minnesota Press.

Branegan, Jay. 1980. "Rogers Park Public Housing Project Halted." *Chicago Tribune*, Oct. 27, p. D1.

Bridges, Khiara M. 2011. *Reproducing Race: An Ethnography of Pregnancy as a Site of Racialization*. Berkeley: University of California Press.

Briscoe, Forrest, and Sean Safford. 2008. "The Nixon in China Effect: Activism, Imitation, and the Institutionalization of Contentious Practice." *Administrative Science Quarterly* 53:460–91.

Brockner, J. 1988. "The Effects of Work Layoffs on Survivors: Research, Theory, and Practice." In *Research in Organizational Behavior*, vol. 10, edited by B. M. Staw and L. L. Cummings, 213–55. Greenwich, CT: JAI.

Brown, Michael K., Martin Carnoy, Elliott Currie, Troy Duster, David B. Oppenheimer, Marjorie M. Shultz, and David Wellman. 2003. *Whitewashing Race: The Myth of the Color-Blind Society*. Berkeley: University of California Press.

Brown-Nagin, Tomiko. 2005. "Elites, Social Movements, and the Law: The Case of Affirmative Action." *Columbia Law Review* 105:1436–528.

Brown-Saracino, Japonica. 2010. *A Neighborhood That Never Changes: Gentrification, Social Preservation, and the Search for Authenticity*. Chicago: University of Chicago Press.

Buck, Thomas. 1972. "CHA Gets OK for 199 Housing Units." *Chicago Tribune*, Feb. 11, p. 2.

Burke, Meghan A. 2012. *Racial Ambivalence in Diverse Communities: Whiteness and the Power of Color-Blind Ideologies*. Lanham, MD: Lexington Books.

Caiazza, Amy, April Shaw, and Misha Werschkul. 2004. *Women's Economic Status in the States: Wide Disparities by Race, Ethnicity, and Region*. Washington, DC: Institute for Women's Policy Research.

Catalyst. 2006. *2005 Catalyst Census of Women Board Directors of the Fortune 500*. New York.

Center for Urban Research and Learning, Loyola University Chicago. 2002. "Gentrification and Affordable Housing in Rogers Park: Community of Change, Community of Opportunity." Chicago.

Chicago Daily Defender. 1963. "Chicago's Growing Racial Crisis." Mar. 4, p. 9.

———. 1966a. "While Others Snarl, Far North Siders Welcome Negroes." Sept. 3.

———. 1966b. "Nazis Plan 'Back to Africa' Englewood March Saturday." Sept. 6.

Chicago Fact Book Consortium. 1984. *Local Community Fact Book, Chicago Metropolitan Area*. Chicago: Chicago Review Press.

———. 1995. *Local Community Fact Book, Chicago Metropolitan Area, 1990*. Chicago: University of Illinois.

Chicago Housing Authority. 2000. "Plan for Transformation: Moving to Work Annual Plan FY 2001." Chicago.

Chicago Rehab Network. 2013. *Rogers Park Housing Fact Sheet*. http://www.chicagorehab.org/resources/docs/fact_books/2013_ca_fact_sheets/rogers_park.pdf. Accessed Mar. 15, 2014.

Chicago Sun-Times. 2000. "Hot Chicago Neighborhoods." May 26, p. 5.

Chicago Tribune. 1956. "Seek Ordinance for 49th Ward Beach Survey." Jan. 8, p. N4.

———. 1957. "Rogers Park Asks Ok for Urban Renewal Site." Nov. 14, p. N8.

———. 1964. "Disappear in Rogers Park." Oct. 8, p. N1.

———. 1968. "Rogers Park Group Urges Open Housing." June 9.

City of Chicago, City Council. 1994. *Journal of the Proceedings of the City Council of the City of Chicago, Illinois*. Nov. 16.

City of Chicago, Department of Community Development. 2010. *Market Profile: Rogers Park*.

City of Chicago, Department of Planning. 1986. *The Now and Future of Rogers Park: Summary Report on the Rogers Park Community Planning Conference.* Chicago.

———. 1988. *Community Assistance Panel Sheridan Road.* Chicago.

Clawson, Rosalee A., Elizabeth R. Kegler, and Eric N. Waltenburg. 2001. "The Legitimacy-Conferring Authority of the U.S. Supreme Court: An Experimental Design." *American Politics Research* 29 (6): 566–91.

Clegg, Roger. 2007. *Statement to the Equal Employment Opportunity Commission Meeting to Launch E-Race Initiative.* Washington, DC: Feb. 28.

Cohen, Michael D., James G. March, and Johan P. Olsen. 1972. "A Garbage Can Model of Organizational Choice." *Administrative Science Quarterly* 17 (1): 1–25.

Colapinto, John. 2003. "Armies of the Right: The Young Hipublicans." *New York Times Magazine,* May 25.

College Board. 2006. *Trends in College Pricing.* Washington, DC.

Collins, Sharon M. 1983. "The Making of the Black Middle Class." *Social Problems* 30 (4): 369–82.

———. 1997a. *Black Corporate Executives: The Making and Breaking of a Black Middle Class.* Philadelphia: Temple University Press.

———. 1997b. "Black Mobility in White Corporations: Up the Corporate Ladder but Out on a Limb." *Social Problems* 44 (1): 55–100.

———. 2011a. "Diversity in the Post–Affirmative Action Labor Market: A Proxy for Racial Progress." *Critical Sociology* 37 (5): 521–41.

———. 2011b. "From Affirmative Action to Diversity: Erasing Inequality from Organizational Responsibility." *Critical Sociology* 37 (5): 517–20.

Condit, Celeste Michelle, and John Louis Lucaites. 1993. *Crafting Equality: America's Anglo-African Word.* Chicago: University of Chicago Press.

Conley, Dalton. 1999. *Being Black, Living in the Red: Race, Wealth, and Social Policy in America.* Berkeley: University of California Press.

Cotter, David A., Joan M. Hermsen, Seth Ovadia, and Reeve Vanneman. 2001. "The Glass Ceiling Effect." *Social Forces* 80 (2): 655–82.

Coulter, Ann. 2009. "At the End of the Day, Diversity Has Jumped the Shark." *Human Events,* Nov. 18. http://www.humanevents.com/article.php?id=34484. Accessed Aug. 15, 2011.

Crain's Chicago Business. 1995. "Helter Shelter: Problems Plague Tax-Credit Housing." May 1.

Crenshaw, Kimberlé Williams. 2007. "'Framing Affirmative Action.'" *Michigan Law Review First Impressions* 105:123–33.

Crenson, Matthew A. 1983. *Neighborhood Politics.* Cambridge, MA: Harvard University Press.

Darrow, Joy. 1973. "Chicago Financing 'Fix' under Probe." *Chicago Daily Defender,* Sept. 10.

Dávila, Arlene. 2001. *Latinos, Inc.: The Marketing and Making of a People.* Berkeley: University of California Press.

Davis, Angela. 1996. "Gender, Class, and Multiculturalism: Rethinking 'Race' Politics." In *Mapping Multiculturalism,* edited by Avery F. Gordon and Christopher Newfield, 40–48. Minneapolis: University of Minnesota Press.

Daye, Charles E. 2000. "Whither 'Fair' Housing: Meditations on Wrong Paradigms, Ambivalent Answers, and a Legislative Proposal." *Washington University Journal of Law and Policy* 3 (241): 242–94.

Deo, Meera E. 2011. "The Promise of *Grutter*: Diverse Interactions at the University of Michigan Law School." *Michigan Journal of Race and Law* 17 (1): 63–118.

Desmond, Matthew, and Mustafa Emirbayer. 2009. "What Is Racial Domination?" *Du Bois Review: Social Science Research on Race* 6 (2): 335–55.

DevCorp North. 2006. *Commercial Corridor Plan for Howard Street and Morse Avenue.* Chicago.

Developing Government Accountability to the People. 2006. *A Report Card for Chicago, 2006.* http://www.uic.edu/depts/pols/ChicagoPolitics/dgap.pdf. Accessed June 4, 2014.

Di Leonardo, Micaela. 1998. *Exotics at Home: Anthropologies, Others, American Modernity.* Chicago: University of Chicago Press.

———. 2008. "New Global and American Landscapes of Inequality." In *New Landscapes of Inequality: Neoliberalism and the Erosion of Democracy in America,* edited by Jane L. Collins, Micaela di Leonardo, and Bret Williams, 3–16. Santa Fe, NM: School for Advanced Research Press.

DiMaggio, Paul. 1997. "Culture and Cognition." *Annual Review of Sociology* 23:263–87.

DiMaggio, Paul, and Walter W Powell. 1983. "The Iron Cage Revisited: Institutional Isomorphism and Collective Rationality in Organizational Fields." *American Sociological Review* 48 (2): 147–60.

DiTomaso, Nancy. 2013. *The American Non-Dilemma: Racial Inequality without Racism.* New York: Russell Sage Foundation.

Diversity, Inc. 2006. "Why You Shouldn't Believe Everything You Read: 5 Studies We Reject." Nov., 74–76.

Dobbin, Frank R. 2009. *Inventing Equal Opportunity.* Princeton, NJ: Princeton University Press.

Dobbin, Frank R., and Alexandra Kalev. 2008. "You Can't Make Me: Resistance to Corporate Diversity Training." Paper presented at the Discoveries of the Discrimination Research Group Conference, Palo Alto, CA.

———. 2013. "The Origins and Effects of Corporate Diversity Programs." In *The Oxford Handbook of Diversity and Work,* edited by Quinetta M. Roberson, 253–79. Oxford: Oxford University Press.

Dobbin, Frank R., Alexandra Kalev, and Erin L. Kelly. 2007. "Diversity Management in Corporate America." *Contexts* 6 (4): 21–8.

Downey, Dennis J. 1999. "From Americanization to Multiculturalism: Political Symbols and Struggles for Cultural Diversity in Twentieth-Century American Race Relations." *Sociological Perspectives* 42 (2): 249–63.

Duany, Andres, Elizabeth Plater-Zyberk, and Jeff Speck. 2000. *Suburban Nation: The Rise of Sprawl and the Decline of the American Dream.* New York: North Point.

Duggan, Lisa. 2003. *The Twilight of Equality? Neoliberalism, Cultural Politics, and the Attack on Democracy.* Boston: Beacon.

Duneier, Mitchell. 2004. "Scrutinizing the Heat: On Ethnic Myths and the Importance of Shoe Leather." *Contemporary Sociology* 33:139–50.

Durkheim, Emile. (1912) 1995. *The Elementary Forms of Religious Life.* New York: Free Press.

Edelman, Lauren B. 1990. "Legal Environments and Organizational Governance: The Expansion of Due Process in the American Workplace." *American Journal of Sociology* 95:1401–40.

———. 1992. "Legal Ambiguity and Symbolic Structures: Organizational Mediation of Civil Rights Law." *American Journal of Sociology* 97 (1): 531–76.

Edelman, Lauren B., Sally Riggs Fuller, and Iona Mara-Drita. 2001. "Diversity Rhetoric and the Managerialization of Law." *American Journal of Sociology* 106 (6): 1589–642.

Edelman, Lauren B., Linda H. Krieger, Scott R. Eliason, Catherine R. Albiston, and Virginia

Mellema. 2011. "When Organizations Rule: Judicial Deference to Institutionalized Employment Structures." *American Journal of Sociology* 117 (3): 888–954.

Edelman, Lauren B., Christopher Uggen, and Howard S. Erlanger. 1999. "The Endogeneity of Legal Regulation: Grievance Procedures as Rational Myth." *American Journal of Sociology* 105 (2): 406–54.

Edelman, Murray. 1974. *Language and Social Problems*. Madison: University of Wisconsin–Madison.

———. 1977. *Political Language: Words That Succeed and Policies That Fail*. New York: Academic.

———. (1964) 1985. *The Symbolic Uses of Politics*. Urbana: University of Illinois Press.

Edgell, Penny. 1998. "Making Inclusive Communities: Congregations and the 'Problem' of Race." *Social Problems* 45 (4): 451–72.

Edney, Hazel. 2002. "Students Lead a 'New' Civil Rights Movement." *Foreign Policy in Focus*, May 16.

Elejalde, Alexia. 2006. "Diversity Next Door; Rogers Park's Mix of Races and Ethnicities Is a Rarity in Chicago Neighborhoods." *Chicago Tribune*, Red Eye Edition, Jul. 19, p. 10.

Ellen, Ingrid Gould. 2000. *Sharing America's Neighborhoods: The Prospects for Stable Racial Integration*. Cambridge, MA: Harvard University Press.

Embrick, David. 2011. "The Diversity Ideology in the Business World: A New Oppression for a New Age." *Critical Sociology* 37 (5): 541–56.

Emerson, Robert M. 1983. *Contemporary Field Research: A Collection of Readings*. Prospect Heights, IL: Waveland.

Emerson, Robert M., Rachel I. Fretz, and Linda L. Shaw. 1995. *Writing Ethnographic Fieldnotes*. Chicago: University of Chicago Press.

Emirbayer, Mustafa. 1997. "Manifesto for a Relational Sociology." *American Journal of Sociology* 103 (2): 281–317.

Espenshade, Thomas J., and Alexandria Walton Radford. 2009. *No Longer Separate, Not Yet Equal: Race and Class in Elite College Admission and Campus Life*. Princeton, NJ: Princeton University Press.

Ewick, Patricia, and Austin Sarat. 2004. "Hidden in Plain View: Murray Edelman in the Law and Society Tradition." *Law and Social Inquiry* 29 (2): 439–63.

Ewick, Patricia, and Susan S. Silbey. 1998. *The Common Place of Law: Stories from Everyday Life*. Chicago: University of Chicago Press.

Fairclough, Norman. 1989. *Language and Power*. London: Longman.

Farley, Reynolds. 2010. "The Waning of American Apartheid?" *Contexts* 10 (3): 36–43.

Farley, Reynolds, and William H. Frey. 1994. "Changes in the Segregation of Whites from Blacks during the 1980s: Small Steps toward a More Integrated Society." *American Sociological Review* 59 (1): 23–45.

Fast Company staff. 2005. "Why We Hate HR." *Fast Company*, Aug. 1. http://www.fast company.com/53319/why-we-hate-hr. Accessed Mar. 25, 2013.

Feagin, Joe R. 2006. *Systemic Racism: A Theory of Oppression*. New York: Routledge.

Fears, Darryl. 2003. "At U-Michigan, Minority Students Find Access—and Sense of Isolation; Affirmative Action Debate Intensifies Emotions on Campus." *Washington Post*, Apr. 1.

Fields, Corey D. (2013) "The Paradoxes of Black Republicans." In *The Social Side of Politics*, edited by Douglas Hartmann and Christopher Uggen, 145–59. New York: W.W. Norton.

Fischer, Claude S. 1975. "Toward a Subcultural Theory of Urbanism." *American Journal of Sociology* 80 (6): 1319–41.

———. 1999. "Uncommon Values, Diversity, and Conflict in City Life." In *Diversity and*

Its Discontents: Cultural Conflict and Common Ground in Contemporary American Society, edited by Neil J. Smelser and Jeffrey C. Alexander, 213–27. Princeton, NJ: Princeton University Press.

Fischer, Claude S., and Michael Hout. 2008. *Century of Difference: How America Changed in the Last One Hundred Years*. New York: Russell Sage Foundation.

Fligstein, Neil. 1990. *The Transformation of Corporate Control*. Cambridge, MA: Harvard University Press.

———. 2001. *The Architecture of Markets: An Economic Sociology of Twenty-First-Century Capitalist Societies*. Princeton, NJ: Princeton University Press.

Fligstein, Neil, and Adam Goldstein. 2010. "The Anatomy of the Mortgage Securitization Crisis." In *Markets on Trial: The Economic Sociology of the U.S. Financial Crisis: Part A*, vol. 30 of *Research in the Sociology of Organizations*, edited by Michael Lounsbury and Paul Hirsch, 29–70. Bingley, UK: Emerald Group.

Ford, Gerald R. 1999. "Inclusive American, under Attack." *New York Times*, Aug. 8, p. 15.

Foucault, Michel. 1972. *The Archaeology of Knowledge and the Discourse on Language*. New York: Pantheon Books.

Fredrickson, George M. 2002. *Racism: A Short History*. Princeton, NJ: Princeton University Press.

Freeman, Alan. 1998. "Antidiscrimination Law from 1954 to 1989: Uncertainty, Contradiction, Rationalization, Denial." In *The Politics of Law: A Progressive Critique*, edited by David Kairys, 285–311. New York: Basic Books.

Freeman, Lance. 2005. "Displacement or Succession? Residential Mobility in Gentrifying Neighborhoods." *Urban Affairs Review* 40 (4): 463–91.

Friedland, Roger, and Robert R. Alford. 1991. "Bringing Society Back In: Symbols, Practices, and Institutional Contradictions." In *The New Institutionalism in Organizational Analysis*, edited by Paul DiMaggio and Walter W. Powell, 232–63. Chicago: University of Chicago Press.

Friedland, Roger, and John W. Mohr. 2004. "The Cultural Turn in American Sociology." In *Matters of Culture: Cultural Sociology in Practice*, edited by Friedland and Mohr, 1–70. Cambridge: Cambridge University Press.

Friere, Paulo. 1970. *Pedagogy of the Oppressed*. London: Continuum.

Frymer, Paul, and John David Skrentny. 2004. "The Rise of Instrumental Affirmative Action: Law and the New Significance of Race in America." *Connecticut Law Review* 36:677–723.

Gamson, William A., and Andre Modigliani. 1987. "The Changing Culture of Affirmative Action." In *Research in Political Sociology*, edited by Richard G. Braungart, 3:137–77. Greenwich, CT: JAI Press.

Gans, Herbert J. 1999. "The Possibility of a New Racial Hierarchy in the Twenty-First-Century United States." In *The Cultural Territories of Race: Black and White Boundaries*, edited by Michèle Lamont, 371–90. Chicago: University of Chicago Press.

Gaventa, John. 1980. *Power and Powerlessness: Quiescence and Rebellion in an Appalachian Valley*. Chicago: University of Chicago Press.

Geertz, Clifford. 1973. *The Interpretation of Cultures*. New York: Basic Books.

Gerteis, Joseph, Douglas Hartmann, and Penny Edgell. 2007. "The Multiple Meanings of Diversity: How Americans Express Its Possibilities and Problems." Paper presented at the annual meetings of the American Sociological Association, New York.

Getz, Ann. 1967. "Rogers Park Tops Welfare Study." *Chicago Tribune*, Feb. 19, p. L1.

Ghaziani, Amin. 2008. *The Dividends of Dissent: How Conflict and Culture Work in Lesbian and Gay Marches on Washington*. Chicago: University of Chicago Press.

——. 2009. "An 'Amorphous Mist'? The Problem of Measurement in the Study of Culture." *Theory and Society* 38 (6): 581–612.

Ghaziani, Amin, and Marc Ventresca. 2005. "Keywords and Cultural Change: Frame Analysis of Business Model Public Talk, 1975–2000." *Sociological Forum* 20 (4): 523–59.

Gioia, Dennis A., Majken Schultz, and Kevin G. Corley. 2000. "Organizational Identity, Image, and Adaptive Instability." *Academy of Management Journal* 25 (1): 63–81.

Gitlin, Todd. 1995. *The Twilight of Common Dreams: Why America Is Wracked by Culture Wars.* New York: Henry Holt.

Glazer, Nathan. 1997. *We Are All Multiculturalists Now.* Cambridge, MA: Harvard University Press.

——. 2005. "Diversity." In *New Dictionary of the History of Ideas*, edited by Maryanne Horowitz, 590–93. Detroit: Charles Scribner's Sons.

Gleason, Philip. 1984. "Pluralism and Assimilationism: A Conceptual History." In *Linguistic Minorities, Policies, and Pluralism*, edited by John Edwards, 221–58. London: Academic.

Gold, Steven J. 2004. "From Jim Crow to Racial Hegemony: Evolving Explanations of Racial Hierarchy." *Ethnic and Racial Studies* 27 (6): 951–68.

Goode, Judith. 2001. "Let's Get Our Act Together: How Racial Discourses Disrupt Neighborhood Activism." In *The New Poverty Studies: The Ethnography of Power, Politics, and Impoverished People in the United States*, edited by Judith Goode and Jeff Maskovsky, 364–98. New York: New York University Press.

Goodwin, Carole. 1979. *The Oak Park Strategy: Community Control of Racial Change.* Chicago: University of Chicago Press.

Graham, Hugh Davis. 1990. *The Civil Rights Era: Origins and Development of National Policy, 1960–1972.* Oxford: Oxford University Press.

——. 1992. "The Origins of Affirmative Action: Civil Rights and the Regulatory State." *Annals of the American Academy of Political and Social Sciences* 523:50–62.

——. 2000. "The Surprising Career of Federal Fair Housing Law." *Journal of Policy History* 12 (2): 215–32.

Grams, Diane. 2010. *Producing Local Color: Art Networks in Ethnic Chicago.* Chicago: University of Chicago Press.

Gramsci, Antonio. 1971. *Selections from the Prison Notebooks.* New York: International.

Green, Denise O'Neil. 2004a. "Fighting the Battle for Racial Diversity: A Case Study of Michigan's Institutional Responses to *Gratz* and *Grutter*." *Educational Policy* 18 (5): 733–51.

——. 2004b. "Justice and Diversity: Michigan's Response to *Gratz, Grutter*, and the Affirmative Action Debate." *Urban Education* 39 (4): 374–93.

Green, Tristin K. 2010. "Race and Sex in Organizing Work: 'Diversity,' Discrimination, and Integration." *Emory Law Journal* 59:585–647.

Green, Tristin K., and Alexandra Kalev. 2008. "Discrimination-Reducing Measures at the Relational Level." *Hastings Law Journal* 59:1435–61.

Greenland, Fiona Rose, Anthony S. Chen, and Lisa M. Stulberg. 2010. "Beyond the Open Door: The Origins of Affirmative Action in Undergraduate Admissions at Cornell and the University of Michigan." Paper presented at the Policy History Conference, Columbus, OH, June 3–6.

Griswold, Wendy. 1987. "A Methodological Framework for the Sociology of Culture." *Sociological Methodology* 17:1–35.

Grodsky, Eric. 2007. "Compensatory Sponsorship in Higher Education." *American Journal of Sociology* 112 (6): 1662–712.

Gronbjerg, Kirsten A., Katy Crossley, Lorri Platek, Natalya Zhezmer, and Toni Migliore. 1993. *Rogers Park: A Tradition of Diversity—Laying the Foundation for Economic Development.* Chicago: Department of Sociology-Anthropology, Loyola University.

Guinier, Lani, and Gerald Torres. 2002. *The Miner's Canary: Enlisting Race, Resisting Power, Transforming Democracy.* Cambridge, MA: Harvard University Press.

Gurin, Patricia, E. Dey, S. Hurtado, and G. Gurin. 2002. "Diversity and Higher Education: Theory and Impact on Educational Outcomes." *Harvard Educational Review* 72 (3): 330–66.

Gurin, Patricia, Jeffrey S. Lehman, and Earl Lewis. 2004. *Defending Diversity: Affirmative Action at the University of Michigan.* Ann Arbor: University of Michigan Press.

Gurin, Patricia, Biren (Ratnesh) Nagda, and Ximena Zuniga. 2013. *Dialogue across Difference: Practice, Theory, and Research on Intergroup Dialogue.* New York: Russell Sage Foundation.

Hacker, Jacob S. 2008. *The Great Risk Shift: The New Economic Insecurity and the Decline of the American Dream.* Oxford: Oxford University Press.

Hacking, Ian. 2005. "Why Race Still Matters." *Daedalus* 134:102–16.

Hallett, Tim. 2010. "The Myth Incarnate: Recoupling Processes, Turmoil, and Inhabited Institutions in an Urban Elementary School." *American Sociological Review* 75 (1): 52–74.

Haltom, William, and Michael McCann. 2004. *Distorting the Law: Politics, Media, and the Litigation Crisis.* Chicago: University of Chicago Press.

Haney-López, Ian F. 2000. "Institutional Racism: Judicial Conduct and a New Theory of Racial Discrimination." *Yale Law Journal* 109:1717–884.

———. 2006. "A Nation of Minorities: Race, Ethnicity, and Reactionary Colorblindness." *Stanford Law Review* 59:985–1064.

Harley, J. B. 1989. "Deconstructing the Map." *Cartographica* 26:1–20.

Harper, Shannon, and Barbara Reskin. 2005. "Affirmative Action at School and on the Job." *Annual Review of Sociology* 31:357–79.

Hartmann, Douglas, Penny Edgell, and Joseph Gerteis. 2005. "American Attitudes about Diversity." Press release on file with author.

Hartmann, Douglas, and Joseph Gerteis. 2005. "Dealing with Diversity: Mapping Multiculturalism in Sociological Terms." *Sociological Theory* 23 (2): 218–40.

Hartstein, Larry. 1994. "New Day for Rogers Park Road: Sheridan Remake Taking Shape." *Chicago Tribune,* Nov. 18.

Harvey, David. 2005. *A Brief History of Neoliberalism.* Oxford: Oxford University Press.

———. 2012. *Rebel Cities: From the Right to the City to the Urban Revolution.* New York: Verso Books.

Haskins, Ron. 2008. "Education and Economic Mobility." In *Getting Ahead or Losing Ground: Economic Mobility in America,* edited by Julia B. Isaacs, Isabel V. Sawhill, and Ron Haskins, 91–104. Washington, DC: Economic Mobility Project, an Initiative of the Pew Charitable Trusts.

Hatton, Erin. 2011. *The Temp Economy: From Kelly Girls to Permatemps in Postwar America.* Philadelphia: Temple University Press.

Hebel, Sara. 2004. "Patrolling Professors' Politics." *Chronicle of Higher Education,* Feb. 13.

Heller, Donald E. 2005. *Condition of Access: Higher Education for Lower Income Students.* Westport, CT: American Council on Education / Praeger Series on Higher Education.

Herring, Cedric. 2009. "Does Diversity Pay? Race, Gender, and the Business Case for Diversity." *American Sociological Review* 74 (2): 208–24.

Hirsch, Arnold R. 1983. *Making the Second Ghetto: Race and Housing in Chicago, 1940–1960.* Cambridge: Cambridge University Press.

Hirschman, Dan, Ellen Berrey, and Fiona Rose-Greenland. 2012. "Dequantifying Diversity: Affirmative Action and Admissions at the University of Michigan." Paper presented at the annual meeting of the American Sociological Association, Denver.

Hochschild, Jennifer. 2002. "Affirmative Action as Culture War." In *Companion to Racial and Ethnic Studies,* edited by David Goldberg and John Solomos, 282–303. Malden, MA: Wiley-Blackwell.

Hochschild, Jennifer, Vesla M. Weaver, and Traci Burch. 2012. *Creating a New Racial Order: How Immigration, Multiracialism, DNA, and the Young Can Remake Race in America.* Princeton, NJ: Princeton University Press.

Hoffman, Steve G. 2011. "The New Tools of the Science Trade: Contested Knowledge Production and the Conceptual Vocabularies of Academic Capitalism." *Social Anthropology* 19 (4): 439–62.

———. 2012. "Academic Capitalism." *Contexts* 11 (4): 12–13.

Hollinger, David A. 2000. *Postethnic America: Beyond Multiculturalism.* New York: Basic Books.

Hopp-Peters, Elizabeth. 1988. "Rogers Park Renaissance Construction, Renovation Set Stage for Comeback." *Chicago Tribune,* Dec. 4, Real Estate, p. 1.

Horton, John. 1995. *The Politics of Diversity: Immigration, Resistance, and Change in Monterey Park, California.* Philadelphia: Temple University Press.

Hout, Michael, Claude S. Fischer, and Mark Chaves. 2013. *More Americans Have No Religious Preference: Key Finding from the 2012 General Social Survey.* Berkeley: Institute for the Study of Societal Issues, University of California, Berkeley.

Howe, Amy. 2013. "Finally! The *Fischer* Decision in Plain English." *Supreme Court of the United States Blog,* June 24. http://www.scotusblog.com/2013/06/finally-the-fisher-decision-in-plain-english/. Accessed July 9, 2013.

Humes, Edward. 2006. *Over Here: How the G.I. Bill Transformed the American Dream.* Orlando: Harcourt.

Hunter, Albert. 1974. *Symbolic Communities: The Persistence and Change of Chicago's Local Communities.* Chicago: University of Chicago Press.

Ihejirika, Maudlyn. 1995. "Time for Another Change, 49th Ward Challengers Say; Moore Defends His Record in Diverse Rogers Park." *Chicago Sun-Times,* Feb. 23, p. 12.

Jackall, Robert. 1988. *Moral Mazes: The World of Corporate Managers.* Oxford: Oxford University Press.

Jackman, Mary R. 1994. *The Velvet Glove: Paternalism and Conflict in Gender, Class, and Race Relations.* Berkeley: University of California Press.

Jacobs, Jane. 1961. *The Death and Life of Great American Cities.* New York: Random House.

Johnston, W. B., and A. H. Packer. 1987. *Workforce 2000: Work and Workers for the Twenty-First Century.* Indianapolis: Hudson Institute.

Jorvasky, Ben. 1992. "Scattered Successes: After 26 Years, the Gautreaux Housing Decision Is beginning to Bear Fruit." *Chicago Reader,* June 11.

Kalev, Alexandra, Frank R. Dobbin, and Erin Kelly. 2006. "Best Practices or Best Guesses? Assessing the Efficacy of Corporate Affirmative Action and Diversity Policies." *American Sociological Review* 71 (4): 589–617.

Kallen, Horace. 1915. "Democracy versus the Melting Pot: A Study of American Nationality." *Nation,* Feb. 25.

Kanter, Rosabeth Moss. 1993. *Men and Women of the Corporation.* New York: Basic Books.

Karabel, Jerome. 2005. *The Chosen: The Hidden History of Admission and Exclusion at Harvard, Yale, and Princeton*. New York: Houghton Mifflin.

Kärreman, Dan, and Mats Alvesson. 2004. "Cages in Tandem: Management Control, Social Identity, and Identification in a Knowledge-Intensive Firm." *Organization* 11 (1): 149–75.

Kelly, Erin, and Frank R. Dobbin. 1998. "How Affirmative Action became Diversity Management: Employer Response to Anti-discrimination Law, 1961–1996." *American Behavioral Scientist* 41 (7): 960–84.

Kennedy, Maureen, and Paul Leonard. 2001. *Dealing with Neighborhood Change: A Primer on Gentrification and Policy Choices*. Washington, DC: Brookings Institution and PolicyLink.

Kertzer, David I. 1988. *Ritual, Politics, and Power*. New Haven, CT: Yale University Press.

Killgore, Leslie. 2009. "Merit and Competition in Selective College Admissions." *Review of Higher Education* 32 (4): 469–88.

Kim, Daniel. 2002. "Rally Targets Racist Views, Ignorance." *Michigan Daily*, Mar. 21, pp. 1A, 7A.

Kim, Soohan, Alexandra Kalev, and Frank R. Dobbin. 2012. "Progressive Corporations at Work: The Case of Diversity Programs." *New York University Review of Law and Social Change* 36 (2): 171–213.

Kirkland, Anna, and Ben Hansen. 2011. "'How Do I Bring Diversity?': Race and Class in the College Admissions Essay." *Law and Society Review* 45 (1): 103–38.

Klinenberg, Eric. 2002. *Heat Wave: A Social Autopsy of Disaster in Chicago*. Chicago: University of Chicago Press.

Konrad, Alison M., and Frank Linnehan. 1995. "Formalized HRM Structures: coordinating Equal Employment Opportunity or Concealing Organizational Practices?" *Academy of Management Journal* 38 (3): 787–820.

———. 1999. "Affirmative Action: History, Effects, and Attitudes." In *Handbook of Gender and Work*, edited by Gary N. Powell, 429–52. Thousand Oaks, CA: Sage.

Krieger, Linda H. 1995. "The Content of Our Categories: A Cognitive Bias Approach to Discrimination and Equal Employment Opportunity." *Stanford Law Review* 47:1161.

Krugman, Paul. 2002. "For Richer." *New York Times*, Oct. 20.

Krysan, Maria. 2011. "Race and Residence: From the Telescope to the Microscope." *Contexts* 10 (3): 38–42.

Kulik, Carol T., and Loriann Roberson. 2008a. "Common Goals and Golden Opportunities: Evaluations of Diversity Education in Academic and Organizational Settings." *Academy of Management Learning and Education* 7 (3): 309–31.

———. 2008b. "Diversity Initiative Effectiveness: what Organizations Can (and Cannot) Expect from Diversity Recruitment, Diversity Training, and Formal Mentoring Programs." In *Diversity at Work*, edited by Arthur P. Brief, 265–317. Cambridge: Cambridge University Press.

Kunda, Gideon. 1992. *Engineering Culture: Control and Commitment in a High-Tech Corporation*. Philadelphia: Temple University Press.

Kymlicka, Will. 1995. *Multicultural Citizenship: A Liberal Theory of Minority Rights*. New York: Oxford University Press.

Lakeside Community Development Corporation. 2006. *The Community Housing Audit: Housing Redevelopment in One Chicago Neighborhood*. Chicago, Oct.

Lakoff, George. 2002. *Moral Politics: How Liberals and Conservatives Think*. Chicago: University of Chicago Press.

Lamont, Michèle, ed. 1999. *The Cultural Territories of Race: Black and White Boundaries*. Chicago: University of Chicago Press.

———. 2000. *The Dignity of Working Men: Morality and the Boundaries of Race, Class, and Immigration*. New York: Russell Sage Foundation.

Lamont, Michèle, and Virág Molnár. 2002. "The Study of Boundaries in the Social Sciences." *Annual Review of Sociology* 28:167–95.

Landry, Bart, and Kris Marsh. 2011. "The Evolution of the New Black Middle Class." *Annual Review of Sociology* 37:373–94.

Lau, Peter F., ed. 2004. *From the Grassroots to the Supreme Court: Brown v. Board of Education and American Democracy*. Durham, NC: Duke University Press.

Lemann, Nicholas. 1991. *Promised Land: The Great Black Migration and How It Changed America*. New York: Alfred A. Knopf.

———. 1999. *The Big Test: The Secret History of the American Meritocracy*. New York: Farrar, Straus, and Giroux.

Lewis, Amanda E. 2003. "Everyday Race-Making: Navigating Racial Boundaries in Schools." *American Behavioral Scientist* 47 (3): 283–305.

———. 2004. "'What Group?': Studying Whites and Whiteness in the Era of 'Color-Blindness.'" *Sociological Theory* 22 (4): 623–46.

Lewis Mumford Center, University of New York at Albany. 2001. *Ethnic Diversity Grows, Neighborhood Integration Lags Behind*. Albany:. http://mumford.albany.edu/census/WholePop/WPreport/MumfordReport.pdf. Accessed July 11, 2014.

Light, Ryan, Vincent J. Roscigno, and Alexandra Kalev. 2011. "Racial Discrimination, Interpretation, and Legitimation at Work." *Annals of the American Academy of Political and Social Science* 634:39–59.

Lipson, Daniel N. 2007. "Embracing Diversity: The Institutionalization of Affirmative Action as Diversity Management at UC-Berkeley, UT-Austin, and UW-Madison." *Law and Social Inquiry* 32 (4): 985–1026.

———. 2008. "Where's the Justice? Affirmative Action's Severed Civil Rights Roots in the Age of Diversity." *Perspectives on Politics* 6 (4): 691–706.

Litvin, Deborah R. 2002. "The Business Case for Diversity and the 'Iron Cage.'" In *Casting the Other: The Production and Maintenance of Inequalities in Work Organizations*, edited by Barbara Czarniawska and Heather Höpfl, 241–77. London: Routledge.

———. 2006. "Diversity: Making Space for a Better Case." In *Handbook of Workplace Diversity*, edited by Alison M. Konrad, Pushkala Prasad, and Judith K. Pringle, 75–94. London: Sage.

Llewellyn, Karl. 1930. "A Realistic Jurisprudence—the Next Step." *Columbia Law Review* 30:431–65.

Lloyd, Richard. 2002. "Neo-Bohemia: Art and Neighborhood Redevelopment in Chicago." *Journal of Urban Affairs* 24 (5): 517–32.

Logan, John. 2011a. *The Persistence of Segregation in the Metropolis: New Findings from the 2010 Census*. Report of the US2010 project.

———. 2011b. *Separate and Unequal: The Neighborhood Gap for Blacks, Hispanics and Asians in Metropolitan America*. Report of the US2010 project, 1–22.

Logan, John, and Harvey Molotch. 1987. *Urban Fortunes: The Political Economy of Place*. Berkeley: University of California Press.

Logan, John, Rachel Bridges Whaley, and Kyle Crowder. 1999. "The Character and Consequences of Growth Regimes: An Assessment of Twenty Years of Research." In *The Urban Growth Machine: Critical Perspectives Two Decades Later*, edited by

Andrew E. G. Jonas and David Wilson, 73–94. Albany: State University of New York Press.

Loveman, Mara. 1999. "Comment: Is Race Essential?" *American Sociological Review* 64 (6): 891–99.

Lowe, Frederick. 1973. "Rogers Park Group Applies Pressure to Secure Housing Loans." *Chicago Tribune*, May 10.

Lukes, Steven. 2004. *Power: A Radical View*. 2d ed. New York: Palgrave-Macmillan.

Lynch, Frederick R. 1997. *The Diversity Machine: The Drive to Change the "White Male Workplace."* New York: Free Press.

Macaulay, Stewart. 1963. "Non-contractual Relations in Business: A Preliminary Study." *American Sociological Review* 28 (1): 55–67.

MacLean, Nancy. 2006. *Freedom Is Not Enough: The Opening of the American Workplace*. New York: Russell Sage Foundation.

———. 2008. "Southern Dominance in Borrowed Language: The Regional Origins of American Neoliberalism." in *New Landscapes of Inequality: Neoliberalism and the Erosion of Democracy in America*, edited by Jane L. Collins, Micaela di Leonardo, and Brett Williams, 21–37. Santa Fe, NM: School for Advanced Research Press.

Maly, Michael T. 2005. *Beyond Segregation: Multiracial and Multiethnic Neighborhoods in the United States*. Philadelphia: Temple University Press.

Maly, Michael T., and Michael Leachman. 1998. "Rogers Park, Edgewater, Uptown, and Chicago Lawn, Chicago." *Cityscape* 4 (2): 130–60.

Mannheim, Karl. 1936. *Ideology and Utopia: An Introduction to the Sociology of Knowledge*. New York: Harcourt, Brace, and World.

Martin, Joanne. 2001. *Organizational Culture: Mapping the Terrain*. Thousand Oaks, CA: Sage.

Marvasti, Amir B., and Karyn D. McKinney. 2011. "Does Diversity Mean Assimilation?" *Critical Sociology* 37 (5): 631–50.

Marx, Anthony W. 1998. *Making Race and Nation: A Comparison of South Africa, the United States, and Brazil*. New York: Cambridge University Press.

Marx, Karl, and Friedrich Engels. 1947. *The German Ideology*. New York: International.

Massey, Douglas S. 2008. *Categorically Unequal: The American Stratification System*. New York: Russell Sage Foundation.

Massey, Douglas S., and Nancy A. Denton. 1993. *American Apartheid: Segregation and the Making of the Underclass*. Cambridge, MA: Harvard University Press.

Matlock, John, Gerald Gurin, and Katrina Wade-Golden. 2003. *The Michigan Student Study: Students' Expectations of and Experiences with Racial/Ethnic Diversity (Synopsis)*. Office of Academic Multicultural Initiatives, University of Michigan. http://www.umich.edu /~oami/mss/downloads/synopsis0103.pdf. Accessed Sept. 19, 2006.

Matney, Malinda M. 2003. "Comparison of University of Michigan Students 1993 (Middle of Generation X) to 2002 (Beginning of Millennial Generation)." *What's On Our Students' Minds* 1 (2). Division of Student Affairs, University of Michigan.

McAdam, Doug. 1982. *Political Process and the Development of Black Insurgency, 1930–1970*. Chicago: University of Chicago Press.

———. 1990. *Freedom Summer*. New York: Oxford University Press.

McAdam, Doug, Sidney Tarrow, and Charles Tilly. 2001. *Dynamics of Contention*. Cambridge: Cambridge University Press.

McCabe, Mike. 1980. "Man, Youth Charged." *Chicago Tribune*, Oct. 24, p. B1.

McCann, Michael. 1994. *Rights at Work: Pay Equity Reform and the Politics of Legal Mobilization*. Chicago: University of Chicago Press.

———. 1996. "Causal versus Constitutive Explanations (or, On the Difficulty of Being So Positive . . .)." *Law and Social Inquiry* 21 (2): 457–82.

Mele, Christopher. 2000. *Selling the Lower East Side: Culture, Real Estate, and Resistance in New York City*. Minneapolis: University of Minneapolis Press.

———. 2013. "Neoliberalism, Race and the Redefining of Urban Redevelopment." *International Journal of Urban and Regional Research* 37 (2): 598–617.

Menand, Louis. 1995. "Diversity." In *Critical Terms for Literary Studies*, edited by Frank Lentricchia and Thomas McLaughlin, 336–53. Chicago: University of Chicago Press.

Metropolitan Planning Council. 1999. *For Rent: Housing Options in the Chicago Region*. Chicago: University of Illinois at Chicago.

Meyer, John, and Brian Rowan. 1977. "Institutionalized Organizations: Formal Structure as Myth and Ceremony." *American Journal of Sociology* 83 (2): 340–63.

Michaels, Walter Benn. 2006. *The Trouble with Diversity: How We Learned to Love Identity and Ignore Inequality*. New York: Metropolitan Books.

Michigan Review. 2002. "Affirmative Action: Dishonest and Discriminatory." Oct. 30, p. 4.

Miller, John J. 2003. "'Diversity' . . . D'oh! Some Tactical Stumbles on the Way to the Michigan Debate." *National Review*, July 28.

———. 2004. "My Fraternity." *National Review Online*, Dec. 2.

Mintzberg, Henry. 1983. *Structure in Fives: Designing Effective Organizations*. Englewood Cliffs, NJ: Prentice-Hall.

Mische, Ann. 2011. "Relational Sociology, Culture, and Agency." In *The Sage Handbook of Social Network Analysis*, edited by John Scott and Peter J. Carrington, 80–98. London: Sage.

Molotch, Harvey. 1972. *Managed Integration: Dilemmas of Doing Good in the City*. Berkeley: University of California Press.

Moore, Wendy Leo, and Joyce M. Bell. 2011. "Maneuvers of Whiteness: 'Diversity' as a Mechanism of Retrenchment in the Affirmative Action Discourse." *Critical Sociology* 37 (5): 597–614.

Morning, Ann. 2011. *The Nature of Race: How Scientists Think and Teach about Human Difference*. Berkeley: University of California Press.

Morning, Ann, and Daniel Sabbagh. 2005. "From Sword to Plowshare: Using Race for Discrimination and Antidiscrimination in the United States." *International Social Science Journal* 57 (183): 57–73.

Morrill, Calvin, and Gary Alan Fine. 1997. "Ethnographic Contributions to Organizational Sociology." *Sociological Methods and Research* 5 (4): 424–51.

Morris, Aldon D. 1984. *The Origins of the Civil Rights Movement: Black Communities Organizing for Change*. New York: Free Press.

Moss, Phillip, and Chris Tilly. 2001. *Stories Employers Tell: Race, Skill, and Hiring in America*. New York: Russell Sage Foundation.

Moynihan, Daniel Patrick. 1960. *The Negro Family: The Case for National Action*. Office of Policy Planning and Research, US Department of Labor, March.

Mumby, Dennis K. 2004. "Discourse, Power, and Ideology: Unpacking the Critical Approach." In *The Sage Handbook of Organizational Discourse*, edited by David Grant, Cynthia Hardy, Cliff Oswick, and Linda Putnam, 237–59. Thousand Oaks, CA: Sage.

Munson, Judy. 1985. "Orr's Independence, Activism Winning Over the 49th." *Chicago Tribune*, Apr. 3, p. G25.

National People's Action. 2010. *The Home Foreclosure Crisis in Chicago: An Assessment of Foreclosures and Their Impacts in 2009*. Chicago.

Nelson, Bryce. 1967. "Ruckus over Race Has Relevance to Other Universities." *Science* 156 (3779): 1209–12.

Nelson, Robert L., Ellen Berrey, and Laura Beth Nielsen. 2008. "Divergent Paths: Conflicting Conceptions of Employment Discrimination in Law and the Social Sciences." *Annual Review of Law and Social Science* 4:103–22.

Nelson, Robert L., and William P. Bridges. 1999. *Legalizing Gender Inequality: Courts, Markets, and Unequal Pay for Women in America.* Cambridge: Cambridge University Press.

Newfield, Christopher, and Avery F. Gordon. 1996. "Multiculturalism's Unfinished Business." In *Mapping Multiculturalism*, edited by Avery F. Gordon and Christopher Newfield, 76–115. Minneapolis: University of Minnesota Press.

Newman, Kathe. 2009. "Post-industrial Widget Flows: Capital Flows and the Production of the Urban." *International Journal of Urban and Regional Research* 33 (2): 314–41.

Nielsen, Laura Beth. 2004. *License to Harass: Law, Hierarchy, and Offensive Public Speech.* Princeton, NJ: Princeton University Press.

Nielsen, Laura Beth, Robert Nelson, and Ellen Berrey. 2013. "Rights on Trial: Employment Civil Rights in Court." Book manuscript on file with author.

Nielsen, Laura Beth, Robert L. Nelson, Ryon Lancaster, and Nicholas Pedriana. 2008. *Characteristics and Outcomes of Federal Employment Discrimination Litigation, 1987–2003.* Chicago: American Bar Foundation.

Nightingale, Carl. 2012. *Segregation: A Global History of Divided Cities.* Chicago: University of Chicago Press.

Nkomo, Stella M. 1992. "The Emperor Has No Clothes: Rewriting 'Race in Organizations.'" *Academy of Management Review* 17 (3): 487–513.

Norton, Michael I., and Samuel R. Sommers. 2011. "Whites See Racism as a Zero-Sum Game That They Are Now Losing." *Perspectives on Psychological Science* 6 (3): 215–18.

Nyden, Philip W., Michael T. Maly, and John Lukehart. 1997. "The Emergence of Stable, Racially and Ethnically Diverse Urban Communities: A Case Study of Nine U.S. Cities." *Journal of Housing Policy Debate* 8:491–534.

Obasogie, Osagie K. 2014. *Blinded by Sight: Seeing Race through the Eyes of the Blind.* Stanford, CA: Stanford University Press.

Office of the Press Secretary, The White House. 2003. *President Bush Discusses Michigan Affirmative Action Case: Remarks by the President on the Michigan Affirmative Action Case.* Jan. 15.

Omi, Michael, and Howard Winant. 1987. *Racial Formation in the United States: From the 1960s to the 1990s.* New York: Routledge.

Orlebeke, Charles J. 2000. "The Evolution of Low-Income Housing Policy, 1949 to 1999." *Housing Policy Debate* 11 (2): 489–520.

Owens, Ann. 2012. "Neighborhoods on the Rise: A Typology of Neighborhoods Experiencing Socioeconomic Ascent." *City and Community* 11 (4): 345–69.

Page, Scott E. 2007. *The Difference: How the Power of Diversity Creates Better Groups, Firms, Schools, and Societies.* Princeton, NJ: Princeton University Press.

Pager, Devah. 2003. "The Mark of a Criminal Record." *American Journal of Sociology* 108 (5): 937–75.

Pattillo, Mary. 2007. *Black on the Block: The Politics of Race and Class in the City.* Chicago: University of Chicago Press.

Peckham, Howard H. 1994. *The Making of the University of Michigan, 1917–1992.* Ann Arbor: University of Michigan, Bentley Historical Library.

Pederson, Jesper Strandgaard, and Frank R. Dobbin. 2006. "In Search of Identity and

Legitimation: Bridging Organizational Culture and Neoinstitutionalism." *American Behavioral Scientist* 49 (7): 897–907.

Pedriana, Nicholas, and Robin Stryker. 2004. "The Strength of a Weak Agency: Enforcement of Title VII of the 1964 Civil Rights Act and the Expansion of State Capacity, 1965–1971." *American Journal of Sociology* 110 (3): 709–60.

Perrow, Charles. 1986. *Complex Organizations: A Critical Essay.* New York: McGraw-Hill.

Pippert, Timothy D., Laura J. Essenburg, and Edward J. Matchett. 2013. "We've Got Minorities, Yes We Do: Visual Representations of Racial and Ethnic Diversity in College Recruitment Materials." *Journal of Marketing for Higher Education* 23 (2): 258–82.

Plaut, Victoria C., Flannery G. Garnett, Laura E. Buffardi, and Jeffrey Sanchez-Burks. 2011. "'What about Me?' Perceptions of Exclusion and Whites' Reactions to Multiculturalism." *Journal of Personality and Social Psychology* 101 (1): 337–53.

Plaut, Victoria C., Kecia M. Thomas, and Matt J. Goren. 2009. "Is Multiculturalism or Colorblindness Better for Minorities?" *Psychological Science* 20:444–46.

Polikoff, Alexander. 1985. "What's in a Name? The Diversity of Racial Diversity Programs." Consultation/Hearing of the United States Commission on Civil Rights, March 6–7.

Pollitt, Katha. 2006. "Show Him the Money." *Nation*, Nov. 6. http://www.thenation.com /article/show-him-money. Accessed Mar. 22, 2014.

Popkin, Susan J., and Mary K. Cunningham. 1999. *Searching for Housing with Section 8 in Chicago Region.* Washington, DC: Urban Institute.

Population Reference Bureau. 2008. "US Labor Force Trends." *Population Bulletin* 63:1–17.

Portes, Alejandro, and Rubén G. Rumbaut. 2006. *Immigrant America: A Portrait.* Berkeley: University of California Press.

Pukelis, Stanley R. 1985. "Why I Live Here: East Rogers Park." *Chicago Sun-Times* July 28, p. 8.Putnam, Robert D. 2007. "*E Pluribus Unum*: Diversity and Community in the Twenty-first Century." *Scandinavian Political Studies* 30 (2): 137–74.

Quigley, John M. 2006. "Housing Policy in the U.S." Working paper of the Berkeley Program on Housing and Urban Policy, University of California, Berkeley.

Raeburn, Nicole C. 2004. *Changing Corporate America from Inside Out: Lesbian and Gay Workplace Rights.* Minneapolis: University of Minnesota Press.

Ragin, Charles C. 1994. *Constructing Social Research: The Unity and Diversity of Method.* Thousand Oaks, CA: Pine Forge.

Randolph, Antonia. 2012. *The Wrong Kind of Different: Challenging the Meaning of Diversity in American Classrooms.* New York: Teachers College Press.

Reardon, Sean F., Rachel Baker, and Daniel Klasik. 2012. *Race, Income, and Enrollment Patterns in Highly Selective Colleges, 1982–2004.* Center for Education Policy Analysis, Stanford University.

Reardon, Sean F., and Kendra Bischoff. 2011. "Growth in the Residential Segregation of Families by Income, 1970–2009." In US2010 Project. Russell Sage Foundation and Brown University.

Reed, Adolph Jr., ed. 1999. *Without Justice for All: The New Liberalism and Our Retreat from Racial Equality.* Boulder, CO: Westview.

Reed, Isaac. 2013. "Power: Relational, Discursive, and Performative Dimensions." *Sociological Theory* 31 (3): 193–218.

Reskin, Barbara, and Debra Branch McBrier. 2000. "Why Not Ascription? Organizations' Employment of Male and Female Managers." *American Sociological Review* 65 (2): 210–33.

Riccucci, Norma M. 1997. "Cultural Diversity Programs to Prepare for Work Force 2000: What's Gone Wrong?" *Public Personnel Management* 26 (1): 35–41.

Richardson, John D., and Karen M. Lancendorfer. 2004. "Framing Affirmative Action: The Influence of Race on Newspaper Editorial Responses to the University of Michigan Cases." *Press/Politics* 9 (4): 74–94.

Ridgeway, Cecilia L. 1997. "Interaction and the Conservation of Gender Inequality: Considering Employment." *American Sociological Review* 62 (2): 218–35.

Rivera, Lauren. 2011. "Ivies, Extracurriculars, and Exclusion: Elite Employers' Use of Educational Credentials." *Research in Social Stratification and Mobility* 29:71–90.

Rochon, Thomas. 1998. *Culture Moves: Ideas, Activism, and Changing Values.* Princeton, NJ: Princeton University Press.

Rojas, Fabio. 2007. *From Black Power to Black Studies: How a Radical Social Movement Became an Academic Discipline.* Baltimore: Johns Hopkins University Press.

Roscigno, Vincent J. 2007. *The Face of Discrimination: How Race and Gender Impact Work and Home Lives.* New York: Rowman and Littlefield.

———. 2011. "Power, Revisited." *Social Forces* 90 (2): 349–74.

Roscigno, Vincent J., Diana L. Karafin, and Griff Tester. 2009. "The Complexities and Processes of Racial Housing Discrimination." *Social Problems* 56 (1): 49–69.

Roscigno, Vincent J., and George Wilson. 2014a. "The Relational Foundations of Inequality at Work I: Status, Interaction, and Culture." *American Behavioral Scientist* 58 (2): 219–27.

———. 2014b. "The Relational Foundations of Inequality at Work II: Structure-Agency Interplay." *American Behavioral Scientist* 58 (3): 375–78.

Royster, Deirdre A. 2003. *Race and the Invisible Hand: How White Networks Exclude Black Men from Blue-Collar Jobs.* Berkeley: University of California Press.

Rubinowitz, Leonard S., and James E. Rosenbaum. 2000. *Crossing the Class and Color Lines: From Public Housing to White Suburbia.* Chicago: University of Chicago Press.

Rutstein, Dagny. 1988. "Good Neighbors, Good Business, Multifaceted Communities Adding Fuel to Renaissance." *Chicago Tribune*, Sept. 21, p. 5.

Ryan, John, James Hawdon, and Allison Branick. 2002. "The Political Economy of Diversity: Diversity Programs in Fortune 500 Companies." *Sociological Research Online* 7 (1). http://www.socresonline.org.uk/7/1/ryan.html.

Ryan, Lori Verstegen, and Marguerite Schneider. 2002. "The Antecedents of Institutional Investor Activism." *Academy of Management Review* 27 (4): 554–73.

Saez, Emmanuel, and Thomas Piketty. 2003. "Income Inequality in the United States, 1913–1998." *Quarterly Journal of Economics* 118 (1): 1–39. Tables and figures updated to 2008 available at http://elsa.berkeley.edu/~saez/.

Saltman, Juliet. 1990. *A Fragile Movement: The Struggle for Neighborhood Stabilization.* New York: Greenwood.

Sampson, Robert. 2012. *Great American City: Chicago and the Enduring Neighborhood Effect.* Chicago: University of Chicago Press.

Sander, Richard H., and Stuart Taylor. 2012. *Mismatch: How Affirmative Action Hurts Students It's Intended to Help, and Why Universities Won't Admit It.* New York: Basic Books.

Sandoval, Juan Onésimo, and Su Li. 2004. "The Multi-cultural Metropolis: Changing Segregation Patterns in the City of Chicago, 1990–2000." Paper presented at the annual meeting of the American Sociological Association, San Francisco.

Sassen, Saskia. 2001. *The Global City: New York, London, Tokyo.* Princeton, NJ: Princeton University Press.

Sauder, Michael, and Wendy Espeland. 2009. "Rankings and Diversity." *Southern California Review of Law and Social Justice* 18 (3): 587–608.

Saussure, Ferdinand de. 1966. *Course in General Linguistics.* New York: McGraw-Hill.

Schmidt, Christopher. 2008. "*Brown* and the Colorblind Constitution." *Cornell Law Review* 94:203–38.

Schuck, Peter H. 2003. *Diversity in America: Keeping Government at a Safe Distance.* Cambridge, MA: Belknap.

Schudson, Michael. 1989. "How Culture Works: Perspectives from Media Studies on the Efficacy of Symbols." *Theory and Society* 18:153–80.

Searcey, Dionne. 1996. "In Rogers Park, All Are Welcome: No One Is Sure Why So Many Ethnic Groups Flock There. But They Just Do." *Chicago Tribune*, Feb. 22, p. 1.

Seguine, Joel. 2006. "U-M among the Best on Several College Rankings." *University Record Online*, Sept. 5. http://www.umich.edu/~urecord/0607/Sept05_06/12.shtml.

Selznick, Philip. 1949. *TVA and the Grass Roots: A Study in the Sociology of Formal Organization.* Berkeley: University of California Press.

Sewell, William H., Jr. 1996. "Historical Events as Transformations of Structures: Inventing Revolution at the Bastille." *Theory and Society* 25 (6): 841–81.

———. 1999. "The Concept(s) of Culture." In *Beyond the Cultural Turn: New Directions in the Study of Society and Culture*, edited by Victoria E. Bonnell and Lynn Hunt, 35–61. Berkeley: University of California Press.

Sharkey, Patrick. 2013. *Stuck in Place: Urban Neighborhoods and the End of Progress toward Racial Equality.* Chicago: University of Chicago Press.

Sharone, Ofer. 2004. "Engineering Overwork: Bell-Curve Management at a High-Tech Firm." In *Fighting for Time: Shifting Boundaries of Work and Social Life*, edited by Cynthia Fuchs Epstein and Arne L. Kalleberg, 191–218. New York: Russell Sage Foundation.

Shiao, Jiannbin Lee. 2005. *Identifying Talent, Institutionalizing Diversity: Race and Philanthropy in Post–Civil Rights America.* Durham, NC: Duke University Press.

Shor, Ira. 1992. *Empowering Education: Critical Teaching for Social Change.* Chicago: University of Chicago Press.

Simon, Bryant. 2010. "Race Doesn't Matter, Race Matters: Starbucks, Consumption and the Appeal of the Performance of Colorblindness." *Du Bois Review: Social Science Research on Race* 7 (2): 271–92.

Singh, Nikhil Pal. 2005. *Black Is a Country: Race and the Unfinished Struggle for Democracy.* Cambridge, MA: Harvard University Press.

Skogan, Wesley G., and Susan M. Hartnett. 1997. *Community Policing, Chicago Style.* New York: Oxford University Press.

Skrentny, John David. 1996. *The Ironies of Affirmative Action: Politics, Culture, and Justice in America.* Chicago: University of Chicago Press.

———. 2002. *The Minority Rights Revolution.* Cambridge, MA: Belknap.

———. 2014. *After Civil Rights: Racial Realism and the Law in the New American Workplace.* Princeton, NJ: Princeton University Press.

Slaughter, Sheila, and Gary Rhoades. 2004. *Academic Capitalism and the New Economy: Markets, State, and Higher Education.* Baltimore: Johns Hopkins University Press.

Small, Mario. 2009. "'How Many Cases Do I Need?': On Science and the Logic of Case Selection in Field-Based Research." *Ethnography* 10 (1): 5–38.

Smith, Vicki. 2001. *Crossing the Great Divide: Worker Risk and Opportunity in the New Economy.* Ithaca, NY: Cornell University Press.

Smock, Kristina. 2004. *Democracy in Action: Community Organizing and Urban Change.* New York: Columbia University Press.

Snow, David A., Robert D. Benford, Holly J. McCammon, Lyndi Hewitt, and Scott Fitzgerald. 2014. "The Emergence, Development, and Future of the Framing Perspective: 25+ Years since 'Frame Alignment.'" *Mobilization* 19 (1): 23–45.

Sobel, Robert. 1993. *The Age of Giant Corporations: A Microeconomic History of American Business, 1914–1992*. Westport, CT: Greenwood.

Sommer, Will. 2012. "Swagger-Jacking: What We Talk about When We Talk about U Street." *Washington City Paper*, Annotated Guide to 2012. http://www.washingtoncity paper.com/articles/43663/swagger-jacking-what-we-talk-about-when-we-talk-about. Accessed Dec. 26, 2012.

Spillman, Lyn. 1997. *Nation and Commemoration: Creating National Identities in the United States and Australia*. Cambridge: Cambridge University Press.

Stainback, Kevin, and Donald Tomaskovic-Devey. 2012. *Documenting Desegregation: Racial and Gender Segregation in Private-Sector Employment since the Civil Rights Act*. New York: Russell Sage Foundation.

Stainback, Kevin, Donald Tomaskovic-Devey, and Sheryl Skaggs. 2010. "Organizational Approaches to Inequality: Inertia, Relative Power, and Environments." *Annual Review of Sociology* 36:225–47.

Steele, Jeffrey. 1996. "Can-Do Spirit Thrives in These 3 Neighborhoods, Diversity Melds into a Sense of Common Good." *Chicago Tribune*, June 19, p. 3.

Sterba, James P. 2009. *Affirmative Action for the Future*. Ithaca, NY: Cornell University Press.

Stevens, Mitchell L. 2007. *Creating a Class: College Admissions and the Education of Elites*. Cambridge, MA: Harvard University Press.

Stevens, Mitchell L., and Josipa Roksa. 2011. "The Diversity Imperative in Elite Admissions." In *Diversity in American Higher Education: Toward a More Comprehensive Approach*, edited by Lisa M. Stulberg and Sharon Lawner Weinberg, 63–73. New York and London: Routledge.

Stinchcombe, Arthur L. 2005. *The Logic of Social Research*. Chicago: University of Chicago Press.

Stohr, Greg. 2004. *A Black and White Case: How Affirmative Action Survived Its Greatest Legal Challenge*. Princeton, NJ: Bloomberg.

Stryker, Robin. 2000. "Legitimacy Processes as Institutional Politics: Implications for Theory and Research in the Sociology of Organizations." *Research in the Sociology of Organizations* 17:179–223.

Stulberg, Lisa M., and Anthony S. Chen. 2014. "The Origins of Race-Conscious Affirmative Action in Undergraduate Admissions: A Comparative Analysis of Institutional Change in Higher Education." *Sociology of Education* 87 (1): 36–52.

———. 2011. "A Long View on 'Diversity': A Century of American College Admissions Debates." In *Diversity in American Higher Education: Toward a More Comprehensive Approach*, edited by Lisa M. Stulberg and Sharon Lawner Weinberg, 51–62. New York: Routledge.

Sturm, Susan. 2001. "Second Generation Employment Discrimination: A Structural Approach." *Columbia Law Review* 101:458–68.

Sturm, Susan, and Lani Guinier. "The Future of Affirmative Action: Reclaiming the Innovative Ideal." *California Law Review* 84 (4): 953–1036.

Sugrue, Thomas J. 1996. *The Origins of the Urban Crisis: Race and Inequality in Postwar Detroit*. Princeton, NJ: Princeton University Press.

Sullivan, James. 1962. "Rogers Pk. Told: Do-It-Yourself to Fight Blight." *Chicago Tribune*, Mar. 25, p. N1.

Suttles, Gerald D. 1972. *The Social Construction of Communities*. Chicago: University of Chicago Press.

———. 1990. *The Man-Made City: The Land-Use Confidence Game in Chicago*. Chicago: University of Chicago Press.

Swan, Elaine. 2010. "Commodity Diversity: Smiling Faces as a Strategy of Containment." *Organization* 17 (1): 77–100.

Swanson, Stevenson. 1980a. "Public Housing Battle Rages." *Chicago Tribune*, Oct. 9, pp. N1–2.

———. 1980b. "Subsidized Housing: Uptown Housing No 'Dumping Ground for Poor.'" *Chicago Tribune*, Nov. 6, pp. N1, N6.

———. 1980c. "Walk to Work Program Key: Loyola Plan Saving a Neighborhood." *Chicago Tribune*, Dec. 4, p. 1.

———. 1981a. "North of Howard Street, 'The First Concern Is Survival.'" *Chicago Tribune*, June 4. p. N-A1.

———. 1981b. "Rogers Park Shelter Survives Protests." *Chicago Tribune*, Mar. 19, p. N1.

———. 1981c. "Tenants Vow Renewed Fight for Rights." *Chicago Tribune*, Jan. 1, p. N-A1.

Swidler, Ann. 1986. "Culture in Action: Symbols and Strategies." *American Sociological Review* 51 (2): 273–86.

———. 2001. "Cultural Expression and Action." In *International Encyclopedia of the Social and Behavioral Sciences*, edited by Neil J. Smelser and Paul B. Baltes, 3063–69. Amsterdam: Elsevier.

Tarrow, Sidney. 1998. *Power in Movement: Social Movements and Contentious Politics*. Cambridge: Cambridge University Press.

Taylor, Paul, and Richard Fry. 2012. *The Rise of Residential Segregation by Income*. Washington, DC: Pew Research Center.

Thomas, David A., and Robin J. Ely. 2001. "Cultural Diversity at Work: The Effects of Diversity Perspectives on Work Group Processes and Outcomes." *Administrative Science Quarterly* 46 (2): 229–73.

Thomas, R. Roosevelt, Jr. 1994. "From Affirmative Action to Affirming Diversity." *Harvard Business Review*, March–April, 107–17.

Thompson, John B. 1984. *Studies in the Theory of Ideology*. Berkeley: University of California Press.

———. 1990. *Ideology and Modern Culture: Critical Social Theory in the Era of Mass Communication*. Stanford, CA: Stanford University Press.

Thornton, Patricia H. 2002. "The Rise of the Corporation in a Craft Industry: Conflict and Conformity in Institutional Logics." *Academy of Management Journal* 45 (1): 81–101.

Thornton, Patricia H., William Ocasio, and Michael Lounsbury. 2012. *The Institutional Logics Perspective: A New Approach to Culture, Structure, and Process*. Oxford: Oxford University Press.

Tilly, Charles. 1999. *Durable Inequality*. Berkeley: University of Berkeley Press.

Tissot, Sylvie. 2011. "Of Dogs and Men: The Making of Spatial Boundaries in a Gentrifying Neighborhood." *City and Community* 10 (3): 265–84.

Tomaskovic-Devey, Donald. 2014. "The Relational Generation of Workplace Inequalities." *Sociological Currents* 1 (1): 51–73.

Tomaskovic-Devey, Donald, and Kevin Stainback. 2007. "Discrimination and Desegregation: Equal Opportunity Progress in U.S. Private Sector Workplaces since the Civil Rights Act." *Annals of the American Academy of Political and Social Sciences* 609 (49): 49–84.

Trautner, Mary Nell, and Samantha Kwan. 2010. "Gendered Appearance Norms: An Analysis of Employment Discrimination Lawsuits, 1970–2008." *Gender and Sexuality in the Workplace* 20:127–50.

Truitt, Brett. 2011. "Half-Black, Half-Hispanic Spider-Man Revealed." *USA Today*, Aug. 2. http://www.usatoday.com/life/comics/2011-08-01-black-spider-man_n.htm. Accessed Sept. 15, 2011.

Turner, Margery Austin, Rob Santos, Diane K. Levy, Doug Wissoker, Claudia Aranda, and Rob Pitingolo. 2013. *Housing Discrimination against Racial and Ethnic Minorities.* Washington, DC: US Department of Housing and Urban Development, Office of Policy Development and Research.

Twine, France Winddance, and Jonathan Warren. 2000. *Racing Research, Researching Race: Methodological Dilemmas in Critical Race Studies.* New York: New York University Press.

University of Michigan. 2001. "Ford Foundation Moves to Promote Defense of Diversity." News and Information Services news release, June 12. http://www.umich.edu/news /index.html?Releases/2001/Ju101/r071201e. Accessed May 25, 2005.

———. 2013. *University of Michigan–Ann Arbor: Freshman Class Profile, Fall 2009–Fall 2013.* http://obp.umich.edu/root/facts-figures/students/. Accessed Mar. 15, 2014.

University of Michigan, Board of Regents. 1970. *Proceedings of the Board of Regents.* Mar. Ann Arbor, MI. http://www.hti.umich.edu/u/umregproc/.

———. 1979. *Proceedings of the Board of Regents.* Feb. Ann Arbor, MI. http://www.hti .umich.edu/u/umregproc/.

———. 1987. *Proceedings of the Board of Regents.* Feb. Ann Arbor, MI. http://www.hti .umich.edu/u/umregproc/.

———. 1988. *Proceedings of the Board of Regents.* Dec. Ann Arbor, MI. http://www.hti .umich.edu/u/umregproc/.

———. 1993. *Proceedings of the Board of Regents.* Jan. Ann Arbor, MI. http://www.hti .umich.edu/u/umregproc/.

———. 1994. *Proceedings of the Board of Regents.* May. Ann Arbor, MI. http://www.hti .umich.edu/u/umregproc/.

University of Michigan, Office of Academic and Multicultural Initiatives. N.d. Michigan Diversity Report: Michigan Student Study: An Assessment of Students' and Alumni's Experiences and Outcomes with Diversity. http://www.oami.umich.edu/images /MSS%20DIVERSITY%20REPORT.pdf, accessed July 10, 2014.University of Michigan, Office of Budget and Planning. 2006a. *University of Michigan–Ann Arbor Estimated Cost of Attendance per Academic Year.*

———. 2006b. *University of Michigan–Ann Arbor Freshman Class Profile, 2002–2006.* http:// sitemaker.umich.edu/obpinfo. Accessed Jan. 17, 2007.

University of Michigan, Office of the President. 1990. *The Michigan Mandate: A Strategic Linking of Academic Excellence and Social Diversity.* Ann Arbor, MI.

University of Michigan, Office of the Registrar. 1999a. "The University of Michigan–Ann Arbor, Enrollment in Degree Credit Programs by Race, Fall 1989–1999." Report 837. http://ro.umich.edu/enrollment/ethnicity.php. Accessed July 10, 2014.

University of Michigan, Office of the Registrar. 1999b. "The University of Michigan–Ann Arbor, Undergraduate Enrollment by Race, Opportunity Program, Entry Type, and State of Residence, Fall 1999." Report 872a. http://ro.umich.edu/enrollment/ethnicity .php. Accessed July 10, 2014.

———. 2003. "The University of Michigan–Ann Arbor Undergraduate Enrollment by School or College, Ethnicity, Class Level, and Gender for Term 1460 (Fall 2003)." Report 836U. http://ro.umich.edu/enrollment/ethnicity.php. Accessed July 10, 2014.

———. 2004a. "The University of Michigan–Ann Arbor, Undergraduate Enrollment by Ethnicity, Comprehensive Studies Program, and Entry Type for Term 1510 (Fall 2004)." Report 872a. http://ro.umich.edu/enrollment/ethnicity.php. Accessed July 10, 2014.

———. 2004b. "The University of Michigan–Ann Arbor Undergraduate Enrollment by School or College, Ethnicity, Class Level, and Gender For Term 1410 (Fall 2004)." Report 836U. http://ro.umich.edu/enrollment/ethnicity.php. Accessed July 10, 2014.

———. 2005a. "University of Michigan Enrollment by School or College and Gender for Term 1560 (Fall 2005)." Report 816. http://ro.umich.edu/enrollment/enrollment .php. Accessed Mar. 15, 2014.

———. 2005b. "The University of Michigan–Ann Arbor, Foreign Student Enrollment by School or College and Class Level for Term 1560 (Fall 2005)." Report 118. http:// ro.umich.edu/enrollment/enrollment.php. Accessed Mar. 15, 2014.

———. 2006. "The University of Michigan–Ann Arbor Undergraduate Enrollment by School or College, Ethnicity, Class Level, and Gender for Term 1610 (Fall 2006)." Report 836U. http://ro.umich.edu/enrollment/ethnicity.php. Accessed July 10, 2014.

———. 2013a. "University of Michigan-Ann Arbor, Enrollment by School or College, Ethnicity, Class Level, and Gender, Fall 2013." Report 836U. http://ro.umich.edu /enrollment/ethnicity.php. Accessed July 10, 2014.

———. 2013b. "University of Michigan-Ann Arbor, Ten Year Enrollment by Ethnicity, Fall of Multiple Years." Report 837. http://ro.umich.edu/enrollment/ethnicity.php. Accessed July 10, 2014.

University of Michigan, Office of Undergraduate Admissions (1974). "University of Michigan: A Report to Michigan Principals and Counselors." Sept.

Urciuoli, Bonnie. 2003. "Excellence, Leadership, Skills, Diversity: Marketing Liberal Arts Education." *Language and Communication* 23 (3–4): 385–408.

US Bureau of Labor Statistics. 2007. *Employment and Earnings.* January.

US Department of Education, National Center for Education Statistics. 2011. *Digest of Education Statistics: 2011.* Washington, DC.

———. 2012. *Higher Education: Gaps in Access and Persistence Study.* Washington, DC.

———. 2013. "Women in the Labor Force: A Databook." February.

U.S. News and World Report. 2005. "America's Best Colleges." Aug. 29.

Vallas, Steven. 2001. "Symbolic Boundaries and the New Division of Labor: Engineers, Workers, and the Restructuring of Factory Life." *Research in Social Stratification and Mobility* 18:3–31.

Vallas, Steven, and Emily Cummins. 2014. "Relational Models of Workplace Inequalities: A Critique and Extension of Three Theoretical Traditions." *American Behavioral Scientist* 58 (2): 228–55.

Valverde, Mariana. 2012. *Everyday Law on the Street: City Governance in an Age of Diversity.* Chicago: University of Chicago Press.

Vaughan, Diane. 1992. "Theory Elaboration: The Heuristics of Case Analysis." In *What Is a Case? Exploring the Foundations of Social Inquiry,* edited by Charles C. Ragin and Howard S. Becker, 173–202. Cambridge: Cambridge University Press.

———. 2004. "Theorizing Disaster: Analogy, Historical Ethnography, and the *Challenger* Accident." *Ethnography* 5 (3): 315–47.

Voyer, Andrea M. 2011. "Disciplined to Diversity: Learning the Language of Multicultur- alism." *Ethnic and Racial Studies* 34 (11): 1874–93.

Wacquant, Loïc. 1997. "For an Analytic of Racial Domination." *Political Power and Social Theory* 2:221–34.

Wade-Golden, Katrina, and John Matlock. 2010. "Working through the Challenge: Critical Lessons Learned for Building and Sustaining a Robust Institutional Diversity Culture." In *Implementing Diversity: Contemporary Challenges and Best Practices at Predominantly White Universities,* edited by Helen A. Neville, Margaret Browne Huntt, and Jorge Chapa, 1–19. Urbana: University of Illinois Center on Democracy in a Multiracial Society.

Waeraas, Arild, and Marianne N. Solbakk. 2009. "Defining the Essence of a University: Lessons from Higher Education Branding." *Higher Education* 57 (4): 449–62.

Wagmiller, Robert L., Jr. 2012. "Blacks' and Whites' Experiences of Neighborhood Racial and Ethnic Diversity: Intercohort Variation in Neighborhood Diversity and Integration in Early and Early Middle Adulthood." *Urban Affairs Review* 49 (1): 32–70.

Walder, Andrew. 2009. "Political Sociology and Social Movements." *Annual Review of Sociology* 35:393–412.

Wall, Wendy L. 2008. *Inventing the "American Way": The Politics of Consensus from the New Deal to the Civil Rights Movement.* New York: Oxford University Press.

Wang, Dean. 2002. Letter to the editor. *Michigan Daily,* Mar. 11.

Weber, Max. 1946. "Science as a Vocation." In *From Max Weber: Essays in Sociology,* edited by H. H. Gerth and C. Wright Mills, 129–56. New York: Oxford University Press.

Welter, Gale Danks. 1982. *The Rogers Park Community: A Study of Social Change, Community Groups, and Neighborhood Reputation.* Chicago: Center for Urban Policy, Loyola University.

Williams, Kim M. 2006. *Mark One or More: Civil Rights in Multiracial America.* Ann Arbor: University of Michigan Press.

Williams, Raymond. 1983. *Keywords: A Vocabulary of Culture and Society.* New York: Oxford University Press.

Wilson, George, and Debra Branch McBrier. 2005. "Race and Loss of Privilege: African American / White Differences in the Determinants of Layoffs from Upper-Tier Occupation." *Sociological Forum* 20 (2): 301–21.

Wilson, William Julius. 1987. *The Truly Disadvantaged: The Inner City, the Underclass, and Public Policy.* Chicago: University of Chicago Press.

———. 1996. *When Work Disappears: The World of the New Urban Poor.* New York: Vintage Books.

Wimmer, Andreas. 2008. "The Making and Unmaking of Ethnic Boundaries: A Multi-Level Process." *American Journal of Sociology* 113 (4): 970–1022.

———. 2009. "Herder's Heritage and the Boundary-Making Approach: Studying Ethnicity in Immigrant Societies." *Sociological Theory* 27 (3): 244–70.

Winant, Howard. 2000. "Race and Race Theory." *Annual Review of Sociology* 26:169–85.

Wingfield, Adia Harvey. 2010. "Are Some Emotions Marked 'Whites Only'? Racialized Feeling Rules in Professional Workplaces." *Social Problems* 57 (2): 251–68.

Wingfield, Adia Harvey, and Renée Skeete Alston. 2014. "Maintaining Hierarchies in Predominantly White Organizations: A Theory of Racial Tasks." *American Behavioral Scientist* 58 (2): 274–87.

Wirth, Louis. 1938. "Urbanism as a Way of Life." *American Journal of Sociology* 44 (1): 1–24.

Wood, Peter. 2003. *Diversity: The Invention of a Concept.* San Francisco: Encounter Books.

Yackley, Sel. 1967. "Peaceful Integration Progresses Smoothly in Rogers Park Area." *Chicago Tribune,* Apr. 20, p. H2.

Yates, Ronald. 1971. "3 Aldermen Oppose Part of Proposed CHA Plan." *Chicago Tribune,* Apr. 24, p. N6.

Zhou, Min. 2004. "Are Asian Americans Becoming White?" *Contexts* 3 (1): 29–37.

Ziemba, Stanley. 1980. "Coalition Battles Subsidized Housing." *Chicago Tribune,* Oct. 16, p. N3.

Zukin, Sharon. 1987. "Gentrification: Culture and Capital in the Urban Core." *Annual Review of Sociology* 13:129–47.

———. 1995. *The Cultures of Cities.* Oxford: Blackwell.

———. 2010. *Naked City: The Death and Life of Authentic Urban Places.* New York: Oxford University Press.

Zweigenhaft, Richard, and G. William Domhoff. 2006. *Diversity in the Power Elite: How It Happened, Why It Matters.* Lanham, MD: Rowman and Littlefield.

The letter *f* following a page number denotes a figure,
and the letter *t* denotes a table.